SURFING UNCERTAINTY

Surfing Uncertainty

Prediction, Action,
and the Embodied Mind

Andy Clark

OXFORD
UNIVERSITY PRESS

Oxford University Press is a department of the University of
Oxford. It furthers the University's objective of excellence in research,
scholarship, and education by publishing worldwide.

Oxford   New York
Auckland   Cape Town   Dar es Salaam   Hong Kong   Karachi
Kuala Lumpur   Madrid   Melbourne   Mexico City   Nairobi
New Delhi   Shanghai   Taipei   Toronto

With offices in
Argentina   Austria   Brazil   Chile   Czech Republic   France   Greece
Guatemala   Hungary   Italy   Japan   Poland   Portugal   Singapore
South Korea   Switzerland   Thailand   Turkey   Ukraine   Vietnam

Oxford is a registered trademark of Oxford University Press
in the UK and certain other countries.

Published in the United States of America by
Oxford University Press
198 Madison Avenue, New York, NY 10016

Library of Congress Cataloging-in-Publication Data
Clark, Andy, 1957—
Surfing uncertainty : prediction, action, and the embodied mind / Andy Clark.
    pages cm
Includes bibliographical references and index.
ISBN 978–0–19–021701–3 (cloth : alk. paper)   1. Prediction (Logic)   2. Metacognition.
3. Uncertainty.   I. Title.
BC181.C534 2016
128'.2—dc23
2015004451

9 8 7 6 5
Printed in the United States of America
on acid-free paper

For Christine Clark and Alexa Morcom
Encoder, Decoder, and Everything in Between

Contents

Preface: Meat That Predicts

> 'They're made out of meat.'
>
> 'Meat?'
>
> 'Meat. They're made out of meat.'
>
> 'Meat?'
>
> 'There's no doubt about it. We picked several from different parts of the planet, took them aboard our recon vessels, probed them all the way through. They're completely meat.'

Such are the opening remarks of the very puzzled non-carbon-based aliens whose conversation is reported in the wonderful short story 'Alien/Nation' by science-fiction writer Terry Bissom (*Omni*, 1991). The aliens' puzzlement increases upon learning that the meaty strangers were not even built by non-meat intelligences and do not harbour even a simple non-carbon-based central processing unit hidden inside their meaty exteriors. Instead, it's *meat all the way down*. Even the brain, as one of them exclaims, is made of meat. The upshot is startling:

> 'Yes, thinking meat! Conscious meat! Loving meat. Dreaming meat. The meat is the whole deal! Are you getting the picture?'

Unable to overcome their initial surprise and disgust, the aliens soon decide to continue their interstellar journey, casting us short-lived meat-brains aside with the inevitable quip 'who wants to meet meat?'.

Such carnophobia aside, the aliens were surely right to be puzzled. Thinking meat, dreaming meat, conscious meat, meat that understands. It seems unlikely, to say the least. Of course, it would be no *less* surprising were we made of silicon, or anything else for that matter. The mystery is, and remains, how mere matter manages to give rise to thinking, imagining, dreaming, and the whole smorgasbord of mentality, emotion, and intelligent action. Thinking matter, dreaming matter, conscious matter: that's the thing that it's hard to get your head—whatever it's made of—around. But there is an emerging clue. It is one clue among many, and even if it's a good one, it won't solve all the problems and puzzles. Still, it's a real clue, and it's also one that provides a handy umbrella under which to consider (and in some cases rediscover) many of the previous clues.

The clue can be summed up in a single word: prediction. To deal rapidly and fluently with an uncertain and noisy world, brains like ours have become masters of prediction—surfing the waves of noisy and ambiguous sensory stimulation by, in effect, trying to stay just ahead of them. A skilled surfer stays 'in the pocket': close to, yet just ahead of the place where the wave is breaking. This provides power and, when the wave breaks, it does not catch her. The brain's task is not dissimilar. By constantly attempting to predict the incoming sensory signal we become able—in ways we shall soon explore in detail—to learn about the world around us and to engage that world in thought and action. Succesful, world-engaging prediction is not easy. It depends crucially upon simultaneously estimating the state of the world and our own sensory uncertainty. But get that right, and active agents can both know and behaviourally engage their worlds, safely riding wave upon wave of sensory stimulation.

Matter, when organized so that it cannot help but try (and try, and try again) to successfully predict the complex plays of energies that are washing across its energy-sensitive surfaces, has many interesting properties. Matter, thus organized, turns out, as we'll see, to be ideally positioned to perceive, to understand, to dream, to imagine, and (most importantly of all) to act. Perceiving, imagining, understanding, and acting are now bundled together, emerging as different aspects and manifestations of the same underlying prediction-driven, uncertainty-sensitive, machinery.

For such properties to fully emerge, however, several more conditions need to be met. The energy-sensitive surfaces whose time-varying (and action-relevant) perturbations are to be predicted need to be many and variegated. In us humans they include eyes, ears, tongues, noses, and the whole of that somewhat neglected sensory organ, the skin. They also include a range of more 'inward-looking' sensory channels, including proprioception (the sense of the relative positions of bodily parts, and the forces being deployed) and interoception (the sense of the physiological conditions of the body, such as pain, hunger, and other visceral states). Predictions concerning these more inward-looking channels will prove crucial in the core account of action, and in accounting for feelings and conscious experiences.

Most important of all, perhaps, the prediction machinery itself needs to operate in a distinctively complex, multilevel, variegated internal environment. In this complex (and repeatedly reconfigurable) neural economy, what gets traded are probabilistic predictions, inflected at every level by changing estimates of our own uncertainty. Here different (but densely interanimated) neuronal populations learn to predict various organism-salient regularities obtaining at many spatial and temporal scales. In so doing they lock on to patterns specifying everything from lines and edges, to zebra stripes, to movies, meanings, popcorn, parking lots, and the characteristic plays of offense and defence by your favourite football team. The world thus revealed is a world tailored to human needs, tasks, and actions. It is a world built of affordances—opportunities for action and intervention. And it is a world that is exploited, time and time again, to reduce the complexities of neural processing by means of canny action routines that alter the problem-space for the embodied, predictive brain.

But where, you might well ask, do all these predictions and estimations of our own sensory uncertainty come from? Even if prediction-based encounters with the play of energies across our sensors are what reveal—as I shall argue they do—a complex structured world apt for engagement and action, the knowledge those predictions reflect still needs to be accounted for. In an especially satisfying twist, it will turn out that meat that constantly attempts (using a multilevel inner organization) to predict the plays of (partially self-caused) sensory data is nicely positioned to learn about those regularities themselves. Learning and online processing are thus supported using the same basic resources. This is because perceiving our body and the world, if this story is correct, involves learning to predict our own evolving sensory states—states that are responding both to the body-in-action and to the world. A good way to predict those changing sensory states is to learn about the world (including our own body and actions) that is causing the changes. The attempt to predict the play of sensory stimulation can thus itself be used gradually to install the very models that will enable the predictions to succeed. The prediction task, as we shall see, is thus a kind of 'bootstrap heaven'.

Meat like this is imagining and dreaming meat too. Such meat becomes able to drive its own internal states 'from the top-down' using the knowledge and connections that enable it to match incoming sensory data with structured predictions. And meat that dreams and imagines is (potentially at least) meat that can harnass its imaginings to reason—to think about what actions it might, or might not, perform. The upshot is a compelling 'cognitive package deal' in which perception, imagination, understanding, reasoning, and action are co-emergent from the whirrings and grindings of the predictive, uncertainty-estimating, brain. Creatures that perceive and act on the basis of such subterranean flows of prediction are active, knowledgeable, imaginative beings in rich cognitive contact with a structured and meaningful world. That world is a world made of patterns of expectation: a world in which unexpected absences are as perceptually salient as any concrete event, and in which all our mental states are coloured by delicate estimations of our own uncertainty.

To complete the picture, however, we must locate the inner prediction engine in its proper home. That home—as the surfing image is also meant to powerfully suggest—is a mobile embodied agent located in multiple empowering webs of material and social structure. To make full and satisfying contact with the thinking and reasoning of agents *like us*, we must factor in the myriad effects of the complex social and physical 'designer environments' in which we learn, act, and reason. Without this environment, our kind of selective response to the world could never emerge or be maintained. It is the predictive brain operating in rich bodily, social, and technological context that ushers minds like ours into the material realm. Here especially, the focus on prediction pays rich dividends, offering new and potent tools for thinking about the moment-by-moment orchestration of neural, bodily, and environmental resources into effective transient problem-solving coalitions. By the end of our story, the predictive brain will stand revealed not as an insulated inner 'inference engine' but an action-oriented engagement machine—an enabling (albeit, as it happens, meaty) node in patterns of dense reciprocal exchange binding brain, body, and world.

A.C.
Edinburgh, 2015

Acknowledgements

This book has benefitted enormously from the help and advice of a large number of people. Very particular thanks go to Karl Friston, Jakob Hohwy, Bill Phillips, and Anil Seth. Your patience and encouragement made this whole project possible. Also to Lars Muckli, Peggy Series, Andreas Roepstorff, Chris Thornton, Chris Williams, Liz Irvine, Matteo Colombo, and all the participants at the Predictive Coding Workshop (School of Informatics, University of Edinburgh, January 2010); to Phil Gerrans, Nick Shea, Mark Sprevak, Aaron Sloman, and the participants at the first meeting of the UK Mind Network held at the Faculty of Philosophy, Oxford University, March 2010; to Markus Werning, Albert Newen, and the organizers and participants of the 2010 meeting of the European Society for Philosophy and Psychology, held at Ruhr-Universität Bochum, August 2010; to Nihat Ay, Ray Guillery, Bruno Olshausen, Murray Sherman, Fritz Sommer, and the participants at the Perception & Action Workshop, Santa Fe Institute, New Mexico, September 2010; to Daniel Dennett, Rosa Cao, Justin Junge, and Amber Ross (captain and crew of the hurricane-Irene-blocked 2011 Cognitive Cruise); to Miguel Eckstein, Mike Gazzaniga, Michael Rescorla, and the faculty and students at the Sage Center for the Study of Mind, University of California, Santa Barbara, where, as a Visiting Fellow in September 2011, I was privileged to road-test much of this material; to all the commentators on my 2013 *Behavioral and Brain Sciences* paper, with special mentions for Takashi Ikegami, Mike Anderson, Tom Froese, Tony Chemero, Ned Block, Susanna Siegel, Don Ross, Peter König, Aaron Sloman, Mike Spratling, Mike Anderson, Howard Bowman, Tobias Egner, Chris Eliasmith, Dan Rasmussen, Paco Calvo, Michael Madary, Will Newsome, Giovanni Pezzulo, and Erik Rietveld; to Johan Kwisthout, Iris van Rooij, Andre Bastos, Harriet Feldman, and all the participants at the Lorentz Center Workshop 'Perspectives on Human Probabilistic Inference' held in Leiden, Netherlands, in May 2014; to Daniel Dennett, Susan Dennett, Patricia and Paul Churchland, Dave Chalmers, Nick Humphrey, Keith Frankish, Jesse Prinz, Derk Pereboom, Dmitry Volkov, and the students from Moscow State University, who in June 2014 discussed these (along with many other) themes on an unforgettable boat trip among the icebergs of Greenland. Thanks also to Rob Goldstone, Julian Kiverstein, Gary Lupyan, Jon Bird, Lee de-Wit, Chris Frith, Richard Hensen, Paul Fletcher, Robert Clowes, Robert Rupert, Zoe Drayson, Jan Lauwereyns, Karin Kukkonen, and Martin Pickering for informative and provocative discussions of some of this material. Thank to my OUP editor Peter Ohlin for his constant interest, help, and support, to Emily Sacharin for her patient work on the figures, to Molly Morrison for final-stages editorial support, and to Lynn Childress for the fantastic copy-editing. Heartfelt thanks to my wonderful partner Alexa Morcom, my amazing mother Christine Clark, the entire Clark and Morcom clans, Borat and Bruno (the cats), and all our friends and colleagues in Edinburgh and beyond. Finally, this one is also in memory of my wonderful brother James ('Jimmy') Clark.

Most of the present text is new, but some chapters reproduce or draw on material from the following published articles:

Whatever next? Predictive brains, situated agents, and the future of cognitive science. *Behavioral and Brain Sciences, 36*(3), 2013, 181–204.

The many faces of precision. *Frontiers in Psychology, 4*(270), 2013. doi:10.3389/fpsyg.2013.00270.

Perceiving as predicting. In D. Stokes, M. Mohan, & S. Biggs (Eds.), *Perception and its modalities*. New York: Oxford University Press, 2014.

Expecting the world: Perception, prediction, and the origins of human knowledge. *Journal of Philosophy, 110*(9), 2013, 469–496.

Embodied prediction. Contribution to T. Metzinger and J. M. Windt (Eds.), *Open MIND Project*. Frankfurt am Maine: MIND Group open access publication. 2015, online at: http://open-mind.net

Thanks to the editors and publishers for permission to use this material here. Sources of figures are credited in the legends.

SURFING UNCERTAINTY

Introduction

Guessing Games

This is a book about how creatures like us get to know the world and to act in it. At the heart of such knowing engagements lies (if these stories are on track) a simple but remarkably powerful trick or stratagem. That trick is trying to guess the incoming sensory stmulations as they arrive, using what you know about the world. Failed guesses generate 'prediction errors' that are then used to recruit new and better guesses, or to inform slower processes of learning and plasticity. Rooted in the dynamics of self-organization, these 'predictive processing' (PP) models deliver compelling accounts of perception, action, and imaginative simulation. They deliver new accounts of the nature and structure of human experience. And they place centre stage a self-fuelling cycle of circular causal commerce in which action continuously selects new sensory stimulations, folding in environmental structure and opportunities along the way. PP thus provides, or so I will argue, the perfect neuro-computational partner for recent work on the embodied mind—work that stresses the constant engagement of the world by cycles of perceptuo-motor activity. The predictive brain, if this is correct, is not an insulated inference engine so much as an action-oriented engagement machine. It is an engagement-machine, moreover, that is perfectly positioned to select frugal, action-based routines that reduce the demands on neural processing and deliver fast, fluent forms of adaptive success.

Prediction is, of course, a slippery beast. It appears, even within these pages, in many subtly (and not-so-subtly) different forms. Prediction, in its most familiar incarnation, is something that a *person* engages in, with a view to anticipating the shape of future events. Such predictions are informed, conscious guesses, usually made well in advance, generated by forward-looking agents in the service of their plans and projects. But that kind of prediction, that kind of conscious guessing, is not the kind that lies at the heart of the story I shall present. At the heart of that story is a different (though not ultimately unrelated) kind of prediction, a different kind of 'guessing'. It is the kind of automatically deployed, deeply probabilistic, non-conscious guessing that occurs as part of the complex neural processing routines that underpin and unify perception and action. Prediction, in this latter sense, is something brains do to enable embodied, environmentally situated agents to carry out various tasks.

This emphasis on prediction has a long history in the sciences of mind.[1] But it is only in the last decade or so that the key elements have come together to offer what is (potentially at least) the first truly unifying account of perception, cognition, and action. Those elements include practical computational demonstrations of the power and feasibility of prediction-driven learning, the emergence of new neuroscientific frameworks that complement the computational ones, and a wealth of experimental results suggesting an inner economy in which predictions, prediction-error signals, and estimates of our own sensory uncertainty play a large and previously underappreciated role. Such work straddles the once-firm divide between accounts that stress the importance of inner, model-building activity and those that recognize the delicate distributions of labour between brain, body, and world.

PP, as I shall describe it, may best be seen as what Spratling (2013) dubs an 'intermediate-level model'. Such a model leaves unspecified a great many important details concerning neural implementation, aiming instead to 'identify common computational principles that operate across different structures of the nervous system [and] provide functional explanations of the empirical data that are arguably the most relevant to neuroscience'. It thus offers a distinctive set of tools and concepts, and a kind of mid-level organizational sketch, as a means of triangulating perception, cognition, emotion, and action. The PP schema is especially attractive because it deeply illuminates the nesting of the neural economy within the much larger nexus of embodied, world-involving action. Applied to a wide variety of both normal and pathological cases and phenomena, PP suggests new ways of making sense of the form and structure of human experience, and opens up an interesting dialogue with work on self-organization, dynamics, and embodied cognition.

Brains like ours, this picture suggests, are predictive engines, constantly trying to guess at the structure and shape of the incoming sensory array. Such brains are incessantly pro-active, restlessly seeking to generate the sensory data for themselves using the incoming signal (in a surprising inversion of much traditional wisdom) mostly as a means of checking and correcting their best top-down guessing. Crucially, however, the shape and flow of all that inner guessing is flexibly modulated by changing estimations of the relative uncertainty of (hence our confidence in) different aspects of the incoming signal. The upshot is a dynamic, self-organizing system in which the inner (and outer) flow of information is constantly reconfigured according to the demands of the task and the changing details of the internal (interoceptively sensed) and external context.

Such accounts make tempting contact with the form and structure of human experience itself. That contact is evident, for example, in the ease which such models accommodate the perceptual strangeness of unexpected sensations (as when we take a sip of tea under the strong expectation of coffee) or the remarkable salience of omissions (as when the note that is suddenly absent from a well-predicted musical sequence seems almost present in experience, before being replaced by a strong sense of a very specific absence). PP models also illuminate a variety of pathologies and disturbances, ranging from schizophrenia and autism to 'functional motor syndromes' (in which expectations and altered assignments of confidence (precision) result in false sensory 'evidence' of illness or injury).

More generally still, the PP framework delivers a compelling and unifying account of familiar human experiences such as the capacity to produce mental imagery, to reason 'off-line' about possible future choices and actions, and to grasp the intentions and goals of other agents. All these capacities, we shall see, emerge naturally from the use of a top-down 'generative model' (more on which shortly) as a means of intelligently guessing (predicting) the play of sensory data across multiple spatial and temporal scales. This same apparatus delivers a firm and intuitive grip upon the nature and possibility of meaning itself. For to be able to predict the play of sensory data at multiple spatial and temporal scales just is, or so I shall argue, to encounter the world as a locus of meaning. It is to encounter, in perception, action, and imagination, a world that is structured, populated by organism-salient distal causes, and prone to evolve in certain ways. Perception, understanding, action and imagination, if PP is correct, are constantly co-constructed courtesy of our ongoing attempts at guessing the sensory signal.

That guessing ploy is of profound importance. It provides the common currency that binds perception, action, emotion, and the exploitation of environmental structure into a functional whole. In contemporary cognitive scientific parlance, this ploy turns upon the acquisition and deployment of a 'multilayer probabilistic generative model'.

The phrase, when first encountered, is a little daunting. But the basic idea is not. It can be illustrated right away, using as a springboard a tale told to me by one of my true philosophical and scientific heroes, Daniel Dennett, while we were rather splendidly marooned in his Maine farmhouse late in the summer of 2011, courtesy of Hurricane Irene. Back in the mid-1980s, Dennett encountered a colleague, a famous palaeontologist who was worried that students were cheating at their homework by simply copying (sometimes even tracing) the stratigraphy drawings he really wanted them to understand. A stratigraphy drawing—literally, the drawing of layers—is one of those geological cross-sections showing (you guessed it) rock layers and layerings, whose job is to reveal the way complex structure has accrued over time. Successful tracing of such a drawing is, however, hardly a good indicator of your geological grasp!

To combat the problem, Dennett imagined a device that was later prototyped and dubbed SLICE. SLICE, named and built by the software engineer Steve Barney,[2] ran on an original IBM PC and was essentially a drawing program whose action was not unlike that of the Etch-a-Sketch device many of us played with as children. Except that this device controlled the drawing in a much more complex and interesting fashion. SLICE was equipped with a number of 'virtual' knobs, and each knob controlled the unfolding of a basic geological cause or process, for example, one knob would deposit layers of sediment, another would erode, another would intrude lava, another would control fracture, another fold, and so on.

The basic form of the homework is then as follows: the student is *given* a stratigraphy drawing and has to *recreate* the picture not by tracing or simple copying but by twiddling the right knobs, in the right order. In fact, the student has no choice here, since the device (unlike an Etch-a-Sketch or a contemporary drawing application) does not support pixel-by-pixel, or line-by-line, control. The *only way* to make geological depictions appear on screen is to find the right 'geological cause' knobs (for example, depositing sediment, then intruding lava) and deploy them with the right intensities. This means twiddling the right knobs, in the right sequence, and with the right intensities ('volumes') so as to recreate the original drawing. Dennett's thinking was that IF a student could do that, then she really did understand quite a lot about how hidden geological causes (like sedimentation, erosion, lava flow, and fracture) conspire to generate the physical outcomes captured by different stratigraphic drawings. In the terminology that I will be using in the rest of this book, the successful student would have to command a 'generative model', enabling her to construct various geological outcomes for herself, based upon an understanding of what causes might be at work and how they would need to interact to yield the target drawing. The target drawing thus plays the role of the sensory evidence that the student needs to re-construct using her best model of the geological domain.

We can take this further by requiring the student to command a *probabilistic* generative model. For a single presented picture, there will often be a number of different ways of combining the various knob twiddlings to recreate it. But some of these combinations may represent far more likely sequences and events than others. To get full marks, then, the student should deploy the set of twiddlings that correspond to the set of events (the set of 'hidden geological causes') that are the *most likely* to have brought about the observed outcome. More advanced tests might then show a picture while explicitly ruling out the most common set of causes, thus forcing the student to find an alternative way of bringing that state about (forcing her to find the *next most likely* set of causes, and so on).

SLICE allows the user to deploy what she knows about geological causes (sedimentation, erosion, etc.) and how they interact to self-generate a stratigraphic image: one that matches the image set in the homework. This stops the cheating. To match the given picture (just a set of pixels after all) by twiddling knobs that create that picture from well-controlled mixtures of hidden causes such as erosion, sedimentation, and fracture *just is* to understand quite a lot about geology and geological causes.

This is a nice—if limited—illustration of a fundamental trick that the brain uses, if the models I will be considering are on track, to make sense of the ongoing play of sensory signals (really, just impinging energies) received from the world. We perceive the world, this suggests, by identifying the set of interacting worldly causes that make most likely the current patterns of energies impinging upon our many (exteroceptive, proprioceptive, and and interoceptive) sensory receptors. In this way, we see the world by (if you will) guessing the world, using the sensory signal to refine and nuance the guessing as we go along.

Notice that the real-world perceptual matching task targets not a single static outcome (as in SLICE) but rather an evolving real-world scene. Matching the incoming signal, in the kinds of cases we will be considering, thus requires knowing how the elements of the scene will evolve and interact across multiple spatial and temporal scales. This can be accomplished courtesy of the multilevel nature of the prediction-mongering neural organization—we shall have a lot more to say about such multilevel architectures in the chapters to follow.

To complete the illustration, we need to remove both the student and as much of the prior knowledge as possible from the equation! The resulting device is SLICE*: a self-sufficient version of SLICE that acquires its own knowledge concerning geological hidden causes. In microcosm at least, using prediction-driven learning in hierarchical (deep, multilayer) architectures, this can be done. The key idea, one that seems to be turning up in very many guises in contemporary cognitive science, is that we also *learn* about the world by attempting to generate the incoming sensory data for ourselves, from the top-down, using the massed recurrent connectivity distinctive of advanced biological brains. This works because good models make better predictions, and we can improve our models by slowly amending them (using well-understood learning routines) so as to incrementally improve their predictive grip upon the sensory stream.

The core idea, as it emerges for the simple but unrealistic (see below) case of passive perception, can now be summarized. To perceive the world is to meet the sensory signal with an apt stream of multilevel predictions. Those predictions aim to construct the incoming sensory signal 'from the top down' using stored knowledge about interacting distal causes. To accommodate the incoming sensory signal in this way is already to understand quite a lot about the world. Creatures deploying this kind of strategy learn to become knowledgeable consumers of their own sensory stimulations. They come to know about their world, and about the kinds of entity and event that populate it. Creatures deploying this strategy, when they see the grass twitch in just that certain way, are *already expecting* to see the tasty prey emerge, and *already expecting* to feel the sensations of their own muscles tensing to pounce. An animal, or machine, that has that kind of grip on its world is already deep into the business of understanding that world. This whole bedrock story about perception and learning is presented in Part I of the present treatment.

But there is something crucial missing from this neat picture of passive perception. What is missing is action, and action changes everything. Our massed recurrent neuronal ensembles are not just buzzing away constantly trying to predict the sensory stream. They are constantly *bringing about* the sensory stream by causing bodily movements that selectively harvest new sensory stimulations. Perception and action are thus locked in a kind of endless circular embrace. This means that we need to make a further—and cognitively crucial—amendment. Our new toy system is a robot (call it Robo-SLICE) that must act in ways responsive to the sensory stimulations it receives. It must act, that is to say, in ways appropriate to the combinations of bodily and environmental causes that (it estimates) make the current sensory data most likely. World-engaging actions are now central to the account, enabling Robo-SLICE actively to seek and select its own sensory stimulations, exposing its receptors to the kinds of energetic inputs that matter for its own survival and for the kinds of goals and purposes to which it has become attuned. Robo-SLICE, moreover, is able to use action upon the world to reduce the complexity of its own inner processing, selecting frugal, efficient routines that trade movement and environmental structure against costly computation.

Imagining Robo-SLICE is a tall order, and the limitations of our little thought experiment are rapidly revealed. For we have not specified any kind of lifestyle, niche, or set of basic concerns for SLICE, and so we have no sense of what might constitute *apt action* in response to the sensory inputs. Nor have we yet shown how the ongoing attempt to predict the sensory signal might *cause* such an agent to act appropriately, sampling its world in ways designed to bring the sensory signal progressively in line with some special subset of its own sensory predictions. This neat trick, which turns some of our sensory predictions into self-fulfilling prophecies, is the subject of Part II of the present treatment.

And we are not there yet. To complete the picture, we will need to endow Robo-SLICE with a capacity to alter the long-term structure of its own social and material environment, so as to inhabit a world in which the 'energetic inputs that matter' are more reliably served up as and when required. Such world-structuring, repeated time and time again, generation by generation, also enables beings like us to build better and better worlds to think in, allowing impinging energies to guide ever-more-complex forms of behaviour and enabling thought and reason to penetrate domains that were previously 'off-limits'. This, then, is Situated Robo-SLICE —an autonomous, active, learning system able to alter its world in ways that improve its thinking and serve (and alter) its needs. This is the subject of Part III of the present treatment.

I want to end this brief Introduction by mentioning some key features and attractions that are just-visible (or so I hope) from the sketch above.

One feature is cognitive co-emergence. The strategy of multilevel sensory prediction simultaneously supports rich, world-revealing forms of perception, is learning-friendly, and looks well-placed to usher imagination (and, as we will later see, more directed forms of mental simulation) onto the biological stage. If we perceive the world by generating the incoming sensory data 'top-down' using stored knowledge about the world to recreate salient aspects of those sensory patterns, then perceiving itself involves a form of understanding: it involves knowing what things are like, and how they are disposed to evolve over time. Imagination is there too, since the capacity to self-generate (at least an approximation to) the sensory signal implies that systems that can perceive the world this way can also generate, off-line, perception-like states for themselves. Such self-generation is simply another use of the same generative-model-style knowledge that enables them to meet incoming sensory stimulations with apt sensory predictions.

Such accounts make deep and suggestive contact with the recent explosion of experimental results favouring the so-called 'Bayesian brain hypothesis': the hypothesis that the brain somehow implements processing that approximates ideal ways of weighing new evidence against prior knowledge. Finding the set of hidden causes that make the current sensory data most likely corresponds to Bayesian inference.

Such brains will not, of course, get everything right, all the time! I was struck recently by the following description by Lt Colonel Henry Worsley, head of a British Army team on an expedition to the North Pole:

> Whiteout days are tricky. That's when the cloud cover gets so low it obscures the horizon. Amundsen called it 'the white darkness'. You have no idea of distance or height. There's a story of him seeing what he thought was a man on the horizon. As he started walking, he realized it was a dog turd just three feet in front of him.[3]

The 'man' percept may well have been globally (i.e., overall, in the kind of world we inhabit and in the light of our state of information) 'Bayes' optimal' given that Amundsen believed that he was looking to a far horizon. Colonel Worsley's brain, that is to say, may have been crunching prior knowledge and present evidence together in the best possible fashion. Nonetheless, that percept of a man on the horizon was really tracking a mere turd. Whenever I use the worrying word 'optimal' in this book, I mean to gesture only at this kind of 'dog-turd optimality'.

Another large-scale feature is integration. The perspective to be explored will allow us to view a number of core cognitive phenomena (perception, action, reason, attention, emotion, experience, and learning) in a unified way, and it will suggest ways of making qualitative and perhaps even quantitative sense of many of the claims of 'embodied and situated' cognitive science. These latter integrations are made possible by a kind of cognitive common denominator in the form of 'ways of rendering increasingly predictable the stream of sensory data'. We can twiddle the knobs in our generative model so as to match the sensory data. But we can also alter the data to make it easier to capture by twiddling the knobs—alterations that may be effected both by our immediate actions, and by longer term bouts of environmental restructuring. This potential unification of work on probabilistic neural processing with work on the role of embodiment and action is, I believe, one of the most attractive features of the emerging framework.

These same accounts open up new avenues for thinking about the shape and nature of human experience. By foregrounding prediction and (importantly) neural estimations of the reliability of those predictions, they cast new light upon a variety of pathologies and disturbances including schizophrenia, autism, and functional motor and sensory symptoms.[4] They also help us to appreciate the large and complex space of neurotypical human experience and may offer hints (especially once we incorporate interoceptive predictions concerning our own evolving visceral states) concerning the mechanistic origins of conscious feelings and experience.

Despite all this, it is perhaps worth stressing that prediction is not the only instrument in the brain's cognitive toolkit. For prediction, at least in the rather specific sense to be explored, involves the recruitment, at quite short timescales, of top-down approximations to the incoming sensory signal using prediction error signals computed during online processing. This is a powerful strategy that may well underlie a wide variety of cognitive and behavioural effects. But it is surely not the only strategy available to the brain, let alone to the active agent. Adaptive response is a many-splendored thing, and multiple strategies must surely combine to keep active agents in touch with their complex, and partially self-constructed, worlds.

But even upon this wider playing field prediction may play a key role, contributing to the moment-by-moment *orchestration* of our many disparate inner and outer resources, as well as in the construction of core forms of intelligent contact with the world. What emerges is a picture in which prediction-based processing (courtesy, we shall see, of variable 'precision-weighting') selects transient neuronal ensembles.

Those transient ensembles recruit, and are constantly recruited by, bodily actions that may exploit all manner of environmental opportunities and structure. In this way, the vision of the predictive brain makes full and fruitful contact with that of the embodied, environmentally situated mind.

Finally, it is important to notice that there are really two stories on offer in the present work. One is an extremely broad vision of the brain as an engine of multilevel probabilistic prediction. The other is a more specific proposal ('hierarchical predictive coding' or Predictive Processing (PP)) concerning just how such a story might be told. It is entirely possible that the broad story will turn out to be correct, even if many of the details of the more specific proposal (PP) turn out to be wrong or incomplete. The added value of pursuing the more specific proposal is twofold. First, that proposal represents the most thoroughly worked out version of the more general story that is currently available. Second, it is a proposal that has already been applied to a large—and ever-increasing—variety of phenomena. It thus serves as a powerful illustration of the potential of some such story to tackle a wide range of issues, illuminating perception, action, reason, emotion, experience, understanding other agents, and the nature and origins of various pathologies and breakdowns.

These are exciting developments. Their upshot is not, I think, yet another 'new science of the mind', but something potentially rather better. For what emerges is really just a meeting point for the best of many previous approaches, combining elements from work in connectionism and artificial neural networks, contemporary cognitive and computational neuroscience, Bayesian approaches to dealing with evidence and uncertainty, robotics, self-organization, and the study of the embodied, environmentally situated mind. By seeing brains as restless, pro-active organs constantly driven to predict and help bring about the play of sensory stimulation, we may be glimpsing some of the core functionality that allows three pounds or so of mobile, body-based brain-meat, immersed in the human social and environmental swirl, to know and engage its world.

Part I

THE POWER OF PREDICTION

1

Prediction Machines

1.1   *Two Ways to Sense the Coffee*

What happens when, after a brief chat with a colleague, I re-enter my office and visually perceive the hot, steaming, mug of coffee that I left waiting on my desk? One possibility is that my brain receives a swathe of visual signals (imagine, for simplicity, an array of activated pixels) that rapidly specify a number of elementary features such as lines, edges, and colour patches. Those elementary features are then fed forward, progressively accumulated, and (where appropriate) bound together, yielding higher and higher level types of information culminating in an encoding of shapes and relations. At some point, these complex shapes and relations activate bodies of stored knowledge, turning the forward flow of sensation into world-revealing perception: the seeing of steaming delicious coffee in (as it happens) a funky retro-green mug. Such a model, though here simplistically expressed, corresponds quite accurately to traditional cognitive scientific approaches that depict perception as a cumulative process of 'bottom-up' feature detection.[1]

Here is an alternative scenario. As I re-enter my office my brain already commands a complex set of coffee-and-office involving expectations. Glancing at my desk, a few rapidly processed visual cues set off a chain of visual processing in which incoming sensory signals (variously called 'driving' or 'bottom-up signals') are met by a stream of downwards (and lateral[2]) predictions concerning the most probable states of this little world. These predictions reflect the buzzing, pro-active nature of much of our ongoing neuronal processing. That torrent of downward-flowing prediction is in the business of pre-emptively specifying the probable states of various neuronal groups along the appropriate visual (and other) pathways. The downwards (and lateral) flow of prediction concerns all aspects of the unfolding encounter and is not limited to simple visual features such as shape and colour. It may include a wealth of multimodal associations and (as we shall see in subsequent chapters) a complex mix of motoric and affective predictions. There ensues a rapid exchange (an energetic dance between multiple top-down and bottom-up signals) in which incorrect downward-flowing 'guesses' yield error signals that propagate laterally and upwards and are used to leverage better and better guesses. When the flow of prediction adequately accounts for the incoming signal, the visual scene is perceived. As this process unfolds, the system is trying to generate (at multiple spatial and temporal scales) the incoming sensory signal for itself. When this succeeds, and a match is established, we experience a structured visual scene.

That, I submit, is how I actually see the coffee. This bare-bones proposal, to be nuanced, refined, and repeatedly augmented as our story unfolds, recalls the catchy (but potentially a little distortive, as we shall see in chapter 6) dictum that *perception is controlled hallucination*.[3] Our brains try to guess what is out there, and to the extent that that guessing accommodates the sensory barrage, we perceive the world.

1.2   *Adopting the Animal's Perspective*

How does all that knowledge—the knowledge that powers the predictions that underlie perception and (as we shall later see) action—arise in the first place? Surely we have to perceptually experience the world *before* we can acquire the knowledge needed to make predictions about it? In which case, perceptual experience cannot require prediction-based processing after all.

To resolve this worry, we will need firmly to distinguish what might be thought of as the mere transduction of energetic patterns via the senses from the kinds of rich, world-revealing perception that result (if this story is on track) when and only when that transduction can be met with apt top-down expectations. The question then becomes: How, on the basis of mere energetic transduction, can apt expectations ever be formed and brought to bear? It is an attractive feature of the story on offer that the *very same process* (attempting to predict the current sensory input) may turn out to underlie both learning and online response.

A good place to start (following Rieke et al., 1997, and Eliasmith, 2005) is by contrasting the perspective of an external observer of some system with that of the animal or system itself. The external observer might be able to see, for example, that certain neurons in the frog's brain fire only when there is a pattern of retinal stimulation that most often occurs when some juicy prey, such as a fly, is within tongue's reach. That pattern of neuronal activity might then be said to 'represent' the presence of the prey. But such descriptions, though sometimes useful, can blind us to a much more pressing problem. This is the problem of how the frog, or any other system of interest, might come to get a grip upon a world at all. To bring this question into better view, we need to adopt (in an innocent sense to be explained shortly) the perspective not of the external observer but of the frog itself. The way to do this is to consider *only the evidence available to the frog*. In fact, even this may be misleading, as it seems to invite us to imagine the world from some kind of frog's eye view. Instead, to adopt the animal's perspective in the sense at issue is to restrict ourselves to what can be known from the flows of energetic stimulation that impinge upon the frog's sensory apparatus. Those energetic stimulations might indeed be caused by what we, as external observers, recognize as a fly. But the only thing that is ever available to the frog's brain is the perturbations to its sensory systems caused by the energies flowing from the world across its many receptors. This means, as Eliasmith (2005, p. 102) points out, that 'the set of possible stimuli is unknown, and an animal must infer what is being presented given various sensory cues'. I would add (to anticpate some of our later discussions) that 'inferring what is being presented' is deeply related to selecting apt actions. The animal's perspective, in this sense, is determined by what information is made available, via changing states of the sensory receptors, to the animal's brain. But the whole point of 'processing' that information is to help select an appropriate action, given the current state of the animal (e.g., how hungry it is) and the state of the world as indexed by those impiniging energies.

It is also worth stressing that the term 'information' is here used simply as a description of 'energy transfer' (see Eliasmith, 2005; Fair, 1979). Talk of information, that is to say, must ultimately be cashed simply in terms of the energies impinging upon the sensory receptors. This is essential if we are to avoid, yet again, the illicit importation of an observer's perspective into our account of how informed observers are naturally possible in the first place. Information talk, thus used, makes no assumptions concerning what the information is about. This is essential, since sorting that out is precisely what the animal's brain needs to do if it is to serve as an empowering resource for the control of an environmentally apt response. It is thus the task of the (embodied, situated) brain to turn those energetic stimulations into action-guiding information.

An early example of 'taking the animal's perspective' in this way can be found, Eliasmith notes, in the work of Fitzhugh (1958) who explored ways to try to infer the nature of the environmental causes from the responses of the animal's nerve fibres alone, deliberately ignoring everything he knew (as an external observer) about the kinds of stimuli to which those fibres might be responding. In this way:

> Just as a brain (or its parts) infer the state of the world from sensory signals, Fitzhugh attempts to determine what is in the world, once he knows a nerve fiber's response to an unknown stimulus. He purposefully limits the information he works with to that available to the animal. The 'extra' information available via the observer's perspective is only used after the fact to 'check his answers'; it is not used to determine what the animal is representing. (Eliasmith, 2005, p. 100)

Fitzhugh faced a formidable task. Yet such, in essence, is the task of the biological brain. The brain must discover information about the likely causes of impinging signals without any form of direct access to their source. All that it 'knows' about, in any direct sense, are the ways its own states (e.g., spike trains) flow and alter. Such states also cause effects in the embodied organism, some of which (an external observer might notice) are effects upon the motion of the sensory transducers themselves. In this way active agents get to structure their own sensory flows, affecting the ebb and flow of their own energetic stimulation. This, we shall later see, is an important additional source of information. But it does not alter the basic situation. It remains correct to say that all the system has direct access to is its own sensory states (patterns of stimulation across its sensory receptors).

How, simply on the basis of patterns of stimulation across the sensory receptors, can embodied, situated brains alter and adapt so as to act as useful nodes (ones that incur considerable metabolic expense) for the origination of adaptive response? Notice how different this conception is to ones in which the problem is posed as one of establishing a mapping relation between environmental and inner states. The task is not to find such a mapping but to infer the nature of the signal source (the world) from just the varying input signal itself.

1.3   Learning in Bootstrap Heaven

Prediction-driven learning provides a remarkably powerful way to make progress under such initially unpromising conditions. The best way to appreciate this is by first recalling the kind of learning that can be achieved by providing a system with an apt 'teacher'. The teacher, of course, is not usually a human agent, but rather some automated signal that tells the learner exactly what it ought to be doing or concluding given the current input. Systems that rely on such signals are said to be 'supervised' learners. The most famous such systems are those relying upon the so-called 'back-propagation of error' (e.g., Rumelhart, Hinton, & Williams, 1986a,b; and discussion in Clark, 1989, 1993). In these kinds of 'connectionist' systems the current output (typically, some kind of cat-egorization of the input) is compared to the correct output (as set-up in some body of labelled or otherwise pre-classified training data) and the connection weights that encode the system's know-how slowly adjusted to bring future response more and more into line. Such processes of slow automatic adjustment (known as gradient descent learning) are able to take systems starting with random assignments of connection weights and gradually—all being well[4]—bring them up to speed.

The development and refinement of connectionist systems was a crucial step in the long lineage leading to the predictive processing (PP) models that we shall shortly be considering. Indeed, predictive pro-cessing (and more generally, hierarchical Bayesian) models are prob-ably best seen as a development within that same broad lineage (for discussion, see McClelland, 2013, and Zorzi et al., 2013). Prior to such work, it was tempting[5] to simply deny that effective and fundamental learning was possible, given only the apparently slim pickings of the sensory evidence. Instead, the bulk of human knowledge might simply have been innate, gradually installed in the shape and functioning of our neural circuits over many millennia.

Connectionist models of learning raised important doubts about such arguments, showing that it was actually possible to learn quite a lot from the statistically rich bodies of sensory data that we actually encountered (for a review, see Clark, 1993). But standard (back-propagation-trained) connectionist approaches were hampered in two ways. The first was the need to provide sufficient amounts of pre-categorized training data to drive supervised learning. The second was the difficulty of training such networks in multilayer forms,[6] since this required distributing the response to the error signal in hard-to-determine ways across all the layers. Prediction-driven learning, applied in multilayer settings, addresses both these issues.

Let's take the training signal first. One way to think about prediction-driven learning is to see it as offering an innocent (that is, ecologically feasible) form of supervised learning. More accurately, it offers a form of self-supervised learning, in which the 'correct' response is repeatedly provided, in a kind of ongoing rolling fashion, by the environment itself. Thus, imagine you are that brain/network, busily transducing signals from the world, able to detect only the ongoing changes in your own sensory registers. One thing you can do, while thus helping yourself to nothing more than the 'animal's perspective', is busily to try to predict the next state of those very registers.

The temporal story here is, however, rather more complex than that makes it seem. It is easiest to think of the process in terms of prediction at discrete time-steps. But, in fact, the story we will explore depicts the brain as engaging in a continuous process of sensory prediction in which the target is a kind of rolling present. The line between 'predicting the present' and 'predicting the very-near-future' is one that simply vanishes once we see the percept itself as a prediction-driven construct that is always rooted in the past (systemic knowledge) and anticipating, at multiple temporal and spatial scales, the future.[7]

The good news about the prediction task is that the world itself will now provide the training signal you need. For the states of your sensory registers *will* change, in ways systematically driven by the incoming signal, as the world around you changes. In this way, the evolving states of your own sensory receptors provide a training signal allowing your brain to 'self-supervise' its own learning. Thus:

> predictive forms of learning are particularly compelling because they provide a ubiquitous source of learning signals: if you attempt to predict everything that happens next, then every single moment is a learning opportunity. This kind of pervasive learning can for example explain how an infant seems to magically acquire such a sophisticated understanding of the world, despite their seemingly inert overt behavior (Elman, Bates, Johnson, Karmiloff-Smith, Parisi, & Plunkett, 1996)—they are becoming increasingly expert predictors of what they will see next, and as a result, developing increasingly sophisticated internal models of the world. (O'Reilly et al. (submitted) p. 3)

The prediction task, thus conceived, is a kind of bootstrap heaven. For example, to predict the next word in a sentence, it helps to know about grammar (and lots more too). But one way to learn a surprising amount about grammar (and lots more too) is to look for the best ways to predict the next words in sentences. This is just the kind of training that the world can naturally provide, since your attempts at prediction are soon followed by the soundform corresponding to (you guessed it) the next word in the sentence. You can thus use the prediction task to bootstrap your way to the grammar, which you then use in the prediction task in future. Properly handled, this kind of bootstrapping (which implements a version of 'empirical Bayes'; see Robbins, 1956) turns out to provide a very potent training regime indeed.

Prediction-driven learning thus exploits a rich, free, constantly available, bootstrap-friendly, teaching signal in the form of the ever-changing sensory signal itself. Whether the task is ecologically basic (e.g., predicting the evolving visual scene so as to spot predators and prey) or more ecologically advanced (e.g., detecting coffee cups or predicting the next word in a sentence) the world can be relied upon to provide a training signal allowing us to compare current predictions with actual sensed patterns of energetic input. This allows well-understood learning algorithms to unearth rich information about the interacting external causes ('latent variables') that are actually structuring the incoming signal. But in practice this requires an additional and vital ingredient. That ingredient is the use of multilevel learning.

1.4   *Multilevel Learning*

Prediction-driven learning operating in hierarchical (multilayer) settings plausibly holds the key to learning about our kind of world: a world that is highly structured, displaying regularity and pattern at many spatial and temporal scales, and populated by a wide variety of interacting and complexly nested distal causes. It is there, where sensory prediction and hierarchical learning combine, that we locate an important computational advance over previous work. That advance has roots in Helmholtz's (1860) depiction of perception as a process of probabilistic, knowledge-driven inference. From Helmholtz comes the key idea that sensory systems are in the tricky business of inferring worldly causes from their bodily (sensory) effects. It is thus a kind of bet on what's out there, constructed by asking how the world would have to be for the sensory organs to be stimulated the way they currently are. Part of what makes this tricky is that a single such pattern of sensory stimulation will be consistent with many different sets of worldly causes, distinguished only by their relative (and context-dependent) probability of occurrence.

Helmholz's insights informed influential work by MacKay (1956), Neisser (1967), and Gregory (1980), as part of the cognitive psychological tradition that became known as 'analysis-by-synthesis' (for a review, see Yuille & Kersten, 2006).[8] In machine learning, such insights helped inspire a cascade of crucial innovations beginning with work on the aptly named 'Helmholz Machine' (Dayan et al., 1995; Dayan and Hinton, 1996; see also Hinton and Zemel, 1994). The Helmholz Machine was an early example of a multilayer architecture trainable without reliance upon experimenter pre-classified examples. Instead, the system 'self-organized' by attempting to generate the training data for itself, using its own downwards (and lateral) connections. That is to say, instead of starting with the task of classifying (or 'learning a recognition model for') the data, it had first to learn how to generate, using a multilevel system, the incoming data for itself.

This can seem an impossible task, since generating the data requires the very knowledge that the system is hoping to acquire. For example, to generate the phonetic structures proper to some public language you would need already to know a lot about the various speech sounds and how they are articulated and combined.[9] Likewise, a system could learn to perform the classification task (taking sound streams as input and delivering a phonetic parse as output) if it already commanded a generative model of phonetically structured speech in the language. But, in the absence of either, where do you begin? The answer seems to be 'gradually, and in both places at once'. The impasse was solved, in principle at least, by the development of new learning routines that made iterated visits to 'bootstrap heaven'.

The key development that made this possible was the discovery of algorithms such as the 'wake-sleep algorithm' (Hinton et al., 1995) that used each task (recognition and generation) gradually to bootstrap the other. This algorithm[10] allowed the system to learn both the recognition and the generation models by training both sets of weights in an alternating fashion, in a process of 'iterative estimation'. The wake-sleep algorithm used its own top-down connections to provide the desired (target) states for the hidden units, thus (in effect) self-supervising the development of its perceptual 'recognition model' using a generative model that tried to create the sensory patterns for itself (in 'fantasy', as it was sometimes said). Importantly, this kind of process could succeed even starting with small random weight assignments throughout (for a useful review, see Hinton, 2007a).

A generative model,[11] in this quite specific sense, aims to capture the statistical structure of some set of observed inputs by inferring a causal matrix able to give rise to that very structure. In the Introduction, we met SLICE* whose acquired generative model combined hidden geological causes such as fracture and lava intrusion so as to best account for (by generating, from the top-down) the pixel patterns in a target geological (stratigraphic) image. A good probabilistic generative model for vision would likewise seek to capture the ways that lower level visual patterns (ultimately, retinal stimulations) are generated by an inferred interacting web of distal causes. A certain pattern of retinal stimulation, encountered in a given context, might thus be best accounted for using a generative model that (as an admittedly simplistic illustration) combines top-level representations of interacting agents, objects, motives, and motions with multiple intermediate layers capturing the way colours, shapes, textures, and edges combine and temporally evolve. When the combination of such hidden causes (which span many spatial and temporal scales) settles into a coherent whole, the system has self-generated the sensory data using stored knowledge and perceives a meaningful, structured scene.

It is again worth stressing that this grip upon the structured distal scene must be generated using only the information available from the animal's perspective. It must be a grip, that is to say, rooted entirely in the combination of whatever pre-structuring (of brain and body) may be present thanks to the animal's evolutionary history and the plays of energetic stimulation that have been registered by the sensory receptors. A systematic means of achieving such a grip is provided by the ongoing attempt to self-generate the sensory signal using a multilevel architecture. In practice, this means that top-down and lateral connections within a multilevel system come to encode a probabilistic model of interacting causes operating at multiple scales of space and time. We recognize objects and states and affairs, if these approaches are correct, by finding the most likely set of interacting factors (distal causes) whose combination would generate (hence predicts, and best accounts for) the incoming sensory data (see, e.g., Dayan, 1997; Dayan et al., 1995; Hinton et al., 1995; Hinton & Ghahramani, 1997; Hinton & Zemel, 1994; Kawato et al., 1993; Mumford, 1994; Olshausen & Field, 1996).

1.5   Decoding Digits

Consider a practical problem that many of us solve daily, often without much conscious effort: the problem of identifying handwritten digits. Granted, there is less and less of this about. But when someone does leave that hastily scrawled sticky-note on the bathroom mirror, it can be essential (or at the very least, a matter of date or no date) to distinguish the numbers. How do we do it?

The machine-learning theorist Geoffrey Hinton describes a benchmark machine-learning system capable of handwritten digit recognition (see Hinton, 2007a, b; Hinton & Nair, 2006; see also Hinton & Salakhutdinov, 2006). The system's task is simply to classify images of handwritten digits (images of handwritten 1s, 2s, 3s, etc.). That is to say, the system aims to take images of highly variable handwritten digits as inputs, and output the correct classification (identifying the digit as an instance of a 1, or a 2, or a 3 ... etc.). The set-up (see Figure 1.1) involves three layers of feature detectors trained on a corpus of unlabelled images of handwritten digits. But instead of attempting directly to train the multilayer neural network to classify the images, the network learns and deploys a probabilistic generative model of the kind described above. It learns a multilayer generative model capable of producing such images for itself, using its top-down connections (followed by some additional fine-tuning). The goal of the learning is

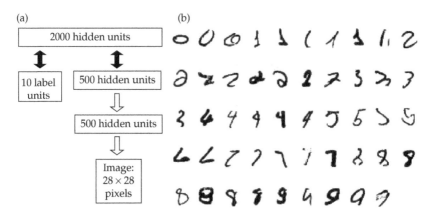

FIGURE 1.1   Learning to Recognize Hand-Written Digits
(a) The generative model used to learn the joint distribution of digit images and digit labels. (b) Some test images that the network classifies correctly even though it has never seen them before.

Source: Hinton, 2007a.

thus progressively to 'adjust the weights on the topdown connections so as to maximize the probability that the network would generate the training data' (Hinton, 2007a, p. 428). The route to successful perception (in this case, handwritten digit recognition) thus goes via a learning strategy that is actually much closer to the active generation of digits (e.g., in computer graphics).

The results were impressive. The trained net gets all the (often badly written) examples shown in Figure 1.1 right, although none were actually in the training data. The network[12] was tested extensively using a benchmark database of 60,000 training images and 10,000 test images. It outperformed all the more standard ('back-propagation' trained) artificial neural networks except those especially 'hand-crafted' to the task. It also performed nearly as well as more computationally expensive methods involving so-called 'support-vector machines'. And most important of all, it did so using a learning routine that echoes, if the stories we will be considering are on track, a key aspect of the functional organization of the brain: the use of top-down connections to generate versions of the very data to which the system seeks to respond.

Such an approach may be applied to any structured domain. Hinton's own variety (which, I should stress, differs in some very important ways from the 'predictive processing' models that we will soon be focussing upon[13]) has been successfully applied to tasks as diverse as document retrieval, predicting the next word in a sentence, and predicting what movies people will enjoy (see Hinton & Salakhutdinov, 2006; Mnih & Hinton, 2007; Salakhutdinov et al., 2007). To begin to appreciate the potential power of such approaches, it helps to note that the entire digit recognition network, Hinton remarks, has only 'about as many parameters as 0.002 cubic millimeters of mouse cortex' and that 'several hundred networks of this complexity would fit within a single voxel of a high resolution fMRI scan' (Hinton, 2005, p. 10). Hinton plays this card humbly, as a means of dramatizing just how far machine learning still has to go. But looked at another way, it invites us to appreciate just how deep a grip on the world that surrounds us a brain as complex as ours, deploying some version of that potent learning strategy, might achieve.

1.6   Dealing with Structure

Prediction-driven multilevel learning also addresses another key shortfall of early ('back-propagation of error' based) connectionist treatments—their lack of a principled means of dealing with structure. This is the need to represent and process 'complex, articulated structures' (Hinton, 1990, p. 47) such as part-whole hierarchies: structures in which elements form wholes that can themselves be elements of one or more larger wholes. Work in 'classical Artificial Intelligence' offered a rather (too) direct solution to this problem. Conventional symbolic approaches used systems of 'pointers' in which one essentially arbitrary digital object could be used to access another, which might itself be used to access another, and so on. Within such a system a symbol could be viewed as 'a small [usually arbitrary] representation of an object that provides an "remote access" path to a fuller representation of the same object'. In this way 'many [small] symbols can be put together to create a "fully-articulated" representation of some larger structure' (both quotes from Hinton, 1990, p. 47). Such systems could indeed represent structured (nested, often hierarchical) relationships in a manner that allowed for easy sharing and recombination of elements. But they proved brittle and inflexible in other ways, failing to display fluid context-sensitive responsiveness, and floundering when required to guide behaviour in time-pressured real-world settings.[14]

The need to deal in a principled manner with structured domains drove much early scepticism (e.g., Fodor & Pylyshyn, 1988) about the connectionist alternative to the use of classical, sentence-like internal representational forms. But jump to the year 2007 and we find Geoffrey Hinton, a machine-learning theorist not given to overstatement, writing that 'the limitations of back-propagation learning can now be overcome by using multilayer neural networks that contain top-down connections and training them to generate sensory data rather than to classify it' (Hinton, 2007a, p. 428). The worries about structure are directly addressed because (as we shall see frequently in the text) prediction-driven learning, as it unfolds in these kinds of multilayer settings, tends to separate out interacting distal (or bodily) causes operating at varying scales of space and time.

This is important since structured domains are ubiquitous in both the natural and human-built world. Language exhibits densely nested compositional structure in which words form clauses that form whole sentences that are themselves understood by locating them in the context of even larger linguistic (and non-linguistic) settings. Every visual scene, such as a city street, a factory floor, or a tranquil lake, embeds multiple nested structures (e.g., shops, shop doorways, shoppers in the doorways; trees, branches, birds on the branches, leaves, patterns on the leaves). Musical pieces exhibit structures in which overarching sequences are built from recurring and recombinant sub-sequences, each of which has structure of its own. The world, we might reasonably suggest, is known by us humans (and doubtless most other animals too) as a meaningful arena populated by articulated and nested structures of elements. Such structured forms of knowing are made possible (in ways we are about to explore) by prediction-driven learning in which top-down connections try to build-up the sensory scene using knowledge about worldy causes operating at multiple spatial and temporal scales.

1.7   Predictive Processing

It is that twist—the strategy of using top-down connections to try to generate, using world knowledge, a kind of virtual version of the sensory data via a deep multilevel cascade—that lies at the heart of 'hierarchical predictive coding' approaches to perception (Friston, 2005; Lee & Mumford, 2003; Rao & Ballard, 1999). Hierarchical predictive coding (or 'predictive processing' (Clark (2013)) combines the use of top-down probabilistic generative models with a specific vision of how and when such influence might operate. Borrowing from commercial work in 'linear predictive coding', that vision depicts the top-down and lateral flow of neural signals as constantly (not just during learning) aiming to predict the current sensory barrage, leaving only any unpredicted elements (in the form of residual 'prediction errors') to propagate information forward within the system (see Brown et al., 2011; Friston, 2005, 2010; Hohwy, 2013; Huang & Rao, 2011; Jehee & Ballard, 2009; Lee & Mumford, 2003; Rao & Ballard, 1999).

Transposed (in ways we are about to explore) to the neural domain, this makes prediction error into a kind of proxy (Feldman & Friston, 2010) for any as-yet-unexplained sensory information. Prediction error here reports the 'surprise' induced by a mismatch between the sensory signals encountered and those predicted. More formally—and to distinguish it from surprise in the normal, experientially loaded sense—this is known as surprisal (Tribus, 1961). As mentioned earlier, I shall describe such systems as engaging in 'predictive processing'. In thus speaking of 'predictive processing' rather than resting with the more common usage 'predictive coding', I mean to highlight the fact that what distinguishes these approaches is not simply the use of the data compression strategy (more on which shortly) known as predictive coding. Rather, it is the use of that strategy in the very special context of hierarchical (i.e., multilevel) systems deploying probabilistic generative models. Such systems exhibit powerful forms of learning and—as we will later see—deliver rich forms of context-sensitive processing and are able flexibly to combine top-down and bottom-up flows of information within the multilayer cascade.

Predictive coding was first developed as a data compression strategy in signal processing (for a history, see Shi & Sun, 1999). Thus consider a basic task such as image transmission. In most images, the value of one pixel regularly predicts the value of its nearest neighbours, with differences marking important features such as the boundaries between objects. That means the code for a rich image can be compressed (for a properly informed receiver) by encoding only the 'unexpected' variation: the cases where the actual value departs from the predicted one. The simplest prediction would be that neighbouring pixels all share the same value (the same grey scale value, for example) but much more complex predictions are also possible. As long as there is detectable regularity, prediction (and hence this particular form of data compression) is possible. It is the deviations from what is predicted that then carry the 'news', quantified as the difference (the 'prediction error') between the actual current signal and the predicted one. This affords major savings on bandwidth, an economy that was the driving force behind the development of the techniques by James Flanagan and others at Bell Labs during the 1950s (for a review, see Musmann, 1979).

Data-compression by informed prediction allows quite modest encodings to be reconstructed into rich and florid renditions of the original sights and sounds. Such techniques figure prominently in, for example, motion-compressed coding for video. This is an especially effective application since so much of the information needed to reconstruct the image in the current frame of a video sequence is already present in the previously processed frame. Take the case of a moving object against a stable background. There, most of the background information for the present frame can be assumed to be the same as the previous frame, with prediction error signalling changes in what is occluded, or camera pans. Nor is the technique limited to such simple cases. Predictable transforms of the moving object can themselves be factored in (as long as the speed, or even the rate of acceleration, remains the same) using so-called motion-compensated prediction error. Thus, all the information required to construct frame 2 of a very simple moving image might already be present in frame 1, with compensation applied for motion. To receive the second frame, you would then just need to transmit a simple message (e.g., informally 'same as before except move everything two pixels to the right'). In principle, every systematic and regular change could be predicted leaving only truly unexpected deviations (e.g., the emergence of an unexpected, previously occluded, object) as the source of residual errors.

The trick is thus trading intelligence and knowledge against the costs of encoding and transmission on the day. Notice that nothing here requires the receiver to engage in processes of *conscious* prediction or expectation. All that matters is that the receiving system be able to reconstruct the incoming signal in ways that make the most of whatever regularities have been detected or that it has proven useful to assume. In this way, animals like us may be saving valuable neural bandwidth by using what we already know to predict as much of the current sensory data as possible. When you seem almost to see your beloved cat or dog when the curtains start to move in just the right way (even if it was, on this occasion, only the wind that was responsible) you may have been using well-trained prediction machinery to start to complete the perceptual sequence, saving on bandwidth and (usually) knowing your world better as a result.

Predictive processing thus combines the use, within a multilevel bidirectional cascade, of 'top-down' probabilistic generative models with the core predictive coding strategy of efficient encoding and transmission. If the predictive processing story is on track, then perception is indeed a process in which we (or rather, various parts of our brains) try to guess what is out there, using the incoming signal more as a means of tuning and nuancing the guessing rather than as a rich (and bandwidth-costly) encoding of the state of the world. This does not mean, of course, that perceptual experience occurs only after all forward-flowing error is eliminated. Full, rich, percepts here take shape only when downward predictions match the incoming sensory signal at many levels. But this matching (as we will later see) is itself a piecemeal matter in which rapid perception of the general nature or 'gist' of a scene may be accomplished using a well-trained feedforward sweep that is sensitive to simple (e.g., low spatial frequency[15]) cues. Richer detail then emerges concurrently with the progressive reduction of residual error signals calculated relative to the ensuing waves of top-down prediction. The ongoing process of perceiving, if such models are correct, is a matter of the brain using stored knowledge to predict, in a progressively more refined manner, the patterns of multilayer neuronal response elicited by the current sensory stimulation. This in turn underlines the surprising extent to which the structure of our expectations (both conscious and non-conscious) may be determining much of what we see, hear, and feel.

In the rest of this book, we will thus be exploring two distinct but overlapping stories. The first is a general, and increasingly well-supported, vision of the brain (and especially the neocortex) as fundamentally an inner engine of probabilistic prediction (see, e.g., Bubic et al., 2010; Downing, 2007; Engel, Fires, et al., 2001; Kvergaga et al., 2007). The other is one specific proposal (hierarchical predictive coding, or 'predictive processing') describing the possible shape and nature of that core process of multilevel probabilistic prediction. This proposal is conceptually elegant, computationally well-grounded, and seems to have a reasonably promising shot at being neurally implemented. As a result, it is being widely applied, with new phenomena being brought under its umbrella at a surprising (sometimes even an alarming) rate. It offers a very comprehensive vision. We should not forget, however, that there are many possible models in this general vicinity.[16]

1.8   Signalling the News

To put some example-based flesh on all this, consider first a demonstration (Hosoya et al., 2005) of the basic predictive coding strategy at work in the retina. The starting point of this account is the well-established sense in which retinal ganglion cells take part in some form of predictive coding, insofar as their receptive fields display centre-surround spatial antagonism, as well as a kind of temporal antagonism. What this means is that neural circuits predict, on the basis of local image characteristics, the likely image characteristics of nearby spots in space and time (basically, assuming that nearby spots will display similar image intensities) and subtract this predicted value from the actual value. What gets encoded is thus not the raw value but the differences between raw values and predicted values. In this way, 'ganglion cells signal not the raw visual image but the departures from the predictable structure, under the assumption of spatial and temporal uniformity' (Hosoya et al., 2005, p. 71). This saves on bandwidth and also flags what is (to use Hosoya et al.'s own phrase) most 'newsworthy' in the incoming signal.

These computations of predicted salience might have been made solely on the basis of average image statistics. Such an approach would, however, lead to trouble in many ecologically realistic situations. Consider the problem faced by 'Mexican Walking Fish', a salamander that frequently moves between a watery environment and dry land. The spatial scales at which nearby points in space and time are typically similar in image intensity vary markedly between such cases, because the statistical properties of the different types of scene vary. This is true in less dramatic cases too, such as when we move from inside a building to a garden or lake. Hosoya et al. thus predicted that, in the interests of efficient, adaptively potent, encoding, the behaviour of the retinal ganglion cells (specifically, their receptive field properties) should vary as a result of adaptation to the current scene or context, exhibiting what they term 'dynamic predictive coding'.

Putting salamanders and rabbits into varying environments, and recording from their retinal ganglion cells, Hosoya et al. confirmed their hypothesis: Within a space of several seconds, about 50% of the ganglion cells altered their behaviours to keep step with the changing image statistics of the varying environments. A mechanism was then proposed and tested using a simple feedforward neural network that performs a form of anti-Hebbian learning. Anti-Hebbian feedforward learning, in which correlated activity across units leads to inhibition rather than to activation (see, e.g., Kohonen, 1989), enables the creation of so-called 'novelty filters' that learn to become insensitive to the most highly correlated (hence most 'familiar') features of the input. This, of course, is exactly what is required to learn to discount the most statistically predictable elements of the input signal in the way dynamic predictive coding suggests. Better yet, there are neuronally plausible ways to implement such a mechanism using amacrine cell synapses to mediate plastic inhibitory connections that in turn alter the receptive fields of retinal ganglion cells (for details, see Hosoya et al., 2005, p. 74) so as to suppress the most correlated components of the stimulus. In sum, retinal ganglion cells seem to be engaging in a computationally and neurobiologically explicable process of dynamic predictive recoding[17] of raw image inputs, whose effect is to 'strip from the visual stream predictable and therefore less newsworthy signals' (Hosoya et al., 2005, p. 76).

1.9   Predicting Natural Scenes

Predictive processing takes this biological emphasis on the newsworthy several steps further, offering a new take on cortical organization itself. In predictive processing schemes the incoming sensory signal is met by a flow of 'guessing' constructed using multiple layers of downward and lateral influence, and residual mismatches get passed forwards (and laterally) in the form of an error signal. At the core of such proposals lies a deep functional asymmetry between forward and backwards pathways—functionally speaking 'between raw data seeking an explanation (bottom-up) and hypotheses seeking confirmation (topdown)' (Shipp, 2005, p. 805). Each layer in such a multilevel

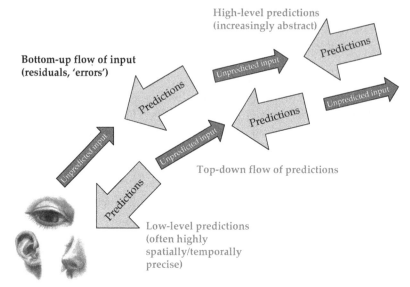

High-level predictions
(increasingly abstract)

Bottom-up flow of input
(residuals, 'errors')

Top-down flow of predictions

Low-level predictions
(often highly
spatially/temporally
precise)

Input

FIGURE 1.2   The Basic Predictive Processing Schema
A highly schematized view of the predictive processing view of information
transfer in the brain. Bottom-up inputs are processed in the context of priors
(beliefs/hypotheses) from layers higher up in the hierarchy. The unpredicted
parts of the input (errors) travel up the hierarchy, leading to the adjustment of
subsequent predictions, and the cycle continues.

Source: Adapted from Lupyan & Clark, In Press

hierarchical system treats activity in the layer below as if it were sensory input, and attempts to meet it with a flow of apt top-down prediction (for this basic schema, see Figure 1.2). There are several worked
examples of this in the literature (see the review by Huang & Rao, 2011).

Rao and Ballard (1999) provide the seminal proof-of-concept. In this
work prediction-based learning targets image patches drawn from natural scenes using a multilayer artificial neural network. The network,
which had no pre-set task apart from that of using the downwards
and lateral connections to match input samples with successful predictions, developed a nested structure of units with simple-cell-like receptive fields and captured a variety of important, empirically observed
effects. At the lowest level, there is some pattern of energetic stimulation, transduced (let's suppose) by sensory receptors from ambient
light patterns produced by the current visual scene. These signals are
then processed via a multilevel cascade in which each level attempts
to predict the activity at the level below it via backward connections.

The backward connections allow the activity at one stage of the processing to return as another input at the previous stage. So long as this
successfully predicts the lower level activity, all is well, and no further
action needs to ensue. But where there is a mismatch, 'prediction error'
occurs and the ensuing (error-indicating) activity is propagated laterally and to the higher level. This automatically recruits new probabilistic representations at the higher level so that the top-down predictions
do better at cancelling the prediction errors at the lower level (yielding rapid perceptual inference). At the same time, prediction error is
used to adjust the longer-term structure of the model so as to reduce
any discrepancy next time around (yielding slower timescale perceptual learning). Forward connections between levels thus carry only
the 'residual errors' (Rao & Ballard, 1999, p. 79) separating the predictions from the actual lower level activity, while backward and lateral
connections (conveying the generative model) carry the predictions
themselves. Changing predictions corresponds to changing or tuning
your hypothesis about the hidden causes of the lower level activity. In
the context of an embodied active animal, this means it corresponds
to changing or tuning your grip on what to do about the world, given
the current sensory barrage. The concurrent running of this kind of
prediction error calculation within a bidirectional hierarchy of cortical
areas allows information pertaining to regularities at different spatial
and temporal scales to settle into a mutually consistent whole in which
each such 'hypothesis' is used to help tune the rest. As the authors put
it, 'prediction and error-correction cycles occur concurrently throughout the hierarchy, so top-down information influences lower-level estimates, and bottom-up information influences higher-level estimates of
the input signal' (Rao & Ballard, 1999, p. 80). In the visual cortex, such a
scheme suggests that backward connections from V2 to V1 would carry
a prediction of expected activity in V1, while forward connections
from V1 to V2 would carry forward the error signal indicating residual
(unpredicted) activity. This kind of functional asymmetry in the role of
forward and backward connections is central to the PP vision.

    To test these ideas, Rao and Ballard implemented a simple bidirec-
tional hierarchical network of such 'predictive estimators' and trained
it on image patches derived from five natural scenes (see Figure 1.3).
Using learning algorithms that progressively reduce prediction error
across the linked cascade and after exposure to thousands of image
patches, the system learned to use responses in the first-level network to extract features such as oriented edges and bars, while the
second-level network came to capture combinations of such features
corresponding to patterns involving larger spatial configurations—for

FIGURE 1.3   Five Natural Images Used for Training the Three-Level
Hierarchical Network Described in the Text

Source: Rao & Ballard, 1999.

example, the alternating stripes of a zebra. In this way the hierarchical predictive coding architecture, using only the statistical properties
of the signals derived from the natural images, was able to induce a
simple generative model of the structure of the input data. It learned
about the presence and importance of features such as lines, edges, and
bars, and about combinations of such features (such as stripes) in ways
that enable better predictions concerning what to expect next, in space
or in time. In Bayes-speak (see Appendix 1), the network maximized
the posterior probability of generating the observed states (the sensory
inputs) and, in so doing, induced a kind of internal model of structure
in the signal source.

The Rao and Ballard model also displayed a number of interesting 'non-classical receptive field' effects, such as end-stopping.
End-stopping (see Rao & Sejnowski, 2002) occurs when a neuron
responds strongly to a short line falling within its classical receptive field but (surprisingly) shows diminishing response as the line
gets longer. Such effects (and with them, a whole panoply of 'context
effects' as we will later see) emerge naturally from the use of hierarchical prediction machinery. The response tails off as the line gets longer
because longer lines and edges were the statistical norm in the natural
scenes to which the network was exposed in training. After training,
longer lines are thus what is first predicted (and fed back, as a hypothesis) by the level-two network. The strong firing of the level-1 'edge
cells' when they are driven by shorter lines thus reflects not successful

feature detection by those cells but rather an earlier stage of error or mismatch since the short segment was not initially predicted by the higher level network.

This example neatly illustrates the dangers of thinking in terms of a simple cumulative flow of feature detection and the advantages of rethinking the flow of processing as a mixture of top-down expectation and bottom-up error correction. It also highlights the way these learning routines latch on to the structure of the world as it is specified by the training data. End-stopped cells are simply a response to the statistics of the natural scenes used in training and reflect the typical length of the lines and edges in those scenes. In a very different world (such as the underwater world of some sea creatures) such cells would have learnt very different responses.

Such approaches assume that the environment generates sensory signals by means of nested interacting causes and that the task of the perceptual system is to invert this structure by learning and applying a hierarchical generative model so as to predict the unfolding sensory stream. Learning routines of this broad kind have been successfully applied in many domains, including speech perception, reading, and recognizing the actions of oneself and of other agents (see Friston, Mattout, & Kilner, 2011; Poeppel & Monahan, 2011; Price & Devlin, 2011). This is not surprising, since the underlying rationale is quite general. If you want to predict the way some set of sensory signals will change and evolve over time, a good thing to do is to learn how those sensory signals are determined by interacting external causes. And a good way to learn about those interacting causes is to try to predict how the sensory signal will change and evolve over time.

1.10   Binocular Rivalry

So far, our examples of predictive processing have been restricted to a few relatively low-level phenomena. As a final opening illustration, however, and one that nicely brings together many of the key elements introduced so far, consider Hohwy et al.'s (2008) hierarchical predictive coding model of binocular rivalry.

Binocular rivalry[18] (see Figure 1.4) is a striking form of visual experience that occurs when, using a special experimental set-up, each eye is presented (simultaneously) with a different visual stimulus. This can be achieved by using two superimposed images rendered using red and cyan graphics, viewed using special glasses with one red and one cyan lens (the same kind of set-up, known as anaglyph 3D, that was once

FIGURE 1.4   Illustration of Binocular Rivalry
Different images are presented to the left and right eyes ('stimulus'). The subject experiences switches from perception of one image (face) to the other (house). Note that 'mixed percepts' (composed of parts of both images) are also temporarily experienced ('piecemeal rivalry').

Source: Schwartz et al., 2012. By permission of The Royal Society.

used for viewing 3D comics or movies). Courtesy of these eye-specific filters, the right eye might be presented with an image of a house while the left receives an image of a face. Under these (extremely—and importantly—artificial) conditions, subjective experience unfolds in a surprising, 'bi-stable' manner. Instead of seeing (visually experiencing) an ongoing merger of the house and face information, subjects report a kind of perceptual alternation between seeing the house and seeing the face. The transitions themselves are not always sharp, and subjects often report a gradual breaking through (see, e.g., Lee et al., 2005) of elements of the other image before it dominates the previous one, after which the cycle repeats.

Binocular rivalry, as Hohwy et al. remind us, has proven to be a powerful tool for studying the neural correlates of conscious visual experience, because the incoming signals remain constant while the percept switches to and fro (Frith et al., 1999). Despite this attention, however, the precise mechanisms at play here are not well understood. Hohwy et al.'s strategy is to take a step back and to attempt to explain the phenomenon from first principles in a way that makes sense of many apparently disparate findings. In particular, they pursue what they dub an 'epistemological' approach: one whose goal is to reveal binocular rivalry as a reasonable (knowledge-oriented) response to an ecologically unusual stimulus condition.

The starting point for their story is, once again, the emerging unifying vision of the brain as an organ of prediction using a hierarchical generative model. Recall that, on these models, the task of the perceiving brain is to account for (to accommodate or 'explain away') the incoming or 'driving' sensory signal by means of a matching top-down prediction. The better the match, the less prediction error then propagates up the hierarchy. The higher level guesses are thus acting as priors for the lower level processing, in the fashion (as remarked earlier) of so-called 'empirical Bayes'.[19]

Within such a multilevel setting, a visual percept is determined by a process of prediction operating across many levels of a (bidirectional) processing hierarchy, each concerned with different types and scales of perceptual detail. All the communicating areas are locked into a mutually coherent predictive coding regime, and their interactive equilibrium ultimately selects a best overall (multiscale) hypothesis concerning the state of the visually presented world. This is the hypothesis that 'makes the best predictions and that, taking priors into consideration, is consequently assigned the highest posterior probability' (Hohwy et al., 2008, p. 690). Other overall hypotheses, at that moment, are simply crowded out: they are effectively inhibited, having lost the competition to best account for the driving signal.

Notice, though, what this means in the context of the predictive processing cascade. Top-down signals will account for (by predicting) only those elements of the driving signal that conform to (and hence are predicted by) the current winning hypothesis. In the binocular rivalry case, however (see Figure 1.4) the driving (bottom-up) signals contain information that suggests two distinct, and incompatible, states of the visually presented world, for example, face at time t at location x and house at time t at location x. When one of these is selected as the best overall hypothesis, it will account for all and only those elements of the driving input that the hypothesis predicts. As a result, prediction error for that hypothesis decreases. But prediction error associated with the elements of the driving signal suggestive of the alternative hypothesis is not thereby suppressed, so it is now propagated up the hierarchy. To suppress *those* prediction errors, the system needs to find another hypothesis. But having done so (and hence, having flipped the dominant hypothesis to the other interpretation), there will again emerge a large prediction error signal, this time deriving from those elements of the driving signal not accounted for by the flipped interpretation. In Bayesian terms (see Appendix 1) this is a scenario in which no unique and stable hypothesis combines high prior and high likelihood. No single hypothesis accounts for all the data, so the system alternates between the two semi-stable states. It behaves as a bi-stable system, minimizing prediction error in what Hohwy et al. describe as an energy landscape containing a double well.

What makes this account different from its rivals (such as Lee et al., 2005) is that where they posit a kind of direct, attention-mediated but essentially feedforward, competition between the inputs, the predictive processing account posits 'top-down' competition between linked sets of hypotheses. The effect of this competition is to selectively suppress the prediction errors associated with the elements of the driving (sensory) signals accommodated by the current winning hypothesis ('face'). But this top-down suppression leaves untouched the prediction errors associated with the remaining (house-signifying) elements of the driving signal. These errors are then propagated up the system. To explain them away the overall interpretation must switch. This pattern repeats, yielding the distinctive alternations experienced during dichoptic viewing of inconsistent stimuli.

But why, under such circumstances, do we not simply experience a combined or interwoven image: a kind of house/face mash-up, for example? Although such partially combined percepts do occur, and may persist for brief periods of time, they are never complete (bits of each stimulus are missing) or stable. Such mash-ups do not constitute a viable hypothesis given our more general knowledge about the visual world. For it is part of that general knowledge that, for example, houses and faces do not occupy the same place, at the same scale, at the same time. This kind of general knowledge may itself be treated as a systemic prior, albeit one pitched at a relatively high degree of abstraction (such priors are sometimes referred to as 'hyperpriors' and we shall have more to say about them in subsequent chapters). In the case at hand, what is thereby captured is the fact that 'the prior probability of both a house and face being co-localized in time and space is extremely small' (Hohwy et al., 2008, p. 691). This, indeed, may be the deep explanation of the existence of competition between certain higher level hypotheses in the first place—these hypotheses must compete because the system has learned that 'only one object can exist in the same place at the same time' (Hohwy et al., 2008, p. 691).

Despite these attractions, the binocular rivalry scenario presented here is incomplete. In particular, it is clear that there are strong attentional components here, whose treatment requires additional resources (to be introduced in chapter 2). Moreover, the active visual exploration of the presented scene—and in particular the fact that we can only visually explore the scene in ways appropriate to one 'reading' at a time—plausibly plays a major role in shaping our experiences.[20] Such augmentations would thus require the larger apparatus that we shall later (Part II) dub 'action-oriented predictive processing'.

1.11   *Suppression and Selective Enhancement*

To successfully represent the world in perception, if these models are correct, depends crucially on quashing sensory prediction error. Perception thus involves accommodating the driving (incoming) sensory signal by matching it with a cascade of predictions pitched at a variety of spatial and temporal scales. To the extent that such matching succeeds, well-predicted aspects of the driving sensory signal are suppressed or dampened—those aspects of the signal, as it is sometimes said, are 'explained away'.[21]

This kind of 'explaining away' is important and central, but it needs very careful handling. It is important as it reflects one characteristic property of predictive processing models. That feature lies at the root of the encoding efficiencies that these models exhibit, since all that then needs to be passed forward through the system is the residual error signal (signifying as-yet-unexplained sensory information) which is what remains once predictions and driving signals have been matched.[22] But there is more to the systemic unfolding that ensues than suppression and dampening alone. For alongside suppression, PP delivers sharpening and selective enhancement.

Fundamentally, this is because PP posits a kind of duplex architecture: one that at each level combines representations of inputs with estimations of error and (see chapter 2) sensory uncertainty. According to this proposal, what really gets suppressed, 'explained away' or cancelled out is thus the error signal, which (in these models) is depicted as computed by dedicated 'error units'. These are linked to, but distinct from, the so-called representation units that encode the causes of sensory inputs. By cancelling out the activity of some of the error units, activity in some of the laterally interacting 'representation' units (which feed predictions laterally and downward) can actually end up being selected and sharpened.

In this way, the predictive processing account avoids any direct conflict with accounts (such as the biased-competition model of Desimone & Duncan, 1995) that posit top-down *enhancements* of selected aspects of the sensory signal. It avoids such conflict because:

> High-level predictions explain away prediction error and tell the error units to "shut up" [while] units encoding the causes of sensory input are selected by lateral interactions, with the error units, that mediate empirical priors. This selection . . . sharpens responses among the laterally competing representations. (Friston, 2005, p. 829)

Such effects are further facilitated by attentional ('precision-weighting') mechanisms that we will meet in chapter 2. For the moment, the point to notice is that the PP account is consistent with both the suppression *and* the selective enhancement of (different aspects of) early cortical response.[23]

What is most distinctive about the predictive processing proposal (and where much of the break from tradition really occurs) is that it depicts the forward flow of information as solely conveying error, and the backward flow as solely conveying predictions. The PP architecture thus achieves a rather delicate balance between the familiar and the novel. There is still a cascade of feature detection, with potential for selective enhancement, and with increasingly complex features dealt with by neural populations that are more distant from the sensory peripheries. But the forward flow of sensory information is now replaced by a forward flow of prediction error. This signifies the sensory information that is as-yet-unexplained. In the more action-oriented terms that will occupy us later (in Parts II and III), it is sensory information that is not yet leveraged to guide apt engagements with the world.

This balancing act between supression and selective enhancement threatens to be quite architecturally demanding. In standard implementations it requires positing the existence of 'two functionally distinct sub-populations, encoding the conditional expectations [representations, predictions] of perceptual causes and the prediction error respectively' (Friston, 2005, p. 829). Functional distinctness need not, of course, imply full physical separation. But a common conjecture in this literature depicts superficial pyramidal cells (a prime source of forward neuro-anatomical connections) as playing the role of error units, passing prediction errors laterally and forwards, while deep pyramidal cells play the role of representation units, passing predictions (made on the basis of a complex generative model) laterally and downward (see, e.g., Friston, 2005, 2009; Mumford, 1992).

It is important to remember that 'error neurons', despite the label, can equally well be conceived as a variety of representation neurons—but ones whose functional role is to encode as yet unexplained (or, more broadly, unaccomodated) sensory information. What they encode is thus specified only relative to a prediction. For example:

> in the early visual cortex, predictor neurons code information about the predicted orientation and contrast at a certain point in the visual field, and error neurons signal mismatches between the observed orientation and contrast and the predicted orientation and contrast. In IT [inferior temporal] cortex, predictor neurons code information about object category; error neurons signal mismatches in predicted and observed object category (den Ouden et al., 2012; Peelen and Kastner, 2011). (Koster-Hale & Saxe, 2013, p. 838)

However it may (or may not) be realized—and for a useful run-down of some key possibilities, see Koster-Hale and Saxe (2013)—predictive processing demands *some* form of functional separation between encodings of prediction and of prediction error.[24] Such separation constitutes a central feature of the architecture, enabling it to combine the suppressive elements resulting from predictive coding with multiple routes to top-down signal enhancement.

1.12   *Encoding, Inference, and the Bayesian Brain*

Neural representations, should the hierarchical predictive processing account prove correct, encode 'probability density functions' in the form of a probabilistic generative model, and the flow of inference respects Bayesian principles (for a brief sketch, see Appendix 1) that balance prior expectations against new sensory evidence. This (Eliasmith, 2007) is a departure from traditional understandings of internal representation, and one whose full implications have yet to be fully understood. It means that the nervous system is fundamentally adapted to deal with uncertainty, noise, and ambiguity, and that it requires some (perhaps several) concrete means of internally representing uncertainty. Non-exclusive options here include the use of distinct populations of neurons, varieties of 'probabilistic population codes' (Pouget et al., 2003), and relative timing effects (Deneve, 2008) (for a very useful review, see Vilares & Körding, 2011).

Predictive processing accounts thus share what Knill and Pouget (2004, p. 713) describe as the 'basic premise on which Bayesian theories of cortical processing will succeed or fail', namely, that 'the brain represents information probabilistically, by coding and computing with probability density functions, or approximations to probability density functions' (p. 713). Such a mode of representation implies that when we represent a state or feature of the world, such as the depth of a visible object, we do so not using a single computed value but using a conditional probability density function that encodes 'the relative probability that the object is at different depths Z, given the available sensory information' (p. 712).

In what sense are such systems truly Bayesian? According to Knill and Pouget, 'the real test of the Bayesian coding hypothesis is in whether the neural computations that result in perceptual judgments or motor behaviour take into account the uncertainty available at each stage of the processing' (2004, p. 713). That is to say, reasonable tests will concern how well a system deals with the uncertainties that characterize the information it actually manages to encode and process, and (I would add) the general shape of the strategies it uses to do so.

There is increasing (though mostly indirect—see below) evidence that biological systems approximate, in multiple domains, the Bayesian profile thus understood. To take just one example, Weiss et al. (2002)—in a paper revealingly titled 'Motion illusions as optimal percepts'—used an optimal Bayesian estimator (the 'Bayesian ideal observer') to show that a wide variety of psychophysical results, including many motion 'illusions,' (see 6.9 following) fall naturally out of the assumption that human motion perception implements just such an estimator mechanism.

Examples could be multiplied (for a balanced review, see Knill & Pouget, 2004). At least in the realms of low-level, basic, and adaptively crucial, computations, biological processing may quite closely approximate Bayes's optimality. But what researchers find in general is not that we humans are—rather astoundingly—'Bayes' optimal' in some absolute sense (i.e., responding correctly relative to the absolute uncertainties in the stimulus), but rather, that we are often optimal, or near optimal, at taking into account the uncertainties that characterize the information that we actually command: the information that is made available by the forms of sensing and processing that we actually deploy (see Knill & Pouget, 2004, p. 713). That means taking into account the uncertainty in our own sensory and motor signals and adjusting the relative weight of different cues according to (often very subtle) contextual clues. Recent work confirms and extends this assessment, suggesting that humans act as rational Bayesian estimators, in perception and in action, across a wide variety of domains (Berniker & Körding, 2008; Körding et al., 2007; Yu, 2007).

Of course, the mere fact that a system's response profile takes this kind of shape does not unequivocally demonstrate that the system is implementing some form of Bayesian reasoning. In a limited domain, even a look-up table that simply associates cues with responses could (Maloney & Mamassian, 2009) yield the same behavioural repertoire as a 'Bayes' optimal' system. Nonetheless, the predictive processing story, if correct, would rather directly underwrite the claim that the nervous system approximates a genuine version of Bayesian inference.[25] Some recent electophysiological studies lend strong support to this broad possibility, revealing distinctive cortical response signatures for Bayesian updating and predictive surprise, and further suggesting that the brain codes and computes weighted probabilities. Summing up these studies the authors conclude:

> Our electrophysiological findings suggest that the brain acts as a Bayesian observer, i.e., that it might adjust probabilistic internal states, which entail beliefs about hidden states in the environment, in a probabilistic generative model of sensory data.
> (Kolossa, Kopp, and Fingscheidt, 2015, p. 233).

1.13   Getting the Gist

Instead of simply representing 'CAT ON MAT', the probabilistic Bayesian brain will encode a conditional probability density function, reflecting the relative probability of this state of affairs (and any somewhat-supported alternatives) given the available information. This estimate reflects both bottom-up influences from multiple sensory channels, and prior information of various kinds. It is worth pausing to examine some of the many ways this delicate top-down/bottom-up dance might unfold.

During the early stages of processing, a PP system will avoid committing itself to any single interpretation, and so there will often be an initial flurry of error signals. Such signals plausibly account for major components of early evoked responses (as measured by EEG recordings using scalp electrodes) as competing 'beliefs' propagate up and down the system. This is typically followed by rapid convergence upon a dominant theme (such as "animals in a natural scene") with further details ("several tigers sitting quietly under the shade of a large tree") subsequently negotiated. The set-up thus favours a kind of recurrently negotiated 'gist-at-a-glance' model, where we first identify the general scene followed by the details. This affords a kind of 'forest first, trees later' approach (Friston, 2005; Hochstein & Ahissar, 2002). These early emerging gist elements may be identified on the basis of rapidly processed (low spatial frequency) cues, as suggested by Bar, Kassam, et al. (2006). Such coarse cues may indicate whether we confront (for example) a cityscape, a natural scene, or an underwater scene, and they may also be accompanied by early emerging affective gist—do we like what we are seeing? See Barrett & Bar, 2009 and discussion in 5.10 following.

Thus imagine you are kidnapped, blindfold, and taken to some unknown location. As the blindfolds are removed, your brain's first attempts at predicting the scene will surely fail. But rapidly processed, low spatial frequency cues soon get the predictive brain into the right general ballpark. Framed by these early emerging gist elements (which might even be identified, in a trained-up system, using an ultra-rapid purely feedforward sweep, see Potter et al., 2014[26]) subsequent processing can be guided by specific mismatches with early attempts to fill in the details of the scene. These allow the system to progressively tune its top-down predictions, until it settles on a coherent overall interpretation pinning down detail at many scales of space and time.

This does not mean, however, that context effects will always take time to emerge and propagate downwards. For in many (indeed, most) real-life cases, substantial context information is already in place when new sensory information arrives. An apt set of priors is thus often already active, poised to impact processing without further delay.

This is important. The brain, in ecologically normal circumstances, is not just suddenly 'turned on' and some random or unexpected input delivered for processing! So there is usually plenty of top-down influence (active prediction) in place even before a stimulus is presented.[27] Over whatever timescale, though, the endpoint (assuming we form a rich visual percept) is the same. The system will have settled into a set of states that make mutually intertwined bets concerning many aspects of the scene, from the general theme all the way down to more spatio-temporally precise information about parts, colours, textures, and orientations.

1.14   Predictive Processing in the Brain

Section 1.9 already displayed a little indirect evidence for predictive processing by the brain in the form of computational simulations that reproduced and explained observed 'non-classical receptive field effects' such as end-stopping. Another such effect (see Rao & Sejnowski, 2002) occurs when an oriented stimulus yields a strong response from a cortical cell, but that response is suppressed when the surrounding region is filled with a stimulus of identical orientation, yet enhanced when the orientation of the central stimulus is orthogonal to those of the surrounding region. A powerful explanation of this result, Rao and Sejnowski (2002) suggest, is once again that the observed neural response here signals *error* rather than well-guessed content. It is thus smallest when the central stimulus is highly predictable from the surrounding ones and largest when it is actively counter-predicted by the surroundings. Similarly, Jehee and Ballard (2009) offer a predictive processing account of 'biphasic response dynamics' in which the optimal stimulus for driving a neuron (such as certain neurons in lateral geniculate nucleus, LGN) can reverse (e.g., from preferring bright to preferring dark) in a short (20 ms) space of time. Once again the switch is very neatly explained as a reflection of a unit's functional role as an error or difference detector rather than a classical feature detector. In such cases, the predictive coding strategy is in full evidence because:

> Low-level visual input [is] replaced by the difference between the input and a prediction from higher-level structures ... higher-level receptive fields ... represent the predictions of the visual world while lower-level areas ... signal the error between predictions and the actual visual input. (Jehee & Ballard, 2009, p. 1)

More generally, consider the case of 'repetition suppression'. Multiple studies (for a recent review, see Grill-Spector et al., 2006) have shown that stimulus-evoked neural activity is reduced by stimulus repetition.[28] Summerfield et al. (2008) manipulated the local likelihood of stimulus repetitions, showing that the repetition-suppression effect is *itself* reduced when the repetition is improbable/unexpected. The favoured explanation is (again) that repetition normally reduces response because it increases predictability (the second instance was made likelier by the first) and thus reduces prediction error. Repetition suppression thus also emerges as a direct effect of predictive processing in the brain, and as such its severity may be expected to vary (just as Summerfield et al. found) according to our local perceptual expectations. In general then, the predictive coding story offers a very neat and unifying explanation of a wide variety of quite low-level contextual effects.

There is an emerging body of supportive fMRI and EEG work dating back to a pioneering fMRI study by Murray et al. (2002) that also reveals just the kinds of relationships posited by the predictive processing story. Here, as higher level areas settled into an interpretation of visual shape, activity in V1 was dampened, consistent with the successful higher level predictions being used to explain away (cancel out) the sensory data. Recent studies confirm this general profile. Alink et al. (2010) found decreased responses for predictable stimuli using variants on an apparent motion illusion, while den Ouden et al. (2010) report similar results using arbitrary contingencies that were manipulated rapidly during the course of their experiments.[29] Adding fuel to these fires, Kok, Brouwer, et al. (2013) experimentally manipulated subjects' expectations about the probable direction of motion of a simple visual stimulus. The studies, using auditory cues that stood in a predictive relationship to moving dots, showed that subject's implicit expectations (as manipulated by the auditory cues) impacted neuronal activity at the very earliest stages of sensory processing. The effects, moreover, went beyond simple speeding up or sharpening of responses, altering what was actually subjectively perceived. The authors concluded, exactly in line (as they note) with predictive processing, that 'our results support an account of perception as a process of probabilistic inference ... wherein integration of top-down and bottom-up information takes place at every level of the cortical hierarchy' (Kok, Brouwer, et al., 2013, p. 16283).

Next, consider the P300, an electrophysiological response that has been linked to the occurrence of unexpected stimuli. In a recent detailed model comparison, the varying amplitude of the P300 was best explained (Kolossa et al., 2013) as an expression of the residual errors between top-down expectation and incoming sensory evidence. Relatedly, predictive processing provides a compelling account of the 'mismatch negativity' (MMN)—a characteristic electrophysiological brain response that is also evoked by the occurrence of an unexpected ('oddball') stimulus, or by the total omission of some expected stimulus, within a learnt sequence. Thus (citing Hughes et al., 2001; Joutsiniemi & Hari, 1989; Raij et al., 1997; Todorovic et al., 2011;

Wacongne et al., 2011; and Yabe et al., 1997), it was recently commented that 'one of the most remarkable properties of the auditory system is that it can generate evoked responses to an absent but expected stimulus' (Wacongne et al., 2012, p. 3671). Omission-based responses (and oddball responses more generally) thus provide further evidence for a predictive-processing-style schema in which 'the auditory system [acquires] an internal model of regularities in auditory inputs, including abstract ones, that are used to generate weighted predictions about the incoming stimuli' (Wacongne et al., 2012, p. 3671). Such responses (which are by no means restricted to the auditory modality) fall neatly into place once we consider them as indexing transient bursts of prediction error signalling—signalling that occurs as part of the normal process by which incoming signals are recognized (see Friston, 2005; Wacongne et al., 2012). The PP account here makes direct contact with striking features of normal human experience. The experiential impact of an unexpected omission (as when a note is missed out of a familiar sequence) can be very bit as perceptually striking and salient as the inclusion of an unexpected note. This is an otherwise puzzling effect that is neatly explained by assuming that the construction of perceptual experience involves expectations based upon our best model of what is likely to occur. We return to this topic in 3.5 following.

At a more architectural level, the central role of generative model based prediction makes sense both of the prevalence of backward neural connectivity and of apparent functional differences between the forward and backward connections—differences that reflect, predictive processing suggests, the divergent functional roles of prediction-error signalling and probabilistic prediction (for some detailed discussion of these functional asymmetries, see Friston, 2002, 2003; and for some recent experimental work on this topic, see Chen et al., 2009).

1.15   Is Silence Golden?

Early work in this broad area (such as the seminal work by Rao & Ballard described above) met with some puzzlement. This is perhaps unsurprising, since the basic story is radically different from the more standard picture of a feedforward (even if attention-modulated) cascade of simple-to-complex feature detection. The puzzlement was famously captured in a commentary from Christoph Koch and Tomaso Poggio bearing the subtitle 'Silence is Golden'. The passage is so perfectly expressive of some quite common first impressions that I hope the reader will forgive a long extract:

> In predictive coding, the common-place view of sensory neurons as detecting certain 'trigger' or 'preferred' features is turned upside down in favor of a representation of objects by the absence of firing activity. This appears to be at odds with [data indicating that neurons] extending from V1 to inferior temporal cortex, respond with vigorous activity to ever more complex objects, including individual faces or paperclips twisted in just the right way and seen from a particular viewpoint.
>
> In addition, what about all of the functional imaging data from humans revealing that particular cortical areas respond to specific image classes, such as faces or three-dimensional spatial layout? Is it possible that this activity is dominated by the firing of . . . cells actively expressing an error signal, a discrepancy between the input expected by this brain area and the actual image? (Both quotes from Koch & Poggio, 1999, p. 10)

There are two main worries being expressed here: first, a worry that these accounts are abandoning representation in favour of silence, since well-predicted elements of the signal are quashed or 'explained away'; second, a worry that the accounts thus seem in tension with strong evidence of increasingly complex representations tokened by activity in higher areas.

Neither worry is ultimately justified. To see why not, recall the architectural story just outlined. Each layer, we saw, must now support two functionally distinct kinds of processing. For simplicity, let's follow Friston (2005) and imagine this as each layer containing two functionally distinct kinds of cell or unit[30]:

> — 'representation units', that encode that layer's current best hypothesis (pitched at its preferred level of description) and that feed that hypothesis down as prediction to the layer below.
>
> — 'error units', that pass activation forward when local within-layer activity is not adequately accounted for by incoming top-down prediction from the layer above.

That means that more and more complex representations are indeed formed, and used in processing, as one moves up the hierarchy. It is just that the *flow* of representational information (the predictions), at least in the purest versions, is all downwards (and sideways). Nevertheless, the upward flow of prediction error is itself a sensitive instrument, bearing fine-grained information about very specific failures of match. That is why it is capable of inducing, in higher areas, complex hypotheses (consistent sets of representations) that can then be tested against the lower level states. As a result, neither of the two early worries raised by Koch and Poggio gets a grip. There are representational populations 'all the way up', and higher-level cells can still respond to ever-more-complex objects and properties. But their activity is determined by the forwards (and lateral) flow of error signals and the states that they select.

Koch and Poggio may, however, be hinting also at a different kind of concern. This is the concern that the bedrock 'predictive coding' image of the brain as 'aiming at silence' (by achieving perfect prediction of sensory inputs) can seem out of kilter with the fundamental profile of animal life itself! For that profile, surely, is to move and explore, forever searching out new inputs demanding new bouts of neural activity. The worry, baldly stated, is that the predictive coding strategy may seem like a recipe for finding a dark corner and staying there, correctly predicting immobility and darkness until all bodily functions cease.

Fortunately (as we shall see in detail in chapters 8 and 9) the threat here is entirely superficial. For the role of perception, on the accounts we shall explore, is simply to drive adaptively valuable action. Many of our moment-by-moment predictions are thus actually predictions (more on this in chapter 6) of restless sensorimotor trajectories, and their job is to keep us moving us around the world in ways that keep us fed and warm, and that serve our needs and projects. Among the most prediction-error inducing states for creatures like us are thus states in which all activity ceases and in which hunger and thirst begin to predominate. By the end of the present treatment, we shall have seen just how the bedrock strategy of prediction error minimization, as it unfolds in active, evolved, information-hungry adaptive agents, itself enforces all the restless, playful, searching, and exploratory forms of behaviour that we know and love.

1.16 Expecting Faces

For the present, however, let's return to the second (more concrete) worry raised by Koch and Poggio—the worry that neural activity, as processing proceeds, does not look to be dominated by the firing of cells expressing error. Consider once again the standard model of perception as the product of processing via a stream of increasingly complex feature-detection, such that responses at the higher levels come to reflect the presence of complex, invariant items such as faces, houses,

etc. What the predictive processing story suggests, we can now clarify, is not that we abandon that model but that we enrich it, by adding
within each layer cells specialized for the encoding and transmission
of prediction error. Some cells at each level are thus responding to
states of the body and world while others are registering errors relative to predictions about those states: predictions flowing laterally and
downwards, from the level above. Is this correct?

The evidence here is only just appearing, but seems to fit the 'predictive processing' profile. Thus consider the well-established finding
(Kanwisher et al., 1997) of increased activity in fusiform face area (FFA)
when shown a face rather than (say) a house. Surely, a critic might say,
this is best explained by simply supposing that neurons in FFA have
learnt to be active complex feature detectors for faces? It is immediately
apparent that this is no longer straightforward, however, given that the
PP story allows that FFA may indeed harbour units that specialize in
the representation of faces, as well as ones that specialize in the detection of errors (mismatches between top-down predictions reaching
FFA and the bottom-up signal). Thus, the difference is that if the predictive coding story is correct, FFA should *also* harbour error units that
encode mismatches with expected (face) activity based upon lateral
and top-down predictions. The predicted presence of both representational and error units in FFA provided a nice opportunity for some
telling empirical tests.

Egner et al. (2010) compared simple feature detection (with and without attention) and predictive processing models of recorded responses
in FFA. The simple feature detection model predicts, just as Koch and
Poggio suggested, that FFA response should simply scale with the presence of faces in the presented image. The predictive processing model,
however, predicts something rather more complex. It predicts that FFA
response should 'reflect a summation of activity related to prediction
("face expectation") and prediction error ("face surprise")' (Egner et al
2010, p. 1601). That is to say, it predicts that the (low temporal resolution) fMRI signal recorded from the FFA should reflect the activity of
both putative kinds of cell: those specializing in prediction ('face expectation') and those specializing in detecting errors in prediction ('face
surprise'). This was then tested by collecting fMRI data from area FFA
while independently varying both the presented features (face vs. house)
and manipulating subject's unconscious degree of face expectation (low,
medium, high) and hence their proper degree of 'face surprise'. To do
this, the experimenters probabilistically paired presentations of face/
house with a 250 ms preceding colour frame cue giving 25% (low), 50%
(medium), or 75% (high) chance of the next image being a face.

The results were clear. FFA activity showed a strong interaction between stimulus and face expectation. FFA response was maximally differentiated only under conditions of low face expectation. Indeed, and quite surprisingly, FFA activity given *either* stimulus (face OR house) *was indistinguishable under conditions of high face expectation*. There is a very real sense then, in which FFA might (had it first been investigated using predictive processing paradigms) have been dubbed a 'face-expectation area'.

The authors conclude that, contrary to any simple feature-detection model, '[FFA] responses appear to be determined by feature expectation and surprise rather than by stimulus features per se' (Egner et al., 2010, p. 16601). The authors also controlled (by further model comparisons) for the possible role of attentional effects. But these could not, in any case, have made much contribution since it was face surprise, not face expectation, that accounted for the larger part of the BOLD (fMRI)[31] signal. In fact, the best-fit predictive processing model used a weighting in which face-surprise (error) units contributed about twice as much[32] to the BOLD signal as did face-expectation (representation) units, suggesting that much of the activity normally recorded using fMRI may be signalling prediction error rather than detected features. This is an important result. In the authors' own words:

> the current study is to our knowledge the first investigation to formally and explicitly demonstrate that population responses in visual cortex are in fact better characterized as a sum of feature expectation and surprise responses than by bottom-up feature detection (with or without attention). (Egner et al., 2010, p. 16607)

1.17   When Prediction Misleads

There is, of course, a downside to all this efficient prediction-based response, and it is nicely illustrated by familiar visual illusions, such as the Hollow Face illusion. Here, the concave inner surface of a 3D face-mask will look—under certain condition—like a normal face: convex, with the nose extending outwards. To get a better sense of how this looks, try the video clips embedded in the short review at http://www.michaelbach.de/ot/fcs_hollow-face/.

Better yet, experience the illusion for yourself using a real three-dimensional mask, of the kind you would use for Halloween. Take the mask and reverse it, so you are looking at the hollow inside rather than the convex (face-shaped) side. If the viewing distance is correct (don't get too close: it needs to be at least around 3 feet away) and the mask is gently illuminated from behind, it will appear as if the mask is not hollow. You will 'see' the nose sticking outwards, when in fact, you are looking into the concave reverse-side of the face impression. Figure 1.5 shows the appearance, under such conditions, of a rotating mask.

The hollow mask illusion, in neurotypical subjects, is powerful and persistent. It is, however, robustly reduced among schizophrenic subjects—an effect that specific disturbances to the predictive processing apparatus may also (see chapter 7) help explain. The hollow mask illusion was first used by the neuroscientist Richard Gregory (see, e.g., Gregory, 1980) to illustrate the power of 'top-down', knowledge-driven influences on perception. Such will effects emerge directly from the operation of the principles of prediction-based learning and processing discussed in previous sections. Our statistically salient experience with endless hordes of convex faces in daily life installs a deep neural 'expectation' of convexness: an expectation that here trumps the many other visual cues that ought to be telling us that what we are seeing is a concave mask.

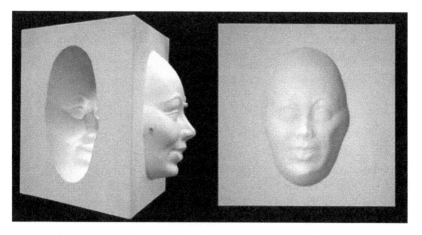

FIGURE 1.5   Hollow Mask Illusion
The leftmost and far right images show the hollow, concave side of a mask rotating on a stand. When viewed from a few feet away, and illuminated from the rear, the concave side appears convex. This demonstrates the power of top-down predictions (we 'expect' faces to be convex) to impact perceptual experience.

Source: Gregory (2001), by permission of the Royal Society.

You might reasonably suspect that the hollow mask illusion, though striking, is really just some kind of psychological oddity. And to be sure, our neural predictions concerning the probable convexity of human faces seem especially strong and potent. But if predictive processing approaches are on track, this general strategy actually pervades human perception. Brains like ours are constantly trying to use what they already know so as to predict the current sensory signal, using the incoming signal to select and constrain those predictions, and sometimes using prior knowledge to 'trump' certain aspects of the incoming sensory signal itself. Such trumping makes good adaptive sense, as the capacity to use what you know to outweigh some of what the incoming signal seems to be saying can be hugely beneficial when the sensory data is noisy, ambiguous, or incomplete—situations that are, in fact, pretty much the norm in daily life.

An interesting upshot of this is that many visual illusions, as mentioned in 1.12, may nonetheless be best understood as 'optimal percepts'. In other words, given the structure and statistics of the world we inhabit, the optimal estimate of the worldly state (the estimate that represents the best possible take on the incoming signal, given what the system already knows) will be the one that, on some occasions, gets things wrong. A few local failures, then, are just the price we pay for being able to get things right, most of the time, in a world cloaked by ambiguity and noise.

1.18   Mind Turned Upside Down

Predictive processing turns a traditional picture of perception on its head. According to that once-standard picture (Marr, 1982) perceptual processing is dominated by the forward flow of information transduced from the world via various sensory receptors. Traditional perceptual neuroscience followed suit, with visual cortex (the most-studied example) being viewed as a hierarchy of neural feature detectors driven from the bottom up. This was a view of the perceiving brain as passive and stimulus-driven, taking energetic inputs from the senses and turning them into a coherent percept by a kind of step-wise build-up, accumulating structure and complexity along the way in a kind of Lego-block fashion. Such views may be contrasted with the increasingly 'active' views that have been pursued over the past several decades of neuroscientific and computational research,[33] including the recent explosion of work on intrinsic neural activity—the ceaseless buzz of spontaneous, correlated neuronal activation that takes place even in the absence of ongoing task-specific stimulation.[34] Much of the brain's activity, all this suggests, is both ongoing and endogenously generated.

Predictive processing plausibly represents the last step in this retreat from a passive, input-dominated, view of the flow of neural processing. According to this emerging class of models, naturally intelligent systems do not passively await sensory stimulation. Instead, they are constantly active, trying to predict (and actively elicit, see Part II) the streams of sensory stimulation before they arrive. Before an 'input' arrives on the scene, these pro-active cognitive systems are already busy predicting its most probable shape and implications. Systems like that are already (pretty much constantly) poised to act, and all they need to process are sensed deviations from the predicted state. It is these calculated deviations from predicted states ('prediction errors') that thus bear much of the information-processing burden, informing us of what is salient and newsworthy within the dense sensory barrage.[35]

Action itself, as we shall see in Part II, then needs to be reconceived. Action is not so much a 'response to an input' as a neat and efficient way of selecting the *next* input, driving a rolling cycle. These hyperactive systems are constantly predicting their own upcoming states and actively moving about so as to bring some of them into being. We thus act so as to bring forth the evolving streams of sensory information that keep us viable and that serve our increasingly recondite ends. With action incorporated, predictive processing implements a comprehensive reversal of the traditional (bottom-up, forward-flowing) schema. The largest contributor to ongoing neural response is the ceaseless anticipatory buzz of downwards-flowing neural prediction that drives perception and action in a circular causal flow. Incoming sensory information is just one further factor perturbing those restless pro-active seas.

As ever-active prediction engines these kinds of brains are not, fundamentally, in the business of 'processing inputs' at all. Rather, they are in the business of predicting their inputs. This pro-active neural strategy keeps us poised for action and (as we shall later see) allows mobile, embodied agents to intervene on the world, bringing about the kinds of sensory flow that keep them viable and fulfilled.

If these stories are on track, then just about every aspect of the passive forward-flowing model is false. We are not cognitive couch potatoes idly awaiting the next 'input', so much as proactive predictavores—nature's own guessing machines forever trying to stay one step ahead by surfing the incoming waves of sensory stimulation.

2

Adjusting the Volume
(Noise, Signal, Attention)

2.1   Signal Spotting

If we look for them, most of us can find shifting face-forms hidden among the clouds. We can see the forms of insects hidden in the patterned wallpaper or of snakes nestling among the colourful swirls of a carpet. Such effects need not imply the ingestion of mind-altering substances. Minds like ours are already experts at self-alteration. When we look for our car keys on the cluttered desk, we somehow alter our perceptual processing to help isolate the target item from the rest. Indeed, spotting the (actual) car keys and 'spotting' the (non-existent) faces, snakes, and insects are probably not all that different, at least as far as the form of the underlying processing is concerned. Such spottings reflect our abilities not just to alter our action routines (e.g., our visual scan paths) but also to modify the details of our own perceptual processing so as better to extract signal from noise. Such modifications look to play a truly major role in the tuning (both long- and short-term) of the on-board probabilistic prediction machine that underpins our contact with the world. The present chapter explores the space and nature of such online modifications, discusses their relations with familiar notions such as attention and expectation, and displays a possible mechanism (the 'precision-weighting' of prediction error) that may be implicated in a wide range of signal-enhancement effects.

2.2 Hearing Bing

Hack number 48 in Tom Stafford and Matt Webb's wonderfully engaging book *Mind Hacks* is called 'Detect Sounds on the Margins of Certainty'. Based on previous experimental work by Merckelbach and van de Ven (2001), the hack invites the reader first to listen to a 30-second soundfile. The reader is instructed that the soundfile contains a hidden sample of Bing Crosby's 'White Christmas', but that the sample is very faint and may begin in the first, second, or third ten-second segment of the soundfile. The intrepid reader might like to try this before continuing, by clicking on Hack 48 at: http://mindhacks.com/book/links/.

Merckelbach and van de Ven (2001) tried this experiment with undergraduate students and found that almost one-third of the students reported detecting the onset of the song. In fact, as you may have guessed by now, there is no White Christmas hidden anywhere in the noise. The ability of some folk to 'detect' the familiar song is just an expression (in this case, a kind of over-extension) of an ability central to perceptual search and perceptual awareness in general: the ability to discount some aspects of a signal, treating them as 'noise', while accentuating other aspects (thus treating them as 'signal'). This ability, deployed under the influence of the strong expectation of a weak 'hard-to-detect' fragment of the familiar song, allows many perfectly normal subjects to enjoy what is in effect an auditory hallucination. The effect can even be amplified, it turns out, by combinations of stress and caffeine (Crowe et al., 2011).

Now consider a second kind of case: sine-wave speech. Sine-wave speech (Remez et al., 1981; Remez & Rubin, 1984) is a degraded replica of recorded speech stripped of most of the normal speech attributes and acoustics. The sine-wave replica preserves only a kind of skeletal outline in which the core (and rather coarse) pattern of dynamic changes in the speech signal is coded as a set of pure tone whistles. You can hear an example by clicking on the first loudspeaker icon at: http://www.mrc-cbu.cam.ac.uk/people/matt.davis/sine- wave-speech/.

Chances are you will not make much of what you hear: to me it sounded like a string of science-fiction beeps of the kind pioneered by the BBC Radiophonic Workshop back in the early 1960s. Others hear something like the incomprehensible inflected whistlings of the moon mice characters from the cult UK children's show The Clangers. But now click on the next loudspeaker and listen to the original sentence, then revisit the sine-wave replica. This time around, your experiential world has altered. It has become (more on this in later chapters) meaningful: a world of clearly intelligible speech. For a lovely selection of demos like this, try: http://www.lifesci.sussex.ac.uk/home/Chris_Darwin/SWS/.

Remember to click the SWS (Sine-Wave Speech) versions first. Once you know what the sentence is it becomes pretty much impossible to 'rehear' it in the original fashion. An apt comparison would be hearing speech in a language you understand and in one you do not. It is almost impossible to hear speech sounds in the former case simply as sounds. Exposure to the original (non-sine-wave) spoken sentence helps prepare you in a similar fashion. Over time, you may even become expert enough at sine-wave speech perception to succeed without prior exposure to the specific acoustically normal sentence. At that point, you have become an expert with a more general skill (a 'native hearer' of sine-wave speech).

Davis and Johnsrude (2007) describe the perception of sine-wave speech as just one instance of the much more pervasive phenomenon of *top-down influence* upon sensory processing. Such influence, if the accounts sketched in chapter 1 are correct, is rooted in the creation and deployment of probabilistic generative models busily trying to predict the flow of sensory input. We see such influence in all modalities and across modalities. A well-worn example is reproduced in Figure 2.1(a). At first sight, all that most people can see is a pattern of light and shadow. But once you have discovered the spotty, shadowed Dalmatian dog that knowledge alters the way you see that picture for the rest of your life. For a less familiar example, take a look at Figure 2.1(b). In such cases,[1] our knowledge about the world (our 'prior beliefs' as realized by generative models commanded by the brain) plays a major role in the construction of the percept. (It is perhaps worth repeating that the term 'belief' is widely used (in this literature) to cover any of the contents of the generative models that guide perception and action. There is no requirement that such beliefs be consciously accessible to the reflective agent. Indeed, for the most part, they will comprise a variety of sub-personal states whose best expressions are probabilistic rather than sentential[2]).

Other, less obvious, examples of cross-modal influence have been mounting up in the literature. An especially striking example is the finding that the perceived colour of a wine can have a large impact on how people (including wine experts) describe the taste of that wine (see Morrot et al., 2001; Parr et al., 2003; and Shankar et al., 2010—the

(a)   (b)

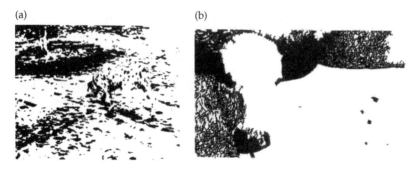

FIGURE 2.1   Hidden Figures
(a) Hidden in the black and white noise is an image (clear enough, once you spot it) of a Dalmatian dog. Clue: the head is near the centre of the image, inspecting the ground.
(b) A less well-known example of the same phenomena. This time it is a cow. Clue: the cow has a big head; it is facing you, with its nose at the bottom of the picture and two black ears in the top left half.

Source: Hidden Cow by John McCrone, CC-BY-SA-3.0. http://creativecommons.org/licenses/by-sa/3.0), via Wikimedia Commons.

latter bearing the rather wonderful title of 'Grape Expectations'). In these experiments, white wines that had been artificially coloured to look red were described, even by experts, using red-wine descriptors such as prune, chocolate, and tobacco. Nor does the influence of prior expectations stop there. Oysters taste better, it seems, when eating is accompanied (even deep inside a landlocked restaurant) by sounds of the sea (Spence & Shankar, 2010).

Predictive processing offers a powerful framework within which to approach and understand a whole pantheon of knowledge-based and contextual effects upon perceptual inference, since it makes what we know (both consciously and, more often, non-consciously) about the world a prime player in the construction of perceptual experience itself. We shall return to questions concerning the construction of conscious experience in chapter 7. For the moment, I want to dwell on something a little more abstract, but quite fundamental to the accounts on offer. That something is crucial to perceptual success (such as spotting the Dalmatian or hearing sine-wave speech), to perceptual play (such as finding face-forms in the clouds) and to some perceptual failures (such as hallucinating the sounds of 'White Christmas'). It is the ability flexibly to extract signal from noise by forming and deploying focused and fine-grained estimates of our own perceptual uncertainty.[3] That ability (the focus of the rest of the present chapter) lies at the heart of the predictive processing (PP) treatment of attention and plays a major role in accounting for both normal and abnormal forms of contact with the world.

2.3   The Delicate Dance between Top-Down and Bottom-Up

The perceptual problems that confront us in daily life vary greatly in the demands they make upon us. For many tasks, it is best to deploy large amounts of prior knowledge, using that knowledge to drive complex proactive patterns of gaze fixation, while for others it may be better to sit back and let the world do as much of the driving as possible. Which strategy (more heavily input-driven or more heavily expectation-driven) is best is also hostage to a multitude of contextual effects. Driving along a very familiar road in heavy fog, it can sometimes be wise to let detailed top-down knowledge play a substantial role. Driving fast along an unfamiliar winding mountain road, we need to let sensory input take the lead. How is a probabilistic prediction machine to cope?

It copes, PP suggests, by continuously estimating and re-estimating its own sensory uncertainty. Within the PP framework, these estimations of sensory uncertainty modify the impact of sensory prediction error. This, in essence, is the predictive processing model of attention. Attention, thus construed, is a means of variably balancing the potent interactions between top-down and bottom-up influences by factoring in their so-called 'precision', where this is a measure of their estimated certainty or reliability (inverse variance, for the statistically savvy). This is achieved by altering the weighting (the gain or 'volume', to use a common analogy) on the error units accordingly. The upshot of this is to 'control the relative influence of prior expectations at different levels' (Friston, 2009, p. 299). Greater precision means less uncertainty and is reflected in a higher gain on the relevant error units (see Friston, 2005, 2010; Friston et al., 2009). Attention, if this is correct, is simply a means by which certain error unit responses are given increased weight, hence becoming more apt to drive response, learning, and (as we shall later see) action. More generally, this means the precise mix of top-down and bottom-up influence is not static or fixed. Instead, the weight given to sensory prediction error is varied according to how reliable (how noisy, certain, or uncertain) the signal is taken to be.

We can illustrate this using our earlier example. Visual input, in the fog, will be estimated to offer a noisy and unreliable guide to the state of the distal realm. Other things being equal visual input should, on a bright day, offer a much better signal, such that any residual error should be taken very seriously indeed. But the strategy clearly needs to be much more finely tuned than that suggests. Thus suppose the fog (as so often happens) briefly clears from one small patch of the visual scene. Then we should be driven to sample preferentially from that smaller zone, as that is now a source of high-precision prediction errors. This is a complex business, since the evidence for the presence of that small zone (right there!) comes only from the (initially low-weighted) sensory input itself. There is no fatal problem here, but the case is worth describing carefully. First, there is now some low-weighted surprise emerging relative to my best current take on the the visual situation (which was something like 'in uniformly heavy fog'). Aspects of the input (in the clear zone) are not unfolding as that take (that model) predicted. However, my fog-model includes general expectations concerning occasional clear patches. Under such conditions, I can further reduce overall prediction error by swopping to the 'fog plus clear patch' model. This model incorporates a new set of precision predictions, allowing me to trust the fine-grained prediction errors computed for the clear zone (only). That small zone is now the estimated source of high-precision prediction errors of the kind the visual system can trust to recruit clear reliable percepts. High-precision prediction errors from the clear zone may then rapidly warrant the recruitment of a new model capable of describing some salient aspects of the local environment (watch out for that tractor!).

Such, in microcosm, is the role PP assigns to sensory attention: 'Attention can be viewed as a selective sampling of sensory data that have high-precision (signal to noise) in relation to the model's predictions' (Feldman & Friston, 2010, p. 17). This means that we are constantly engaged in attempts to predict precision, that is, to predict the context-varying reliability of our own sensory prediction error, and that we probe the world accordingly. This kind of 'predicted-precision based' probing and sampling also underlies (as we will see in Part II) the PP account of gross motor activity. For the present, the point to notice is that in this noisy and ambiguous world, we need to know when and where to take sensory prediction error seriously, and (more generally) how best to balance top-down expectation and bottom-up sensory input. That means knowing when, where, and how far, to trust specific prediction error signals to select and nuance the model that is guiding our behaviour.

An important upshot is that the knowledge that makes human perception possible concerns not only the layered causal structure of the (action-salient—more on that later) distal world but the nature and context-varying reliability of our own sensory contact with that world. Such knowledge must form part and parcel of the overall

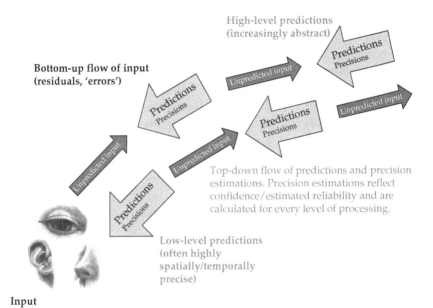

High-level predictions
(increasingly abstract)

Predictions
Precisions

Bottom-up flow of input
(residuals, 'errors')

Predictions
Precisions

Unpredicted input

Predictions
Precisions

Unpredicted input

Unpredicted input

Predictions
Precisions

Top-down flow of predictions and precision
estimations. Precision estimations reflect
confidence/estimated reliability and are
calculated for every level of processing.

Unpredicted input

Predictions
Precisions

Low-level predictions
(often highly
spatially/temporally
precise)

Input

**FIGURE 2.2   The Basic Predictive Processing Schema, This Time with
Precision-Weighting**
This is the same highly schematized view of the PP architecture shown in
chapter 1, but with precision-weighting added to the mix. Now, the impact
of select prediction error signals is modulated by varying estimates of their
current reliability and salience

Source: Adapted from Lupyan & Clark, 2014.

generative model. For that model must come to predict both the shape
and multiscale dynamics of the impinging sensory signal and the
context-variable reliability of the signal itself (see Figure 2.2). The familiar idea of 'attention' now falls into place as naming the various ways
in which predictions of precision tune and impact sensory sampling,
allowing us (when things are working as they should) to be driven by
the signal while ignoring the noise. By actively sampling where we
expect (relative to some task) the best signal to noise ratio, we ensure
that the information upon which we perceive and act is fit for purpose.

2.4   Attention, Biased Competition, and Signal Enhancement

Attention, if these stories are on track, names the means or process
by which an organism increases the gain (the weighting, hence the
forward-flowing impact) on those prediction error units estimated to

provide the most reliable sensory information relative to some current task, threat, or opportunity. More formally, the suggestion is that
'attention is the process of optimizing synaptic gain to represent the
precision of sensory information (prediction error) during hierarchical inference' (Feldman & Friston, 2010, p. 2). The general idea is thus
that patterns of neuronal activation (among the so-called 'representation units') encode systemic guesses concerning task-relevant states of
the world, while changes in the gain (i.e., changes in the weighting or
'volume') on the associated error units[4] reflect the brain's best estimate
of the relative precision of the top-down 'guessing' and the bottom-up
sensory information. Precision-weighting thus delivers the system's
best estimate of the trustworthiness of the sensory information itself.
This means that 'top-down predictions are not just about the content
of lower-level representations but also about our [the brain's] confidence in those representations' (Friston, 2012, p. 238). It is thought that
these top-down estimates of precision alter the post-synaptic gain on
prediction error units (commonly identified with superficial pyramidal cells; see, e.g., Mumford, 1992; Friston, 2008). Thus we read that:

> Physiologically, precision corresponds to the postsynaptic gain
> or sensitivity of cells reporting prediction errors (currently
> thought to be large principal cells that send extrinsic efferents
> of a forward type, such as superficial pyramidal cells in cortex).
> (Friston, Bastos, et al., 2015, p.1)

In sum, these alterations in gain[5] track the estimated reliability (statistically, the inverse variance) of select prediction errors. Such errors
encode all the sensory information that remains to be explained (or
that has not yet been leveraged for the control of action). Precision thus
estimates the reliability of the signals that carry the news, to repeat the
handy metaphor used in chapter 1.

Estimating precision and altering the gain on prediction error
accordingly brings an immediate and hugely important benefit. It allows
the PP approach fluidly to combine the superficially contradictory
effects (see 1.11) of signal suppression and signal enhancement. Signal
suppression is, of course, the familiar effect of predictive coding methods of data compression. Lower-level activity that is well-predicted by
a winning higher-level model is quashed or 'explained away' (because
there is no news there), and so no signal propagates forward through
the system. The superficially contradictory effect is salience-based signal enhancement. Observed effects here include facilitation (speeding
up of evoked responses; see Henson, 2003) and sharpening (in which
some cells cease to be active, allowing others to dominate the response;
see Desimone, 1996). Precision-weighting allows PP to combine these

effects in a very flexible manner, since increases in post-synaptic gain implement a facilitation effect, which then 'boosts prediction errors that inform the best hypothesis about the cause of sensory input (Gregory, 1980) while suppressing alternative hypotheses; namely *it sharpens neuronal representations*' (Friston, 2012a, p. 238, italics in original). Kok, Jehee, and de Lange (2012) find just such sharpening effects, revealing expectation-based enhancement in some aspects of early sensory response paired (just as the PP model suggests) with overall reductions in neural activity. Such expectation-induced sharpening was shown to be behaviourally potent, yielding better performance on a simple task involving the detection of subtle differences in the orientation of a stimulus.

Such sharpening is the familiar mainstay of 'biased competition' models (Desimone & Duncan, 1995). Such models posit—much as the name suggests—a competition for upstream neuronal representation in which only 'winning' lower level cells (with small receptive fields) are allowed to drive higher level cells (with larger receptive fields). Attention, the biased competition models suggests, should be identified with this process of competition: a competition whose outcome is determined both by the nature of the task and by the properties of the stimuli competing for the representational resources. Many observed effects (e.g., Reynolds et al., 1999; Beck & Kastner, 2005, 2008) clearly conform to the biased competition model. Some electrophysiological (ERP) components, for example (see Bowman et al., 2013) are increased when a target appears repeatedly in the same location. Additionally (again, see Bowman et al., 2013), there are visual search experiments in which distractors, despite their rarity, yield little evoked response yet pre-described, frequently appearing, targets deliver large ones. Can such effects be explained directly by the attention-modulated precision-weighting of residual error?

An fMRI study by Kok et al. (2012) lends elegant support to the predictive processing model of such effects by showing that these are just the kinds of interaction between prediction and attention that the model of precision-weighted prediction error suggests. In particular, Kok et al. show that predicted stimuli that are unattended and task-irrelevant result in reduced activity in early visual cortex (the 'silencing' of the predicted, as mandated by simple predictive coding) but that 'this pattern reversed when the stimuli were attended and task-relevant' (Kok et al., 2012, p. 2). The study manipulated spatial attention and prediction by using independent prediction and spatial cues (for further details, see the original paper by Kok et al.) and found that attention reversed the silencing effect of prediction upon the sensory signal, in just the way the precision-weighting account would specify. Thus, when attention and prediction were congruent (when the independent attention cue selected the spatial hemifield in which the predicted stimulus did, in fact, occur), attention enhanced neural response in V1, V2, and V3 for the predicted over the unpredicted stimuli. When they were incongruent (that is, the predicted stimulus did not occur at the attended spatial location), no enhancement occurred, and response to the predicted stimulus was reduced in V1. In addition, the response to unpredicted stimuli was the same whether they occurred on the attended or unattended side. Finally, there was a large response in V1, V2, and V3 for the unexpected omission of a stimulus in the attended hemifield. This whole pattern is best explained, the authors argue, by the attention-modulated precision-weighting of prediction error in which attention increases the downstream impact of selected prediction error units. Attention and expectation thus look to operate as distinct elements within the inferential cascade in the way PP suggests. Attention enhances (increases the gain on) the neural responses associated with select prediction errors, while expectation dampens those neural responses that are in line with the expectation.

The ability of the PP account to encompass various forms of attentional enhancement has also been demonstrated using computer simulations of the Posner paradigm (Posner, 1980). In the Posner paradigm (see Figure 2.3) subjects fixate a central point (so the experiment probes so-called 'covert attention') and are presented with a visual cue that often (but not always) indicates the location of a forthcoming target stimulus. For example, the cue may be valid over 80% of trials. Trials with a valid cue are called 'congruent trials' and trials where this is not the case (where the cue is invalid, and hence does not correctly predict the stimulus) are called 'incongruent trials'. The paradigm thus manipulates our contextual expectations, since the cue creates a context in which the appearance of the stimulus in the cues location becomes more likely. The main finding, unsurprisingly, is one of facilitation: valid cues speed up detection of the target stimulus while targets presented on incongruent trials are perceived more slowly, and with less confidence. Feldman and Friston (2010) present a detailed, simulation-based model in which precision-modulated prediction error is used to optimize perceptual inference in a way that reproduces both the ERP and psychophysical responses found in human subjects. Valid cues establish what was sometimes known as 'attentional set' by increasing the gain on the prediction error units

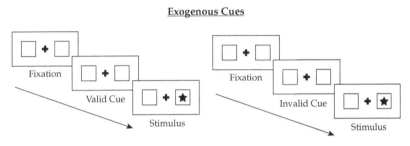

FIGURE 2.3   The Posner Paradigm

Source: Licensed under the Creative Commons Attribution 3.0 License en.wikipedia.
org/wiki/File:Posner_Paradigm_Figure.png.

associated with the cued spatial location. This then constitutes a systemic 'expectation' of a good signal-to-noise ratio for information from that spatial region and thus speeds up the process, once the target appears, of recruiting the right hypothesis (roughly 'target there') thus recapitulating the facilitation effect. Invalidly cued targets yield low-weighted early prediction error, hence take significantly longer to recruit the right hypothesis ('target over there') and are perceived with lower confidence.

This general take on attention is phenomenologically compelling. Try to attend long and hard to a single word on this page. The experience, or so it seems to me, is initially one of increased local clarity, closely followed by a state of decaying clarity while remaining alert. There is at that point a tendency to entrain action, perhaps using shifts of covert attending or micro-saccades to further explore the fixated word. The longer all this goes on *without* the emergence of any new, different, or clearer information the harder it becomes to sustain the process of attending.[6] Attention thus presents itself as bound up, experientially, with both the expectation of and the search for new and better information.

2.5   Sensory Integration and Coupling

The precision-weighting of prediction error turns out to be a very versatile tool, and one that will play a variety of roles as our story unfolds. For the present I merely note, without much amplification, two such additional roles. The first concerns sensory integration. Often, when confronting the world, the brain receives sensory signals from a variety of sources. For example, we may see and hear an approaching car. In such cases, the two sources of sensory input need to play delicately balanced roles in determining our perceptual experience of salient (indeed, often survival-relevant!) environmental states such as the car's location and speed of approach. Automatic estimations of the relative precision of the two sensory signals enable the brain to integrate the two sources of information, using each source in the best way given the larger context. Such integration depends both upon specific (sub-personal) expectations concerning the sight and sound of typical cars and also upon more general expectations such as the expectation (a systemic 'hyperprior') that whenever auditory and visual estimations of the spatial location of a signal source are reasonably close, the best overall hypothesis is that there is a single source—in this case, a rapidly moving car. Such hyperpriors can also mislead, as demonstrated by the projection of sound onto a ventriloquist's dummy. But in ecologically central cases, they enable the optimal combination of multiple sources of sensory data. There is thus a potent interaction between the process of hypothesis selection and the precision-weighting of various sources of sensory input.

Estimated precision also helps to determine the moment-by-moment flow of information between neural areas (thus helping to determine changing patterns of 'effective connectivity'; see Friston, 1995, 2011c). This second role will prove important when we later consider the context-sensitive and task-specific recruitment of variable mixes of neural (and indeed extra-neural, see Part III) resources. Thus, to take a very simple example, it might sometimes be best to allow visual information to dominate when selecting a behavioural response (e.g., in the presence of known auditory distractors) and that can be achieved by assigning low-precision to auditory prediction errors and higher precision to visual ones.[7] For example, den Ouden et al. (2010) offer an account of variations in the strength of coupling (i.e., influence) between cortical areas that depicts variably precision-weighted prediction error as the key tool controlling such couplings 'on the fly' according to (contextualized) task-demands. The same broad apparatus may also adjudicate between multiple systems (such as the prefrontal cortex and the dorsolateral striatal system) capable of determining online response. In just this vein Daw, Niv, and Dayan (2005, p. 1704) describe those systems as subject to a 'Bayesian principle of arbitration ... according to uncertainty' such that the sub-system currently estimated to provide the most accurate predictions gets to drive behaviour and choice. Such principles will loom large when we consider (in Part III) possible relations between the predictive processing framework and the shape and nature of the entire embodied, encultured, and environmentally embedded cognitive architecture that we call 'mind'.

2.6   A Taste of Action

The full role of precision (and precision expectations) in the predictive processing story cannot be appreciated, however, without at least previewing the treatment of action. This is unsurprising, since (as we shall see) PP makes a strong proposal concerning the cognitive centrality of a complex looping interplay between perception and action. In fact, so complex, central, and looping is the interplay that perception will emerge (Part II) as inseparable from action, and the theoretical divisions between sensory and motor processing will themselves be called into question.

All that lies before us. For present purposes, it will suffice to introduce one core element of that richer, more action-oriented story. That element (already hinted at in the comments about selecting actions above) concerns the role of action as a tool for *precision-expectation-based sensory sampling.* That is hard to parse and a bit of a mouthful, but the idea is both simple and astonishingly powerful. Consider a case in which there are two models in close competition to account for the sensory signal. One model reduces prediction error more than the other, but the prediction error it reduces is estimated as unreliable. The other model, though it reduces less absolute error, reduces error that is estimated to be highly reliable. The 'best bet' in such circumstances is usually (though see Hohwy, 2012, for some important caveats) to endorse the model that reduced the more reliable error signals. If the two competing models were, simplistically, 'cat in porch' and 'burglar in porch',[8] this could be a matter of some practical import.

But how do we determine the reliability or otherwise of the signal? It is here that action (a special kind of action) plays a key cognitive role. For part of the generative model that I have (very coarsely) glossed as 'burglar in porch' includes expectations concerning the best way to *sample* the environment so as to yield reliable information concerning that very possibility. It includes, for example, expectations concerning the best way to scan the scene, foveating first one location then another, so as to *reduce uncertainty concerning that very hypothesis*. Assuming the hypothesis is correct (there is a burglar there) this process will yield a sequence of precise prediction errors that both refine and confirm my dire suspicion, revealing perhaps a glint of metal (a torch? a gun?) and the outline of a dark roll-neck sweater. The process iterates, as the hypotheses 'torch' and 'gun' now need to be assessed. There too, my generative model includes expectations concerning the best way to engage (sample) the sensory scene so as to reduce uncertainty. These expectations engage action in a way that is perfectly continuous (as we will see in Part II) with the PP account of perception. Perception and action here form a virtuous, self-fuelling, circle in which action serves up reliable signals that recruit percepts that both determine and become confirmed (or disconfirmed) in action.

2.7   Gaze Allocation: Doing What Comes Naturally

There is a larger story here too, concerning the way attention is distributed during the performance of natural tasks. A natural task, as I shall use the term, is pretty much any well-learned task that we might perform during the course of our ordinary daily activities. Natural tasks thus include boiling the kettle, walking the dog, shopping, running, and eating lunch. What matters about such tasks (and what distinguishes them from many laboratory-based experimental paradigms) is that they provide the full, rich set of sensory cues that we have come (during learning) to expect in those specific situations. This matters, since it allows task-specific knowledge to play a much more important role driving (for example) proactive visual saccades in which our eyes move anticipatorily to the places relevant information will next be found, and opening the door to many other forms of active intervention whose common purpose is to yield better information just-in-time to guide relevant actions. Human performance on natural tasks cannot be explained, it now seems clear, by simple bottom-up models in which gaze fixation (a natural correlate of the sequential disposition of attention) is determined by low-level visual[9] salience. This is in opposition to early suggestions that simple stimulus features, pre-attentively extracted, might drive our gaze/attention around the scene. To be sure, such features (a dot of red among a sea of green dots, a sudden flash, or a vertical line among a sea of horizontals) will capture attention. But attempts to define so-called 'salience maps' in such essentially bottom-up terms (e.g., Koch & Ullman, 1985) have provided scant leverage for explaining the disposition of gaze and attention during the performance of normal, everyday tasks. Using a mixture of real-world walking and walking in virtual (but reasonably realistic) environments, Jovancevic et al. (2006) and Jovancevic-Misic and Hayhoe (2009) showed that simple feature-based salience maps failed to predict where and when gaze would shift around the scene. Similar results were obtained by Rothkopf, Ballard, and Hayhoe (2007), who showed that simple salience maps made false predictions and failed to explain the observed patterns of fixation in almost all cases. In fact:

> Humans looked at mainly the objects with only 15% of fixations directed to the background. In contrast, the salience model predicted that more than 70% of fixations should have been directed to the background. (Tatler et al., 2011, p. 4)

Tatler et al. drive the point home noting that:

> In ball sports, the shortcomings of feature-based schemes become even more obvious. Saccades are launched to regions where the ball will arrive in the near future (Ballard & Hayhoe, 2009; Land & McLeod, 2000). Crucially, at the time that the target location is fixated, there is nothing that visually distinguishes this location from the surrounding background of the scene. Even without quantitative evaluation, it is clear that no image-based model could predict this behavior. (Tatler et al., 2011, p. 4)

Looking ahead, to currently empty (no relevant stimulus present) locations is a pervasive feature of gaze allocation during the performance of natural tasks and has been experimentally confirmed for tasks including tea-making (Land et al., 1999) and sandwich-making (Hayhoe et al., 2003). In the sandwich case (check this next time you cut a sandwich!) subjects look where the knife makes its first contact with the bread, then keep looking just ahead of the current cutting point as the knife moves forwards.

Faced with this endemic failure to account for the shape of daily performance in natural tasks, one response, Tatler et al. note, is to keep the low-level salience map but add some mechanism of top-down modulation. Such hybrid approaches are suggested by Navalpakkam and Itti (2005) and by Torralba et al. (2006). Other work seeks to replace the low-level salience map with other constructs such as the so-called 'priority map' (Fecteau & Munoz, 2006) that fluidly integrates low- and high-level cues in a task-specific (that is to say, prior knowledge-dependent) way. Most promising of all, however (or so I would suggest) are approaches that fundamentally reorient the discussion, bringing perception and action into intimate coupling (Fernandes et al., 2014) and making uncertainty reduction the driving force behind gaze allocation and attentional shift. Prime examples include Sprague et al. (2007), Ballard and Hayhoe (2009), and Tatler et al. (2011) and the growing corpus of work on attention and precision-weighting reviewed in the present chapter.[10] At the heart of all these approaches lies the simple but profound insight that:

> Observers have learned models of the dynamic properties of the world that can be used to position eye gaze in anticipation of a predicted event [and that] action control must proceed on the basis of predictions rather than perceptions. (Tatler et al., 2011, p. 15)

Such models develop with experience. Learner drivers, Tatler et al. note, allocate their gaze just in front of the car as they take a corner, while seasoned drivers look further ahead, fixating road locations up to 3 seconds ahead of their speed of travel (Land & Tatler, 2009). Cricketers likewise anticipate the bounce of the ball (Land & McLeod, 2000). All these cases of 'pro-active saccades' (saccades that land on the right location in advance) depend on the agent commanding and deploying task-specific knowledge. Such bodies of knowledge (which PP casts in the form of probabilistic generative models) reflect, first and foremost, properties of the dynamic environment itself. They also reflect the action capacities (including the response speeds, etc.) of the individual agent. That properties of the environment play a major role is demonstrated by the large degree of overlap between the scan patterns of different individuals performing the same well-learnt tasks (Land et al., 1999). In addition, Hayhoe et al. (2003) show that information is typically retrieved just-in-time for action, in ways that leave information in the environment until just the right moment (see also discussion in Clark, 2008, chapter 1, and in chapter 8 following).

Precision-weighted PP accounts are ideally placed to bring all these elements together in a single unifying story: one that places neural prediction and the reduction of uncertainty centre-stage. This is because PP treats action, perception, and attention as (in effect) forming a single mechanism for the context- and task-dependent combination of bottom-up sensory cues with top-down expectations. Crucially, these top-down expectations now include expectations of precision, which drive the action system to sample the scene in ways that reduce uncertainty where, and when, it matters. Gaze allocation is thus driven by learnt generative models that combine expectations about unfolding events with action-entraining expectations concerning the best ways to sample the scene so as to reduce uncertainty at task-critical junctures.

The PP account also unifies the treatment of exogenous and endogenous attention, revealing low-level 'pop-out' effects as conceptually continuous with high-level inner model-based effects. In the former case, attention is captured by stimuli that are strong, unusual (the red spot among the sea of green ones), bright, sudden, etc. These are all cases where an evolved system should 'expect' a good signal-to-noise ratio. The effect of learning is conceptually similar. Learning delivers a grip on how to sample the environment in task-specific ways that yield high-quality sensory information. This reduces uncertainty and streamlines performance of the task. It is this latter kind of knowledge that is brought to bear in endogenous attention, perhaps (see Feldman & Friston, 2010, pp. 17–18) by increasing the baseline firing rate of select neuronal populations.

Before moving on, I should enter an important caveat concerning 'natural tasks'. For simplicity, I have here concentrated on a few well-learnt (possibly over-learnt) tasks such as driving and making a sandwich. But the PP account also delivers fluent and rapid learning about new situations when those situations are built from known elements and structures. That means that we can rapidly become 'expert observers' of (modestly) brand new scenes. For example, when watching a theatre play we rapidly get to grips with the novel arrangements of people and objects on stage, learning what is plot-salient and thus where (and when) we most need to reduce uncertainty, pro-actively allocating gaze and attention accordingly.

2.8   Circular Causation in the Perception-Attention-Action Loop

An important upshot of all this is that the generative model that underlies perception includes key action-driving expectations concerning *prospective confirmation*. That is to say, it includes (sub-personal) expectations concerning how things should unfold assuming some current perceptual hypothesis (the one dictating our ongoing perceptual awareness) is correct. Such expectations concern both what will happen (i.e., what perceptual inputs will result) if we sample the world in line with the hypothesis and what signal-to-noise ratios will result. In the latter case, the brain is betting on what might be dubbed *prospective precision*, that is, the anticipated signal-to-noise ratio consequent upon sampling the scene by moving our eyes, other sensory organs, or even our whole body. Thus a sequence of saccades to locations expected to deliver high-precision information of the kind predicted by some specific perceptual hypothesis (and not predicted by nearby rivals) provides excellent evidence that the hypothesis is correct and warrants keeping it alive and 'in the driving seat'. But should things fail to fall into place (should the results of the perceptual 'experiment' appear to falsify the hypothesis) those error signals can be used to recruit a different hypothesis, in the manner described earlier.

This has an immediate and interesting consequence that will continue to occupy us as the story unfolds. It means that perception, attention, and embodied action work together to drive the agent in self-fuelling cycles of active perception in which we probe the world according to systemic 'beliefs' concerning that which our own actions are about to reveal. This leads to what Friston, Adams, et al. (2012) describe as 'the circular causality that lies behind perception', namely, that:

> The only hypothesis that can endure over successive saccades is the one that correctly predicts the salient features that are sampled. . . . This means that the hypothesis prescribes its own verification and can only survive if it is a correct representation of the world. If its salient features are not discovered, it will be discarded in favor of a better hypothesis. (Friston, Adams, et al., 2012, p. 16)

'Salient features' are features that, when sampled, minimize uncertainty concerning the current perceptual hypothesis (they are the ones that, when things unfold as expected, maximize our confidence in the hypothesis). Active agents are thus driven to sample the world so as to (attempt to) confirm their own perceptual hypotheses. The current winning percept should then be able to 'maintain itself by selectively sampling evidence for its own existence [correctness]' (p. 17). Such sampling indeed implies a kind of 'saliency map': but it is not a map determined by low-level, attention-grabbing visual features[11] but by relatively high-level knowledge concerning the world and the distribution of salient, precise, sensory information.

Friston, Adams, et al. demonstrate this core effect using a simple simulation (see Figure 2.4) in which an artificial agent samples a visual scene in ways driven by various perceptual hypotheses. Here, the agent commands three models that it tries to fit to the stimulus, settling upon the model that correctly predicts the sensory data consequent upon one pattern of saccade.[12] After a few early probes, the simulated agent sequentially fixates the points that confirm the hypothesis that the source of the input is an upright face. Figure 2.5 shows the system's behaviour when presented with an image that fits none of its known models. Under those conditions, no model (no hypothesis) prescribes a pattern of fixations able to confirm itself, so sensory uncertainty cannot be quashed and no model can be selected. No percept is then in a position to 'maintain itself by selectively sampling evidence for its own existence [correctness]' (Friston, Adams, et al., 2012, p. 17). Under such unpromising conditions, the scene is sampled in a wandering fashion and no clear stable percept is produced. Such failures, assuming the brain believes it is getting high-quality (precise) sensory information would, however, drive increased plasticity allowing a new model to be acquired and applied (see section 2.12).

Summing up, PP posits core perception-attention-action loops in which internal models of the world and their associated precision expectations play key action-driving roles. Working together these determine a (frequently self-fulfilling) process of exploratory, epistemically mandated, sensing and acting: a process in which a winning hypothesis (a winning 'take on the world') causes us to sample the scene in ways that reflect both the hypothesis itself and our own context-varying states of sensory uncertainty.

2.9   *Mutual Assured Misunderstanding*

There is, however, a possible dark side to all this too. The dark side emerges when subtly misguided estimations of precision lead us to harvest sensory information in ways that work against the formation of a good (veridical) picture of how things are. Siegel (2012) describes just such a possible scenario. It is a scenario in which 'Jill believes, without justification, that Jack is angry at her ... When she sees Jack, her belief makes him look angry to her'. In such cases, our active top-down model causes us to discard some elements of the signal (treating them as mere 'noise') and amplify others. Normally—as seen in the cases above—this leads to more accurate perception, in noisy and ambiguous circumstances. In the case of angry-looking Jack, however, our belief

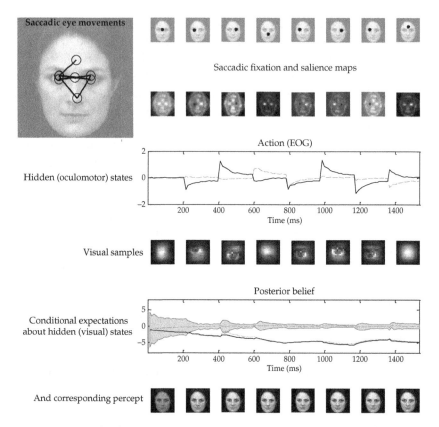

FIGURE 2.4 This figure shows the results of the first simulation by Friston, Adams, et al. (2012), in which a face was presented to an agent, whose responses were simulated using the PP schema described in the text. In this simulation, the agent had three internal images or hypotheses about the stimuli it might sample (an upright face, an inverted face, and a rotated face). The agent was presented with an upright face and its conditional expectations were evaluated over 16 (12 ms) time bins until the next saccade was emitted. This was repeated for eight saccades. The ensuing eye movements are shown as dots at the location (in extrinsic coordinates) at the end of each saccade in the upper row. The corresponding sequence of eye movements is shown in the insert on the upper left, where the circles correspond roughly to the proportion of the image sampled. These saccades are driven by prior beliefs about the direction of gaze based upon the saliency maps in the second row. Note that these maps change with successive saccades as posterior beliefs about the hidden states, including the stimulus, become progressively more confident. Note also that salience is depleted in locations that were foveated in the previous saccade. These posterior beliefs provide both visual and proprioceptive predictions that suppress visual prediction errors and drive eye movements, respectively. Oculomotor responses are shown in the third row in terms of the two hidden oculomotor states corresponding to vertical and horizontal

primes us to deploy a model that (in part by altering the precision we assign to various aspects of the prediction error signal) 'discovers' visual evidence for the—false and ungrounded—hypothesis that Jack is angry. This is just like hearing the song 'White Christmas' 'hidden' in the noise. The upshot is that our visual experience itself (not some add-on judgment) then represents Jack as looking angry, adding fuel to the fire of our earlier suspicions.

Action and perception are here locked into a *mutually misleading* cycle. This is because the primed 'angry-Jack' hypothesis gets to control (in ways we will explore in more detail in later chapters) the *actions* that then probe the world for confirming evidence of Jack's anger. We saccade around Jack's face looking for subtle evidence, we look for tension in his limb movements, oddities in his choice of words, etc. And since we have upped the precision on signals carrying information about subtle 'signs' of anger and (thereby) reduced it on veridical signs of normality, we may well find the very 'evidence' we were looking for. In a real-world setting, Teufel, Fletcher, and Davis (2010) show that our active top-down models of other people's current mental states and intentions do indeed influence how we physically perceive them to be, affecting our base perception of their gaze direction, motion onset, form of motion, etc. (for many more examples of the effects of top-down knowledge upon perception, see Goldstone, 1994; Goldstone & Hendrickson, 2010; Lupyan, 2012).

To cement the tragedy, the fact that Jack and Jill are both PP agents (hence beings whose percepts are deeply prediction-penetrated) may rapidly make things worse. For Jill's probes and suspicions are not invisible to Jack himself, and her body language is a little tense. Jack thinks (wrongly) 'Perhaps Jill is angry with me?'. Now the scenario

---

displacements. The associated portions of the image sampled (at the end of each saccade) are shown in the fourth row. The final two rows show the posterior beliefs in terms of their sufficient statistics and the stimulus categories, respectively. The posterior beliefs are plotted here in terms of conditional expectations and the 90% confidence interval about the true stimulus. The key thing to note here is that the expectation about the true stimulus supervenes over its competing expectations and, as a result, conditional confidence about the stimulus category increases (the confidence intervals shrink to the expectation). This illustrates the nature of evidence accumulation when selecting a hypothesis or percept that best explains sensory data. For full details of the experiment and results, see the original paper by Friston, Adams, et al., 2012.

Source: From Friston, Adams, et al., 2012, by permission.

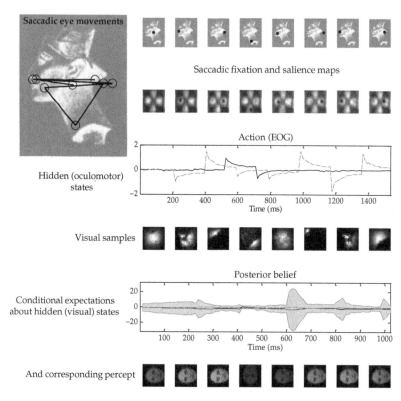

Saccadic eye movements

Saccadic fixation and salience maps

Action (EOG)

Hidden (oculomotor) states

Visual samples

Posterior belief

Conditional expectations about hidden (visual) states

And corresponding percept

FIGURE 2.5 This figure uses the same format as the previous figure, but shows the result of presenting an unknown (unrecognizable) face—the image of the ancient Egyptian queen Nefertiti. Because the simulated agent has no internal image or hypothesis that can produce veridical predictions about salient locations to foveate, it cannot resolve the causes of its sensory input and is unable to assimilate visual information into a precise posterior belief about the stimulus. Saccadic movements are generated by a saliency map that represents the most salient locations based upon a mixture of all internal hypotheses about the stimulus. Irrespective of where the agent looks, it can find no posterior beliefs or hypothesis that can explain the sensory input. As a result, there is a persistent posterior uncertainty about the states of the world that fail to resolve themselves. The ensuing percepts are poorly formed and change sporadically with successive saccades.

Source: From Friston, Adams, et al., 2012, by permission.

repeats, To Jack, Jill now looks a little angry and sounds a little angry. Jill then detects even more signs of tenseness (perhaps they are now real) in Jack, and the cycle of mutual (originally misplaced) prediction escalates. Mutual prediction, as we shall later see, can greatly enhance interpersonal understanding. But when coupled with the profound effects of expectation upon perception and action, it can also provide a worrying recipe for self-fulfilling psycho-social knots and tangles.

Nor is this dark side restricted to cases of multiple interacting human agents. Increasingly, our best tools and technologies are in the business of predicting our own needs, requests, and patterns of use. Google anticipates search requests according to past patterns and information about present location, and offers advice and options even before we ask for them. Amazon uses powerful collaborative filtering techniques to make suggestions based on past purchases. Such innovations extend the realm of mutual prediction to include webs of humans and machines, each of which are now busily anticipating the other. Unless checked or controlled this could lead, as in the so-called 'filter bubble' scenario described in Pariser (2011), to increasingly restricted explorations of the space of opportunities.[13]

2.10   Some Worries about Precision

A brief sketch of the basic PP account of attention appeared in Clark (2013). This was a target article in the peer-review journal *Behavioral and Brain Sciences*, and as such was accompanied by a variety of commentaries from leading figures in the field. Bowman et al. (2013) was one such commentary. In addition to some worries concerning biased competition (see 2.4), Bowman et al. were concerned that the precision-based account seemed best suited to explaining spatial, rather than feature-based, attention. Feature-based attention, Bowman et al. noted, allows us to enhance response to a given feature even when it appears at an unpredicted location. Thus, to borrow their example, the command to find an instance of bold type may result in attention being captured by a nearby spatial location. If we then (as PP suggests) increase the precision-weighting upon prediction error from that spatial location, doesn't that suggest that the precision-weighting of select prediction error signals is a *consequence* of attending rather than its *causal mechanism*?

This is a nice puzzle, and it reveals something important about the apparatus on offer. For the resolution of the puzzle lies, I suggest, in the manipulation of precision-weighting at different levels of the processing regime. Feature-based attention corresponds, intuitively, to increasing the gain on the prediction error units associated with the identity or configuration of a stimulus (e.g., increasing the gain on units reporting prediction errors pertaining to the distinctive geometric pattern of a four-leaf clover). Boosting that response (by giving added weight to the relevant kind of sensory prediction error) should enhance detection of that featural cue. Once the cue is provisionally detected, the subject can fixate the right spatial region, now under conditions of 'four-leaf-clover-there' expectation. Residual error is then amplified for that feature at that location, and high confidence in the presence of the four-leaf clover can (if you are lucky!) be obtained. Note that attending to the wrong spatial region (e.g., due to incongruent spatial cueing) will actually be counterproductive in such cases. Precision-weighted prediction error is thus able to encompass both mere-spatial and feature-based signal enhancement.

Additional worries were raised by Block and Siegel (2013) who suggested that predictive processing is unable to offer any plausible or distinctive account of very basic results such as the attentional enhancement of perceived contrast (Carrasco, Ling, & Read, 2004). In particular, Block and Siegel suggested that the PP model failed to capture changes due to attending that *precede* the calculation of error, and that it falsely predicts a magnification of the changes that follow from attending (consequent upon upping the gain on some of the prediction error). It is worth looking at this case in a little detail.

Carrasco, Ling, and Read (2004) report experiments in which subjects fixate a central spot with contrast gratings to the left and right. The gratings differ in absolute (actual) contrast. But when subjects are cued to attend (even covertly) to the lower contrast grating, their perception of the contrast there is increased, yielding the (false) judgment that, for example, an attended 70% (actual value) contrast grating is the same as an unattended 82% grating. Block and Siegel suggest that the predictive processing account cannot explain the initial effect here (the false perception of an 82% contrast for the covertly attended 70% contrast grating) as the only error signal—and this is where they misconstrue the story—is the difference between the stable pre-attentive 70% registration and the post-attentive 82% one. But this difference was not available until after attention had done its work! Worse still, once that difference is available, shouldn't it be amplified once more, as gain on the relevant error units is now increased?

This is an ingenious challenge, but it is based on a revealing misconstrual of the precision-weighting proposal. It is not the case that PP posits an error signal calculated on the basis of a difference between the unattended contrast (registered as 70%) and the subsequently attended contrast (now appearing to be 82%). Rather, what attention alters is the expectation of precise sensory information from the attended spatial location. Precision is the inverse of the variance, and it is our 'precision expectations' that attention here alters. What seems to be happening, in the case at hand, is that the very fact that we covertly attend to the grating on the left (say) increases our expectations of a precise sensory signal. Under such conditions, the expectation of precise information induces an inflated weighting for sensory error and our subjective estimate of the contrast is distorted as a result.[14]

The important point is that the error is not computed, as Block and Siegel seem to suggest, as a difference between some prior (in this case unattended) percept and some current (in this case attended) one. Instead, it is computed directly for the present sensory signal itself, but *weighted* in the light of our expectation of precise sensory information from that location. Expectations of precision are what, according to PP, is being manipulated by the contrast grating experiment, and PP thus offers a satisfying (and distinctive) account of the effect itself. This same mechanism explains the general effect of attention on spatial acuity.

Block and Siegel also argue that it 'makes no sense to take the error signal to be the sensory input', at least once an agent is awake, alert, and has a grip on what is around her. But the claim is not, of course, that the agent perceives an error signal. (Similarly, no conventional theorist should say that the agent typically perceives the flow of sensory information itself, rather than the world that it makes available.) According to PP, the agent perceives what is around her, but does so *courtesy* of the forward (and lateral) flow of error and the downward (and lateral) flow of prediction.

In sum, predictive processing depicts attention as increasing the gain on select prediction errors. Attention thus forms an integral aspect of the inferential cascade that constitutes the normal perceptual process. Endogenous attention here corresponds to processes of volitional control that impact the gain on prediction errors associated with some task-relevant feature (e.g., the shape of the four-leaf clover) or some selected spatial location. Exogenous attention corresponds to the more automatic processing that ups the gain on select prediction errors during the fluent performance of a well-learnt task, or in response to some ecologically salient cue (such as a flash of light, a motion transient, or a sudden noise). Such ecologically salient cues tend to produce strong sensory signals, and such signals are implicitly 'expected' to display a high signal-to-noise ratio. There is thus a kind of hyperprior in play: an expectation of precision for stronger signals, that plausibly mandates increasing the gain on associated prediction error (see Feldman & Friston, 2010, p. 9; see also Hohwy, 2012, p. 6). Finally, expectations of precision were also seen to guide exploratory actions, determining (for example) patterns of saccade that track the regions of the scene where more precise information is most likely to be found

Uniting perception and action in a single self-fuelling loop, estimates of precision thus enable the flexible task-varying combination of bottom-up sensory information (conveyed by prediction error) and top-down generative-model-based expectation.

2.11   *The Unexpected Elephant*

Understanding the role of precision and precision expectations may be especially important for revealing the complex links between non-conscious ('sub-personal') prediction and the shape and flow of personal-level daily experience. For example, there seems to be an initial disconnect between neural-surprise ('surprisal': the implausibility of some sensory state given a model of the world) and agent surprise. This is evident from the simple fact that the percept that, overall, best minimizes surprisal (hence minimizes prediction errors) 'for' the brain may well be, for me the agent, some highly surprising and unexpected state of affairs—imagine, for example, the sudden unveiling of a large and doleful elephant elegantly smuggled onto the stage by a professional magician. The appearance of a radical disconnect here is, however, illusory, as a slightly more detailed account reveals.

As the magician waves away the cover, coarse rapidly processed visual cues recruit the hypothesis (elephant) best able to minimize sensory prediction error. The perception/action loop is immediately engaged, driving a series of visual saccades that sweep the scene in elephant-specific ways (e.g., foveating where the trunk should be). That visual search will, if the hypothesis is correct, yield high-precision confirmation of that very hypothesis.[15] Suppose the sweep fulfils all systemic expectations. The agent now commands a reliable model that has survived the acid test of high-precision prediction error. The elephant percept is at that point the one that best respects what the cognitive system knows and expects about the world, and what it knows and expects about the results of its own interventions (here, visual saccades) upon the world. The elephant-on-stage percept is thus the winning hypothesis *given* the current combination of driving inputs, precision expectations, and assigned precision (reflecting, as we saw, the brain's degree of confidence in the sensory signal).

Given the right driving signal and a high enough assignment of precision, top-level theories of an initially agent-unexpected kind can thus win out so as to explain away that highly weighted tide of incoming sensory evidence. The sight of the doleful elephant emerges as the best (most likely, least 'surprisal-ing') percept available, given the inputs, the priors, and the estimated precision of sensory prediction error. Nonetheless, systemic priors did not render that percept very likely in advance, hence (perhaps) the value to the agent of the actual feeling of surprise. The *feeling of surprise*, that is to say, might be a way of preserving useful information that would otherwise be thrown away—the information that, prior to the present evidence-led bout of inference, the perceived state of affairs was estimated as highly improbable.

This is all (usually) good news, as it means we are not slaves to our expectations. Successful perception requires the brain to use stored knowledge and expectations (Bayesian priors) to minimize prediction error. But we remain able to see very (agent-) surprising things, in conditions where the brain assigns high reliability to sensory prediction error (hence high reliability to the driving sensory signal). Importantly, that requires other high-level theories, though of an initially agent-unexpected kind, to win out so as to explain away the highly weighted sensory evidence.

2.12   *Some Pathologies of Precision*

What happens, though, if this balancing act goes wrong? What happens if the mechanisms of precision-weighting develop a glitch and the balance between top-down expectation and bottom-up sensing becomes compromised? Here, it seems to me, the predictive processing scenario suggests promising new ways of thinking about the large and varied space of human mentality. We shall see more of this in subsequent chapters. But we can already glimpse the potential in an impressive body of recent work addressing delusions and hallucination in schizophrenia (Corlett, Frith, et al., 2009; Fletcher & Frith, 2009).

Recall the unexpected sighting of the elephant described in the previous section. Here, the system already commanded an apt model able to 'explain away' the particular combination of driving inputs, expectations, and precision (weighting on prediction error) that specified the doleful, grey presence. But such is not always the case. Sometimes, dealing with ongoing, highly weighted sensory prediction error may require brand new generative models gradually to be formed (just as in normal learning). This might hold the key, as Fletcher and Frith (2009) suggest, to a better understanding of the origins of hallucinations and delusion (the two so-called 'positive symptoms') in schizophrenia. These two symptoms are often thought to involve two mechanisms and hence two breakdowns, one in 'perception' (leading to the

hallucinations) and one in 'belief' (allowing these abnormal perceptions to impact top-level belief). Thus Coltheart (2007) notes—correctly
and importantly—that perceptual anomalies alone will not typically
lead to the strange and exotic belief complexes found in delusional
subjects. But must we therefore think of the perceptual and doxastic
components as strictly independent?

A possible link emerges if perception and belief formation, as the
present story suggests, both involve the attempt to match unfolding
sensory signals with top-down predictions. Importantly, the impact
of such attempted matching is precision-mediated in that the systemic effects of residual prediction error vary according to the brain's
confidence in the signal. With this in mind, Fletcher and Frith (2009)
canvass the possible consequences of disturbances to a hierarchical
Bayesian system such that prediction error signals are falsely generated and—more important—highly weighted (hence accorded undue
salience for driving learning).

There are a number of potential mechanisms whose complex interactions, once treated within the overarching framework of prediction
error minimization, might conspire to produce such disturbances.
Prominent contenders include the action of slow neuromodulators such
as dopamine, serotonin, and acetylcholine (Corlett, Frith, et al., 2009;
Corlett, Taylor, et al., 2010). In addition, Friston (2010, p. 132) speculates
that fast, synchronized activity between neural areas may also play a
role in increasing the gain on prediction error within the synchronized
populations.[16] The key idea, however implemented, is that understanding the positive symptoms of schizophrenia requires understanding
disturbances in the generation and (especially) the weighting of prediction error. The suggestion is that malfunctions within that complex
economy (perhaps fundamentally rooted in abnormal dopaminergic
functioning) yield wave upon wave of persistent and highly weighted
'false errors' that then propagate all the way up the hierarchy forcing,
in severe cases (via the ensuing waves of neural plasticity) extremely
deep revisions in our model of the world. The improbable (telepathy, conspiracy, persecution, etc.) then becomes the least surprising,
and—because perception is itself conditioned by the top-down flow of
prior expectations—the cascade of misinformation reaches back down,
allowing false perceptions and bizarre beliefs to solidify into a coherent and mutually supportive cycle.

Such a process is self-entrenching. As new generative models take
hold, their influence flows back down so that incoming data is sculpted by
the new (but now badly misinformed) priors so as to 'conform to expectancies' (Fletcher & Frith, 2009, p. 348). False perceptions and bizarre

beliefs thus form an epistemically insulated self-confirming cycle. This, then, is the darker side of a highly potent cognitive strategy. The predictive processing model merges—usually productively—perception, belief, and learning within a single overarching economy: one within which dopamine along with other mechanisms and neurotransmitters controls the 'precision' (the weighting, hence the impact on inference and on learning) of prediction error itself. But when things go wrong, false inferences spiral and feed back on themselves. Delusion and hallucination then become entrenched, being both co-determined and co-determining. We see milder versions of this everywhere, both in science (Maher, 1988) and in everyday life. We tend to see what we expect, and we use that to confirm the model that is both generating our expectations, and sculpting and filtering both our observations and our estimates of their reliability.

The same broadly Bayesian framework can be used (Corlett, Frith, et al., 2009) to help make sense of the ways in which different drugs, when given to healthy volunteers, can temporarily mimic various forms of psychosis. Here, too, the key feature is the ability of the predictive coding framework to account for complex alterations in both learning and experience contingent upon the (pharmacologically modifiable) way driving sensory signals are meshed, courtesy of precision-weighted prediction errors, with prior expectancies and (hence) ongoing prediction. The psychotomimetic effects of ketamine, for example, are said to be explicable in terms of a disturbance to the prediction error signal (perhaps caused by AMPA upregulation) and the flow of prediction (perhaps via NMDA interference). This leads to a persistent prediction error and—crucially—an inflated sense of the importance or salience of the associated events, which in turn drives the formation of short-lived delusion-like beliefs (Corlett, Frith, et al., 2009, pp. 6–7; see also Gerrans, 2007). The authors go on to offer accounts of the varying psychotomimetic effects of other drugs (such as LSD and other serotonergic hallucinogens, cannabis, and dopamine agonists such as amphetamine) as reflecting other possible varieties of disturbance within a hierarchical predictive processing framework.[17]

This fluid spanning of levels constitutes, it seems to me, one of the key attractions of the present framework. We here move from considerations of normal and altered states of human experience, via computational models (highlighting precision-weighted prediction-error-based processing and the top-down deployment of generative models), to the implementing networks of synaptic currents, neural synchronies, and chemical balances in the brain. The hope is that by thus offering a new, multilevel account of the complex, systematic interactions among inference, expectation, learning, and experience, these models may one day deliver a better understanding even of our own agent-level experience than that afforded by the basic framework of 'folk psychology'. Such an outcome (see also chapter 7) would constitute a vindication of the claim (P. M. Churchland, 1989, 2012, P. S. Churchland, 2013) that adopting a 'neurocomputational perspective' might one day lead us to a deeper understanding of our own lived experience.

2.13   Beyond the Spotlight

Attention has often been depicted as a kind of mental spotlight (see, e.g., Crick, 1984) whose deployment reflects the competition (due to limited resources) for high-quality neural processing. The predictive processing model of attention shares some features with the spotlight model, while departing from it in other ways. It shares the depiction of attention as tied up with the search for precise (low-uncertainty) sensory information. Pointing a spotlight creates (as noted by Feldman & Friston, 2010) the very conditions under which high-quality sensory information can be obtained from a spatial location. But attention is not, PP suggests, itself a *mechanism* so much as a *dimension* of a much more fundamental resource.[18] It is a pervasive dimension of the generative models we (our brains) bring to bear to predict the flow of sensory data. But it is a special dimension, since it concerns not simply the nature of the external causes of the incoming sensory data (the signal) but the precision (statistically, the inverse variance) of the sensory information itself.

The generative model, by including estimates of current precisions and of the precisions that would result from visual saccades and other actions, directly entrains swathes of information-gathering behaviours. It makes predictions concerning not just how the signal should evolve (if the world is indeed thus-and-so) but also what incoming signals should be actively solicited and given the greatest weight as processing unfolds. It is by varying such weightings that we can bias select sensory channels during multimodal processing, flexibly alter the moment-to-moment flow of information between neural areas, and (most generally) alter the balance of power between the bottom-up sensory signal and top-down expectations. Such alterations accomplish the various 'special effects' (seeing faces in clouds, hearing sine-wave speech, or even hallucinating 'White Christmas') described in the early sections of this chapter.

Adding precision-encoded estimations of our own sensory uncertainty to the emerging picture also allows us to combine, in a fluent and flexible manner, the best of two superficially opposed worlds. One is the world of signal-suppression, the core feature of standard predictive coding. Here, expected signal elements are 'explained away' and stripped of forward-flowing causal efficacy. The other is the world of signal enhancement and biased competition. This is a world in which 'mission-critical' signal elements are amplified and enhanced, and their forward-flowing effects magnified. By weighting forward-flowing prediction error signals according to their expected precision the PP framework combines the best of both these worlds, enhancing some responses while suppressing others.

Attention, action, and perception are now joined in mutually supportive, self-fuelling loops. Weighted prediction error signals drive us to sample the world in ways that both reflect and test the hypotheses that are generating the predictions that are driving the actions. The resulting intimacy of perception, attention, and action forms one of the core themes of the present treatment and offers our best hope yet of an account of neural processing able to illuminate the profound cognitive entanglement of brain, body, and world.

3

The Imaginarium

3.1 Construction Industries

Perception, our story suggests, is a process that is both constructive and steeped in prediction. Perception of this stripe—the kind that reveals a structured world of interacting distal causes—has an important and (mostly) life-enhancing spin-off. For such perceivers are thereby imaginers too: they are creatures poised to explore and experience their worlds not just by perception and gross physical action but also by means of imagery, dreams, and (in some cases) deliberate mental simulations.

This is not to claim, of course, that every system that we might intuitively think of as in some form of sensory contact with its world is able to do these things. Doubtless there exist many simple systems (such as light-following robots or bacteria that follow chemical gradients) that use sensory inputs to select apt responses without deploying internally represented models to predict the shape of the incoming signal. Such systems would not, or so I shall argue, enjoy perceptual experiences as of a richly structured external world, nor would they be capable of mental states such as dreaming or imagining. But perceivers like us, if PP is correct, can use stored knowledge to generate a kind of multilevel virtual analogue of the driving sensory signal as it unfolds across multiple layers and types of processing.

The links to imagination and dreaming are then close at hand, for such systems command a generative model capable of reconstructing the sensory signal using knowledge about interacting causes in the world. That process of reconstruction, tuned and deployed in the presence of the sensory signal, paves the way for processes of outright construction, able to form and evolve in the absence of the usual sensory flow. Nearby too are capacities to engage in what some theorists call 'mental time-travel': remembering (reconstructing) the past and predicting the possible shapes of the future. Working together, these various 'construction industries' allow us to make better choices and select better actions. From the simple seeds of a generative-model-based account of online perception, there thus emerges a striking (and strikingly familiar) cognitive form. It is a form in which perception, imagination, understanding, and memory come as a kind of cognitive package deal—a package deal that locates the present where it experientially belongs, at the productive meeting point between past influence and informed future choice.

3.2   Simple Seeing

Consider the image in Figure 3.1. This is the so-called 'Cornsweet Illusion'. To most people, the central paired tiles appear to be very different shades of grey–an appearance that, as the second picture reveals, is illusory. The illusion occurs because (as we saw in chapters 1 and 2) our visual experiences do not simply reflect the current inputs, but are greatly informed by 'priors' (prior beliefs, usually taking the form of nonconscious predictions or expectations) concerning the world. In this case, the prior is that surfaces tend to be equally reflectant rather than becoming gradually brighter or darker towards their own edges. The brain's best guess is thus that the central pairing involves two differently reflective surfaces (two different shades of grey) illuminated by differing amounts of light. The illusion occurs because the image displays a highly atypical combination of illuminance and reflectance properties and the brain uses what it has learnt about typical patterns of illumination and reflectance to infer (falsely in this case) that the two tiles must be different shades of grey. In the world we actually live in, these particular prior beliefs or neural expectations are provably 'Bayes optimal'—that is, they represent the globally best method for inferring the state of the world from the ambient sensory evidence (Brown &

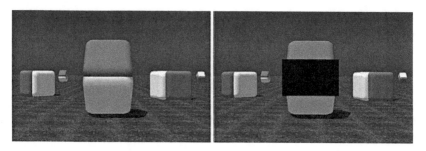

FIGURE 3.1 Cornsweet Illusion Set Up
The first image (*left*) depicts a typical Cornsweet illusion set up. The centres of the two tiles comprising the central pairing appear to be different shades of grey. The second image (*right*) reveals that they are in fact the same shade of grey.

Source: D. Purves, A. Shimpi, & R. B. Lotto (1999). An empirical explanation of the Cornsweet effect. *Journal of Neuroscience, 19*(19), 8542–8551.

Friston, 2012). The brain thus generates our perceptual experiences by combining prior knowledge (including, as we saw in chapter 2, knowledge about context) with incoming sensory evidence.

3.3 Cross-Modal and Multimodal Effects

This basic effect explains a surprisingly wide variety of familiar perceptual phenomena. One such phenomenon is the widespread existence of cross- and multimodal context effects on early 'unimodal' sensory processing. The discovery of such effects constitutes one of the major findings of contemporary sensory neuroscience (see, e.g., Hupe et al., 1998; Murray et al., 2002; Smith & Muckli, 2010). Thus, Murray et al. (2002) display the influence of high-level shape information on the responses of cells in early visual area V1, while Smith and Muckli (2010) show similar effects (using as input partially occluded natural scenes) even on wholly non-stimulated (that is to say, not directly stimulated via the driving sensory signal) visual areas. In addition, Murray et al. (2004) showed that activation in V1 is influenced by a top-down size illusion, while Muckli et al. (2005) and Muckli (2010) report activity relating to an apparent motion illusion in V1. Even apparently 'unimodal' early responses are influenced (Kriegstein & Giraud, 2006) by information derived from other modalities and hence will commonly reflect a variety of multimodal associations. Strikingly, even the expectation that a relevant input will turn out to be in one modality (e.g., auditory) rather than another (e.g., visual) turns out to improve performance, presumably by enhancing 'the weight of bottom-up input for perceptual inference on a given sensory channel' (Langner et al., 2011, p. 10).

This whole smorgasbord of context effects flows very naturally from the PP model. If so-called visual, tactile, or auditory sensory cortex is actually operating using a cascade of feedback from higher levels to actively predict the unfolding sensory signals (the ones originally transduced using the various dedicated receptor banks of vision, sound, touch, etc.), then we should not be in the least surprised to find extensive multimodal and cross-modal effects (including these kinds of 'filling-in') even on 'early' sensory response. One reason this will be so is that the notion of 'early' sensory response is in one sense now misleading, for expectation-induced context effects will simply propagate all the way down the system, priming, generating, and altering 'early' responses as far down as V1. Any statistically valid correlations, registered within the 'metamodal' (or at least, increasingly information-integrating) areas towards the top of the processing hierarchy, can inform the predictions that then cascade down, through what were previously thought of as much more unimodal areas, all the way to the areas closer to the sensory peripheries. Such effects are inconsistent with the idea of V1 as a site for simple, stimulus-driven, bottom-up feature-detection using cells with fixed (context-inflexible) receptive fields. But they are fully consistent with (indeed, mandated by) models that depict V1 activity as constantly negotiated on the basis of a flexible combination of top-down predictions and driving sensory signal. Reflecting on this new vision of 'early' sensory processing, Lars Muckli writes that

> It is conceivable that V1 is, first of all, the target region for cortical feedback and then, in a second instance, a region that compares cortical feedback to incoming information. Sensory stimulation might be the minor task of the cortex, whereas its major task is to . . . predict upcoming stimulation as precisely as possible. (Muckli, 2010, p. 137)

3.4   Meta-Modal Effects

The visual word form area (VWFA) is an area within the ventral stream that responds to proper letter strings: the kind that might reasonably form a word in a given language. Response in this brain area was already known to be independent of surface details such as case, font, and spatial location. In an important neuroimaging (fMRI) study, Reich et al. (2011) found evidence that VWFA is actually tracking something even more abstract than visual word form. It appears to be tracking word form regardless of the modality of the transducing stream. Thus, the very same area is activated in congenitally blind subjects during Braille reading. The fact that the early input here is tactile rather than visual makes no difference to the recruitment of VWFA. This supports the idea (Pascual-Leone & Hamilton, 2001) of such brain areas as 'metamodal operators' that are 'defined by a given computation that is applied regardless of the sensory input received'.

This fits neatly, as Reich et al. (2011, p. 365) themselves note, with the PP image in which higher levels of the cortical hierarchy learn to track the 'hidden causes' that account for, and hence predict, the sensory consequences of distal states of affairs. Reich et al. speculate that much activity in VWFA might thus reflect modality-transcending predictions about the sensory consequences of words. VWFA, that is to say, seems to be generating top-down predictions using modality-transcending models of word-hood. The meta-modality of VWFA would then 'explain its ability to apply top-down predictions to both visual and tactile stimuli' (Reich et al., 2011, p. 365).

Another nice example, this time from the action domain, is provided by Wolpert, Miall, and Kawato (1998) who note that elements of an individual's hand-writing style are preserved even when different effectors (such as the right or left hand, or even the toes) are used.[1] Abstract high-level motor commands must be unpacked in different ways as cascading predictions get closer and closer to the effector systems themselves. But at the higher levels, it seems, there is substantial motoric information encoded in effector-spanning forms.

In sum, the PP framework offers a powerful way of accommodating all manner of cross-, multi-, and meta-modal effects on perception. It depicts the senses as working together to provide feedback to a linked set of prediction devices that are attempting to track unfolding states of the world across multiple spatial and temporal scales. This delivers a very natural account of efficient multimodal cue integration and allows top-down effects to penetrate even the lowest (earliest) elements of sensory processing. (If that sounds epistemically worrying to you—perhaps because you suspect that too much top-down influence would make us see whatever we expect to see, rather than what is 'really there'—never fear. What is actually on offer is a very delicate balancing act indeed, as we will see in chapter 6.)

3.5   *Perceiving Omissions*

A further advantage of the predictive processing story (as mentioned in 1.14) is that it provides a powerful account of the full spectrum of 'omission-related responses'. The theoretical importance of such responses was noticed long ago by the Soviet psychologist Eugene Sokolov, in pioneering studies of the orienting reflex—the immediate 'attending' reaction typically provoked by unexpected changes in the environment. Sokolov noted that repeated exposures led to reduced response and dubbed this effect 'habituation'. One might have thought of this as some kind of brute physical effect due to some form of low-level sensory adaptation. Sokolov noticed, however, that even a *reduction* in the magnitude of some habituated stimulus could engage 'dishabituation' and prompt a renewed response.[2] Sokolov concluded that the nervous system must learn and deploy a 'neuronal model' that is constantly matched to the incoming stimulus, since what is attracting the animal's attention is now a reduction in the physical signal itself.

An extreme version of such a scenario occurs when an expected signal simply fails to materialize. For example, if we hear a regular series of beats and then a beat is omitted, we are perceptually aware (quite vividly aware) of its absence. Moreover, there is a familiar sensation of 'almost experiencing' the onset of the omitted item—as if we started to hear (or see, or feel) the very thing that, an instant later, we vividly notice has not occurred.

Accounts that posit the 'top-down' use of a generative model as a means of meeting the incoming sensory signal with apt expectations are ideally (perhaps uniquely) well-placed to explain both responsiveness to omission and the peculiar phenomenology of omission. A compelling example is provided by Adams et al. (2013) using simulation studies of the generation and recognition of birdsong. In these experiments (see Figure 3.2), a hierarchical predictive processing network responded to short sequences of simulated chirps (sequences displaying characteristic frequencies and volumes) using the kind of multilayer prediction machinery described in previous chapters. The simulations were then repeated but omitting part (the last three chirps) of the original signal. At the first missing chirp, the network responded with a strong burst of prediction error. This strong burst of error, the authors note, is generated in the complete absence of any guiding sensory input, since 'at this point there is no sensory input to predict and the prediction error is generated entirely by top-down predictions' (Adams et al., 2013, p. 10). Moreover, a closer analysis of the network's responses showed that, at the very moment where the first missing

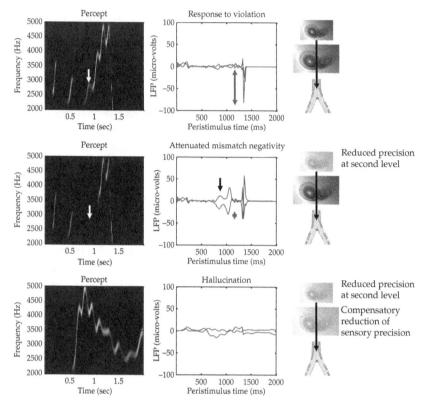

FIGURE 3.2 Omission-Related Responses

The left-hand panels show the predicted sonograms based upon posterior expectations, while the right-hand panels show the associated
(precision-weighted) prediction error at the sensory level. The top panels
show a normal omission-related response due to precise top-down predictions that are violated when the first missing chirp is not heard. This
response is attenuated, when the (log) precision of the second level is reduced
to two (middle row). This renders top-down predictions more sensitive to
bottom-up sensory evidence and sensory prediction errors are resolved
under reduced top-down constraints. At the same time, the third chirp—that
would have been predicted on the basis of top-down (empirical) prior
beliefs—is missed, leading to sensory prediction errors that nearly match
the amplitude of the prediction errors elicited by the omission. The lower
row shows predictions and prediction errors when there is a compensatory
decrease in sensory log precision from two to minus two. Here, there is a
failure of sensory prediction errors to entrain high-level expectations and
subsequent false inference that persists in the absence of any stimuli.

Source: From Adams, Stephan, et al., 2013, by permission.

chirp should have occurred, the system generated a *transient (illusory) percept*. This percept (the systemic best-guess at the state of the world) was not strong, but the timing was correct with respect to the missing chirp. In other words, the network first dimly 'perceived' (imagined) the missing chirp, before responding with a strong error signal as soon as the actual absence of such a signal became apparent. Such results nicely model (Adams et al., 2013, pp. 10–11) the so-called 'mismatch negativity'—the P300[3] neuronal response found in EEG studies using oddball or omitted stimuli—a result that also makes physiological sense given that such studies are most sensitive to the responses of the kinds of cell (superficial pyramidal cells) most plausibly implicated as reporting prediction errors.

In a revealing further manipulation (again, see Figure 3.2), Adams et al. reduced the precision of sensory prediction error at an upper level (level 2) of the multilayer network. The effect of this, as we saw in chapter 2, is to reduce the system's confidence in its own top-down predictions. Under these conditions, the chirp that was previously hardest to detect (the third chirp) is completely missed and a prediction error generated. However, since the system (with reduced level 2 precision) is now less confident in its predictions, this error is not as large as it would have been under normal conditions. This may correspond, the authors note, to the kind of reduced neuronal (and behavioural) responses to oddballs and omissions found in schizophrenic subjects. This account of such responses is interesting since it suggests that

> attenuated mismatch or violation responses in chronic schizophrenia may not reflect a failure to detect surprising events but reflect a failure to detect unsurprising (predictable) events. In other words, they may reflect the fact that every event is surprising. (Adams et al., 2013, p. 11)

One way a system might try to compensate for such pan-surprisingness is to effectively downgrade its confidence in the sensory signal itself. Reducing the estimated precision of the sensory signal has complex effects that we will further explore in subsequent chapters. In the simple birdsong study, such a reduction resulted in the total abolition of omission-related response and radical failures correctly to infer the structure of the distal environment from the sensory signal. Under such circumstances, auditorily encountered songs were tracked only roughly, with distorted structure and frequency. This is inevitable since under those conditions 'sensory information is not afforded the precision needed to constrain or entrain top-down predictions' (Adams et al., 2013, p. 12). This corresponds to the genesis of hallucinations, here emerging as quasi-perceptual states that are insufficiently controlled by top-down prediction and apt estimations of our own sensory uncertainty.

3.6   Expectations and Conscious Perception

The PP model has implications (more on which in chapter 7) for the study of the neural underpinnings of conscious sensory awareness.

We can creep up on this with some mundane reflections. It is intuitively obvious that, for example, a familiar song played using a poor radio receiver will sound much clearer than an unfamiliar one. Whereas we might have thought of this, within a simple feed-forward feature-detection framework, as some kind of *memory* effect, it now seems just as reasonable to think of it as a genuinely *perceptual* one. The clear-sounding percept, after all, is constructed in just the same way as the fuzzy-sounding percept, albeit using a better set of top-down predictions (priors, in the Bayesian translation of the story). That is to say—or so I would suggest—the familiar song really does sound clearer. It is not that memory *later* does some filling-in that affects, in a backward-looking way, how we judge the song to have sounded. Rather, the top-down effects bite in the very earliest stages of processing, leaving us little conceptual space (or so it seems to me) to depict the effects as anything other than enhanced-but-genuine perception. Thus imagine we discover a creature whose auditory apparatus is highly tuned to the detection of some biologically relevant sound. Imagine too that that tuning consists largely in a strong set of priors for that sound, such that the creature can detect it despite considerable noise in the ambient signal (a kind of cocktail party effect). Surely we would simply describe this as a case of acute perception? Then we must say the same, it seems to me, of the music-lover hearing a familiar song from a low-quality radio.

Can we avoid a slippery slope here, as we progressively degrade the driving signal and up-regulate the expectations? The lucky imaginar whose confabulations just happen perfectly to predict the external world is not truly *perceiving* her world at all. She is just a lucky guesser.

Two factors conspire to save us from being forced to accept such an agent into the ranks of the true perceivers. First, we should consider the counterfactuals. If you were just lucky that the distal world is currently as predicted, then *were* the worldly states to be different, you would fail to track them. This already distinguishes the lucky predictor from the normal predictive processing agent. Second, we must add the availability of attention. Attention, as we saw in the previous chapter, ups the gain on aspects of the error signal. That means we can indeed focus (if we decide to do so) on the fuzziness of the sound of the bad radio, upping the gain on select sensory prediction error to reveal the finer form of the sound-stream. The PP agent may then agree that the radio is past its prime and in dire need of replacement. Counterfactual robustness plus the availability of attention-based gain on sensory prediction error thus allows us to distinguish 'lucky hallucinations' from veridical prediction-driven percepts.

The role of prediction in the construction of conscious perceptual experience is nicely demonstrated in work by Melloni et al. (2011). Melloni et al. show that the onset time required to form a reportable conscious percept varies according to our expectations—they show, in other words, that expectation can speed up conscious awareness. Using electroencephalographic (EEG) signatures, it was calculated that conscious perception could occur as rapidly as 100ms faster for a well-predicted stimulus, and hence that 'the signatures of visibility are not bound to processes with a strict latency but depend on the presence of expectations' (Melloni et al., 2011, p. 1395). Such a result is best explained, Melloni et al. suggest, by appeal to a hierarchical predictive coding framework in which 'conscious perception is the result of a hypothesis test that iterates until information is consistent across higher and lower areas' (p. 1394).

3.7   The Perceiver as Imaginer

Animals capable of forming rich, world-revealing percepts are, if the predictive processing story is on track, animals that understand their worlds and that are poised to imagine them too. The argument for this is straightforward. An important feature of the internal models that power such approaches is that they are *generative* in nature. That is to say, the knowledge (model) encoded at an upper layer[4] must be such as to render activity in that layer capable of predicting the response profile at the layer below. That means that the model at layer N + 1 becomes capable, when operating within the context of the larger system, of generating the sensory data (i.e., the input as it would there be represented) at layer N (the layer below) for itself. Since this story applies all the way down to layers that are attempting to predict activity in early processing areas , that means that such systems are fully capable of generating 'virtual' versions of the sensory data for themselves.

This is, in one sense, unsurprising. As Hinton (and for similar comments, see Mumford, 1992) notes, 'vivid visual imagery, dreaming, and the disambiguating effect of context on the interpretation of local image regions … suggests that the visual system can perform top-down generation' (Hinton, 2007b, p. 428). In another sense, it is quite remarkable. It means that perception—at least, as it occurs in creatures like us—is co-emergent with something functionally akin to imagination. By 'creatures like us', I here mean creatures capable of rich, world-revealing perception: creatures able to perceive a complex distal environment populated by interacting hidden causes. In my own case, such hidden causes include rainstorms, primroses, and poker hands. In the case of my two cats (Bruno and Borat), they seem to include[5] cat-treats, mice, and moths. Bruno, Borat, and Clark, I suggest, are all deploying generative models to capture regularities in their sensory input at multiple spatial and temporal scales. Obviously, a simple robot that locomotes to a light source need not, and probably should not, deploy a multilayered generative model to do so. Instead, the need for generative models emerges most clearly when systems must deal with complex structures of hidden causes in domains characterized by noise, ambiguity, and uncertainty.

The claim I wish to defend, more carefully stated, is thus that animals[6] able to perceive a complex external world of interacting causes using the characteristic resources of prediction-driven learning will be animals capable of the endogenous generation of sensory-like states. It does not seem far-fetched to suggest that dreaming, imagining, and mental imagery thus became available as part and parcel of the very same cognitive package that delivered our grip on a structured (organism-salient) external world. This does not mean that every such animal can, by some deliberate act of will, bring such imaginings about. Indeed, it seems very likely that for most creatures acts of deliberate imagining (which I suspect may require the use of self-cueing via language) are simply impossible. But creatures that are thus enabled to perceive a structured world possess the neural resources to generate, from the top-down, approximations to those same sensory states. There thus emerges a deep duality between online perception (as enabled by the predictive processing architecture) and capacities for the endogenous generation of quasi-sensory states.

3.8 'Brain Reading' During Imagery and Perception

Strong fMRI evidence for such a duality emerged in a study by Reddy et al. (2010). The starting point for the study was a set of well-known results showing that mental imagery and online visual perception activate many of the same early processing areas (e.g., Kosslyn et al., 1995; Ganis et al., 2004). Such results have been replicated many times and also extended to include areas such as Lateral Occipital Cortex (LOC). This is an extra-striate area that responds strongly to shapes and objects, including letter-forms such as 'X' and 'O', preferring them to simple textures or scrambled objects. Stokes et al. (2009) showed LOC to be active both when subjects perceived and when they imagined the letters 'X' and 'O'.

Such results lend intuitive support to the idea of a deep computational duality between perception and imagination, but they are also compatible with many weaker accounts. They speak to an overlap of brute geographical location (many of the same areas 'lighting up' during online perception and offline imagination and recall) but that does not yet establish the kind of deeper functional overlap predicted by the PP class of models.

The Reddy et al. study directly addresses this issue, building upon recent successes in what is sometimes called 'brain reading'. In brain reading (e.g., Haxby et al., 2001; Kamitani & Tong, 2005; Norman et al., 2006), investigators attempt to reconstruct properties of a stimulus from fMRI data (the BOLD signal tracking hemodynamic response) concerning the neural activity that the stimulus evokes. That means plotting multivoxel[7] response patterns and using them to infer (to decode) properties of the stimulus that brought them about.

The experimenter is here in roughly the position of the biological brain itself. Her task—made possible by powerful mathematical and statistical tools—is to take patterns of neural activation[8] and, on that basis alone, infer properties of the stimulus. Such properties range from identifying the class to which the stimulus—which is typically an image—belongs (e.g., is it a face, a fruit, a tool?), to selecting which specific image from a predefined set evoked the response, to (most recently, and most impressively) actually reconstructing, as far as possible, the presented image itself. We shall see an example of the first type shortly. A nice example of the second type (fMRI-based image selection) can be found in Kay et al. (2008) who were able to infer which novel natural image (from a set of 120) a subject had been perceiving while being scanned. An example of the third (active reconstruction) type can be found in Miyawaki et al. (2008).

Interestingly, the tools and approaches used to perform the third task—the image reconstruction task—increasingly look to recapitulate the kinds of strategies used by the biological brain itself. The most promising approaches thus use a Bayesian method that combines information in the measured response with prior information concerning the structure and even the semantic contents of natural images—for an example, see Naselaris et al. (2009). The use of such prior information (just as in predictive processing) turns out to have a large and beneficial effect upon the quality of the image reconstruction. Taking this one step further, van Gerven et al. (2010) use a version of the architecture used in the digit recognition example discussed in chapter 1 (a 'deep belief network'; see Hinton et al., 2006) to reconstruct perceived handwritten greyscale digits from the fMRI data. The authors conclude (p. 3139) that 'hierarchical generative models can be used for neural decoding and offer a new window into the brain'.

The Reddy et al. experiment did not, however, involve image selection or image reconstruction. It addressed instead the much simpler problem of image classification. The first goal (in line with previous work) was to use pattern-classification techniques to decode category information concerning *viewed* images, determining whether the subject, when scanned, was perceiving images of tools, food, faces, or buildings. The second goal was to use the same techniques to determine whether subjects, when scanned, were *imagining* tools, food, faces, or buildings. Assuming this proved possible, the third and final goal was to determine how the voxel-level 'codes' for the imagined objects related to those for the 'same' object when it is actually perceived. For the decoding, the experimenters used a well-understood method (linear support vector machines) to learn the mappings between voxel-patterns and the four categories (food, tools, faces, and buildings). This was done for both perceived and imagined objects, and recordings were made both from early visual areas (V1, V2) and higher ones (FFA, PPA, and some distributed recordings).

Both forms of decoding (decoding what was seen and what was imagined) proved possible, though—and we shall return to this very shortly—decoding from the earliest, retinotopically mapped areas was possible only during actual viewing and not during imagery. In ventral-temporal cortex, by contrast, decoding proved possible under both conditions (actual viewing and imagery). Reddy et al. then addressed the third (and for our purposes the most interesting) question: what relation, if any, existed between the neural states implicated in the imagery condition and those implicated in the perceptual condition. This question bears directly upon our earlier conjectures concerning the deep duality of perception and imagination.

To address this question, Reddy et al. used an ingenious method. They took the trained-up classifier for perception and used it as the decoder under the imagery condition, and vice versa (taking the trained-up classifier for imagery and using it to decode online perception). Remarkably, each classifier worked for the other condition. In other words, it was possible to use the 'imagery decoder' to classify a currently viewed item, and the 'percept decoder' to classify a merely imagined item. This suggests that the two tasks are not simply sharing coarse neural resources, but are sharing the fine-grained use of those resources too. More specifically, it shows the existence of substantial overlap between the fine-grained[9] multi-voxel activation patterns (in ventral-temporal cortex) that encode the scenes when they are perceived and when they are merely imagined. An additional analysis showed that the role of the various voxels (their weighted contributions to classification success within a given category) was similar, and that the two conditions (imagery and online perception) shared key 'diagnostic voxels' (p. 6). The authors conclude that

> The use of pattern classification techniques ... indicated that actual viewing and mental imagery shared the same representations at the level of fine-grained multivoxel activation patterns in object-responsive ventral–temporal cortex [thus demonstrating] a high level of similarity between the fine-grained representations involved in perception and imagery of natural object categories. (Reddy et al., 2010, p. 7)

Such results lend strong support to the idea, central to predictive processing, that perception depends heavily upon a top-down generative capacity.

Nonetheless, there are clearly many differences, both experiential and functional, between perception and processes (such as mental imagery and perhaps dreaming) that are being driven purely from the top-down. Another aspect of the Reddy et al. study, briefly mentioned earlier, is revealing in this regard. For despite the demonstration of overlapping coding for perception and imagery in ventral-temporal cortex, decoding from earlier (V1 and V2) retinotopically mapped populations, though possible under the perceptual condition, was not possible under the imagery condition. Otherwise put, activity in those early areas was fMRI-'readable' as belonging to one of the four image classes only when the subject was actually engaged in online viewing and not when merely imagining. This may be linked (as Reddy et al. themselves intimate) to the fact that, on the whole, mental imagery seems less vivid and less detailed (less realistic) than online perception. A possible explanation, consistent with a body of superficially rather conflicting results concerning the ability of areas such as V1 to participate in mental imagery (see, e.g., Cui et al., 2007; Wheeler et al.,

2000) is that it is possible to drive V1 from the top down, but that this only occurs when the task itself demands a fine grain of imagined detail.

Perhaps in the more typical run of things imagery (unlike rich forms of hallucination) involves only the higher levels of the generative model? A possible mechanism for modulating such effects is readily available within PP in the form of the precision weighting of prediction error (see chapter 2). Assigning a low precision to prediction errors calculated for the early (high spatial and temporal resolution) stages of processing means that no systemic effort is expended upon bringing those states into line with downward-flowing predictions. Under such conditions, it seems plausible that the system would generate a stable percept that simply ignores lower-level details, entraining them (by upping the relevant precision-weightings) only when the task demands.

Online perception may also have special features. Plausibly, we can resolve prediction errors in online perception at a very high level of detail (grain) as when we attend, say, to the fine details of the patterning of a complex wallpaper or the bark of a tree.[10] Such stable, rich granularity may simply not be available in standard cases of mental imagery.[11]

Other ('blunter') low-level responses may, however, be more easily entrained. Laeng and Sulutvedt (2014) show, surprisingly, that the act of imagining can even impact pupil dilation and shrinkage. In this work, subjects were exposed to images of triangles of varying brightness. During exposure, the subject's pupils responded in the usual fashion, by dilating (widening) when the images were darker, and shrinking when they were lighter. When asked to imagine the same triangles, the same pupillary responses of dilation and shrinkage occurred. This result is striking since pupil size is something over which most subjects cannot exercise any form of conscious control, leading the experimenters to comment that 'the observed pupillary adjustments to imaginary light present a strong case for accounts of mental imagery as a process based on brain states similar to those that arise in perception' (p. 188). Such responses might serve, the authors suggest, to prepare the eyes for anticipated (perhaps potentially damaging or dangerously inadequate) levels of light.

3.9   Inside the Dream Factory

Such intimate links binding perception and imagination are suggestive with regard to dreaming too. They suggest, most obviously, that dream-states, like imagery, involve the top-down (generative-model-based) activation of many of the same states as occur during ordinary perception. Such a claim needs, however, to be handled with care. For the neural system, operating in the absence of the availability of 'hypothesis-checking action' and of ongoing driving external inputs, will be unable to support the same kinds of stability and richness of experienced detail that daily sensory engagements offer.

In the absence of the driving sensory signal, there is no stable ongoing information (in the form of reliable, estimated-as-high-precision, prediction error) about low-level perceptual detail available to constrain the system, and hence no pressure to create or maintain a stable hypothesis at the lower levels of processing. In waking life, by contrast, the persisting external scene is repeatedly sampled, according to precision expectations, in ways that provide vital stabilizing pressure and that help create (as we saw in chapter 2) distinctive, self-sustaining percepts. In the absence of reliable sensory input, the estimated precision for such low-level states will be greatly reduced. Since precision-weighting involves promoting some aspects of the processing cascade against others, this implies an increase in the expected precision of other (higher level) states. The overall effect is thus temporarily to insulate unfolding internal predictions from reality testing against sensory states. In this way 'internal brain dynamics become sequestered from the sensorium' (Hobson & Friston, 2012, p. 87).

During sleep, this process is accompanied by some dramatic alterations in the chemical states of the brain. The three dominant states for the human brain are waking, REM (Rapid Eye Movement) sleep, and non-REM (NREM) sleep. Each state has clear physiological, pharmacological, and experiential correlates. In waking, we can occupy many states, from eyes-closed imagistic musing to eyes-open, alert engagement with the external environment. In REM sleep our dreams (at least as evidenced by subsequent report) are vivid, but their logic is weak. Here is a typical enough report:

> I was at a conference and trying to get breakfast but the food and the people in line kept changing. My legs didn't work properly and I found it a great effort to hold my tray up. Then I realized why. My body was rotting away and liquid was oozing from it. I thought I might be completely rotted before the end of the day, but I thought I should still get some coffee if I still had the strength. (Excerpt quoted in Blackmore, 2004, p. 340)

Here is another description, this time from Helena Bonham-Carter, while she was expecting a baby with movie director Tim Burton: 'I dreamed I gave birth to a frozen chicken. In my dream, I was very pleased with a frozen chicken' (quote from Hirschberg, 2003). In NREM sleep, if we dream at all, the dreams (again, as evidenced by waking report) are more like faint and mundane thoughts or fuzzy rememberings. All these states (waking, REM-sleep, NREM sleep) are correlated with specific patterns of neuro-chemical activity. A useful tool for displaying the pattern is Hobson's AIM model (Hobson, 2001). The AIM model characterizes the different states as points in a three-dimensional space, whose axes are:

1. Activation Energy
2. Input Source
3. Modulation

Normal wakefulness is characterized by high activation (as measured by EEG for example) corresponding to fairly intense experience, external input sources (the brain is receiving and processing a rich stream of sensory signals from the world, rather than being shut down and largely recycling its own activity), and a distinctive mode. Modulation here names a balance between brain chemicals, especially amines and cholines. Amines are neurotransmitters such as noradrenaline and serotonin, whose action is known to be essential for normal waking consciousness (they are essential to the processes that enable us direct attention, reason things through, and decide to act). When these are shut off, and other neurotransmitters (cholines, such as acetylcholine) dominate, we experience delusions and hallucinations (if we are awake) and vivid, uncritical dreaming (if we are asleep). In this way it is the amine/choline balance that mostly determines how signals and information (whether externally or internally generated) will be dealt with and processed. In REM sleep, the aminergic systems are deactivated and the cholinergic hyperactive. This is a highly altered cognitive state. Only extreme forms of psychosis or serious medical or recreational drug use can induce this kind of state in non-sleeping humans.[12]

This is not to suggest (far from it) that the best state for a human mind would be one of almost-complete aminergic dominance. Indeed, the power, subtlety, and beauty of wakeful human intelligence seem to have much to do with the precise details of the ever-shifting balance between the two systems. But in normal waking the mode (defined as the ratio between the activity of the two systems) leans towards the aminergic. In REM sleep, with acetycholine dominating, experience is increasingly dissociative, unanchored by sensory input, and beyond volitional control.

From the predictive processing perspective, the role of such changes in neuromodulatory balance is to gate (probably via shifts in precision-weighting; see chapter 2) the internal flow of prediction error. This rather neatly explains, in broad outline at least, the very different flavours of waking and dreaming experience. Thus,

> when we go to bed and close our eyes, the postsynaptic gain of sensory prediction error units declines (through reduced aminergic modulation) with a reciprocal increase in the precision of error units in higher cortical areas (mediated by increased cholinergic neurotransmission). . . . The ensuing sleep state is one in which internal predictions are sequestered from sensory constraints. (Hobson & Friston, 2012, p. 92)

In a similar fashion, Fletcher and Frith suggest that

> Perhaps the dream state arises from disruptions in hierarchical . . . processing such that sensory firing is not constrained by top-down prior information and inferences are accepted without question owing to an attenuation of the prediction-error signal from lower to higher levels. (Fletcher & Frith, 2009, p. 52)

Hobson and Friston (2009, section 4.2.1) further speculate that the sleep state offers an opportunity for the brain to engage in 'post-synaptic pruning'—removing redundant or low-strength connections so as to reduce the complexity of the generative model itself. The idea here (more on this in chapters 8 and 9) is that reducing prediction error while awake and alert sometimes results in models that, although able to capture the sensory patterns, are nevertheless overly complex. Such models effectively treat too much of the signal as data and not enough as noise. They thus 'overfit' the specific data and (thereby) fail to generalize to new situations.

Sleep, thanks to the altered balances just described, provides an opportunity to remedy this. During sleep, the brain's model is insulated from further sensory testing but can still be improved by simplification and streamlining. This is because the quantity that is minimized by the brain is actually (as we will see in chapter 9) prediction error plus model complexity. During sleep, precise prediction errors are not generated, so the balance shifts towards the reduction of model complexity. Sleep may thus allow the brain to engage in synaptic pruning so as to improve (make more powerful and generalizable) the knowledge enshrined in the generative model (see Tononi & Cirelli, 2006; Gilestro, Tononi, & Cirelli, 2009; Friston & Penny, 2011).[13] The resulting links between sleep and good cognitive housekeeping are intuitive and may offer special comfort to those that feel 7 hours is simply not enough! For if Hobson and Friston are right, then 'taking the brain off-line to prune exuberant associations established during wakefulness may be a necessary price we pay for having a sophisticated cognitive system that can distil complex and subtle associations from sensory samples' (Hobson & Friston, 2012, p. 95).

3.10   PIMMS and the Past

The bulk of our story so far has focused upon the use of stored knowledge to predict what might be thought of as a kind of 'rolling present'. Obviously, these processes of prediction depend heavily upon past experiences. But that dependence does not (yet) involve the actual recollection of past experiences. Instead, the past there exists only as it is crystallized into the agent-inaccessible form of altered probability density distributions used to meet and to organize the incoming sensory flow. Creatures like us, however, appear to benefit from a further trick. This is the trick of (from time to time) being able to recall specific concrete events that may be relevant to the task at hand. A crucial point of contact here is the observation that such 'episodic recall' involves learnt associations between items and spatio-temporal contexts. Constraints and opportunities involved in predicting items from contexts, and contexts from items, then provide tools that might (when deployed in the right admixtures) enable a kind of prediction-based reconstruction of episodic memory itself.

Thus consider a recent predictive processing account of multiple memory systems due to Henson and Gagnepain (2010). Henson and Gagnepain's concern is with the contrasting memory systems often dubbed 'recollection' and 'familiarity'. Recollection occurs when a subject, presented with a test item, recalls the episodic context of their past exposure to that item. Such a subject may report the occasion and modality of the original encounter or other surrounding details. Familiarity, by contrast, is present when a subject is unable to recall such details but is nonetheless aware that they have encountered that very item before. Familiarity and recollection are thus both different from (though intertwined with) the kind of semantic memory present simply in virtue of knowing what an object is (e.g., 'it's a clothes brush'). Recollection and familiarity look (though see Johnson et al., 2009) to implicate different neural sub-systems, with the hippocampus playing a special role in the former, and perihinal cortex (in the medial temporal lobe) playing a key role in the latter (see, e.g., Diana et al., 2007).

Henson and Gagnepain's central concern is, however, not with these different roles per se but with patterns of between-area interaction. Their suggestion is that different patterns of interaction (different patterns of effective connectivity and hence of functional coupling[14]) between areas can help explain the varying behavioural and neuroimaging profiles associated with recollection and familiarity. With this in mind, they formulate and defend PIMMS: a 'predictive interactive multiple-memory system' model. The model posits three 'memory systems' distinguished largely by the kinds of representational content in which they specialize. They are labelled (following Tulving & Gazzaniga, 1995) 'episodic' (here associated with recollection, and physiologically with the hippocampus), 'semantic' (here associated with familiarity, and physiologically with perihinal cortex), and 'perceptual' (associated with occipito-temporal cortex, hence specific sensory modalities such as the visual ventral pathway). The key novelty in the PIMMS model is that ongoing feedback links the three systems both during encoding and retrieval, and that different patterns of recurrent interaction at both points account for the observed differences in the behavioural and physiological data.

PIMMS depicts the effects of recollection and familiarity as explained by differing patterns of information flow within a predictive processing hierarchy in which, in the now-familiar fashion 'the role of feedback from one system is to predict the activity in "lower" systems in this hierarchy' (Henson and Gagnepain, 2010, p. 1319). This hierarchy has the hippocampus at the top, the perihinal cortex below, and occipito-temporal cortex below that. Differing levels within the predictive bi-directional hierarchy come to specialize (as we have seen) in making predictions of different kinds, capturing regularities at different spatio-temporal scales. Within such an architecture, the PIMMS model depicts the hippocampus as the top level, concerned to 'optimize the mutual predictability between items (represented in perihinal cortex) and contexts (presumably represented in multiple regions depending on the type of context)' (p. 1321). Such optimization—and this is the crucial move—renders items predictable from contexts and contexts predictable from items. A familiar object in a novel context would thus induce high prediction error, since the mutual predictability would be low. Hippocampal prediction error, they suggest, drives episodic encoding which is implemented by altering the synaptic weights on connections between the hippocampus and the appropriate (e.g., perihinal) cortical populations. Within the trained hierarchy, backwards connections then allow specifics to be predicted from contexts, while forward flowing error drives both encoding and retrieval.

Episodic and semantic memory systems, if this is correct, are linked in a web of mutual internal prediction. Within this web, context-specifying information encoded in the hippocampus attempts to predict item-based representations in perihinal cortex and more 'perceptual' representations in occipito-temporal cortex. Differing patterns of prediction error and prediction error resolution then realize various flavours of familiarity and recollection. Familiarity occurs when a presented item induces low prediction error (hence high 'processing fluency', Jacoby and Dallas, 1981) in areas specializing in item-recognition but—importantly, though this is not explicitly modelled in PIMMS—where that fluency is accompanied by a kind of (statistically second-order) assessment that such fluency is surprising.[15] Recollection, by contrast, occurs when there is high mutual predictability linking the item to a specific context. If the function of the hippocampus is, as suggested, to optimize mutual predictability between items and contexts, various bodies of fMRI data (for the details, see Henson & Gagnepain, 2010, pp. 1320–1322) also fall neatly into place.

The PIMMS model is both incomplete and speculative.[16] I include it here simply as an illustration of some rather more general ideas and principles. Most important, it suggests that the surface appearance of multiple, distinct neural systems subserving different functions (here, different kinds of memory) may be subtly misleading. Rather than a mere motley of different systems, we may confront a web of statistically sensitive mutual influence that combines context with content, and balances specialization against integration. Within that web, moment-by-moment performance depends on the creation and maintenance of task-specific patterns of effective connectivity (here linking semantic, perceptual, and episodic sub-systems; see Figure 3.3). Such patterns may themselves be consequent upon the estimated (task-relevant) precision of various prediction errors. In this way, the calculation and use of precision-weighted prediction error may constitute a general principle of neural functioning, serving not merely to drive and nuance perceptual recognition but to select and orchestrate whole ensembles of neural[17] (and sometimes extra-neural; see Part III) resources.

3.11   Towards Mental Time Travel

Mental time-travel (Suddendorf & Corballis, 1997, 2007) occurs when an agent recalls events from the past or imagines events in the future.

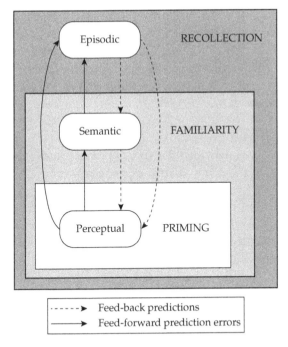

FIGURE 3.3   PIMMS Model of Memory

Encoding, storage, and retrieval are parallel and interactive. Recollection and familiarity entail interactions between these multiple memory systems.

Source: Henson & Gagnepain, 2010.

Such capacities may be based, Suddendorf and Corballis argue, in a more general capacity to imagine experiences using what Hassabis and Maguire (2009, p. 1263) describe as 'the construction system of the brain'. Such an approach is attractive and fits neatly with two converging themes in cognitive neuroscience. The first is the contemporary view of memory as a reconstructive process in which current goals and context, as well as previous episodes of recall, contribute greatly to what is recalled. The second is the wealth of imaging data suggesting substantial—though by no means total—overlap between the neural machinery used to recall the past and to imagine the future (see Okuda et al., 2003; Szpunar et al., 2007; Szpunar, 2010; Addis et al., 2007). Such overlap is nicely dramatized by Ingvar (1985) whose talk of 'remembering the future' highlights the role of neural structures implicated in episodic memory for imagining possible future scenarios. Episodic memory, as we just saw, is the kind of remembering that involves in some sense 're-living' a past experience (as when we remember

a specific, perhaps painful, encounter with a neighbour's dog). It is usually contrasted (Tulving, 1983) with 'semantic memory', which concerns
concepts, features, and properties (dogs usually have four legs, bark,
and come in a wide variety of shapes and forms). Semantic memory
is also rooted in our past experience, but it shapes our current grip on
the world rather than mentally transporting us backwards or forwards
in time.

Further evidence for shared neural substrates for mental time
travel into the past and into the future comes from work on memory impairments. Certain forms of amnesia are correlated with
problems in imagining the future. Hassabis et al. (2007) report that
four out of five hippocampal amnesics were impaired in imagining
novel events—asked to construct new versions of everyday scenes,
their efforts produced less detail, and that detail was less well organized into coherent spatial structure. Schacter et al. (2007) report
that a specific pattern of age-related deterioration in recall (sparse-
ness of episode-specific detail; see Addis et al., 2008) marches in step
with a similar pattern in age-related future thinking. Such evidence
leads them to defend a 'constructive episodic simulation hypothesis'
implicating a shared neural system that supports the 'flexible recombination of details from past events into novel scenarios'. It is this
future-oriented system, rather than episodic memory per se that, they
suggest, is the true bearer of adaptive value. The brain, they conclude,
is 'a fundamentally prospective organ that is designed to use information from the past and the present to generate predictions about the
future' (Schacter et al., 2007, p. 660). This may be the deep reason why
episodic memory is fragile, patchy, and reconstructive since 'a memory system that simply stored rote records would not be well-suited
to simulating future events' (Schacter and Addis, 2007a, p. 27; see also
Schacter and Addis, 2007b).

Schacter and Addis, like Suddendorf and Corballis, are especially
interested in the relations between episodic memory and a certain
form of 'personal, episodic' future thinking: one in which we mentally
project ourselves ahead in time by simulating our own possible future
experiences. I think we may now flag this as another important and
distinctive manifestation of what already looks, from the PP perspective, to be a quite fundamental alignment between perception, recall,
and imagination. Such alignment flows directly, or so I have been arguing, from the basic prediction-and-generative-model-based perspective
on perception: a perspective that may thus offer an even broader framework within which to conceptualize the relations between recall (of
various kinds) and imagination (of various kinds).

More generally, what seems to be emerging is a view of memory as intimately bound up with constructive processes of neural pre-diction and (hence) imagination. As one leading theorist of memory comments:

> If memory is fallible and prone to reconstructive errors, that may be because it is oriented towards the future at least as much as towards the past . . . similar neural systems are involved in both autobiographical memory and future thinking, and both rely on a form of imagination. (Fernyhough, 2012, p. 20)

3.12   A Cognitive Package Deal

PP offers an attractive 'cognitive package deal' in which perception, understanding, dreaming, memory, and imagination may all emerge as variant expressions of the same underlying mechanistic ploy—the ploy that meets incoming sensory data with matching top-down prediction. At the heart of the package lies the ability to use downwards connec-tions to self-generate perception-like states. The very same 'perceptual' machinery, driven from the top-down but insulated from entrainment by the driving sensory signal, then accounts for imagery and dream-ing, and may pave the way for 'mental time-travel' as we assemble cues and contexts able to reconstruct the past and preconstruct the future. This also paves the way for more deliberate forms of reasoning, as we shall later see.

The resulting intimacy among some of our core mental facul-ties is striking. Perception (rich, world-revealing perception) occurs when the probabilistic residue of past experience meets the incom-ing sensory signal with matching prediction. Such prediction may be thin and unidimensional, or richly structured—capturing multi-modal regularities at many temporal and spatial scales. In its most sophisticated expressions, it may involve the reconstruction (or imaginative preconstruction) of rich webs of spatio-temporal con-text. Local, parochial perception thus phases gently into richer and richer forms of understanding, apt to support new forms of agency and choice. In place of any sharp distinction between perception and various forms of cognition, PP thus posits variations in the mixture of top-down and bottom-up influence, and differences of tempo-ral and spatial scale within the internal models that are structur-ing the predictions.[18] Creatures thus endowed have a *structured grip* on their worlds: a grip that consists not in the symbolic encoding of quasi-linguistic 'concepts' but in the entangled mass of multiscale probabilistic expectations used to predict the incoming sensory signal.

Such a picture is, however, radically incomplete. The crucial task—to which we now turn—is to locate the neural engines of prediction where they truly really belong: nested within the larger organizational forms of the active body, and enmeshed in the transformative structures of our material, social, and technological worlds.

Part II

EMBODYING PREDICTION

4

Prediction-Action Machines

> Try to feel as if you were crooking your little finger, whilst keeping it
> straight. In a minute it will fairly tingle with the imaginary change of
> position; yet it will not sensibly move, because it's not really moving
> is also a part of what you have in mind. Drop this idea, think of the
> movement purely and simply, with all brakes off, and presto! it takes
> place with no effort at all.
>
> —William James[1]

4.1 Staying Ahead of the Break

To surf the waves of sensory stimulation, predicting the present is simply not enough. Instead, we are built to engage the world. We are built
to act in ways that are sensitive to the contingencies of the past, and
that actively bring forth the futures that we need and desire. How does
a guessing engine (a hierarchical prediction machine) turn prediction
into accomplishment? The answer that we shall explore is: by predicting the shape of its own motor trajectories. In accounting for action,
we thus move from predicting the rolling present to predicting the
near-future, in the form of the not-yet-actual trajectories of our own
limbs and bodies. These trajectories, predictive processing suggests,
are specified by their distinctive sensory (especially proprioceptive)
consequences. In ways that we are about to explore, predicting these
(non-actual) sensory states actually serves to bring them about.

Such predictions act as self-fulfilling prophecies. Expecting the
flow of sensation that *would* result *were* you to move your body so as
to keep the surfboard in that rolling sweet spot results (if you happen
to be an expert surfer) in that very flow, locating the surfboard right
where you want it. Expert prediction of the world (here, the dynamic

ever-changing waves) combines with expert prediction of the sensory flows that would, in that context, characterize the desired action, so as to bring that action about. This is a neat trick. It intersects with powerful yet frugal computational models of motor control, and it has extensions and implications that will occupy us for the next several chapters. Those extensions and implications range all the way from accounts of agency and experience to accounts of the disturbed or atypical states found in schizophrenia and autism.

As these accounts of action and agency unfold, a curious thing happens. Approaches that once looked like competitor-templates for understanding mind and behaviour emerge as complementary aspects of a single overarching cognitive ploy. Revisiting familiar themes from this perspective, we discover that computationally frugal solutions stressing embodiment, action, and the exploitation of bodily and environmental opportunities emerge quite naturally from a predictive processing (PP) framework involving cascading inference, internal generative models, and ongoing estimations of our own uncertainty. Such approaches are often presented[2] as deeply opposing visions of the human (and animal) mind. But from the vantage point on offer they are increasingly revealed as coordinated (and mutually coordinating) elements in a single adaptive ensemble.

4.2   Ticklish Tales

Why can't you tickle yourself? That was the question famously asked by Blakemore, Wolpert, and Frith (1998).[3] Their answer, drawing upon a substantial body of previous work on sensorimotor learning and control,[4] invoked two basic elements each of which appeared (in less restricted forms) in the account of perception pursued in Part I.

The first basic element is the (now familiar) idea of a generative model, here appearing as a 'forward model of the motor system' used to predict the sensory consequences of self-generated movement. The second is a version of the 'predictive coding' proposal according to which the systemic impact of well-predicted sensory inputs is reduced or eliminated. Putting these together for the special case of attempted self-tickling suggested a simple but compelling schema in which the 'attenuation of self-produced tactile stimulation is due to the sensory predictions made by an internal forward model of the motor system' (Blakemore, Wolpert, and Frith (2000), p. R11).

The would-be self-tickler, Blakemore et al. argued, commands a 'forward model' of the likely sensory consequences of her own motor commands. When she sets out to self-tickle, a copy of the motor command (known as the 'efference copy'; Von Holst, 1954) is processed using the forward model. This model captures (or 'emulates'; see Grush, 2004) the relevant biodynamics of the motor plant, enabling a rapid prediction of the likely feedback from the sensory peripheries. It does this by encoding the relationship between motor commands and predicted sensory outcomes. The motor command is captured using the efference copy which, fed to the forward model, yields a prediction of the sensory outcome (sometimes called the 'corollary discharge'). Comparisons between the actual and the predicted sensory input were thus enabled, and these offered a potential source of useful information for distinguishing self-induced motion (the sensory outcomes of which would be very precisely predicted) from sensory effects rooted in the operation of external factors and forces. Such comparisons would also enable the nervous system to dampen or even remove the components of sensory feedback attributable to our own self-induced movements, as seems to occur when we perceive the visual scene as essentially stable despite the rather large ongoing sensory fluctuations caused by movements of the head and eyes (for a classic discussion, see Sperry, 1950).[5] If, as seems intuitive, the feeling of ticklishness requires a certain element of surprise (not concerning the mere fact of being tickled, so much as the detailed ongoing shape of the stimulation), we now have the bones of an explanation of the elusiveness of the self-induced tickle.

The barrier to self-tickling, this suggests, is akin to the barrier to telling yourself a joke: funny as it may be, the punch-line is just never going to be enough of a surprise. By deploying a precise model of the mapping from our own motor commands to sensory (bodily) feedback, we deprive ourselves of the ability to self-stimulate in a sufficiently unpredictable fashion and we dampen our own sensory responses to the ongoing stimulation.

Such dampening is indeed widely observed. Some fish, for example, generate electrical fields and sense disturbances in those fields indicating the presence of prey (Sawtell et al., 2005; Bell et al., 2008). To do so, they need to discount the much larger disturbances created by their own movements. The solution, once again, looks to involve the use of a predictive forward model and some form of attendant sensory attenuation.

The same pair of mechanisms (forward-model-based prediction and the dampening of resulting well-predicted sensation) have been invoked to explain the unsettling phenomenon of 'force escalation' (Shergill, Bays, Frith, & Wolpert, 2003). In force escalation, physical exchanges (playground fights being the most common exemplar) mutually ramp up via a kind of step-ladder effect in which each person believes the other one hit them harder. Shergill et al. describe experiments that suggest that in such cases each person is truthfully reporting their own sensations, but that those sensations are skewed by the attenuating effects of self-prediction. Thus, 'self-generated forces are perceived as weaker than externally generated forces of the same magnitude' (Shergill et al., 2003, p. 187). This was shown using experiments in which an external device applied a force to a subject's (left index) fingertip, and the subject was then asked to match the force to which they had just been exposed by using their right index finger to push on their left one (via a force transducer allowing accurate measurement of the force applied). Subjects repeatedly overestimated the force required to obtain a match (hence the paper's memorable title 'Two Eyes for an Eye'). The discrepancy was striking: 'Despite the stimuli being identical at the level of peripheral sensation, the perception of force is reduced by about a half when the force is self-generated' (Shergill et al., 2003, p. 187). It is easy to imagine the snowballing effects of such diminished perception of self-generated forces when two agents engage in (what they each believe to be) a tit-for-tat exchange of blows or, for that matter, other kinds of physical interaction.

One way to improve accuracy in such cases is to require the subject to respond using a more indirect method, thus bracketing the precise forward modelling (and attendant sensory dampening) that accompanies normal bodily action. When asked to match the force by using their finger to move a joystick controlling force output, subjects were better able (Shergill et al., 2003, p. 187) to match the original force. A similar manipulation is available for the would-be self-tickler. Blakemore, Frith, and Wolpert (1999) used a robotic interface (as shown in Figure 4.1) both to interpose time-delays and to vary the trajectory of motion linking the subject's own action to the resulting stimulation. As these delays and variations increased, so too did the subjects' 'ticklishness rating' for the resulting stimulation. Such manipulations attempt to outwit the precise forward model, forcing the subject to react as if to an unpredictable external stimulus.

Interestingly, the normal dampening of self-predicted sensations is disturbed in schizophrenia. Schizophrenic subjects perform more accurately than neurotypical ones on the force-matching task (Shergill et al., 2005) and are also more capable of 'self-tickling' (Blakemore et al., 2002). They are also, as we noted earlier, less susceptible to the Hollow Face illusion described in 1.17. The reduction of sensory attenuation in schizophrenia may help explain the emergence, in schizophrenic subjects, of various delusions concerning agency, such as the feeling

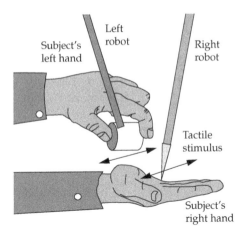

FIGURE 4.1   Diagram of Experimental Setup

A tactile stimulus constituting a piece of foam attached to the end of a robotic manipulator was positioned above the subjects' right palm. The subjects gripped a cylindrical object with the thumb and index finger of their left hand. This object was held directly above the tactile stimulus and was attached to a second robotic device. In the externally produced tactile stimulus condition, the right robot was programmed to produce the sinusoidal (smooth, repetitive, oscillating) tactile stimulus movement on the subjects' right hand. In all the self-produced tactile stimulus conditions, the subjects were required to move the object held in their left hand sinusoidally which, via two robots, produced the same movement of the tactile stimulus above their right hand. Delays and trajectory perturbations could be introduced between the movement made by the left hand and the resultant movement of the right robot.

Source: From Blakemore, Frith, & Wolpert, 1999.

that your actions are under the control of another agent (Frith, 2005). Under-attenuated sensations resulting from self-produced movements will be unusually 'surprising', and hence may be misattributed to external influences. More generally still, there is a negative correlation, in normal subjects, between the amount of sensory attenuation and the tendency to form delusional beliefs (Teufel et al., 2010).

4.3   *Forward Models (Finessing Time)*

Why bother to develop a forward model in the first place? Not, presumably, as an evolved mechanism for force escalation or a defence against the dubious practice of self-tickling. Instead, the use of a forward model turns out to be essential to overcome a variety of signalling delays that would otherwise impede fluid motion. This is because:

> Delays are present in all stages of sensorimotor system, from the delay in receiving afferent sensory information, to the delay in our muscles responding to efferent motor commands. Feedback of sensory information (that we take to include information about the state of the world and consequences of our own actions) is subject to delays arising from receptor dynamics as well as conduction delays along nerve fibers and synaptic relays.

The upshot, according to Franklin and Wolpert, is that:

> we effectively live in the past, with the control systems only having access to out-of-date information about the world and our own bodies, and with the delays varying across different sources of information. (Both quotes from Franklin & Wolpert, 2011, pp. 425–426)

Forward models provide a powerful and elegant solution to such problems, enabling us to live in the present and to control our bodies (and well-practiced tools; see Kluzik et al., 2008) without much sense of ongoing struggle or effort. Such models, moreover, can be learnt and calibrated using the kinds of prediction-based learning scheme reviewed in the opening chapters, since 'forward models can be trained and updated using prediction errors, that is by comparing the predicted and actual outcome of a motor command' (Wolpert & Flanagan, 2001, p. 729).

Why, finally, should the sensations that succumb to fine-grained prediction using such forward models be attenuated and those that escape such prediction be enhanced? The standard answer (which we touched on earlier) is that self-prediction enables us to filter the barrage of sensory data, enhancing that which is externally generated, delivering stable percepts in the face of small motions of the head and eye, and dampening responses to more predictable, and perhaps thus less ecologically pressing, stimuli (see, e.g., Wolpert & Flanagan, 2001). Thus Stafford and Webb (2005), summing up the evolutionary rationale for the kinds of model-based dampening effect revealed by the tickling and force escalation cases, comment that:

> Our sensory systems are constantly bombarded with sensory stimulation from the environment. It is therefore important to filter out sensory stimulation that is uninteresting—such as the results of our own movements—in order to pick out, and attend to, sensory information that carries more evolutionary

importance, such as someone touching us. ... The predictive system protects us and tickling may just be an accidental consequence. (Stafford & Webb, 2005, p. 214)

In a similar vein Blakemore, Frith, and Wolpert, summing up the role of model-based dampening during self-produced movement suggest that:

prediction-based modulation acts as a filter on incoming sensory signals that can enhance the afference-to-reafference ratio (akin to increasing the signal-to-noise ratio). This modulation of incoming sensory input might have the effect of accentuating features of importance (for example, those due to external events). (Blakemore, Frith, & Wolpert, 1999, pp. 555–556)

These are, of course, versions of the rationale that motivates the much more general 'predictive processing' proposal itself. That proposal, grounded in the bedrock of hierarchical generative models and made flexible by the additional ploy (see chapter 2) of precision-weighting prediction error, provides a larger framework able to absorb and reproduce many key insights from classical work on forward models and motor control. More importantly, though, it reproduces them in a way that reveals a much richer network of connections between perception and action, and that (as we'll later see) repairs a revealing problem with the accounts we have just been considering.

The problem with those accounts is that attenuating prediction error using veridical predictions from the forward model does not sufficiently explain the sensory attenuation itself. If prediction error is attenuated by top-down predictions emanating from a forward model, then, once these predictions are in place, the sensory stimulations should still be registered perceptually. Successfully predicting, for example, the flow of visual states as I saccade around a highly familiar scene does not in any way render me experientially blind! A more complete solution (as we will see in chapter 7) turns not solely upon the role of the forward model but also upon another (less explored) effect of variable precision weighting.[6] For the moment, however, our concern is with some core issues concerning motor control itself.

4.4   Optimal Feedback Control

Motor control, at least in the dominant 'internal model based' formulations, requires the development and use not simply of a forward model but also of a so-called *inverse model* (Kawato, 1999). Where the forward model maps current motor commands to predicted sensory effects, the inverse model (also known as a controller) 'performs the opposite transformation … determining the motor command required to achieve some desired outcome' (Wolpert, Doya, & Kawato, 2003, p. 595). According to these 'auxiliary forward model' (Pickering & Clark, 2014) accounts, the action command sends efference copy to a forward model of the action. In such a model, action commands are given as input, and the projected sensory consequences of those commands are generated as output. This forward model could simply involve a look-up table, but is more likely to involve calculations (e.g., approximations to the laws of mechanics), which are in general computed before the action is performed. As a simple analogy, I turn my radiator up from 'off' to half-way. Well before the radiator heats up, I predict (based on repeated experience with my central heating) that it will take 5 minutes to heat by 10°C (using very simple equations, e.g., increase of 2°C per minute, for each 30° turn). I can act upon the prediction right away (e.g., take my coat off) or compare the prediction with the results, and learn from any discrepancy via my *inverse model* (e.g., turn the knob further). Such accounts ('Auxiliary Forward Model' architectures, see Figure 4.2) thus posit two distinct models: an inverse model (or optimal control model) that converts intentions into motor commands, and a forward model that converts motor commands into sensory consequences (which are compared with actual outcomes for online error correction and learning).

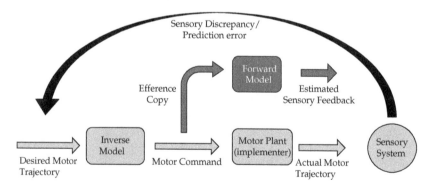

FIGURE 4.2   Auxiliary Forward Model (AFM) Architecture
In this architecture, the output of the inverse model is a motor command, copied to the forward model, which is used to estimate sensory feedback.

Source: From Pickering & Clark, 2014.

Learning and deploying an inverse model appropriate to some task is, however, generally much more demanding than learning the forward model and requires solving a complex mapping problem (linking the desired end-state to a nested cascade of non-linearly interacting motor commands) while effecting transformations between varying co-ordinate schemes (e.g., visual to muscular or proprioceptive, see, e.g., Wolpert, Doya, & Kawato, 2003, pp. 594–596).

Recent work on 'optimal feedback control' (for a review, see Franklin & Wolpert, 2011, pp. 428–429) represents a sophisticated and successful development of this framework. It makes extensive use of so-called 'mixed cost-functions'[7] as a means of selecting one trajectory or movement from the many (indeed, infinitely many) that would achieve a goal, and it combines feedforward and feedback control strategies in an efficient way (for some nice examples, see Todorov, 2004; Harris & Wolpert, 2006; Kuo, 2005). In particular, such strategies allow the planning and the execution of movement to be accomplished at the same time, since 'a feedback control law is used to resolve moment-by-moment uncertainties, allowing the system to best respond to the current situation at each point in time' (DeWolf & Eliasmith, 2011, p. 3). This differs from more traditional approaches in which planning and execution are distinct processes.

Another advantage of the feedback control strategy is that it identifies a 'redundant sub-space' within which variability does not affect task completion. The feedback controller only bothers to correct deviations that move the system outside this space of allowable variation. This is the so-called 'minimum intervention principle' of Todorov (2009). Such systems are also able to make maximal use of their own intrinsic or 'passive' dynamics. We shall return to this topic in Part III, but the key point is that they can compute the cost of an action as the difference between what the system would do (how the motor plant would behave) with and without the control signal. Completing this list of virtues, extensions of the paradigm allow for the combination of pre-learnt control sequences to deal with novel circumstances by 'quickly and cheaply creating optimal control signals from previously learned optimal movements' (DeWolf & Eliasmith, 2011, p. 4). The upshot is a kind of compositional grammar for pre-learnt motor commands. Operating in hierarchical settings (in which higher levels encode compressed representations of trajectories and possibilities) such systems are able to control extremely complex behaviours using efficient and recombinable neural resources. Formally, optimal feedback control theory (see especially Todorov & Jordan, 2002; Todorov, 2008) displays the motor control problem as mathematically equivalent to Bayesian inference (see Appendix 1). Very roughly—again, see Todorov 2008 for a detailed account—you treat the desired (goal) state as observed and perform Bayesian inference to find the actions that get you there. For our purposes, all that matters about Bayesian inference here is that it is a form of probabilistic reasoning that takes into account the uncertainty of the data, combining that with prior beliefs about the world and about the motor system (as encoded by a generative model) in order to deliver (here, relative to some cost function) optimal control (see, e.g., Franklin & Wolpert, 2011, pp. 427–429).

This mapping between perception and action emerges also in some recent work on planning (e.g., Toussaint, 2009). The idea, closely related to these approaches to simple movement control, is that in planning we imagine a future goal state as actual then use Bayesian inference to find the set of intermediate states (which can now themselves be whole actions) that get us there. There is thus emerging a fundamentally unified set of computational models which, as Toussaint (2009, p. 28) comments, 'do not distinguish between the problems of sensor processing, motor control, or planning'. Such theories suggest that perception and action are in some deep sense computational siblings and that:

> The best ways of interpreting incoming information via perception, are deeply the same as the best ways of controlling outgoing information via motor action ... so the notion that there are a few specifiable computational principles governing neural function seems plausible. (Eliasmith, 2007, p. 380)

4.5　Active Inference

The PP model introduced in Part I combines very naturally (while suggesting some provocative twists) with these emerging approaches to action and to motor control.[8] Work on optimal feedback control exploits the fact that the motor system (like visual cortex) displays complex hierarchical structure. Such structure allows complex behaviours to be specified, at higher levels, in compact ways whose implications can be progressively unpacked at the lower levels. The intuitive difference, however, is that in the case of motor control we imagine a downwards flow of information, whereas in the case of visual cortex, we imagine an upwards flow. Vision, on that intuitive picture, takes complex energetic stimuli and maps them onto increasingly compact encodings, whereas motor control takes some compact encoding and progressively unpacks it into a complex set of muscle commands. Descending pathways in motor cortex, this traditional picture suggests, should correspond functionally to ascending pathways in visual cortex. This is not, however, the case. Within motor cortex the downwards connections (descending projections) are 'anatomically and physiologically more like backwards connections in the visual cortex than the corresponding forward connections' (Adams et al., 2012, p. 1). This is suggestive. Where we might have imagined the functional anatomy of a hierarchical motor system to be some kind of mirror-image of that of the perceptual system, the two seem much more closely aligned.[9] The explanation, PP suggests, is that the downwards connections are, in both cases, taking care of essentially the same kind of business: the business of predicting sensory stimulation.

PP, as we saw in Part I, already subverts the traditional picture with respect to perception. The compact higher-level encodings are now part of an apparatus trying to predict the plays of energy across the sensory surfaces. The same story applies, PP suggests, to the motor case. The difference is that motor control is, in a certain sense, *subjunctive*. It involves predicting the non-actual proprioceptive trajectories that would ensue were we performing some desired action. Reducing prediction errors calculated against these non-actual states then serves (in ways we are about to explore) to make them actual. We predict the proprioceptive consequences of our own action and this brings the action about.

The upshot is that the downwards (and lateral) connections, in both motor and sensory cortex, are carrying complex predictions, and the upwards connections carrying prediction errors. This explains the otherwise 'paradoxical' (Adams, Shipp, & Friston, 2013, p.611) fact that the functional circuitry of motor cortex does not seem to be inverted with respect to that of sensory cortex. Instead, the very distinction between motor and sensory cortex is eroded—both are in the business of top-down prediction, though what kind of thing they are predicting is (of course) different. Motor cortex here emerges, ultimately, as a multimodal sensorimotor area issuing predictions in both proprioceptive and other modalities.

The core idea (Friston, Daunizeau, et al., 2010) is thus that there are two ways in which biological agents can reduce prediction error. The first (as seen in Part I) involves finding the predictions that best accommodate the current sensory inputs. The second is by performing *actions that make our predictions come true*—for example, moving around and sampling the world so as to generate or discover the very perceptual patterns that we predict. These two processes can be constructed (we shall see) using the same computational resources. In the normal course of events, they work seamlessly together, as seen in microcosm in the discussion of gaze allocation in chapter 2 (2.6 to 2.8). The upshot is that:

> the perceptual and motor systems should not be regarded as separate but instead as a single active inference machine that tries to predict its sensory input in all domains: visual, auditory, somatosensory, interoceptive and, in the case of the motor system, proprioceptive. (Adams, Shipp, & Friston, 2013, p. 614)

'Active Inference' (Friston, 2009; Friston, Daunizeau, et al., 2010) then names the combined mechanism by which perceptual and motor systems conspire to reduce prediction error using the twin strategies of altering predictions to fit the world, and altering the world to fit the predictions. This general schema may also—perhaps more transparently—be labelled 'action-oriented predictive processing' (Clark, 2013). In the case of motor behaviours, the key driving predictions now have a subjunctive flavour. They are, Friston and colleagues suggest, predictions of the proprioceptive patterns that would ensue were the action to be performed. 'Proprioception' names the inner sense that informs us about the relative locations of our bodily parts and the forces and efforts that are being applied. It is to be distinguished from exteroceptive (i.e., standard perceptual) channels, such as vision and audition, and from interoceptive channels informing us of hunger, thirst, and the states of the viscera. Predictions concerning the latter will play a large role when we later consider the construction of feelings and emotions. For the moment, however, our concern is with simple motor action. To make such action come about, the motor plant behaves (Friston, Daunizeau, et al., 2010) in ways that cancel out proprioceptive prediction errors. This works because the proprioceptive prediction errors signal the difference between how the bodily plant is currently disposed and how it would be disposed were the desired actions being performed. Proprioceptive prediction error will thus persist until the actual disposition of the motor plant is such as to yield (moment-by-moment) the projected proprioceptive inputs. In this way, predictions of the unfolding proprioceptive patterns that would be associated with the performance of some action actually bring that action about. This kind of scenario is neatly captured by Hawkins and Blakeslee (2004), who write that:

> As strange as it sounds, when your own behaviour is involved, your predictions not only precede sensation, they determine sensation. Thinking of going to the next pattern in a sequence causes a cascading prediction of what you should

experience next. As the cascading prediction unfolds, it generates the motor commands necessary to fulfil the prediction. Thinking, predicting, and doing are all part of the same
unfolding of sequences moving down the cortical hierarchy.
(Hawkins & Blakeslee, 2004, p. 158)

Friston and colleagues go further, however, by suggesting that (precise)
proprioceptive predictions directly elicit motor actions. This means
that motor commands have been replaced by (or as I would rather
say, implemented by) proprioceptive predictions. According to active
inference, the agent moves body and sensors in ways that amount to
actively seeking out the sensory consequences that their brains expect.
Perception, cognition, and action—if this unifying perspective proves
correct—work together to minimize sensory prediction errors by selectively sampling and actively sculpting (by motion and by intervention)
the stimulus array.

    This erases any fundamental computational line between percep-
tion and the control of action. There remains, to be sure, an obvious
(and important) difference in direction of fit. Perception here matches
neural; hypotheses; to sensory inputs, and involves 'predicting the
present', while action brings unfolding proprioceptive inputs into line
with neural predictions. The difference, as Anscombe (1957) famously
remarked,[10] is akin to that between consulting a shopping list to select
which items to purchase (thus letting the list determine the contents
of the shopping basket) and listing some actually purchased items
(thus letting the contents of the shopping basket determine the list).
But despite this difference in direction of fit, the underlying form of
the neural computations is now revealed as the same. Indeed, the main
difference between motor and visual cortex, on this account, lies more
in what kind of thing (for example, the proprioceptive consequences of
a trajectory of motion) is predicted rather than how it is predicted. The
upshot is that:

    The primary motor cortex is no more or less a motor cortical
    area than striate (visual) cortex. The only difference between
    the motor cortex and visual cortex is that one predicts retino-
    topic input while the other predicts proprioceptive input from
    the motor plant. (Friston, Mattout, & Kilner, 2011, p. 138)

Perception and action here follow the same deep logic and are implemented using versions of the same computational strategy. In each case,
the systemic imperative remains the same: the reduction of ongoing
prediction error. In perception, this occurs when a top-down cascade

successfully matches the incoming sensory data. In action, it occurs when physical motion cancels out prediction errors by producing the trajectory that yields some predicted sequence of proprioceptive states. Action thus emerges as a kind of self-fulfilling prophecy in which neural circuitry predicts the sensory consequences of the selected action. Those consequences do not immediately obtain, however, so prediction error ensues: error that is then quashed by moving the body so as to bring about the predicted sequence of sensations.

These ways of putting things can, however, make it sound as if perception and action are unfolding separately, each busily pursuing their own direction of fit. This would be a mistake. Instead, PP agents are constantly attempting to accommodate the sensory flux by recruiting an interwoven mesh of percepts and apt world-engaging actions. Our percepts, if this is correct, are not action-neutral 'hypotheses' about the world so much as ongoing attempts to parse the world in ways apt for the engagement of that world. To be sure, not all prediction errors can be *resolved* by actions—some must be resolved by getting a better grip on how things are. But the point of that exercise is to put us in touch with the world in a way that will enable us to select better actions. This means that even the perceptual side of things is deeply 'action-oriented'. This is unsurprising since the only point of perceptual inference is to prescribe action (which changes sensory samples, which entrain perception). What we thus encounter is a world built of action-affordances. This will emerge more clearly in the remainder of the text. For the moment, the point to notice is that prediction error, even in the so-called 'perceptual' case, may best be seen as encoding sensory information that has not yet been leveraged for the control of apt world-enaging action.

4.6   Simplified Control

These prediction-based approaches to the control of action share many key insights with the important work on forward models and optimal feedback control described earlier. In common is the core emphasis on the prediction-based learning of a forward (generative) model able to anticipate the sensory consequences of action. In common too (as we shall later see in more detail) is a distinctive angle upon the experience of agency: one that traces that experience, just as the 'tickling tales' had already started to suggest, in part to the delicacy of the match between prediction and the actual sensory flow. But active inference as it is being developed by Friston and others (see, e.g., Friston, 2011a; Friston,

Samothrakis, & Montague, 2012) differs from these approaches in two key respects.

First, active inference dispenses with the inverse model or controller and along with it the need for efference copy of the motor command. Second, it dispenses with the need for cost or value functions as a means of enforcing speed, accuracy, energetic efficiency, and so on.[11] This all sounds quite dramatic, but in practice it amounts mostly to a reallocation of existing duties: a reallocation in which cost or value functions are 'folded in' to the context-sensitive generative models that simultaneously prescribe recognition and action. Nonetheless this reallocation is conceptually attractive. It fits neatly with important insights from real-world robotics and the study of situated action, and may help us to think better about the space of solutions to complex problems of action selection and motor control.

Action is here reconceived as a direct consequence of expectations (spanning multiple temporal and spatial scales) about trajectories of motion. The upshot is that 'the environment causes prior beliefs about motion ... while these beliefs cause the sampled environment' (Friston & Ao, 2012, p. 10). Such approaches highlight a kind of circular causality that binds what the agent knows (the probabilistic 'beliefs'[12] that figure in the generative model) to actions that select inputs that confirm those very beliefs. Our expectations here 'cause the sampled environment', as Friston and Ao put it, but only in the metaphysically innocent sense of driving actions that selectively disclose predicted sensory stimulations.

It is in this way that the agent by action calls forth the very world that she knows.[13] This, as we shall see in Part III, brings action-oriented predictive processing into close and productive contact with work on self-organizing dynamical systems, offering a new take on core elements of the so-called 'enactivist' vision: a vision in which minds are active constructors of the very worlds they reveal. At short timescales, this is just the process of active sampling described earlier. We sample the scene in ways that reflect and seek to confirm the grip upon the world that structured the sampling. This is a process that only the 'fit' hypotheses (assuming that is understood in a suitably action-oriented manner) survive. At longer timescales (see Part III) this is the process by which we build designer environments that install new predictions that determine how we behave (how we sample that very environment). We thus build worlds that build minds that expect to act in those kinds of worlds.

For the moment, however, the most important thing to notice is that the forward-motor model is now simply part of a larger and more complex generative model associating predictions with their sensory consequences. Motor cortex here specifies not motor commands, traditionally understood, but rather the sensory consequences of movements. Of special importance here are predictions about *proprioceptive* sensory consequences that implicitly minimize various energetic costs. Subject to the full cascade of hierarchical top-down processing, a simple motor command then unfolds into a complex set of predictions concerning proprioceptive effects. These drive behaviour, and they cause us to sample the world in the ways that the current winning 'hypothesis' dictates. Such predictions can be couched, at the higher levels, in terms of desired states or trajectories specified using extrinsic (world-centred, limb-centred) coordinates. This is possible because the required translation into intrinsic (muscle-based) coordinates is then devolved to what are essentially classical reflex arcs set up to quash proprioceptive prediction errors. Thus:

> if motor neurons are wired to suppress proprioceptive prediction errors in the dorsal horn of the spinal cord, they effectively implement an inverse model, mapping from desired sensory consequences to causes in intrinsic (muscle-based) coordinates. In this simplification of conventional schemes, descending motor commands become topdown predictions of proprioceptive sensations conveyed by primary and secondary sensory afferents. (Friston, 2011a, p. 491)

The need for a distinct inverse model/optimal control calculation now seems to have disappeared. In its place we find a more complex forward model mapping prior beliefs about desired trajectories to sensory consequences, some of which (the 'bottom level' proprioceptive ones) are automatically fulfilled using classical reflex arcs. Nor, as mentioned earlier, is there any need for efference copy in these schemes. This is because descending signals are already (just as in the perceptual case) in the business of predicting sensory consequences. So-called 'corollary discharge' (encoding predicted sensory outcomes) is thus endemic and pervades the downwards cascade since 'every backward connection in the brain (that conveys topdown predictions) can be regarded as corollary discharge, reporting the predictions of some sensorimotor construct' (Friston, 2011a, p. 492).

4.7   Beyond Efference Copy

This proposal may, on first encounter, strike the reader as quite radical. Isn't an appreciation of the functional significance of efference copy one of the major success stories of contemporary cognitive and computational neuroscience? In fact, most (perhaps all) of the evidence often assumed to favour that account is, on closer examination, simply evidence of the pervasive and crucial role of forward models and corollary discharge—it is evidence, that is to say, for just those parts of the traditional story that are preserved (and in fact are made even more central) by PP.

For example, Sommer and Wurtz's influential (2008) review paper, whose focus is on the mechanisms that allow us to distinguish the sensory effects of our own movements from those due to environmental change, makes very little mention of efference copy as such. Instead, it makes widespread use of the more general concept of corollary discharge—though as those authors also note, the two terms are often used interchangeably in the literature. A more recent paper, Wurtz et al. (2011), mentions efference copy only once, and then does so only to merge it with discussions of corollary discharge (which then occurs 114 times in the text). Similarly, there is ample reason to believe (just as the standard story suggests) that the cerebellum plays a special role here, and that that role involves making or optimizing perceptual predictions about upcoming sensory events (Bastian, 2006; Roth et al., 2013; Herzfeld & Shadmehr, 2014). But such a role is, of course, entirely consistent with the PP picture. The moral, I suggest, is that it is the general concept of forward models and corollary discharge, rather than the more specific one of efference copy as we defined it earlier, that currently enjoys the clearest support from both experimental and cognitive neuroscience.

Efference copy figures prominently, of course, in one particular set of computational proposals. These proposals concern (in essence) the positioning of forward models and corollary discharges within a putative larger cognitive architecture involving multiple paired forward and inverse models. In these 'paired forward-inverse model' architectures (see, e.g., Wolpert & Kawato, 1998; Haruno, Wolpert, & Kawato, 2003) motor commands are copied to a stack of separate forward models used to predict the sensory consequences of actions. But acquiring and deploying such an architecture, as even its strongest advocates concede, poses a variety of extremely hard computational challenges (see Franklin & Wolpert, 2011). The PP alternative neatly sidesteps many of those costs.

The PP proposal is that a subset of predicted sensory consequences (predicted proprioceptive trajectories) are acting as motor commands already. As a result there are no distinct motor commands to copy, and no efference copies as such. But one could, I suggest, equally well describe those forward-model-based predictions of proprioceptive trajectories as 'implicit motor commands': motor commands that operate (in essence—more on this below) by specifying results rather than by specifying fine-grained limb and joint control. These implicit motor commands (proprioceptive predictions) also influence the even-wider range of predictions concerning the exteroceptive sensory consequences of upcoming actions.

Much of the functionality that is normally attributed to the action of efference copy is thus preserved, including the forward-model-based explanation of core phenomena such as the finessing of time delays (Bastian, 2006) and the stability of the visual world despite eye movements (Sommer & Wurtz, 2006, 2008). The difference is that the heavy lifting that is usually done by the use of efference copy, inverse models, and optimal controllers is now shifted to the acquisition and use of the predictive (generative) model (i.e., the right set of prior probabilistic 'beliefs'). This is potentially advantageous if (but only if) we can reasonably assume that these beliefs 'emerge naturally as top-down or empirical priors during hierarchical perceptual inference' (Friston, 2011a, p. 492). The computational burden thus shifts to the acquisition of the right set of priors (here, priors over trajectories and state transitions), that is, it shifts the burden to acquiring and tuning the generative model itself.

4.8   Doing Without Cost Functions

The second important difference (from the 'optimal feedback control' schema) is that active inference sidesteps the need for cost or value functions as a means of selecting and sculpting motor response. Once again, it does this (Friston, 2011a; Friston, Samothrakis, & Montague, 2012) by, in essence, folding these into the generative model whose probabilistic predictions combine with sensory inputs to yield behaviours.

Simple examples of cost or value functions (that might be applied to sculpt and select motor behaviours) include minimizing 'jerk' (the rate of change of acceleration of a limb during some behaviour) and minimizing rate of change of torque (for these examples, see Flash & Hogan, 1985, and Uno et al., 1989, respectively). Recent work on optimal feedback control, as noted earlier, minimizes more complex 'mixed cost functions' that address not just bodily dynamics but also systemic noise and the required accuracy of outcomes (see Todorov, 2004; Todorov & Jordan, 2002).

Such cost functions (as Friston, 2011a, p. 496, observes) help resolve the many-one mapping problem that afflicts classical approaches to motor control. There are many ways of using one's body to achieve a certain goal, but the action system has to choose one way among the many. Such devices are not, however, needed within the framework on offer, since 'in active inference, these problems are resolved by prior beliefs about the trajectory (that may include minimal jerk) that uniquely determine the (intrinsic) consequences of (extrinsic) movements' (Friston, 2011a, p. 496). Simple cost functions are thus folded into the expectations that determine trajectories of motion.

But the story does not stop there. For the very same strategy here applies to the notion of desired consequences and rewards at all levels. Thus we read that 'crucially, active inference does not invoke any "desired consequences". It rests only on experience-dependent learning and inference: experience induces prior expectations, which guide perceptual inference and action' (Friston, Mattout, & Kilner, 2011, p. 157). Apart from a certain efflorescence of corollary discharge, in the form of downward-flowing predictions, we here seem to confront something of a desert landscape:[14] a world in which value functions, costs, reward signals, and perhaps even desires have been replaced by complex interacting expectations that inform perception and entrain action.[15] But we could equally say (and I think this is the better way to express the point) that the functions of rewards and cost functions are now simply absorbed into a more complex generative model. They are implicit in our sensory (especially proprioceptive) expectations and they constrain behaviour by prescribing their distinctive sensory implications.

Intrinsically rewarding 'appetitive' stimuli (to take the most obvious example) are thus not to be eliminated from our ontology—instead, they are simply reconceived as stimuli that, once identified, 'elicit obligatory volitional and autonomic responses' (Friston, Shiner, et al., 2012, p. 17). Conceptually, what matters here is that behaviours are depicted as brought about by the interaction of our beliefs (sub-personal webs of probabilistic expectation) with the environment. Reward and pleasure are then consequences of some of those interactions, but they are not (if this—admittedly quite challenging—part of the story is correct) causes of those interactions. Instead, it is the complex expectations that drive behaviour, causing us to probe and sample the world in ways that may often deliver reward or pleasure. In this way 'reward is a perceptual (hedonic) consequence of behavior, not a cause' (Friston, Shiner, et al., 2012, p. 17).

Notice that there is no overall computational advantage to be gained by this reallocation of duties. Indeed, Friston himself is clear that:

> there is no free lunch when replacing cost functions with prior beliefs [since] it is well-known [Littman et al., 2001] that the computational complexity of a problem is not reduced when formulating it as an inference problem. (Friston, 2011a, p. 492)

Nonetheless it may well be that this reallocation (in which cost functions are treated as priors) has conceptually and strategically important consequences. It is easy, for example, to specify whole paths or trajectories using prior beliefs about (you guessed it) paths and trajectories! Scalar reward functions, by contrast, specify points or peaks. The upshot is that everything that can be specified by a cost function can be specified by priors over trajectories, but not vice versa, and (more generally) that cost functions can usefully be treated as consequences rather than causes.

Related concerns have led many working roboticists to argue that explicit cost-function-based solutions are inflexible and biologically unrealistic, and should be replaced by approaches that entrain actions in ways that implicitly exploit the complex attractor dynamics of embodied agents (see, e.g., Thelen & Smith, 1994; Mohan & Morasso, 2011; Feldman, 2009). One way very roughly to imagine this broad class of solutions (and for a longer discussion, see Clark, 2008, chapter 1) is by thinking of the way you might control a wooden marionette simply by moving the strings attached to specific body parts. In such cases, 'the distribution of motion among the joints is the "passive" consequence of the ... forces applied to the end-effectors and the "compliance" of different joints' (Mohan & Morasso, 2011, p. 5). Such solutions aim (in line with PP) to 'circumvent the need for kinematic inversions and cost-function computations' (Mohan, Morasso, et al., 2013, p. 14). As proof of principle, Mohan, Morasso, et al. implemented and tested their ideas in a series of robotic simulations using the humanoid iCub robot, noting that in these experiments action itself is driven by a kind of internal forward-model-based simulation. All this suggests a tempting confluence between the PP approach and the pursuit of computationally frugal means of motor control. We shall have more to say about this kind of story in chapter 8.

Solutions that make maximal use of learnt or inbuilt 'synergies' and the complex biomechanics of the bodily plant can be very fluently implemented (see Friston, 2011a; Yamashita & Tani, 2008) using the resources of active inference and (attractor-based) generative models. For example, Namikawa et al. (2011) show how a generative model with multi-timescale dynamics enables a fluent and decomposable (see also Namikawa & Tani, 2010) set of motor behaviours. In these simulations:

> Action per se, was a result of movements that conformed to the proprioceptive predictions of . . . joint angles [and] . . . perception and action were both trying to minimize prediction errors throughout the hierarchy, where movement minimized the prediction errors at the level of proprioceptive sensations. (Namikawa et al., 2011, p. 4)

Another example (that we briefly met earlier) is the use of downward-flowing prediction to avoid the need to transform desired movement trajectories from extrinsic (task-centred) to intrinsic (e.g., muscle-centred) coordinates: an 'inverse problem' that is said to be complex and ill-posed (Feldman, 2009; Adams, Shipp, & Friston, 2013, p. 8). In active inference the prior beliefs that guide motor action already map predictions couched (at high levels) in extrinsic frames of reference onto proprioceptive effects defined over muscles and effectors, simply as part and parcel of ordinary online control. In this way:

> Active inference dispenses with this hard [inverse] problem by noting that a hierarchical generative model can map predictions in extrinsic coordinates to an intrinsic (proprioceptive) frame of reference. This means the inverse problem becomes almost trivial—to elicit firing in a particular stretch receptor one simply contracts the corresponding muscle fibre. In brief, the inverse problem can be relegated to the spinal level, rendering descending afferents from M1 [primary motor cortex] predictions as opposed to commands— and rendering M1 part of a hierarchical generative model, as opposed to an inverse model. (Adams, Shipp, & Friston, 2013, p. 26)

Motor commands are thus replaced (see Figure 4.2) by descending proprioceptive predictions, whose origins may lie at the highest (multimodal or meta-modal) levels but whose progressive (context-sensitive) unpacking proceeds all the way to the spinal cord, where it is finally cashed out via classical reflex arcs (see Shipp et al., 2013; Friston, Daunizeau, et al., 2010).

By reconceiving cost functions as implicit in bodies of expectations concerning trajectories of motion, such solutions avoid the need to solve difficult (often intractable) optimality equations during online processing.[16] Moreover, courtesy of the more complex generative model, these solutions fluidly accommodate signalling delays, sensory noise, and the many-one mapping between goals and motor programs. Arguably, then, more traditional approaches that involve the explicit computation of costs and values make unrealistic demands on online processing, fail to exploit helpful (e.g. passive dynamic) characteristics of the physical plant, and lack biologically plausible implementations.

These various advantages come, however, at a familiar cost. For here too the PP story shifts much of the burden onto the acquisition of those prior 'beliefs'—the multilevel, multimodal webs of probabilistic expectation that together drive perception and action. The PP bet is, in effect, that this is a worthwhile trade-off since PP describes a biologically plausible architecture maximally suited to installing and subsequently tuning the requisite suites of generative-model based prediction through embodied interactions with the world.

We can now summarize the main differences between these approaches to motor control. PP posits a single integrated forward model (see Figure 4.3) driving action, where more standard approaches (Figure 4.2) depict the action-related forward model as a kind of additional resource. According to the more standard ('auxiliary forward model', see Pickering & Clark, 2014) account, the forward model is quite distinct from the apparatus that actually drives online action. It is a (simplified) model of some of the effects of that apparatus. Such a model is free to depart considerably in form from whatever governs the true kinematics of the agent. Furthermore, the outputs of the forward model do not actually cause movements: they are just used to finesse

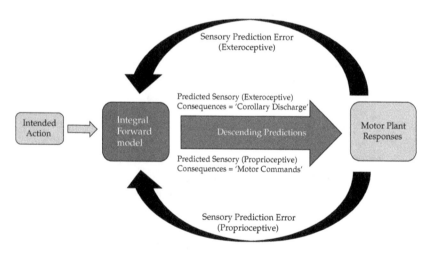

FIGURE 4.3   **Integral Forward Model (IFM) Architecture**
In this architecture, predictions from the forward model act as action commands and there is no need for an efference copy as such.

Source: From Pickering & Clark, 2014.

and predict outcomes, and in learning. According to the PP ('Integral Forward Model', see Pickering & Clark, 2014) account, however, the forward model itself controls our motor acts, via a web of descending predictions that determine set points for reflexes.

4.9   Action-Oriented Predictions

Notice that many of the probabilistic representations inhering in the generative model will now be, in the terms of Clark (1997), 'action-oriented'. They will represent how things are in a way that, once suitably modulated by the precision-weighting of prediction error, also prescribes (in virtue of the flows of sensation they predict) how to act and respond. They are thus representations (as we shall see in more detail in chapters 8–10 following) of *affordances*—environmental opportunities for organism-salient action and intervention. Action, within such a schema, provides a powerful form of prediction-based structuring of the information flow (Pfeifer et al., 2007; Clark, 2008). Action is also conceptually primary, since it provides the only way (once a good world model is in place and aptly activated) to actually alter the sensory signal so as to reduce prediction error.[17] An agent can reduce prediction error without acting, by altering what she predicts. But only action can reduce error by systematically changing the input itself. These two mechanisms must work in delicate harmony to ensure behavioural success.

This very broad story about action, it is worth noticing, could be accepted even by those who may wish to reject the rather particular model in which proprioceptive predictions play the role of motor commands—perhaps because they wish to retain the more familiar apparatus of efference copy, cost functions, and paired forward and inverse models. For all that the broader view of prediction and action here asserts is that (i) action and perception each depend upon probabilistic hierarchical generative models and (ii) perception and action work together, in regimes characterized by complex circular causal flow, so as to minimize sensory prediction errors. Action and perception, such a view suggests, are similarly and continuously constructed around the evolving flow of prediction error. This, I suggest, is the fundamental insight about action suggested by work on the predictive brain. The direct exploitation of proprioceptive predictions as motor commands simply provides one possible neuronal implementation of this much broader schema—albeit one that Friston and colleagues consider to be highly plausible[18] given known facts concerning the physiology of the motor system (Shipp et al., 2013).

4.10   Predictive Robotics

With this in mind, it is worth scouting some broader applications of prediction-based processing routines as tools for the acquisition of motor and cognitive skills by mobile robots. Much of this work has been conducted within the paradigm of 'cognitive developmental robotics' (CDR)[19] (see Asada et al., 2001, 2009). The core idea here is that the artificial control structure that acts as the agent's 'brain' should develop by a process of ongoing embodied interaction with the agent's environment (including other agents).[20] Thus, we read that:

> The key aspect of CDR is its design principle. Existing approaches often explicitly implement a control structure in the robot's 'brain' that was derived from a designer's understanding of the robot's physics. According to CDR, the structure should reflect the robot's own process of understanding through interactions with the environment. (Asada et al., 2001, p. 185)

Let's take simple motor learning first. Park et al. (2012) describe work using the humanoid robot AnNAO. In this work, simple motor sequences are learnt using prediction error minimization within a hierarchical (Bayesian) system. The robot begins by 'experiencing' random movements similar to so-called 'motor babbling' (Meltzoff & Moore, 1997) in human infants. In motor babbling, the infant explores its personal space of action by, in effect, randomly issuing motor commands and then sensing (seeing, feeling, sometimes tasting) what happens. Such learning, as noted by Caligiore et al. (2008) in another robotic study in this area, is an instance of what Piaget (1952) called the 'primary circular-reaction hypothesis' according to which early random self-experimentation sets up associations between goals, motor commands, and sensory states enabling the later emergence of effective goal-directed action. Standard forms of Hebbian learning (Hebb, 1949) can mediate the formation of such links, resulting in the acquisition of a forward model associating actions and their expected sensory consequences.[21] Park et al. (2012) then piggy-backed upon such early learning, training their robot to produce three target action sequences. These were trajectories of motion defined using a sequence of desired action states plotted as sequences of inner state-transitions. The robot was able to learn and reproduce the target action sequences and did so despite the presence of potentially confusing overlaps between sub-trajectories within the trained sequences.

In phase two of this experiment, the robot used a hierarchical (multilayer) system in which higher layers end up learning about longer sequences, and movements result from the combination of top-down prediction and bottom-up sensing. The most probable transition at a given level is thus impacted by top-down information concerning the longer sequence of which the movement is a part. Using this layered approach, the robot was able to learn a simplified version of 'object permanence', predicting the position of a visually presented object (a moving dot) even when it was temporarily occluded by another object.

Phase three extended the story to encompass (a very simple version of) learning by motor imitation. This is an extremely active area in both robotics and cognitive computational neuroscience (for nice introductions, see Rao, Schon, & Meltzoff, 2007; Demiris & Meltzoff, 2008). Park et al. used two identical humanoid robots (this time built using the DARwin-OP[22] robotic platform) that were placed so that each of their visual systems captured the actions of the other. One robot acted as teacher, moving its arms so as to produce a pre-programmed motor routine. The other robot (the 'infant') had to learn this routine from observation alone. This proves possible because the infant robot was trained to develop a 'self-image' linking visual images of its own gross motions to sequences of internal action commands. Once this (thin) self-image is in place, observed motions from the teacher robot can be matched to the memorized self-image and thus linked to internal action commands (Figure 4.4). This routine will only work, however, insofar as the target system (the teacher) is sufficiently 'like' the learner (the 'infant'). This 'like me' assumption (Meltzoff, 2007a, b) may later be relaxed as the agent's generative model increases in complexity and content, but it may be necessary to get the imitation learning process going at the outset (for some excellent discussion and a variety of further robotic studies, see Kaipa, Bongard, & Meltzoff, 2010).

Prediction-based learning thus provides an especially potent resource for bridging between simple sensorimotor skills and higher cognitive achievements such as planning, imitation, and the offline simulation of behaviour (see chapter 5).

4.11   Perception-Cognition-Action Engines

Readers familiar with the science-fiction book (or the movie) *Ender's Game* will recall how what at first seemed to be mere simulations were

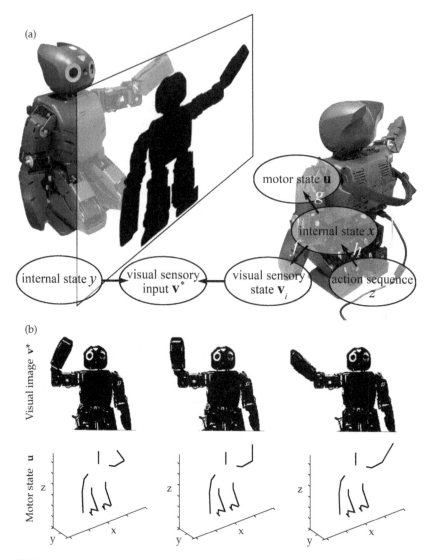

FIGURE 4.4 Structure of Imitation Learning
(a) The target system (left robot) produces image sequence (v^*) from internal state sequence (y). The agent system (right robot) follows by mapping the image sequence (v^*) to the memorized self-image of (vi) whose internal action states x is known. The target's visual sequence produces a sequence of internal action states in agent. The agent trains this sequence to build action sequences (z) and reproduces the action to real motor state u. (b) The agent sees visual images of target robot (up), and the motor state of the agent is derived from the image (down).

Source: From Park et al., 2012.

clandestinely being used to drive physical starships in a real battle situation. This, it seems to me, is one way to think of the core PP proposal concerning action. For action, if this aspect of the story is on track, comes about as a direct result of forward-model-based simulations. Action-oriented extensions of the basic predictive processing story, as the opening quote from William James suggests, thus have much in common with what are sometimes known as 'ideomotor' accounts of action. According to such accounts (Lotze, 1852; James, 1890) the very idea of moving, when unimpeded by other factors, is what brings the moving about. In other words:

> In the ideomotor view, in a sense, causality, as present in the real world, is reversed in the inner world. A mental representation of the intended effect of an action is the cause of the action: here it is not the action that produces the effect, but the (internal representation of the) effect that produces the action. (Pezzulo et al., 2007, p. 75)

In the approach favoured by Friston and colleagues, this emerged as the idea that we learn to associate our own movements with their distinctive proprioceptive consequences. Actions are thus controlled and enabled by proprioceptive prediction, quashing proprioceptive prediction error by moving the body to fit the predictions.

Such approaches make extensive use of the forward-model construct from classical work on motor control, but now recast as part and parcel of a more encompassing generative model. This replicates the many benefits of the use of forward models while treating motor control using the very same apparatus that (in Part I) was invoked to explain perception, understanding, and imagination. The 'cognitive package deal' announced at the end of chapter 3 is thus enriched, with motor control flowing from the same core architecture of generative-model-based sensory prediction. This hints at the possibility of shared computational machinery for action generation and for reasoning about possible actions (either our own or those of other agents)—a theme that will loom large in the next chapter.

This is an attractive package, but it brings with it a cost. It is now our acquired expectations (the complexes of sub-personal prediction implied by a generative model) that carry most of the explanatory, and computational, burden. This may, however, turn out to be an empowering rather than a limiting factor. For PP describes a biologically plausible architecture just about maximally well-suited to installing the requisite suites of prediction through embodied interactions with the training environments that we encounter, perturb, and—at several slower timescales—actively construct. This is an especially potent recipe since much of 'higher cognition', or so I shall later (Part III) argue, is made possible only by our history of encounters with the increasingly exotic sensory flows created by our own culturally crafted 'designer' environments.

The emerging picture is one in which perception, cognition, and action are manifesations of a single adaptive regime geared to the reduction of organism-salient prediction error. Once-crisp boundaries between sensory and motor processing now dissolve: actions flow from percepts that predict sensory signals some of which entrain actions that recruit new percepts. As we engage the world with our senses, percepts and action recipes now co-emerge, combining motor prescriptions with rolling efforts at knowing and understanding. Action, cognition, and perception are thus continuously co-constructed, simultaneously rooted in the cascading predictions that constitute, test, and maintain our grip upon the world.

5

Precision Engineering: Sculpting the Flow

5.1 Double Agents

The image of the brain as a probabilistic prediction machine places context and action centre stage. It requires us to abandon the last vestiges of the 'input-output' model according to which environmental stimuli repeatedly impinge upon a richly organized but essentially passive system. In its place we find a system that is constantly active, moving restlessly from one state of expectation to another, matching sensory states with predictions that harvest new sensory states in a rolling cycle.

Within this complex, shifting nexus, action leads a kind of double life. Actions (like any other regularity in the world) need to be understood. But our own actions are also consequences, if the story rehearsed in chapter 4 is correct, of the sensory expectations encoded in the generative models we deploy. This yields an opportunity. Perhaps our predictions of other agents can be informed by the very same generative model that structures our own patterns of action and response? We may sometimes grasp the intentions of other agents, this suggests, by deploying appropriately transformed versions of the multilayered sets of expectations that underlie our own behaviour. Other agents are thus treated as context-nuanced versions of ourselves.[1] This offers insight into the development and deployment of 'mirror neurons' and (more generally) 'mirror systems': neural resources implicated both in the performance of actions and in the observation of the 'same' actions when performed by others.

The present chapter explores this strategy, using it as a core illustration of something much more general and powerful—the use, within PP, of altered assignments of precision to reconfigure patterns of effective connectivity within the brain.

5.2   Towards Maximal Context-Sensitivity

We can start by considering familiar cases of context-sensitive response, such as that illustrated in Figure 5.1.

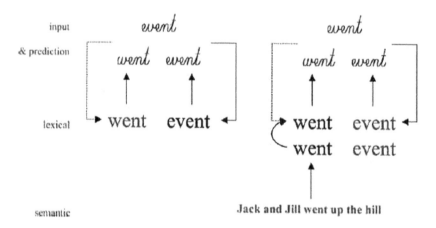

FIGURE 5.1   Schematic Illustrating the Role of Priors in Biasing toward One Representation of an Input or Another

(*Left*) The word 'event' is selected as the most likely cause of the visual input. (*Right*) The word 'went' is selected as the most likely word that is (1) a reasonable explanation for the sensory input and (2) conforms to prior expectations based on semantic context.

Source: Friston, 2002.

In Figure 5.1, we effortlessly read the top sentence as 'Jack and Jill went up the hill' despite the fact that the word 'went' is badly rendered. It is, in fact, structurally identical with the better rendered word form 'event' in the second sentence. This fact is, however, only evident upon quite close inspection. This is due to the strong influence of top-down priors that are helping to determine the best overall 'fit', reconciling the sensory evidence with our probabilistic expectations. In ignoring (courtesy of strong predictions from the level above) the structural deformity of 'went' in the top sentence, 'we tolerate a small error at the lower level to minimize overall prediction error' (Friston, 2002, p. 237). For another example of such top-down influence on perceptual appearances, see Figure 5.2.

Such effects are familiar enough. They are examples of the kind of context-sensitivity displayed by early artificial neural networks constructed using the connectionist 'interactive activation' paradigm.[2] Within the predictive processing paradigm, such context-sensitivity becomes (in a sense to be pursued below) pervasive and 'maximal'.[3]

FIGURE 5.2   Another Example in which Local Contextual Cues Set Up Prior Expectations
In the context of reading the A, the B hypothesis makes the raw visual data most probable. In the context of reading the 12, the 13 hypothesis makes the very same raw visual data most probable. For some further discussion of this example, see Lupyan & Clark, in press.

This is due to the combination of hierarchical form with flexible 'precision-weighting', as introduced in chapter 2. That combination renders context-sensitivity fundamental, systematic, and endemic in ways that have major implications (see also Phillips & Singer (1997), Phillips, Clark, & Silverstein (2015)) for neuroscience and for our understanding of the nature and origins of intelligent response. To creep up on this, reflect that (in the simple example given above): 'If we recorded from the "went" unit under top-down expectation of "event", we might conclude it was now selective for "event"' (Friston, 2002, p. 240). Downwards-flowing influence, in the PP setting, thus has a major impact on the selectivity of lower level response (for some more examples, see Friston & Price, 2001). As a result, 'the representational capacity and inherent function of any neuron, neuronal population, or cortical area is dynamic and context-sensitive [and] neuronal responses, in any given cortical area, can represent different things at different times' (Friston & Price, 2001, p. 275).

The PP architecture here combines, in a pervasive and fluent way, two of the most striking characteristics of neural organization. The two characteristics are functional differentiation (sometimes misleadingly called 'specialization') and integration. Functional differentiation means that local neural assemblies will come to exhibit different 'response profiles' where these reflect 'a combination of intrinsic local cortical biases and extrinsic factors including experience and the influence of functional interactions with other regions of the brain' (Anderson, 2014, p. 52). These response profiles will help determine the kinds of task for which the assembly might be recruited. But this, as Anderson rightly stresses, need not imply specialization in the more standard sense of (for example) there being regions that specialize in fixed tasks such as face recognition or mind reading. Integration (of the rather profound kind exhibited by the neural economy) means that those functionally differentiated areas interact dynamically in ways that allow transient task-specific processing regimes (involving transient coalitions of neural resources) to emerge as contextual effects repeatedly reconfigure the flow of information and influence.

Such effects become pervasive and systematic as a direct result of the hierarchical organization implied by the basic PP model. In that model multiple functionally differentiated subpopulations exchange signals to find a best overall hypothesis, with the signals from each higher population providing rich contextualizing information for the level or levels directly below, based on its own probabilistic priors ('expectations'). This downwards (and lateral) flow of prediction makes large differences, as we just saw, to the moment-by-moment responsiveness of the units that receive it. Moreover, as we saw in chapter 2, the efficacy of specific top-down or bottom-up influences is *itself* modifiable by systemic estimates of precision that raise or lower the gain on specific prediction error signals. This means that the patterns of downwards-flowing influence are (in ways we are about to explore) themselves dynamically reconfigurable according to task and context. The upshot is that flows of prediction and prediction error signals implement a flexible, dynamically reconfigurable cascade in which contextual information from every higher level can play a role in sculpting selectivity and response 'all the way down'.

5.3   Hierarchy Reconsidered

Recall that, in the standard implementation of PP[4] higher level 'representation units' send predictive signals laterally (within level) and downwards (to the next level down) thus providing priors on activity at the subordinate level. In this way backwards (top-down) and lateral connections combine to 'exert a modulatory influence on lower or equivalent stages of cortical transformations and define a hierarchy of cortical areas' (Friston & Price, 2001, p. 279). This kind of cortical hierarchy supports (as we saw in chapter 1) the bootstrapping-style learning that induces empirical priors.[5] Such a hierarchy is simply *defined* by these patterns of interaction. The core requirement is only that there be a reciprocally connected structure of feedback and feedforward connections with asymmetric functional roles. In a little more detail, what is required is that neuronal populations exchange signals using distinct feedforward, feedback, and lateral connections, and that within those webs of influence functionally asymmetric resources handle predictions and prediction error signals.

   In a seminal study, Felleman and Van Essen (1991) describe an anatomical hierarchy (for Macaque visual cortex) whose structure and features map nicely onto those required by this broad schema (for discussion, see Bastos et al., 2012, 2015). Such a hierarchy leaves plenty of room for additional—and functionally salient—complexity. For example, the notion of local recurrent signal exchange between adjoining hierarchical levels is consistent with the existence of multiple parallel streams delivering what Felleman and Van Essen (1991) dubbed 'distributed hierarchical processing'. In such schemes multiple areas may coexist at a single 'level' of the hierarchy, and there may also be long-range connections that entirely skip some intervening levels.

The ground-breaking studies by Felleman and Van Essen were limited, however, by the absence of a measure of hierarchical distance. This introduced substantial indeterminacy into the ordering of areas that emerged from the work (see Hilgetag et al., 1996, 2000), a shortfall that has since been remedied using new data on connectivity (Barone et al., 2000). More recently, Markov et al. (2013, 2014) used neural tracing data and network models to explore the web of inter-area and feedforward/feedback connections in Macaque visual cortex. Their studies suggest that feedback and feedforward connections are indeed both anatomically and functionally distinct, and that feedforward and feedback pathways 'obey well-defined distance rules' (Markov et al., 2014, p. 38), thus confirming the basic PP requirements of hierarchical structure and feedback/feedforward functional asymmetry.

Nonetheless, these studies also introduce substantial complexities to any simple image of feedback and feedforward connections in a fixed cortical hierarchy, revealing networks of connections that display a 'bow-tie' structure combining high-density local communications (in a kind of 'core'—the knot at the centre of the bow-tie shown in Figure 5.3) with sparser long-range connections to rest of the cortex. These long-range connections allow densely connected local processing packets ('modules') to enter into temporary task- and context-varying coalitions (see Park & Friston, 2013; Sporns, 2010, Anderson, 2014).

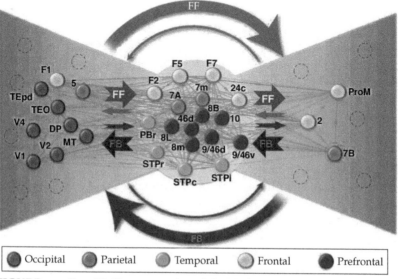

FIGURE 5.3 Bow-Tie Representation of the High-Density Cortical Matrix
Source: Markov et al., 2013, by permission.

Such organizational forms are also consistent with a higher level 'rich club' organization (Van den Heuvel & Sporns, 2011) in which certain well-connected local 'hubs' are themselves heavily mutually interconnected (rather like an exclusive country club for movers and shakers). What emerges is a daunting picture of multiscale dynamical complexity.

This is important. The simple image of processing within a cortical hierarchy may seem to imply a rigid, fixed, serial, flow of information—a kind of neural stepladder with an inevitably problematic 'top level' end point. The PP architecture, it is worth stressing, has very different implications. Unlike traditional feedforward models (of the kind rightly critiqued by Churchland et al., 1994), the PP architecture supports an ongoing, concurrent two-way flow of information. This means that processing at any given higher level is not 'waiting' for processing at the level below to finish before beginning to exert its influence. Moreover, the perceptual processing hierarchy is probably best imagined (Mesulam, 1998; Penny, 2012) as a kind of sphere (see Figure 5.4) rather than a stepladder. Sensory stimulations perturb the sphere at the peripheries and are met by a constellation of predictions whose recruitment is context- and task-dependent. Within the sphere, there are structures and structures-of-structures. But the evolving flow

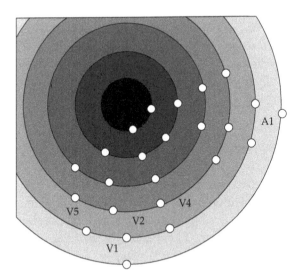

FIGURE 5.4   Cortical Architecture Depicting Multimodal Areas in the Centre and Unimodal Sensory Processing Regions on the Periphery
Visual regions are shown at the bottom and auditory regions are on the right.

Source: Penny, 2012, and based upon Mesulam, 1998.

of information and influence is not fixed. Instead, PP suggests (as we shall shortly see) a variety of potent mechanisms for reconfiguring patterns of moment-by-moment 'effective connectivity' according to task and context. The PP use of hierarchy is thus highly consistent with a picture of the brain as a complex ever-active dynamical system: one whose moment-by-moment signal-passing structure is context-sensitive, fluid, multiply reconfigurable, and constantly changing at many interacting structural and temporal scales (Singer, 2013; Bastos et al., 2012, 2015). Flexible precision-weighting provides, as we shall soon see in more detail, the key systemic tool that allows the combination of a bedrock two-way hierarchical model with the context-sensitive generation of 'hypotheses', and with context-variable patterns of inter-level (and inter-area) influence.

Within such a constantly active system, higher levels are often depicted (see, e.g., Sherman & Guillery, 1998) as 'modulating' the activity at lower levels. It is increasingly unclear, however, if 'modulation' is really the best way of describing the many quite dramatic ways in which ongoing probabilistic prediction here impacts the flow of processing and response. Recent evidence suggests that when two areas are hierarchically proximate (such as V1/V2) 'feedback connections can drive their targets just as strongly as feedforward connections' (Bastos et al., 2012, p. 698). Within the PP framework, this means that top-down predictions are capable, under the right circumstances, of forcing downstream response in ways that can radically revise, or even undo, 'driving' feedforward influence. At the same time, the notion of 'modulation' remains in some ways apt, insofar as the functional role of downwards (and laterally) flowing prediction is to provide essential contextualizing information.

5.4   Sculpting Effective Connectivity

Basic context effects, within the PP framework, flow inevitably from the use of higher level probabilistic expectations to guide and nuance lower level response. This guidance involves expectations concerning the most likely patterns of unfolding activity at the level below. But such expectations, as we saw in chapter 2, are intertwined with context-based assessments of the reliability and salience of different aspects of the sensory information itself. These assessments of reliability and salience determine the *weighting* (precision) given to different aspects of the prediction error signal at different levels of processing. This provides a powerful means of sculpting the larger patterns of 'effective connectivity' that modify the internal flow of influence and information according to task and context.

'Effective connectivity'[6] names 'the influence one neural system exerts over another' (Friston, 1995, p. 57). It is to be distinguished from both structural and functional connectivity. 'Structural connectivity' names the gross pattern of physical linkages (the web of fibres and synapses) that—perhaps working in concert with more diffuse 'volume signalling' mechanisms (Philipides et al., 2000, 2005)—allow neurons to interact across space and time. 'Functional connectivity' describes observed patterns of temporal correlation between neural events. The closely related notion of 'effective connectivity' then aims to reflect short-term patterns of causal influence between neural events, thus taking us beyond simple observations of undirected—and sometimes uninformative—correlation. One useful way to think about the relation between functional and effective connectivity is thus to conceive of:

> the [electrophysiological] notion of effective connectivity . . . as the experiment and time-dependent, simplest possible circuit diagram that would replicate the observed timing relationships between the recorded neurons. (Aertsen & Preissl, 1991, quoted in Friston, 1995, p. 58)

Functional and effective connectivity patterns alter rapidly as we perform our cognitive tasks. Structural change, by contrast, is a slower[7] process, since it is, in effect, reconfiguring the reconfigurable network itself (by altering the underlying communicative skeleton that supports other, more rapid, forms of momentary reconfiguration).

In recent years, the use of neuroimaging paired with new analytic techniques has made the study of the patterns of effective connectivity increasingly viable. Such techniques include structural equation modelling, applications of 'Granger causality', and Dynamic Causal Modelling (DCM).[8] In a rather satisfying twist, DCM (Friston et al., 2003; Kiebel et al., 2009) takes the same core strategy used (if PP is correct) by the brain to model the world and applies it to the analysis of the neuroimaging data itself. DCM relies upon a generative model to estimate (infer) the neural sources given some set of imaging data, and uses Bayesian estimation to reveal changing patterns of effective connectivity. In this way DCM first estimates intrinsic connections between sources, then the changes in connections due to some form of external (typically experimental) perturbation.

Nonlinear extensions of DCM (Stephan et al., 2008) allow the estimation not just of how effective connectivity changes with experimental manipulations (alterations of task and context) but of how those new patterns of effective connectivity are brought about, that is, 'how the connection between two neuronal units is enabled or gated by activity in other units' (Stephan et al., 2008, p. 649). Such gating involves what Clark (1997, p. 136) dubbed 'neural control structures', where these may be defined as any neural circuits, structures, or processes whose role is to control the shape of the inner economy rather than (directly) to track external states of affairs or control bodily action. In just this vein, Van Essen et al. (1994) suggest an analogy with the division of processes in a modern factory, where much effort and energy must be spent to ensure the proper internal trafficking of materials before the construction of any actual products.

Neural gating hypotheses come in many forms, including the postulation of special populations of information-routing 'control neurons' (Van Essen et al., 1994), the canny use of re-entrant processing (Edelman, 1987; Edelman & Mountcastle, 1978), and the development of 'convergence zones' (Damasio & Damasio, 1994). The latter are essentially hubs in which many feedback and feedforward loops converge, and which are thus able to 'direct the simultaneous activation of anatomically separate regions' (p. 65). Such conjectures fit naturally with an emerging body of work that demonstrates the surprising extent to which 'large-scale brain systems can reconfigure their functional architecture in a context-dependent manner' (Cocchi et al., 2013, p. 493; see also Cole et al., 2011; Fornito et al., 2012).

Within the PP framework, gating is principally achieved by the manipulation of the precision-weighting assigned to specific prediction errors. The primary effect of this (as we saw in chapter 2 above) is to systematically vary the relative influence of top-down versus bottom-up information by increasing the gain ('volume') on selected error units. This provides a way to implement a rich set of attentional mechanisms whose role is to bias processing so as to reflect estimates of the reliability and salience of (different aspects of) both the sensory signal and the generative model itself.[9] But those same mechanisms offer a promising means of implementing fluid and flexible forms of large-scale gating among cortical populations. To see this, we need only note that very low-precision prediction errors will have little or no influence upon ongoing processing and will fail to recruit or nuance higher level representations. Altering the distribution of precision-weightings thus amounts, in effect, to altering the 'simplest circuit diagram' (Aertsen & Preissl, 1991) for current processing. The neural mechanisms of attention are here identical with the neural mechanisms that alter patterns of effective connectivity.

This is an intuitive result (see also Van Essen et al., 1994), especially if we consider that the specific means by which such alterations may be effected are many, and that their detailed functional implications may vary in different parts of the brain. Possible implementing mechanisms for the precision-weighting of prediction error (which, in PP, amounts to the control of post-synaptic gain) include the action of various 'modulatory neurotransmitters' such as dopamine, serotonin, acetylcholine, and noradrenalin (Friston, 2009). Frequencies of oscillation must also play a major role (see Engel et al., 2001; Hipp et al., 2011). For example, synchronized pre-synaptic inputs look to result in increased post-synaptic gain. In particular, it has been suggested that 'Gamma oscillations can control gain by affording synchronized neuronal discharges a greater influence on the firing rate of downstream neurons' (Feldman & Friston, 2010, p. 2). These mechanisms also interact, since (to take just one example) gamma oscillations respond to acetylcholine. In general, it seems possible that bottom-up signalling (which in predictive processing encodes prediction error and is hypothesized to originate in superficial pyramidal cells) may be communicated using gamma-range frequencies while top-down influence may be conveyed by beta frequencies (see Bastos et al., 2012, 2015; Buffalo et al., 2011). Thus, while the notion of sculpting patterns of effective connectivity by means of 'precision-weighted prediction error' is simple enough, the mechanisms that implement such effects may be multiple and complex, and they may interact in important but as yet underappreciated ways.

Further support for this general idea (the idea of precision-based reconfiguring of large-scale patterns of effective connectivity) was recently provided by an fMRI study analyzed using nonlinear DCM. In this study (den Ouden et al., 2010), specific prediction error signals in one (striatal) neural area modified the coupling between other (visual and motor) areas. In this experiment, auditory cues (high or low 'beeps') differentially predicted visual targets in ways that altered over time. The subjects' task was rapidly to discriminate (with a motor response) the visual stimuli predicted (in ways that varied over time) by the auditory cues. Speed and accuracy increased (as one would expect) with predictability. Using DCM (and assuming a Bayesian learning model that provided the best fit, taking model complexity into account, to the data; see den Ouden et al., 2010, p. 3212), the experimenters found that failures of prediction (caused by the changing contingencies) systematically altered the strength of the visuomotor coupling in a way that was 'gated by the degree of prediction error encoded by the putamen' and that 'prediction error responses in the putamen [modulate] information transfer from visual to motor areas ... consistent with ... a gating role of the striatum' (both quotes, p. 3217). The amount and precision of prediction error computed by the striatum thus delicately controls the strength (efficacy) of the visuomotor connection, orchestrating the moment-by-moment interplay between visual and motor regions. This is an important result, demonstrating that 'trial-by-trial prediction error responses in a specific region modulate the coupling among other regions' (den Ouden et al., 2010, p. 3217).

The most important effect of ongoing activity within a predictive hierarchy is thus that it supports a vision of the brain as restless: almost constantly in some (changing) state of active expectation whose implications for the flow and processing of sensory input we are only just beginning to appreciate.

5.5   Transient Assemblies

The PP architecture, we have seen, combines functional differentiation with multiple (pervasive and flexible) forms of informational integration. This suggests a new slant upon the vexed notion of cognitive 'modularity' (see, e.g., Fodor, 1983, and for discussion, Barrett & Kurzban, 2006; Colombo, 2013; Park & Friston, 2013; Sporns, 2010, Anderson, 2014). Changing patterns of influence among neural populations (and between larger scale regions) are here determined by precision-weighted prediction error signals, hence by estimates of both the salience and the relative uncertainty associated—for a given task at a given time—with activity in different neural regions and different neuronal populations. Such systems display great context-sensitivity while benefiting from a kind of emergent 'soft modularity'. Distinctive, objectively identifiable,[10] local processing organizations now emerge and operate within a larger, more integrative, framework in which functionally differentiated populations and sub-populations are engaged and nuanced in different ways so as to serve different tasks (for more on this general multiuse picture, see Anderson, 2010, 2014).

PP thus implements an architecture ideally suited to supporting the formation and dissolution of what Anderson (2014) nicely dubs TALoNS—Transiently Assembled Local Neural Subsystems. TALoNS act in some ways like modules or components. But they are formed and reformed 'on the fly', and their functional contributions vary according to their location within larger webs of processing. PP implements just such a fully flexible cognitive architecture and offers a picture of neural dynamics that is highly sensitive, at multiple timescales, both to varying task-demands and to the estimated reliability (or otherwise) of specific bodies of top-down expectation and bottom-up sensory input.[11]

Neural representations here 'become a function of, and dependent upon, input from distal cortical areas' (Friston and Price, 2001, p. 280). This is a potent source of flexibility, since the flow of input from such areas is *itself* subject to rapid restructuring by prediction error signals elsewhere in the brain. When these features combine, the result is an architecture in which there are distinct, functionally differentiated, components and circuits but whose constantly shifting dynamics are (to borrow a phrase from Spivey, 2007) 'interaction dominated'. The highly negotiable flows of influence thus constructed are themselves action-responsive (enforcing various forms of 'circular causation' linking perception and action), and the space of dynamical possibilities is further enriched (as we shall see in Part III) by all manner of bodily and worldly tricks for structuring our own inputs and restructuring problem spaces. The representational economy thus supported is firmly grounded in sensorimotor experience yet benefits (as we shall soon see) from various forms of abstraction consequent upon hierarchical learning. The result is a dauntingly complex system: one that combines a deeply context-flexible processing regime with a rich web of brain-body-world loops to yield negotiable and hugely (almost unimaginably) plastic flows of information and influence.

5.6   Understanding Action

That burgeoning complexity is nowhere more evident, it seems to me, than in our abilities to make sense of our own and others' actions. Human infants, around the age of 4, possess not only a sense of themselves as individual agents with specific needs, wants, and beliefs but also a sense of others as distinct agents with *their* own needs, wants, and beliefs. How might this be achieved? The discovery of 'mirror neurons' has seemed, to many, to deliver a substantial part of the answer. It may be, however, that the existence of mirror neurons is more of a symptom than an explanation, and that flexible, context-sensitive, predictive processing provides a more fundamental mechanism. Understanding the actions of others, if this is correct, is just one manifestation of a much more general capacity for flexible, context-sensitive response.

Mirror neurons were first discovered in area F5 (a premotor area) of the macaque monkey (Di Pellegrino et al., 1992; Gallese et al., 1996; Rizzolatti et al., 1988, 1996). These neurons responded vigorously when the monkey performed a certain action (examples include taking an apple from a box, or picking up a raisin using a well-aimed precision grip). The experimenters were surprised to see, however, that those same neurons also responded vigorously when the monkey merely *observed* the same kind of action being performed by another agent. Neurons with this dual profile have also been found in monkey parietal cortex (Fogassi et al., 1998, 2005). In addition 'mouth mirror neurons' (Ferrari et al., 2003) respond when a monkey sucks juice from a dispenser (a syringe) and when the monkey sees a human performing the same action. At a larger scale, 'mirror systems' (overlapping resources used for generating, observing, and imitating actions) have been found in humans brains using neuroimaging techniques such as fMRI (Fadiga et al., 2002; Gazzola & Keysers, 2009; Iacoboni, 2009; Iacoboni et al., 1999; Iacoboni et al., 2005).

Mirror neurons (and the larger 'mirror systems' in which they participate) captured the imagination of cognitive scientists because they suggested a way to use knowledge of the 'meaning' of our own actions as a kind of lever for understanding the actions of others. Thus, suppose we grant that, when I reach for the raisin using a precision grip, I know (in some simple, first-order way) that my action is all about getting and ingesting the attractive morsel. Then, if the very same sub-populations of mirror neurons fire when I see *you* reaching for the raisin using just such a precision grip, perhaps I thereby become informed about *your* goals and intentions—your desire, to be blunt, for that raisin. Such a window into the minds of others agents would be very useful, enabling me better to anticipate your next moves and perhaps even to derail them, acquiring the raisin for myself by some rapid intervention. In some such way, mirror neurons have been thought to offer a 'fundamental mechanism' for explaining what Gallese, Keysers, and Rizzolatti (2004) call our 'experiential understanding of others' actions' and especially (see Rizzolatti & Sinigaglia, 2007) their goals and intentions.

'Experiential understanding' here names some kind of deep, primary, or 'embodied' understanding that enables us to appreciate the meaning of an observed action by a process of 'direct matching' (Rizzolatti & Sinigaglia, 2007) or 'resonating' (Rizzolatti et al., 2001, p. 661) involving my own motor representations of the same actions. Observing your action leads me, if this is correct, to simulate or partially activate the goal/motor act routine that (in me) would lead to the observed activity. In this way, it is claimed, 'we understand the actions of others by means of our own "motor knowledge" [and] this knowledge enables us immediately to attribute an intentional meaning to the movements of others' (Rizzolatti & Sinigaglia, 2007, p. 205).

None of this, however, can be quite as simple as that makes it sound. This is because performing that task involves solving an especially complex version of the so-called 'inverse problem'. This is the problem (a simple version of which we already encountered in 4.4) of taking an outcome-specifying input (here, the observation of a sequence of motor movements made by another agent) and using it to find the commands (here, the neural states specifying various high-level goals and intentions) that gave rise to it. The problem, as usual, is the multiplicity of possible mappings between observed movements and the high-level states (encoding goals and intentions) that gave rise to them. Thus, 'if you see someone in the street raise their hand, they could be hailing a taxi or swatting a wasp' (Press, Heyes, & Kilner, 2011). Or, to repeat the colourful example from Jacob and Jeannerod (2003), is the man in the white coat holding the knife to a human chest intending to perform a grisly murder or a life-saving operation—is it Dr Jekyll or Mr Hyde? Such intentions are not transparently present in motor sequences alone, since there is no unique mapping between such sequences and the intentions behind them. Jacob and Jeannerod (see also Jeannerod, 2006, p. 149) thus worry that simple movement-based matching mechanisms must fail to get a grip on what they call 'prior goals and intentions'.

What this suggests is that whatever mechanism might under-lie the posited process of 'direct matching' or 'resonating', it cannot be one that relies solely on the feedforward ('bottom-up') flow of sensory information. Instead, the path from the basic observed kinematics to the appreciation of the agent's intention must be very flexibly mediated by the prior state of the system. One way to achieve this is by meeting the incoming stream of sensory information using downwards-flowing activity that reflects what the observer already knows about the larger context in which the other agent's movements are being produced. Now recall the picture (chapter 4) of self-produced action. When we act, if that picture is correct, we predict the flow of sensory data that will result. That prediction involves a process of multilevel 'settling' in which many neural areas exchange signals until a kind of overall concord (minimizing error at all levels) is achieved. Such concord is doubtless imperfect and temporary, since error is never zero and the brain is constantly in flux. But while it is (more or less) achieved, there is harmonization between areas encoding information about basic movement com-mands (low-level kinematics), resulting multimodal sensory inputs, and our own ongoing goals and purposes. Those goals and purposes, likewise, are encoded as a distributed pattern across many levels of processing, and must encompass both 'local' goals such as turning a switch, and more distal ones such as illuminating the room, and even more distal ones, such as lighting up the room. It is this whole web of mutually supportive structure, distributed across many neural areas, whose probable configurations are specified by the learnt generative model that enables us to predict the sensory consequences of our own actions.

The PP take on mirror system activity should now be coming into clearer view. For suppose we deploy that same generative model (but see 5.8 for some tweaks and caveats) to meet the stream of sensory information specifying another agent's activity? Then here too, the brain will be forced to find a set of mutually consistent activity, spanning many neural areas, accommodating both prior expectations and the sensory evidence. Applying this picture to the puzzle case of Jekyll and Hyde, Kilner et al. (2007) note that:

> In this scheme, the intention that is inferred from the observation of the action now depends upon the prior information received from a context level. In other words, if the action was observed taking place in an operating theatre there would be a large prediction error for the intention 'to hurt' and a smaller prediction error for the intention 'to cure'. The prediction error would be the same at all other levels of the hierarchy for the two intentions. By minimising the overall prediction error the MNS [Mirror Neuron System] would infer that the intention of the observed movement was to cure. Therefore, the MNS is capable of inferring a unique intention even if two intentions result in identical movements. (Kilner et al., 2007, p. 164)

In the absence of all context-specifying information, no mechanism (of course) can distinguish the intention of curing from that of hurting. PP provides, however, a plausible mechanism (illustrated in Figure 5.5) for allowing what we already know (enshrined in the generative model used to predict the sensory consequences of our own actions) to make context-reflecting inferences concerning the intentions behind the actions of other (similar) agents.[12]

5.7   Making Mirrors

All this suggests a somewhat deflationary view of mirror neurons themselves. The deflationary view (Heyes, 2001, 2005, 2010) depicts the 'mirroring property' of individual neurons as, in essence, a direct result of processes of associative learning. According to this account, 'each

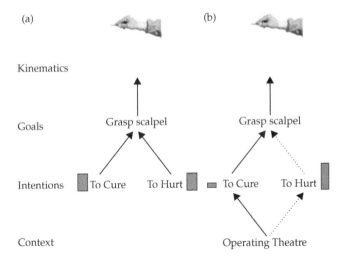

FIGURE 5.5   Examples of the Predictive Coding Account of the Mirror Neuron System (MNS)

Here we consider four levels of attribution in an example hierarchy of the MNS: kinematics, goal, intention, and context. In (a) an action-observation is considered in the absence of a context, in (b) the identical action is observed but now in the context of an operating theatre. The bars depict the level degree of prediction error. In (a) both intentions predict identical goals and kinematics and therefore the prediction error is identical in both schemes. In this case, the model cannot differentiate between the intentions causing the action. In (b) the context causes a large prediction error for the goal 'to hurt' and a small prediction error for the goal 'to cure'. In this case, the model can differentiate between the two intentions.

Source: Kilner et al., 2007, p. 164.

mirror neuron is forged through sensorimotor experience—correlated experience of observing and executing the same action' (Heyes, 2010, p. 576).

Such experience abounds, since we often observe an action which we ourselves are executing. Thus:

> whenever a monkey performs a grasping action with visual guidance, the activation of motor neurons (involved in the performance of grasping) and visual neurons (involved in the visual guidance of grasping) is correlated. Through associative learning, this correlated activation gives the grasping motor neurons additional, matching properties; they become mirror neurons, firing not only when grasping is executed, but also when it is observed. (Heyes, 2010, p. 577)

In the same way, we may reach for the cup and observe the hand shapings that result, or blow the trumpet and hear the sound that emerges. Under such conditions (see Figure 5.6), the correlated activity of motor and sensory neurons causes some neurons to become multiply tuned, responding both to execution and to passive observation. Such

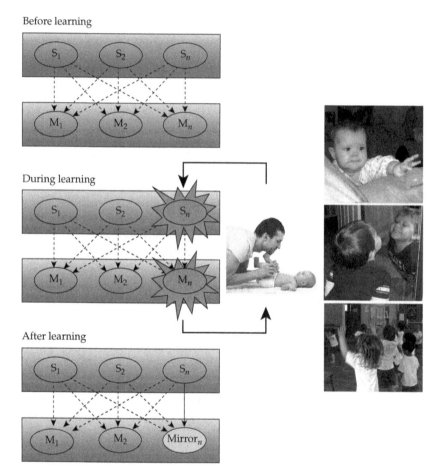

FIGURE 5.6 Associative Sequence Learning

Before learning, sensory neurons (S1, S2, and Sn), which are responsive to different high-level visual properties of an observed action, are weakly and unsystematically connected (dashed arrows) to some motor neurons (M1, M2, and Mn), which discharge during the execution of actions. The kind of learning that produces mirror neurons occurs when there is correlated (i.e., contiguous and contingent) activation of sensory and motor neurons that are each responsive to similar actions.

Source: Press, Heyes, & Kilner, 2011; photo of father and baby ©Photobac/Shutterstock.com.

associations inform the generative model that we use to produce and understand our own actions, and that is then available for use when we observe the actions of other (sufficiently similar) agents.

This shows (see Press, Heyes, & Kilner, 2011) just how mirror neurons and mirror systems may contribute to the flexible understanding of the actions of other agents. They do so not by directly (but mysteriously) specifying the goals or intentions of others but by participating in the same bidirectional multilevel cascades that enable us to predict the evolving sensory signal across many spatial and temporal scales. When error is minimized at all levels, the system has settled on a complex distributed encoding that encompasses low-level sensory data, intermediate goals, and high-level goals: Jekyll is seen as wielding the scalpel in such-and-such a manner, intending to cut, and hoping to cure.

5.8 Whodunit?

There is, however, a complication (but within it hides an opportunity). When I reach for the coffee cup, my cascading neural prediction includes, as a major component, the multiple proprioceptive sensations of strain and extension characteristic of that very reach. These predictions, as we saw in chapter 4, are (PP claims) what bring the reach about. But such predictions should not be carried over, willy-nilly, to the case where I am observing the motions of another agent.

There are two broad solutions to this kind of puzzle. The first involves the creation of a brand-new model (generative model fragment) dedicated to predicting the target events.[13] This is an expensive solution, though it is one that may be forced upon us from time to time (e.g., if I am observing the behaviour of some hugely alien being or a bacterium). It would be more efficient, however, to make maximal use of any overlap between the generative model that constructs my own actions and the one needed to make sense of the actions of others. This is not (conceptually, at least) as hard as it sounds, for we have already secured the main tool required. That tool is once again the precision-weighting of aspects of the prediction error signal. Precision-weighting, we have seen, implements a swathe of mechanisms for both automatic and effortful attending, and for varying the balance between 'top-down' expectation and 'bottom-up' sensory evidence. But it also, as we saw in 5.4, provides a general and flexible means for contextual gating, allowing different neuronal populations to form soft-assembled coalitions (patterns of effective connectivity) responsive to current needs, goals, and circumstances. Given this tool, differences between the predictions apt for the case of self-generated action and those apt for observing and understanding other agents can be systematically dealt with by altering our precision expectations, and thus treating the various self/other distinctions as just further layers of context.

The prime targets for such alteration are our own proprioceptive predictions. Given some cues that inform me that I am watching another agent, the precision-weighting (the gain) on proprioceptive prediction error relative to those aspects of the observed scene should be set low.[14] For according to PP it is the minimization of proprioceptive prediction error that directly drives our own actions, as those high-precision predictions become fulfilled by the motor plant. With the gain on proprioceptive prediction error set low, we are free to deploy the generative model geared to the production of our own actions as a means both of predicting the visual consequences of another's actions and understanding their intentions.[15] Under such conditions, the complex interdependencies between other aspects of the generative model (those relating high-level aims and intentions to proximal goals and to the shape of the unfolding movements) remain active, allowing prediction error minimization across the cortical hierarchy to settle on a best overall guess concerning the intentions 'behind' the observed behaviour.

The upshot is that 'we can use the same generative model, under action or observation, by selectively attending to visual or proprioceptive information (depending upon whether visual movement is caused by ourselves or others)' (Friston, Mattout, & Kilner, 2011, p. 156). By contrast, when engaged in self-generated action, the precision-weighting on the relevant proprioceptive error must be set high. When proprioceptive prediction error is highly weighted yet suitably resolved by a stack of top-down predictions (some of which reflect our goals and intentions), we feel that we are the agents of our own actions. Core aspects of the much-discussed 'sense of agency'[16] (in normal subjects, with well-functioning proprioceptive systems) depend upon this, and mistakes in both the generation of prediction errors and the assignment of precision-weighting to such errors are increasingly thought to underlie many illusions of action and control, as we shall see in detail in chapter 7.[17]

More generally, the implication is that the neural representations that underlie our own intentional motor actions and those that are active when we model the motor behaviour of other agents are substantially the same, and that 'exactly the same neuronal representation can serve as a prescription for self-generated action, while, in another context, it encodes a perceptual representation of the intentions of another' (Friston, Mattout, & Kilner, 2011, p. 150). The clear differences in functionality are here traced not to the core representations but to the estimations of precision that nuance their effects, reflecting the different contexts in play. Mirroring properties may thus be consequences of the operation of a hierarchical predictive processing regime that posits shared representations for perception and action and within which 'the brain does not represent intended motor acts or the perceptual consequences of those acts separately; the constructs represented in the brain are both intentional and perceptual [having] both sensory and motor correlates' (p. 156). Such representations are essentially meta-modal high-level associative complexes linking goals and intentions to sensory consequences. Those states have differing constellations of modality-specific implications (some proprioceptive, some visual, etc.) according to the context in which they occur: implications that are implemented by varying the precision-weighting of different aspects of the prediction error signal.

5.9   Robot Futures

This same broad trick could be used to allow us—as in the mental time-travel cases introduced in chapter 3—to imagine our own future courses of action, in ways that might serve planning and reasoning. For here too, a similar problem arises. Take some animal that commands a rich and powerful generative model enabling it to predict the sensory signal across many temporal and spatial scales. Such an animal already seems well-placed to use that model 'offline' (see Grush, 2004) so as to engage in mental time-travel (see chapter 3) imagining possible future unfoldings and selecting an action accordingly. But the deep intimacy of perception and action here breeds a striking problem. For according to the process model outlined earlier, predicting the proprioceptive consequences of a certain trajectory of arm motion (to take a very simple example) is how we bring that trajectory about.

 The solution, once again, may lie in the canny (learnt) deployment of precision-weighting. Suppose we again lower the weighting on (select aspects of) the proprioceptive error signal, while simultaneously entering a high-level neural state whose rough-and-ready folk-psychological gloss might be something like 'the cup is grasped'. Motor action is entrained by high-precision proprioceptive expectations and cannot here ensue. But here too, all the other intertwined elements in the generative model remain poised to act in the usual way. The result should be a 'mental simulation' of the reach and an appreciation of its most

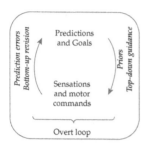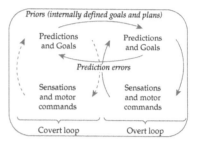

FIGURE 5.7 Covert Loops

Covert loops allow for the running of imaginary actions that produce a sequence of 'fictive actions' and hence of predictions relative to future (rather than present) states of affairs.

Source: Pezzulo, 2012.

likely consequences. Such mental simulations provide an appealing way of smoothing the path from basic forms of embodied response to abilities of planning, deliberation, and 'offline reflection'.[18] Such simulations constitute what Pezzulo (2012) describes as a 'covert loop'. The covert loop (see Figure 5.7):

> works off-line via the suppression of overt sensory and motor processes (in the active inference framework, this requires the suppression of proprioception). This permits running imaginary actions that produce a sequence of fictive actions and of predictions relative to future (rather than present) states of affairs. Fictive actions and predictions can be optimized via free energy [prediction error] minimization but without overt execution: they are not just "mind wandering" but are truly controlled towards goals specified at higher hierarchical levels. Prospection and planning are thus optimization processes that support the generation of distal and abstract goals (and associated plans), beyond current affordances. (Pezzulo, 2012, p. 1)

Here too, the core idea remains independent of the full process model in which motor commands are implemented by proprioceptive predictions. More fundamental than this is the notion that action production, action understanding, and the capacity to simulate possible actions might all be supported by context-nuanced tweaks to a single generative model grounded in the agent's own sensorimotor repertoire.

This idea has been studied, in microcosm, using a variety of simulations. Thus, Weber et al. (2006) describe a hybrid generative/predictive model of motor cortex that provides just this kind of multiple functionality. In this work, a generative model that enables a robot to perform actions doubles as a simulator enabling it to predict possible chains of perception and action. This simulation capacity is then used to enable a simple but challenging behaviour in which the robot must dock at a table in a way that enables it to grasp a visually detected object. Since most modes of table docking are inappropriate to the task, this provides a nice opportunity to base docking behaviour upon the results of the robot's own 'mental simulations' (see Figure 5.8).

Related ideas are pursued by Tani et al. (2004) and by Tani (2007). Tani and colleagues describe a set of robotic experiments using 'recurrent neural networks with parametric biases' (RNNPBs): a class of networks that implement prediction-based hierarchical learning. The guiding idea is that prediction-based hierarchical learning here solves a

FIGURE 5.8   The Robot from Weber et al. (2006), Performing the 'Docking' Action
Note that it cannot reach the orange fruit if it approaches the table at an angle, because of its short gripper and its side columns. This corresponds perhaps to situations where fingers, arm, or hand are in an inappropriate position for grasping.

Source: Weber et al., 2006.

crucial problem. It allows a system to combine a real sensorimotor grip on dealing with its world with the emergence of higher level abstractions that (crucially) develop in tandem with that grip. This is because learning here yields representational forms, at higher processing levels, that allow the system to predict the regularities that are governing the neural patterns (themselves responding to energetic stimulations at the sensory peripheries) present at the lower levels.

These are all examples of 'grounded abstractions' (for this general notion, see Barsalou, 2003; Pezzulo, Barsalou, et al., 2013) that open the door to more compositional and strategic operations, such as solving novel motor problems, mimicking the observed behaviour of other agents, engaging in goal-directed planning, and pre-testing behaviours in offline imagery. Such grounded abstractions do not float free of their roots in embodied action. Instead, they constitute what might be thought of as a kind of 'dynamical programming language' for those interactions: a language in which, for example, 'continuous sensory-motor sequences are automatically segmented into a set of reusable behavior primitives' (Tani, 2007, p. 2). Tani et al. (2004) show that robots equipped (as a result of learning-driven self-organization) with such primitives are able to deploy them so as to imitate the observed behaviour of another. In another experiment, they show that such primitives also facilitate the mapping of behaviours onto simple linguistic forms, so that a robot can learn to follow a command to, for example, point (using its body), push (using its arm), or hit (with its arm) in ways that target designated objects or spatial locations.

This set of studies is further extended in Ogata et al. (2009), who tackle the important problem of viewpoint translation using an RNNPB simulation in which one robot views and then imitates the object-manipulation behaviour of another agent, applying a set of learnt transformations to its own self-model. In this experiment in 'cognitive developmental robotics', 'the other individual is regarded as a dynamic object that can be predicted by projecting/translating a self-model' (Ogata et al., 2009, p. 4148)

Such demonstrations, though restricted in scope, are revealing. The emergence of 'reusable behaviour primitives' shows that features such as compositionality, reusability, and recombinability (features once associated with the brittle, chunky symbol structures of classical Artificial Intelligence) can arise quite naturally as a result of probabilistic prediction-driven learning in hierarchical settings. But the resulting abstractions are now richly grounded in the past experience and sensorimotor dynamics of the agent.

5.10   *The Restless, Rapidly Responsive, Brain*

Context, it seems, is everything. Not just 'Jekyll versus Hyde' but even 'self versus other' are here emerging as manifestations of a capacity to reshape and nuance our own processing routines according to the context in which we find ourselves. But context, of course, must itself be recognized, and it is usually recognized in context!

There is no unfortunate regress here. In the typical case, we are provided with many reliable cues (both external and internal) that recruit the correct subsets of neural resources for fine-tuning by means of the residual prediction error signal. Clear external cues (the operating theatre cues, in the case of Jekyll versus Hyde) are the obvious example. But my own ongoing neural state (encoding information about my goals and intentions) provides another type of cue, already setting up all manner of contextualizing influence, as will the many fine-grained effects of my own bodily motion upon the play of sensory information (see O'Regan & Noe, 2001). Two further ingredients complete the picture. One is the availability of ultra-rapid forms of 'gist processing' able to deliver contextualizing cues within a few hundred milliseconds of encountering a new scene. The other, which cannot really be overstressed, is the ongoing activity of the restless ever-expecting brain.

We saw, way back in chapter 1 (section 13), how the PP schema favoured a recurrently negotiated 'gist-at-a-glance' model, where we first identify the general scene followed by the details. We stressed too that the guiding hand of context is (in ecologically normal cases) seldom absent from our mindset. We are almost always in some more-or-less apt state of sensory expectation. The brain thus construed is a restless, pro-active (Bar, 2007) organ, constantly using its own recent and more distant past history to organize and reorganize its internal milieu in ways that set the scene for responses to incoming perturbations.

Moreover, even in the rare cases where we are forced (perhaps due to some clever experimental design) to process a succession of unrelated sensory inputs, there are canny tricks and ploys that support ultra-rapid extraction of the broad meaning or 'gist' of the scene. Such ultra-rapid gist extraction can deliver, even in otherwise elusive cases, the context relative to which apt precision expectations may be calculated: context that thus forges networks of effective connectivity able to corral new, soft-assembled coalitions of neural resources that both select and nuance the models used to meet the forward flow of sensory information.

Ultra-rapid gist extraction is by no means the sole preserve of the visual modality. But the mammalian visual system is especially well-understood, and here benefits from the combined resources of two rather different processing streams: the fast magnocellular pathway, whose projections from V1 constitute the so-called 'dorsal visual stream', and the slower parvocellular pathway, whose projections from V1 create the so-called 'ventral visual stream'. These are the streams made famous by Milner and Goodale (see, e.g., Milner & Goodale, 2006) in their 'dual visual systems' account. Within the context of a prediction-driven neural economy, it is thought that these streams provide, respectively:

> A fast, coarse system that initiates top-down predictions based on partially processed visual input, and a slower, finer subsystem that is guided by the rapidly activated predictions and refines them based on slower arriving detailed information. (Kveraga et al., 2007, p. 146)

There is also a third, konicellular stream, though its role remains unclear at the time of writing (see Kaplan, 2004). The magnocellular and parvocellular streams each display the kind of hierarchical organization described earlier. But they are also densely and repeatedly cross-connected, creating a dazzling web of forward, backward, and sideways influence (DeYoe & van Essen, 1988) whose combined effect is (Kveraga et al. suggest) to allow the low-spatial frequency information rapidly processed by the dorsal stream to provide context-suggesting information to guide object and scene recognition.

These early stages of rapid 'guessing' yield rough and ready 'analogies' (in the vocabulary of Bar, 2009) for the present input. By this the authors mean only that the rapidly processed cues support the retrieval, based on past experience, of a kind of high-level skeleton: a skeleton that can (in most cases) suggest *just enough* about the likely form and content of the scene to allow the fluent use of residual error rapidly to reveal whatever additional detail the task demands (see Figure 5.9). Such skeleton contents are not restricted to simple facts concerning the nature of the scene (city scene, office scene, animal-in-motion, etc.) but will include (Barrett & Bar, 2009) rapidly retrieved elements of the 'affective gist' of the scene or event, based upon our previous affective reactions. In this way:

> When the brain detects visual sensations from the eye in the present moment, and tries to interpret them by generating a prediction about what those visual sensations refer to or stand for in the world, it uses not only previously encountered patterns of sound, touch, smell and tastes, as well as semantic

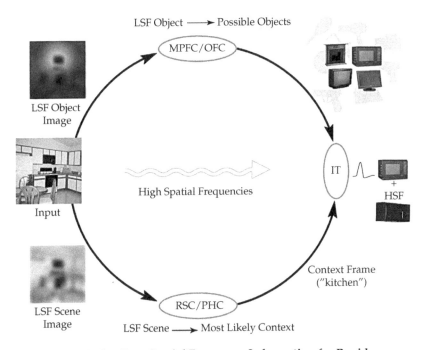

FIGURE 5.9   Using Low Spatial Frequency Information for Rapid Guessing

In parallel to the bottom-up systematic progression of the image details along the visual pathways, there are quick projections of low spatial frequency (LSF) information, possibly via the magnocellular pathway. This coarse but rapid information is sufficient for generating an 'initial guess' about the context and about objects in it. These context-based predictions are validated and refined with the gradual arrival of higher spatial frequencies (HSFs) (Bar, 2004). MPFC, medial prefrontal cortex; OFC, orbital frontal cortex; RSC, retrosplenial complex; PHC, parahippocampal cortex; IT, inferior temporal cortex. The arrows are unidirectional in the figure to emphasize the flow during the proposed analysis, but all these connections are bidirectional in nature.

Source: From Bar, 2009, by permission.

> knowledge. It also uses affective representations—prior expe-
> riences of how those external sensations have influenced inter-
> nal sensations from the body. (Barrett & Bar, 2009, p. 1325)

As processing proceeds, affect and content are here co-computed: intertwined throughout the process of settling upon a coherent, temporarily stable interpretation of the scene. To experience the world, this suggests, is not merely to settle upon a coherent understanding spanning many spatial and temporal scales. It is to settle upon a coherent, multilevel, affectively rich understanding. Such understandings are directly poised to entrain appropriate actions and responses. As we pass from context to context, our brains are constantly active attempting to prepare us to process and respond to each situation. That means activating a succession of 'mindsets' (Bar, 2009, p. 1238) using coarser cues to recruit more detailed guesses, and priming rich bodies of stored knowledge concerning the nature and shape of the opportunities for action and intervention that may be on offer.

The prediction-based account here makes contact, Bar (2009) notes, with two other major research traditions in recent cognitive science. The first concerns the automatic activation (by simple cues such as a word or facial expression) of stereotypes that impact behaviour (see, e.g., Bargh et al., 1996, and, for a rich retrospective, Bargh, 2006). Here, the link is straightforward: the rapid and automatic activation of broad sets of predictions provides a mechanism capable of subsuming these effects, along (as we have seen) with many others.

The second, which is a little less straightforward, concerns the so-called 'default network'. This is a set of neural regions said to be robustly active when we are not engaged in any specific task (when we are allowing our minds to wander freely, as it were) and whose activity is suppressed when attention is focused upon specific elements of the external environment (see Raichle & Snyder, 2007; Raichle et al., 2001). One possible interpretation of this 'resting state activity' profile is that it reflects the ongoing process of building and maintaining a kind of background, rolling 'mindset' preparing us for future bouts of action and choice. Such ongoing activity would reflect our overall world model and include our agent-specific sets of 'needs, goals, desires, context-sensitive conventions and attitudes' (Bar, 2009, p. 1239). This would provide the baseline sets of expectations that are themselves already active when we process even the roughest, coarsest sets of sensory cues from the external (or indeed the internal) environment. Such ongoing endogenous activity is functionally potent and has been invoked (to take a different example) to explain why subjects respond differently to the very same stimulus[19] in ways that are systematically linked to spontaneous pre-stimulus neuronal activity (Hesselmann et al., 2008). Putting all this together we arrive at a picture in which the brain is never passive, not even before the arrival of the coarse cues that drive ultra-rapid gist recognition. The 'resting state', thus construed, is anything but restful. Instead, it too reflects the ceaseless activity of the neural machinery whose compulsive prediction-mongering maintains us in constant yet ever-changing states of expectation.[20]

5.11   Celebrating Transience

PP depicts a complex but rapidly reconfigurable cognitive architecture in which transient coalitions of inner (and outer, see Part III) resources take shape and dissipate under the influence of multiple mechanisms of neural gain control. Such mechanisms implement 'neural gating' regimes in which the flow of influence between brain areas is dynamically alterable, and in which the relative influence of top-down and bottom-up information may be constantly varied according to estimations of our own sensory uncertainty.[21] The result is an architecture able to combine functionally differentiated circuits with highly context-sensitive (and 'interaction-dominated') modes of processing and response.

Underlying this potent combination are complex, acquired bodies of 'precision expectations' whose role is to alter the patterns of influence that obtain between various systemic elements. In the case of observing and understanding other agents, the most important role of these precision expectations is to down-weight proprioceptive prediction error, allowing multilevel prediction to unfold without directly entraining action. Such down-weighting may also provide a means of 'virtual exploration', allowing us to imagine non-actual scenarios as a guide to reasoning and choice.

Most importantly (and most generally) variable precision-weightings sculpt and shift the large-scale flow of information and influence. They thus provide a means for repeatedly reconfiguring patterns of effective connectivity, so that the 'simplest circuit diagram' underlying neural response is itself a moving target, constantly altering in response to rapidly processed cues, self-generated action, changing task demands, and alterations in our own bodily (e.g. interoceptive) states. The brain thus construed is a morphing, buzzing, dynamical system forever reconfiguring itself so as better to meet the incoming sensory barrage.

6

Beyond Fantasy

6.1 Expecting the World

If brains are probabilistic prediction machines, what does that suggest about the mind–world relation? Would it mean, as some have suggested, that we experience only a kind of 'virtual reality' or 'controlled hallucination'? Or are we, courtesy in part of all that prediction-heavy machinery, put more directly in touch with what might (opaquely and problematically) be called 'the world itself'? What is the relation, moreover, between what we *seem* to perceive, and the probabilistic inner economy? We seem to perceive a world of determinate objects and events, a world populated by dogs and dialogues, tables and tangos. Yet underlying those perceptions (if our stories are on track) are encodings of complex intertwined distributions of probabilities, including estimations of our own sensory uncertainty.

Approaching such questions without due regard for the importance of action and our own action repertoires would lead us very badly astray. For it is the guidance of world-engaging action, not the production of 'accurate' internal representations, that is the real purpose of the prediction error minimizing routine itself. This changes the way in which we should think about both the mind–world relation and the shape and reach of the probabilistic inner economy. Knowing our world must now fall into place as part of a larger systemic matrix whose pivot and core is embodied action and the kinds of fast, fluent response needed for adaptive success. Exploring PP in this larger setting is the task of the rest of this book.

6.2   Controlled Hallucinations and Virtual Realities

Chris Frith, in his wonderful (2007) book on the predictive, Bayesian brain, writes that:

> Our brains build models of the world and continuously modify these models on the basis of the signals that reach our senses. So, what we actually perceive are our brain's models of the world. They are not the world itself, but, for us, they are as good as. You could say that our perceptions are fantasies that coincide with reality. (Frith, 2007, p. 135)

This recalls the slogan that we met back in chapter 1, that 'perception is controlled hallucination'.[1] It is controlled hallucination, so the thought goes, because it involves using stored knowledge to generate a 'best multilevel top-down guess'. This is the guess, defined across multiple spatial and temporal scales, that best accounts for the incoming sensory signal. In just this vein, Jakob Hohwy writes that:

> One important and, probably, unfashionable thing that this theory tells us about the mind is that perception is indirect . . . what we perceive is the brain's best hypothesis, as embodied in a high-level generative model, about the causes in the outer world. (Hohwy, 2007a, p. 322)

In a later work, Hohwy describes this relationship using the notion of a 'virtual reality'. Conscious experience, Hohwy suggests:

> arises as the upshot of the brain's appetite for making the best sense it can of the current sensory input, even if that means weighting prior beliefs very highly. This fits with the idea that conscious experience is like a fantasy or virtual reality constructed to keep the sensory input at bay. It is different from the conscious experience that is truly a fantasy or virtual reality, which we enjoy in mental imagery or dreaming, because such experiences are not intended to keep sensory input at bay.

But it is nevertheless at one remove from the real world it is
representing. (Hohwy, 2013, pp. 137–138)

There is something right about all this and something (or so I shall
argue) profoundly wrong. What is right is that the accounts on offer
depict perception as *in some sense* an inferential process (as originally
proposed by Helmholtz, 1860; see also Rock, 1997): one that cannot help
but interpose *something* (the inference) between causes (such as sensory
stimulations or distal objects) and effects (percepts, experiences). Such
processes can go wrong, and the resulting states of fantasy, delusion,
and error have often be taken as compelling evidence for an 'indirect'
view (see, e.g., Jackson, 1977) of our perceptual contact with the world.

Moreover, the bulk of our normal, successful, daily perceptual
contact with the world—if the prediction machine models are on the
mark—is determined as much by our expectations concerning the
sensed scene as by the driving signals themselves. Even more strikingly, the forward flow of sensory information[2] here consists only in the
propagation of error signals, while richly contentful predictions flow
downwards and sideways, interacting in complex non-linear fashions
via the web of reciprocal connections. A key result of this pattern of
influence, as noted back in chapter 1, is much greater efficiency in the
use of neural encodings, because: 'An expected event does not need
to be explicitly represented or communicated to higher cortical areas
which have processed all of its relevant features prior to its occurrence'
(Bubic et al., 2010, p. 10). In ecologically normal circumstances, the
role of moment-by-moment perceptual contact with the world is thus
'merely' to check and when necessary correct the brain's best guessing
concerning what is out there. This is a challenging vision. It depicts our
(mostly non-conscious) expectations as a major source[3] of the contents of
our perceptions: contents that are, however, constantly being checked,
nuanced, and selected by prediction error signals sensitive to the evolving sensory input.

Despite all this, I think we should resist the claim that what we
perceive is best understood as a kind of hypothesis, model, fantasy,
or virtual reality. The temptation to think so, it seems to me, rests on
two mistakes. The first mistake is to conceive of inference-based routes
to adaptive response as introducing a kind of representational veil
between agent and world. Instead, it is only the structured probabilistic know-how distilled from prediction-driven learning that enables us
to *see through the veil of surface statistics* to the world of distal interacting
causes itself.[4] The second mistake is a failure to take sufficient account
of the role of action, and of organism-specific action repertoires, in both

selecting and constantly testing the ongoing stream of prediction itself. Rather than aiming to reveal some kind of action-neutral image of an objective realm, prediction-driven learning delivers a grip upon *affordances*: the possibilities for action and intervention that the environment makes available to a given agent.[5] Taken together, these points suggest that the probabilistic inference engine in the brain does not constitute a *barrier* between agent and world. Rather, it provides a unique tool for encountering a world of significance, populated by human affordances.

6.3   The Surprising Scope of Structured Probabilistic Learning

It is a natural consequence of prediction-based learning that the learner uncovers (when all is working correctly) the weave of interacting distal causes that—given her action repertoire and interests—characterizes the interact-able environment in which learning occurs. In this way prediction-based learning brings into view a structured external world, built of persisting (though often temporally evolving) objects, properties, and complex nested causal relations. As a result, 'the recognition system "inherits" the dynamics of the environment and can predict its sensory products accurately' (Kiebel, Daunizeau, & Friston, 2009, p. 7).

The full power and scope of hierarchical prediction-driven learning in active agents remains to be determined. It is limited by time, by data, and—perhaps most important—by the nature of the neural approximations involved. It is already clear, however, that tractable forms of hierarchical prediction-driven inference are able to uncover deep structure and even the kinds of abstract, high-level regularities that once seemed to cry out for the provision of large quantities of innate knowledge. The general principle at work here is by now familiar. We assume that the environment generates sensory signals by means of nested interacting (distal) causes and that the task of the perceptual system is to invert this structure by learning and applying a hierarchical generative model so as to predict the unfolding sensory stream. The flow of sensation (bound, as we saw, in constant circular causal commerce with the flow of action) is predictable just to the extent that there is spatial and temporal pattern in that flow. But such pattern is a function of properties and features of the world and of the needs, form, and activities of the agent. Thus, the pattern of sensory stimulation reaching the eye from, say, an observed football game is a function of the lighting conditions, the structured scene, and the head and eye movements of the observer. It is also a function of a variety of more abstract interacting features and forces, including the patterns of offense and defence characteristic of each team, the current state of play (there are strategic alterations when one team is far behind, for example), and so on. The beauty of the various waves of work in computational neuroscience and machine learning described in previous chapters is that they begin to show how to learn about such complex stacks of interacting causes without requiring (though they may readily exploit) extensive prior knowledge. This should fundamentally reconfigure our thinking about the debate between nativism and empiricism, and about the nature and possibility of 'carving nature at the joints'.

Thus consider Tenenbaum et al.'s (2011) account of Hierarchical Bayesian Models (HBMs).[6] An HBM is one in which multiple layers of processing are interanimated in an especially potent way, with each layer attempting to account for the patterns of activation (encoding some probability distribution of variables) at the level below. This, of course, is precisely the kind of architecture described, at the so-called 'process' level,[7] by hierarchical predictive coding. When such a system is up and running, mini-hypotheses at all the multiple levels settle into the mutually consistent set that best accounts for the incoming sensory signal, taking into account what the system has learnt and the present sensory evidence, including, we saw, the system's best estimation of the reliability of that evidence. In the Bayesian terms introduced in chapter 1, each layer is learning 'priors' on the level below. This whole multilayer process is tuned by the incoming sensory signals and implements the strategy known as 'empirical Bayes' allowing the system to acquire its own priors from the data, as learning proceeds.

Such multilayer learning has an additional benefit, in that it lends itself very naturally to the combination of data-driven statistical learning with the kinds of systematically productive knowledge representation long insisted upon by the opponents of early work in connectionism and artificial neural networks.[8] HBMs (unlike those early forms of connectionism) implement processing hierarchies suitable for representing complex, nested, structured relationships (for some nice discussion, see Friston, Mattout, & Kilner, 2011; Tani, 2007; and the discussion in 5.9). To see this in microcosm, recall SLICE*, the idealized stratiography program described in the Introduction. SLICE* effectively embodied a productive and systematic body of knowledge concerning geological causes. For SLICE* can produce the full set of geological outcomes allowed by the possible combinations and recombinations of hidden causes represented in its generative model.

By combining the use of multilayer generative models with powerful forms of statistical learning (indeed, using that learning to induce those very models), we thus secure many of the benefits of both early connectionist ('associationist') and more classical ('rule-based') approaches. Moreover, there is no need to fix on any single form of knowledge representation. Instead, each layer is free to use whatever form of representation best enables it to predict and (thus) account for the activity at the level below.[9] In many cases, what seems to emerge (as Tenenbaum et al. are at pains to stress) are structured, productive bodies of knowledge that are nonetheless acquired on the basis of multistage learning driven by statistical regularities visible in the raw training data. Early learning here induces overarching expectations (e.g., very broad expectations concerning what kind of things matter most for successful categorization within a given domain). Such broad expectations then constrain later learning, reducing the hypothesis space and enabling effective learning of specific cases.

Using such routines, HBMs have recently been shown capable of learning the deep organizing principles for many domains, on the basis of essentially raw data. Such systems have learnt, for example, about the so-called 'shape bias' according to which items that fall into the same object-category (like cranes, balls, and toasters) tend to have the same shape: a bias that does not apply to substance categories such as gold, chocolate, or jelly (Kemp et al., 2007). They have also learnt about the kind of grammar (context-free or regular) that will best account for the patterns in a corpus of child-directed speech (Perfors et al., 2006), about the correct parsing into words of an unsegmented speech stream (Goldwater, Griffiths, & Johnson, 2009), and generally about the shape of causal relations in many different domains (e.g., diseases cause symptoms, and not vice versa, Mansinghka et al., 2006). Recent work has also shown how brand new categories, defined by new causal schemas, can be spawned when assimilation to an existing category would require an overly complex—hence effectively 'ad hoc'—mapping (Griffiths, Sanborn, et al., 2008). Such approaches have also been shown (Goodman et al., 2011) to be capable of rapidly learning highly abstract domain-general principles, such as a general understanding of causality, by pooling evidence obtained across a wide range of cases. Taken together, this work demonstrates the unexpected power of learning using HBMs.[10] Such approaches allow systems to infer the high-level structure specific to a domain, and even the high-level structures governing multiple domains, by exposing an apt multilevel system to raw data.

An important point to notice is that HBMs here allow the learner to acquire the schematic relations characteristic of a domain before 'filling in' the details concerning individual exemplars. In this way, for example:

> a hierarchical Bayesian model of grammar induction may be able to explain how a child becomes confident about some property of a grammar even though most of the individual sentences that support this conclusion are poorly understood. (Kemp et al., 2007, p. 318)

Similarly, the shape bias for objects may be learnt before learning the names of any of the individual objects. The bias emerges early as the best high-level schema, and once in place it enables rapid learning about specific exemplars falling into that group. This is possible in cases where 'a child has access to a large number of . . . noisy observations [such that] any individual observation may be difficult to interpret but taken together they may provide strong support for a general conclusion' (Kemp et al., 2007, p. 318). Thus, the authors continue, one might have sufficient evidence to suggest that visual objects tend to be 'cohesive, bounded, and rigid (cf. Spelke, 1990)' before forming any ideas about individual concrete objects such as balls, discs, stuffed toys, and so on.

This is, of course, precisely the kind of early learning pattern that is easily mistaken as evidence of the influence of innate knowledge about the world. The mistake is natural since the high-level knowledge is tailored to the domain and allows subsequent learning to proceed much more easily and fluently than might otherwise be expected. But instead of thus relying on rich bodies of innate knowledge, HBM-style learners are capable of inducing such abstract structuring knowledge from the data. The central trick, as we have seen, is to use the data itself in a kind of multistage manner. First, the data is used to learn priors that encode expectations concerning the large-scale shape of the domain (what Tenenbaum et al., 2011, call the 'form of structure' within the domain). Suitably scaffolded by this structure of large-scale (relatively abstract) expectations, learning about more detailed regularities becomes possible. In this way, HBMs actively unearth the abstract structural expectations that enable them to use raw data to learn finer and finer grained models (supporting finer grained sets of expectations).

Such systems—like PP systems more generally—are also able to induce their own so-called 'hyperpriors' from the data. Hyperpriors (here used interchangeably with 'overhypotheses', see Kemp et al., 2007) are essentially 'priors upon priors' embodying systemic expectations concerning very abstract (at times almost 'Kantian') features of the world. For example, one highly abstract hyperprior might demand that each set of multimodal sensory inputs has a single best explanation. This would enforce a single peak for the probabilistic distributions consequent upon sensory stimulation, so that we always saw the world as being in one determinate state or another, rather than (say) as a superposition of equiprobable states. Such a hugely abstract hyperprior might be a good candidate for innate specification. But it might equally well be left to early learning, since the need to use sensory input to drive actions, and the physical impossibility of acting in two very different ways at once, could conceivably[11] drive an HBM to extract even this as a general principle governing inference.

HBMs, and the various process models (including PP) that might implement them, absolve the Bayesian theorist of the apparent sin of needing to set the right priors in advance of successful learning. Instead, in the manner of empirical Bayes, a multilayer system can learn its own priors from the data. This also delivers maximal flexibility. For although it is now easy to build abstract domain-structure reflecting knowledge (in the form of various hyperpriors) into the system, it is also possible for the system to acquire such knowledge, and to acquire it in advance of the more detailed learning that it both streamlines and makes possible. Innate knowledge thus conceived remains partially 'developmentally open' in that aspects of it can be smoothed and refined, or even completely undone, by data-driven learning using the same multilayer process (for some nice discussion, see Scholl, 2005).

Of course, as King Lear famously commented, 'nothing will come of nothing', and, as hinted above, even the most slimline learning system must always start with some set of biases.[12] More important, our basic evolved structure (gross neuroanatomy, bodily morphology, etc.) may itself be regarded as a particularly concrete set of inbuilt (embodied) biases that form part of our overall 'model' of the world (see Friston, 2011b, 2012c, and discussion in 8.10). Nonetheless, multilayer Bayesian systems have proven capable of acquiring abstract, domain-specific principles without building in many of the rather specific kinds of knowledge (e.g., about the importance of shape for learning about material objects) that were previously thought essential for fluent learning in different domains. Such systems can acquire, sometimes from raw sensory data, knowledge of quite abstract organizing principles—principles that then allow them to make increasingly systematic sense of that very data.

6.4   Ready for Action

The discussion in 6.3 is, however, radically incomplete. It is radically incomplete because most current work on HBMs treats knowing the world on the model of passive perception. But perception and action, as constructed using the PP schema, were seen to be both co-determined and co-determining (see chapters 2, 4 and 5 above). In these broader frameworks, what we do depends upon what we perceive, and what we perceive is constantly conditioned by what we do. This results in the rather specific forms of circular causality described in 2.6 and in chapter 4. Here, high-level predictions entrain actions that both test and confirm the predictions, and that help sculpt the sensory flows that recruit new high-level predictions (and so on, in a rolling cycle of expectation, sensory stimulation, and action).

How should we think of this rolling cycle? The wrong model, it seems to me, would be to depict the rolling cycle as a slightly fancy (because circular) version of the classical sense-think-act cycle in which sensory stimulation must be fully processed, and a structured world of external objects revealed, before actions are selected, planned, and (ultimately) executed. Such a 'sense-think-act' vision has informed much work in cognitive psychology and cognitive science. It is nicely described (and then roundly rejected) by Cisek (2007) who notes that:

> According to this view, the perceptual system first collects sensory information to build an internal descriptive representation of objects in the external world (Marr 1982). Next, this information is used along with representations of current needs and memories of past experience to make judgments and decide upon a course of action (Newell & Simon 1972; Johnson-Laird 1988; Shafir & Tversky 1995). The resulting plan is then used to generate a desired trajectory for movement, which is finally realized through muscular contraction (Miller et al. 1960; Keele 1968). In other words, the brain first builds knowledge about the world using representations which are independent of actions, and this knowledge is later used to make decisions, compute an action plan and finally execute a movement. (Cisek, 2007, p. 1585)

There are many reasons to be wary of such a model (see Clark, 1997; Pfeifer & Bongard, 2006, and further discussion in Part III following). But among the most compelling is the need to be ready to respond fluently to unfolding—and potentially rapidly changing—situations. Such readiness seems ecologically mandated for creatures who must be poised to grasp opportunities and avoid dangers at short notice, and who may be acting in competition with others, including (at times) their own conspecifics. Creatures equipped with ever-active, predictive brains are, of course, already (quite literally) 'ahead of the game', as brains like that are—as we have seen—constantly guessing the ongoing stream of sensory input, including the inputs that should result from their own next actions and worldly interventions. But the story does not end there.

One powerful strategy, which combines very neatly (or so I shall argue) with the image of the ever-active predictive brain, involves rethinking the classical sense-think-act cycle as a kind of mosaic: a mosaic in which each shard combines elements of (what might classically be thought of as) sensing and thinking with associated prescriptions for action. At the heart of this mosaic vision (whose roots lie in the active vision paradigm, see Ballard, 1991; Churchland et al., 1994) lies the simultaneous computation of multiple probabilistically infected 'affordances': multiple possibilities for organism-salient action and intervention.

The flagship statement of this view is the 'affordance competition hypothesis' (Cisek, 2007; Cisek & Kalaska, 2010). Such a view is motivated by a large set of otherwise anomalous neurophysiological data (for a full review, see Cisek & Kalaska, 2010) including:

1. The chronic failure to find inner representations of the world of the kind predicted by a full 'passive reconstruction' model in which the goal of, for example, visual processing is to generate a single rich, unified, action-neutral representation of the scene apt for subsequent use in planning and decision-making.
2. The pervasive effects of attentional modulation, resulting in the enhancement and suppression of different aspects of ongoing neural activity according to task and context (so that neural response seems geared to current behavioural needs rather than to the construction of an action-neutral encoding of the state of the external world).
3. Increasing evidence that neural populations involved in ongoing planning and decision-making are also involved in motor control, and (more generally) that regional cortical responses fail to respect the classical theoretical divisions between perception, cognition (e.g., reasoning, planning, and deciding), and motor control.

Thus, large bodies of work in visual neuroscience suggest that multiple different bodies of information are continuously computed in parallel and partially integrated when (but only when and to whatever extent) some current action or response demands. A familiar example here is the separation of visual information into distinct (though overlapping) ventral and dorsal streams: streams linked, it is increasingly clear, by ongoing, task-sensitive, patterns of informational exchange (see, e.g.,

Milner & Goodale, 1995, 2006; Schenk & McIntosh, 2010; Ungerleider & Mishkin, 1982). Within the neural economy, such fractionation and partiality seems to be the rule, not the exception, characterizing processing within each stream as well as between the streams, and in other parts of the brain (see, e.g., Felleman & Van Essen, 1991; Stein, 1992).

There is also ample evidence for the pervasive effects of attention, reflecting context and task, as well as internal context in the form of interoceptive states such as hunger and boredom. Such effects have been shown to modulate neural responses at every level of the cortical hierarchy and in some sub-cortical (e.g., thalamic) areas too (Boynton, 2005; Ito & Gilbert, 1999; O'Connor et al., 2002; O'Craven et al., 1997; Treue, 2001).

Finally, increasing and highly suggestive evidence challenges the view of core cognitive capacities (such as planning and deciding) as neurophysiologically distinct from the circuitry of sensorimotor control. For example, decisions concerning eye movements and the execution of eye movements recruit highly overlapping circuits in lateral intraparietal area (LIP), frontal eye fields (FEF), and the superior colliculus—the latter being, as Cisek and Kalaska (2011, p. 274) nicely note, 'a brainstem structure that is just two synapses away from the motor neurons that move the eye' (for these results, see Coe et al., 2002; Doris & Glimcher, 2004; and Thevarajah et al., 2009, respectively). In the same vein, a perceptual decision task (one in which the decision is reported by an arm movement) revealed marked responses within premotor cortex corresponding to the process of deciding upon a response (Romo et al., 2004). Quite generally, wherever a decision is to be reported by (or otherwise invokes) some motor action, there looks to be an entwining of perceptuo-motor processing and decision-making, leading Cisek and Kalaska to suggest that 'decisions, at least those reported through actions, are made within the same sensorimotor circuits that are responsible for planning and executing the associated action' (Cisek & Kalaska, 2011, p. 274). In cortical associative regions such as posterior parietal cortex (PPC), Cisek and Kalaska go on to argue, activity does not seem in any way to respect the traditional divisions between perception, cognition, and action. Instead we find neuronal populations that trade in shifting and context-responsive combinations of perceiving, deciding, and acting, and in which even single cells may participate in many such functions (Andersen & Buneo, 2003).

Further support for such a view is provided by Selen et al. (2012). In this study subjects were shown a display of moving dots (a 'dynamic random dot display') and asked to decide whether the dots were mostly moving to the left or to the right. Such decisions are known to depend very sensitively upon both the coherence and the duration of the motion of the dots, and the experimenters varied these parameters while probing the subjects' decision states by requiring decisions at unpredictable times after stimulus onset. The subjects' task was to respond as soon as the display stopped and to do so by means of a motor response (moving a handle to a target). At that time, a small perturbation was applied to the subject's elbow, causing a stretch reflex response which was measured using electromyography (EMG), a technique that records the electrical potentials associated with muscular activity. This provided a quantifiable measure of the state of the motor response effector (the arm) at the time of the probe. Importantly, the decision task itself here is remarkably well-behaved, so that subjects' choices are tightly linked to the fine details of the evolving evidence (the precise mixes of coherence and duration displayed by the moving dots). The experimenters showed that the changing muscular reflex gains and the decision variable (representing the integrated effects of coherence and duration) co-evolved in a way quite incompatible with classical 'sequential flow' models. In sequential flow models the motor action reporting a decision is taken to be independent from, and computed subsequent upon, the decision itself. By contrast, Selen et al. found that the reflex gains at each moment reflected the evolving decision state itself. The results fitted very neatly with the notion (more on which below) of an *affordance competition* in which both possible motor responses are being simultaneously prepared, and in which 'the human brain does not wait for a decision to be completed before recruiting the motor system but instead passes partial information to prepare in a graded fashion for a probable action outcome' (Selen et al., 2012, p. 2277). The reflex gains, that is to say, 'do not simply reflect the outcome of the decision but instead are privy to the brain's deliberations as a decision is being formed' (p. 2284).

The presence of continuous flow from the decision process to the motor system makes sense if we assume that the overall goal is to be as pro-actively ready as possible to perform whichever response the evolving evidence suggests. Such pro-active readiness, to be genuinely useful, must necessarily be multiple and graded. It must allow many possible responses to be simultaneously partially prepared, to degrees dependent upon the current balance of evidence—including estimations of our own sensory uncertainty—as more and more information is acquired (for a similar story applied to phonological choice, see Spivey et al., 2005, see also Spivey et al., 2008).

In a revealing closing comment, Selen et al. speculate that this may flow not simply from the pragmatic advantages of such action-readiness but also from a 'deeper connection between the brain's apparatus for evaluating evidence and the control of motor functions', adding that 'the flow demonstrated in our experiment may be part of a larger bidi-rectional interplay between the brain processes that underlie deci-sion making and motor control' (p. 2285). Similarly, Cisek and Kalaska comment that:

> The distinctions among perceptual, cognitive, and motor systems may not reflect the natural categories of neural com-putations that underlie sensory-guided behavior [and that] the framework of serial information processing may not be the optimal blueprint for the global functional architecture of the brain. (Cisek & Kalaska, 2010, p. 275)

As an alternative blueprint, Cisek and Kalaska explore the 'Affordance Competition Hypothesis' (introduced by Cisek, 2007) according to which:

> the brain processes sensory information to specify, in paral-lel, several potential actions that are currently available. These potential actions compete against each other for further pro-cessing, while information is collected to bias this competition until a single response is selected (Cisek, 2007, p. 1585)

The idea here is that the brain is constantly computing—partially and in parallel—a large set of possible actions and that such partial, paral-lel, ongoing computations involve neural encodings that fail to respect familiar distinctions between perceiving, cognizing, and acting. The reason for this is that the neural representations involved are, as Cisek and Kalaska (2011, p. 279) put it, 'pragmatic' insofar as 'they are adapted to produce good control as opposed to producing accurate descriptions of the sensory environment or a motor plan'. All this makes good eco-logical sense, allowing time-pressed animals to partially 'pre-compute' multiple possible actions, any one of which can then be selected and deployed at short notice and with minimal further processing.

Large bodies of neurophysiological data lend support to such a view. For example, Hoshi and Tanji (2007) found activity in monkey premotor cortex correlated with the potential movements of either hand in a bimanual reaching response task in which the monkey had to wait upon a cue signalling which hand to use (see also Cisek & Kalaska, 2005). Similar results have been obtained for the preparation of visual saccades (Powell & Goldberg, 2000) and using behavioural and lesion studies of reaching behaviour in human subjects (Castiello, 1999; Humphreys & Riddoch, 2000). In addition, as we saw in the previ-ous section, there is intriguing evidence that 'decisions about actions emerge within the same populations of cells that define the physical properties of those actions and guide their execution' (Cisek & Kalaska, 2011, p. 282).

The picture that here emerges is one of neural encodings that are *fundamentally* in the business of action control. Such encodings represent how the world is in ways that are entwined, at multiple levels, with information about how to act upon the world. Many such 'action-oriented' (see Clark, 1997) takes upon the world are being prepared, the Affordance Competition hypothesis suggests, at every moment, although only a few make it beyond the threshold for control of actual motor response.[13]

6.5   Implementing Affordance Competition

All of these insights are neatly accommodated, or so I shall now suggest, using the distinctive resources of the predictive processing model of neural organization. To do so, we leverage three key properties of the predictive processing framework. The first concerns the probabilistic nature of the representations that support perception and action. The second concerns the computational intimacy of perception, cognition, and action. The third concerns the distinctive forms of circular causal interaction between organism and environment that result. Affordance competition then emerges as a natural consequence of probabilistic action-oriented prediction.

Recall (1.12) that the probabilistic Bayesian brain encodes conditional probability density functions, reflecting the relative probability of some state of affairs given the available information. At every level, then, the underlying form of representation remains thoroughly probabilistic, encoding a series of deeply intertwined bets concerning what is 'out there' and (our current focus) how best to act. Multiple competing possibilities for action are thus constantly being computed, though only winning (high precision) proprioceptive predictions get to act as motor commands as such.

In the model of action suggested by Friston and colleagues (see chapters 4 and 5), high precision proprioceptive prediction errors bring about motor actions. The very same neural populations that would be involved (when proprioceptive prediction error is given high precision) in the generation of action may thus be deployed 'offline' (again, see chapter 5) as a means of generating motor simulations suitable for reasoning, choice, and planning. This provides a compelling account of the many overlaps between the neural populations implicated in the control of action and those involved in reasoning, planning, and imagination. In planning, however, we must attenuate or inhibit the descending prediction errors that would normally (on the active inference model) drive our muscles. This effectively insulates us from the world allowing us to use hierarchical generative models to predict in a counterfactual ('what if') mode. Issues concerning sensory attenuation will also loom large (as we will see in chapter 7) in the context of self-made acts and attributions of agency.

Finally, and perhaps most important, action (recall chapter 4) now involves a potent form of circular causality in which the representations that are recruited to account for current sensory stimulations simultaneously determine actions that result in new patterns of sensory stimulation, that recruit new motor responses, and so on. This means that we confront—exactly as the Affordance Competition hypothesis suggests—an economy in which multiple competing probabilistic bets are constantly being made, within what is essentially a circularly causal perception-action machine.

PP thus implements the distinctive circular dynamics described by Cisek and Kalaska using a famous quote from the American pragmatist John Dewey. Dewey rejects the 'passive' model of stimuli evoking responses in favour of an active and circular model in which 'the motor response determines the stimulus, just as truly as sensory stimulus determines movement' (Dewey, 1896, p. 363). This idea is nicely clarified in another quote from elsewhere in the same article, where Dewey writes of seeing as an 'unbroken act' which:

> is as experienced no more mere sensation than it is mere motion (though the onlooker or psychological observer can interpret it into sensation and movement), it is in no sense the sensation which stimulates the reaching; we have, as already sufficiently indicated, only the serial steps in a coordination of *acts*. But now take a child who, upon reaching for bright light (that is, exercising the seeing-reaching coordination) has sometimes had a delightful exercise, sometimes found something good to eat and sometimes burned himself. *Now the response is not only uncertain, but the stimulus is equally uncertain; one is uncertain only so far as the other is.* The real problem may be equally well stated as either to discover the right stimulus, to constitute the stimulus, or to discover, to constitute, the response. (Dewey, 1896, p. 367, emphasis in original)

Dewey's descriptions elegantly prefigure the complex interplay, highlighted by predictive processing, between altering our predictions to fit the evidence ('perception') and seeking out the evidence to fit our predictions ('action'). But it also suggests (rightly, I think) that we really ought not to conceive these, within the predictive processing framework, as competing strategies.[14] Rather, the two strands constantly work hand in hand to reveal a world that is, in a certain sense, constituted in action. For actions now disclose evidence that leads to more actions, and our experience of the world is constituted by this ongoing cycle.

These circular causal loops play two, often overlapping, roles. One role is, of course, pragmatic. A high-level perceptual state as of an oncoming vehicle on the wrong side of the road will recruit motor commands that rapidly move the steering wheel, resulting in new perceptual states that (according to their content) must fine-tune, or attempt to negate the selected course of action. The other role is epistemic. Movements of the head and eyes are rapidly deployed to test and confirm the hypothesis (oncoming vehicle on collision course) itself. Only hypotheses able to withstand such automatically generated tests will be maintained and strengthened (see Friston, Adams, et al., 2012). In this way we sample the world so as to minimize uncertainty about our own predictions.

To see how this looks in practice, reflect that early, ambiguous flurries of sensory stimulation will generate prediction errors that recruit multiple competing perceptual hypotheses. These hypotheses are not, however, action-neutral. Instead, each hypothesis already speaks to the two forms of action just described. Each hypothesis, that is to say, includes information about how to act upon the world so as to confirm or disconfirm the hypothesis, and (courtesy of the context-reflecting bodies of precision expectations) about how to behave in the world supposing the hypothesis proves correct. Subject to various constraints of task and timing, a good strategy will be to allow the most promising hypothesis to launch some cheap epistemic action (such as a rapid sequence of saccades) able to confirm or disconfirm the hypothesis. As such cycles unfold, perceiving will be intimately bound up with various forms of motor planning and action selection, resulting in the distinctive neurophysiological signatures described earlier.

Spivey (2007) paints a rich picture of such continuous circular causal webs and depicts their dynamics as one of constant journeying towards ever-changing, never-quite reached stable end-points. By way of illustration, Spivey asks us to consider the interactions between eye movements (motor productions, albeit on a fast, small, scale) and the cognitive processes that might be said—in some ways misleadingly, as we are about to see—to guide them. In real-world settings, Spivey notes:

> the brain does not achieve a stable percept, then make an eye movement, then achieve another stable percept, then make another eye movement, and so on. The eyes often move during the process of attempting to achieve a stable percept. This means that before perception can finish settling into a stable state, oculomotor output changes the perceptual input by placing new and different information on the foveas. (Spivey, 2007, p. 137)

Visual perception is thus constantly conditioned by visuomotor action, and visuomotor action is constantly conditioned by visual perception. As far as successful behaviour is concerned, what counts are the perceptuomotor trajectories that result. It is these trajectories, not the stability or even the veracity of the percepts spun off along the way, that constitute agentive behaviour and that determine the success or failure of our attempts to engage the world.

In sum, perceptuomotor trajectories emerge and are maintained within circular causal webs. Within those webs, estimated uncertainty and the demands of action mediate strong forms of affordance competition. This is because estimations of precision, and the pragmatic and epistemic actions they imply, function (Cisek & Kalaska, 2011, p. 282) to 'enhance the most behaviorally salient information in the environment to bias sensorimotor systems towards the most behaviorally relevant possible actions'. Precision estimations position a hypothesis to gain control of behaviour, at which point it must become self-fuelling (engaging confirmatory circular causal commerce) or perish. Precision estimations, working in the context of lateral (within level) inhibition among competing hypotheses, position a hypothesis to gain control of behaviour, at which point it must become self-fuelling (engaging confirmatory circular causal commerce) or perish. All this delivers, I suggest, a particularly clear and vibrant sense in which many neural representations must be 'pragmatic', as well as establishing a larger framework in which affordance competition emerges as a natural consequence of probabilistic action-oriented prediction.

6.6   Interaction-Based Joints in Nature

All this has implications for the debates concerning the nature of our perceptual contact with the world. Probabilistic prediction-driven learning provides a mechanism able (when all is going well) to see past superficial noise and ambiguity in the sensory signal, revealing the shape of the distal realm itself. In that (restricted) sense it provides a powerful mechanism for 'carving nature at the joints'. But many of those joints, it now seems clear, are *interaction-based*: they are defined with respect to an active organism characterized by specific needs and possibilities for action and intervention. Our perceptual 'take' on the world is thus constantly conditioned by our own 'action repertoire' (König et al., 2013) in interaction with our needs, projects, and opportunities.

This simple (but profound) fact results in large reductions of computational complexity by helping to select, at any given moment, what features to process, and what things to try to predict. From the huge space of possible ways of parsing the world given the impinging energetic flux, our brains try to predict the patterns that serve our needs and that fit our action repertoires. This may well result (as we will see in detail in chapter 8) in the use of simple models whose power resides precisely in their failing to encode every detail and nuance present in the sensory array. This is not a barrier to true contact with the world—rather, it is a prerequisite for it. For knowing the world, in the only sense that can matter to an evolved organism, means being able to act in that world: being able to respond quickly and efficiently to salient environmental opportunities.

Among the many things that brains like ours need to predict, an important subset concerns the sensory consequences of our own actions. Once this is taken on board, the intimacy of sensory and motor processing is, as König et al. (2013) note, unsurprising. Moreover, the sensory consequences of our own actions are deeply informed by basic facts about our embodiment, such as our size, the placement of sensors and the reach of effectors, and so on. Such influence is dramatically displayed by an analysis (Betsch et al., 2004; Einhäuser et al., 2009) of the statistical structure of the visual inputs obtained (using a head-mounted camera) from the perspective of a freely moving cat exploring some outdoor environments. The same gross external realm, when explored (see Figure 6.1) from the perspective of the cat, produced sequences of natural images whose statistical structure included a predominance of horizontal contours, altered spatial distribution of contrast, and various effects attributable to the surprising speed of cat head movements.

The statistics of natural scenes, as those scenes are encountered in action by a given type of animal, also become written in the patterns of cortical activity (both spontaneous and evoked) that the animal displays. This has been neatly demonstrated by Berkes et al. (2011) in work on the V1 activity of awake ferrets. This activity was analyzed at various stages during the development of the ferrets, and under three

FIGURE 6.1   The World from a Cat's Perspective
(a) The cat is exploring an outside park area on one of its walks. The cable, twisted with the leash, connects to the VCR in the backpack. (b–e) Four typical pictures taken from the videos are shown. (b) The horizon divides the image into a bright, low-contrast upper image region (sky) and a darker, lower region of high contrast (stones). (c) The cat's view of the pond shows richly detailed plant structures and low-contrast water regions. (d) On close inspection by the cat, blades of grass are evenly spread over the entire image. (e) During a walk in the nearby forest the upper half is dominated by dark, vertically oriented trees in front of the bright sky. The lower half of the image representing the forest floor consists of many objects (branches, leaves) arranged in all possible orientations.

Source: Betsch et al. 2004.

conditions: viewing movies of natural scenes, in darkness, and viewing movies of unnatural scenes. The study found that the similarity between spontaneous and evoked response increased dramatically with age, but *only* in respect of responses evoked by natural scenes. This pattern of results is best explained, the authors argue, by a 'progressive adaptation of internal models to the statistics of natural stimuli at the neural level' (Berkes et al., 2011, p. 83). In other words, the ferret's spontaneous neural activity patterns slowly adapt, over developmental time, to reflect the 'prior expectations of [an] internal model' (p. 87).

Adopting the Bayesian perspective, the authors suggest that spontaneous cortical activity reflects the multilevel structure of prior expectations that constitute the inner model, and stimulus-evoked activity the posterior probability—the probability that some specific combination of environmental causes gave rise to the sensory input, hence the animal's 'best guess' at the current state of the world. This diagnosis was reinforced by tests on mature ferrets exposed to movies of unnatural scenes, where much greater divergences between spontaneous and evoked activity were recorded. Spontaneous cortical activity, Berkes et al. conclude, here shows all the hallmarks of a gradually adapting internal model of the ferret's world.

How might such a model be used to guide action? Within PP, selection from within the action repertoire of a given agent is accomplished by context- and task-reflecting assignments of precision. Such assignments control synaptic gain according to estimations of the uncertainty of sensory signals. In particular (see Friston, Daunizeau, Kilner, & Kiebel, 2010, and discussion in chapters 4 and 5) the precision weighting of proprioceptive prediction error is thought to implement a kind of 'motor attention' that is necessarily involved in the preparation of any motor action. Attention thus acts to 'boost the gain of proprioceptive channels during motor preparation' (Brown, Friston, & Bestmann, 2011, p. 2). At the same time, it is the precision-weighting upon all aspects of sensory prediction error that together determines which sensorimotor loops win the competition for the control of behaviour. The upshot, exactly in line with the Affordance Competition hypothesis, is to select one among the various behavioural responses already suggested (hence partially activated) by current context and organismic state. Mechanisms that implement the precision-weighting of proprioceptive prediction error thus serve to select 'salient representations that have affordance [i.e.] sensorimotor representations that predict both perceptual and behavioural consequences' (Friston, Shiner, et al., 2012, p. 2). What we do is determined, this model suggests, by precise (highly weighted) prediction errors that help select among (while simultaneously responding to) competing higher level hypotheses, each of which implies a whole swathe of sensory and motor predictions. Such high-level hypotheses are intrinsically affordance-laden: they represent both how the world is and how we might act in that very world (they are thus a species of what Millikan (1996) has called 'Pushmi-pullyu representations': states having both descriptive and imperative contents). Perception, by recruiting salient affordance-laden representations, puts us in touch with a world already parsed for action and intervention.

Plausibly, it is only *because* the world we encounter must be parsed for action and intervention that we encounter, in experience, a relatively unambiguous, determinate world at all. Subtract the need for action and the broadly Bayesian framework can seem quite at odds with the phenomenal facts about conscious perceptual experience: our world, it might be said, does not look as if it is encoded as an intertwined set of probability density distributions. Instead, it looks unitary and, on a clear day, unambiguous. In the context of an active world-engaging system, however, such an outcome makes adaptive sense. For the point of all that probabilistic betting is to drive action and decision, and action and decision lack the luxury of being able to keep all options indefinitely alive. Instead, affordance competition must be repeatedly resolved and actions selected. Precision-weighted prediction error provides a tool for biasing processing by selecting the most salient sensorimotor representations—the ones most apt to drive behaviour and response.

Biological systems, as mentioned earlier, may be informed by a variety of learned or innate 'hyperpriors' concerning the general nature of the world. One such hyperprior might be that the world is usually in one determinate state or another. To implement this, the brain might use a form of probabilistic representation in which, despite the presence of continual competition, each distribution has a single peak (meaning that each overall sensory state has a single best explanation). One fundamental reason that our brains appear only to entertain unimodal (single peak) posterior beliefs may thus be that—at the end of the day—these beliefs are in the game of informing action and behaviour, and we can only do one thing at one time. The use of such a representational form would amount to the deployment of an implicit formal hyperprior[15] (formal because it concerns the form of the probabilistic representation itself) to the effect that our uncertainty can be described using such a unimodal probability distribution. Such a prior makes adaptive sense, given the kinds of brute fact about action mentioned above (e.g., we can only perform one action at a time, choosing to grasp the pen for writing or for throwing, but not both at once).

6.7   *Evidentiary Boundaries and the Ambiguous Appeal to Inference*

Prediction error minimization takes place behind what Hohwy (2013, 2014) describes as an 'evidentiary boundary.' Our agentive access to the world, he argues, is bounded by the prediction error minimizing routine as it is applied to the flow of interoceptive, exteroceptive, and proprioceptive signals. Such consdierations lead Hohwy to depict PP as imposing a firm and neurocentric boundary upon the cognizing mind. Thus we read that:

> PEM should make us resist conceptions of [the mind-world] relation on which the mind is in some fundamental way porous to the world, or viewed as embodied, extended or enactive. Instead, the mind appears to be secluded from the world, it seems to be more neurocentrically skull-bound than embodied or extended, and action itself is more an inferential process on sensory input than enactive coupling with the body and environment. (Hohwy 2014, p.1)

Howhy (2013, pp. 219–221, 2014) offers a variety of interlocking considerations meant to support this vision of the secluded, neurocentric mind. At the heart of them all lies the observation that prediction error minimizing routines are defined over sensory signals so that "from inside the skull the brain has to infer the hidden causes of its sensory input" (Hohwy 2013, p.220). The guiding theme is thus one of inferential seclusion—the mind, it is argued, is that which operates behind the veil of transduced sensory information, inferring complex 'hidden causes' as the best explanation of changing (and partially self-induced) patterns of sensory stimulation. By contrast, Hohwy suggests:

> Views of mind and cognition that emphasize openness, embodiment, and active extension into the environment seem to be biased against this inferential conception of the mind. (Hohwy 2014, p.5)

But embodied views are not, of course, biased against the (surely unassailable) claim that *something* important is being done by the brain when agents engage their worlds in the kinds of ways distinctive of flexible, adaptive, intelligent response. So where might the putative tension lie? It lies principally in the notion, repeatedly stressed by Hohwy, that what the brain does is best construed as a form of inference. But here we need to be very careful indeed. For the notion of inference in play here is actually far less demanding than it initially appears.

To see this, consider what was at issue in early debates concerning vision and the embodied mind. Here, according to a typical review paper published in the mid-1990's:

> The key insight . . . is that the task of vision is not to build rich inner models of a surrounding 3-D reality, but rather to use visual information efficiently and cheaply in the service of real-world, real-time action. (Clark 1999, p. 345)

One alternative—mostly pursued by research programs in 'ecolog-ical psychology'—is to use sensing as a channel allowing us to lock-on to simple invariants in the sensory flow.[16] Used in this way, sensing delivers an action-based *grip* upon the world, rather than an action-neutral reconstruction apt for detached reasoning. Such a grip may intrinsically involve organismic action as when—to take the famous example from McBeath and Shaffer (1995)—the baseball outfielder runs so as to keep the image of the ball stationary on the retina. By thus act-ing in ways that continuously cancel out any apparent optical accelera-tion, the outfielder ensures (see Fink, Foo, and Warren 2009) that she will meet the ball where it descends to the pitch. In such cases, behav-ioural success is not the outcome of reasoning defined over a kind of inner replica of the external world. Rather, it is the outcome of percep-tion/action cycles that operate by keeping sensory stimulations within certain bounds.

Such cases will occupy us further in chapter 8. What mat-ters for present purposes is that these kinds of strategy are *radically non-reconstructive*. They do not use sensing, moment-by-moment, to build an inner model that recapitulates the structure and richness of the real-world, and that is thus able to stand-in for that world for the purposes of planning, reasoning, and the guidance of action. Instead, here-and-now behaviour is enabled by using sensing in the special way described above—as a channel to enable the organism to co-ordinate its behaviours with select aspects of the distal environment.

Such non-reconstructive roles for perception are often cast in bald opposition to the inferential, secluded vision. Thus Anderson (2014) describes non-reconstructive approaches as an alternative to main-stream (inferential, reconstructive) approaches in which perception is cast as analogous to scientific inference and in which:

> from incomplete and fragmentary data, one generates hypoth-eses (or models) for the true nature of the world, which are then tested against and modified in light of further incoming sensory stimulation. (Anderson 2014, p. 164)

Such traditional approaches, Anderson continues, depict cognition as "post-perceptual. . . . representation-rich, and deeply decoupled from the environment".

Non-reconstructive accounts of the role of sensing suggest a viable alternative and one that, Anderson suggests, significantly alters our understanding of our own epistemic situation. Instead of engaging the world on the basis of a rich inner model constructed behind the closed doors of sensing, non-reconstructive solutions show how to achieve behavioural goals by maintaining a delicate dance between sensing and action. One signature of this kind of grip-based non-reconstructive dance is that it suggests a potent reversal of our ordinary way of thinking about the relations between perception and action. Instead of seeing perception as the control of action, it becomes fruitful to think of action as the control of perception (Powers 1973, Powers et al., 2011). Thus (re)-conceived, the problem becomes "not ... choosing the right response in light of a given stimulus but ... choosing the right stimulus in light of a given goal" (Anderson, 2014, p. 182–3).

But, as Hohwy himself correctly notes, there is absolutely nothing in the PP vision that conflicts either with this vision of actions whose role is to harvest perceptions or (more generally) with the idea of non-reconstructive strategies as one means of promoting behavioural success. Such strategies are, in fact, quite naturally accommodated since the best ways to minimize long-term prediction error will often be both frugal and action-involving. Thus we read that:

> It is a mistake to think that just because the brain only does inference, it must build up its internal model like it was a following a sober physics textbook. As long as prediction error is minimized on average and over the long run, it doesn't matter which model is doing it. For this reason a model that predicts linear optical trajectories is entirely feasible and can easily be preferable to a more cumbersome series of computations. This is particularly so if it is a less complex model, with fewer parameters, since prediction error in the long run is helped by minimal complexity. (Hohwy, 2014, p. 20)

This is revealing. Hohwy here (and elsewhere[17]) recognizes that often, the PP framework will stand opposed to more 'intellectualist' stories that depict moment-by-moment behavioural success as the product of inferences defined over rich internal models whose role is to allow the cognizer to 'throw away the world'. Instead, the role of the inner model is, in many cases, to spot the contexts in which some more frugal, action-involving, procedure will work (for lots more on this hybrid picture, see chapter 8). This means that 'inference', as it functions in the PP story, is not compelled to deliver internal states that bear richly reconstructive contents. It is not there to construct an inner realm able to to stand in for the full richness of the external world. Instead, it may deliver efficient, low-cost strategies whose unfolding and success depend delicately and continuously upon the structure and ongoing contributions of the external realm itself, as exploited by various forms of action and intervention.

Relatedly, Hohwy frequently speaks of PP-style systems as seeking out the *hypotheses* that best explain the sensory information. Heard in one way, this is again correct. The prediction error minimizing system must find the multilevel set of neuronal states that best *accommodate* (as I will now put it) the current sensory barrage. But this, I suggest, is far preferable to talk of 'finding the right hypothesis' as such talk again invites unwanted and potentially misleading baggage. Accommodating the current sensory barrage may take many forms, some of which involve low-cost methods of selecting actions that re-shape the sensory signal or function to maintain it within pre-set bounds. Accommodating the incoming signal thus need not imply anything like settling upon a description of the external situation, or finding a proposition or set of propositions that best describes or predicts that incoming signals. Indeed, at the most fundamental level, the task of PP systems is not to retrieve apt descriptions. The fundamental task, using prediction errors as the lever, is to find the neural activity patterns that most successfully accommodate current sensory states by means of world-enaging action.

6.8 Don't Fear the Demon

Why does Hohwy, despite often stressing the importance of a 'non-intellectualist' reading of PP, insist that it promotes a neurocentric, secluded vision of the mind? The reason seems to be that he links the secluded, inferential vision to something quite different and (I shall argue) rather alien to much of the discussion in hands-on embodied cognitive science. He links it to the mere possibility of evil-demon style global skepticsm—the possibility that we might be fooled into believing we are embodied agents acting in a real world, when 'really' we are merely brains being fed whatever sequence of sensory signals is needed to maintain the illusion. It is this mere possibility that, in Hohwy's treatment, suffices to establish a robust 'veil of tranduction' which positions the world as we know it on the far side of an important, agent-impermeable, evidentiary boundary.

Thus, in response to the suggestion that PP is consistent with (and indeed actively predicts) the use of fast and frugal strategies that use sensing in the special way described above, Hohwy writes that

> the incoming visual signal drives action but ... this driving in fact does rely on a veil of transduction, namely the evidentiary boundary within which there is ample inference, and beyond which lies nothing but inferred causes. (2014, p. 21).

To demonstrate this, Hohwy invokes the spectre of Cartesian (evil demon-style) skepticism. But this, it seems to me, is something of a red herring. The skeptical claim is simply the claim that, were the play of sensory stimulations being received and (apparently) harvested by the brain to remain fixed, so too would our experience of the world. For all we know, then, our physical bodies might be hanging immobile in some Matrix-like energy web, kept alive and fed whatever sensory stimulations are required to make it seem as if we are running to catch flyballs and arguing about the powers of evil demons. But this mere possibility (even if it is accepted) in no way casts doubt upon the key claims associated with work in embodied cognitive science. Consider running to catch that flyball. This (in the Matrix/vat) would involve feeding the brain the complex, action-sensitive unfolding sensory streams that would normally ensue were an embodied agent actually running so as to cancel the optical acceleration of the ball. The mere fact that this is what would be required supports what really matters here, which is the non-reconstructive account of fly-ball interception.

What the skeptical challenges suggest is thus a very different sense of 'inferential seclusion' from the one at issue in debates between reconstructive and non-reconstructive approaches to perception and action. For those debates (the ones about the shape of the perception-action nexus) were not about whether we might be fooled, by some clever manipulation, into misconstruing our own worldly situation. Instead, they were about how best to understand, from within our current scientific perspective, the role of the sensory stream in enabling apt forms of world-engaging action. At issue was the question whether apt actions are always and everywhere computed by using sensing to get enough information into the system to allow it to plot its response by exploring a rich, internally represented recapitulation of the distal world. Non-reconstructive approaches (much more on which in chapter 8) demonstrate the viability of alternative, more computationally frugal, behaviourally interactive, solutions. They do not imply—nor do they seek to imply—the falsity of the skeptical hypothesis. That is an orthogonal question that would demand a full philosophical treatment in its own right.[18]

The image of the mind as secluded behind an inferential curtain is thus importantly ambiguous. If it means only that the world, insofar as we know and experience it, is that which is both experientially specified and actively engaged by the ongoing flow of (partially self-induced) sensory stimulations, then PP indeed mandates a certain kind of seclusion. But seclusion, in this rather limited sense, does not imply the richly reconstructive model of perception according to which our actions are selected by processes of reasoning defined over the contents of rich inner models whose role is to replace the external world with a kind of inner simulacrum.[19]

The mere fact that neural processing is organized around prediction error minimization routines thus puts no real pressure upon the claim that lies at the heart of recent work on the embodied mind. For what that work most fundamentally rejects is the richly reconstructive model of perception. The appearance of conflict arises from an ambiguity in the notions of inference and seclusion themselves. For these notions may seem to imply the presence of a rich inner recapitulation of the distal environment, with a consequent downgrading of the role of action and upgrading of the role of reasoning defined over that inner model. Nothing in PP, however, mandates this. Instead, PP strongly suggests that brains like ours will, wherever possible, exploit simple strategies that rely heavily on world-engaging action, delivering new sensory stimulations just-in-time to support behavioral success. Such strategies are the focus of chapter 8.

6.9   Hello World

The PP schema does not merely fail to impose any worrisome barrier[20] between the agent and the world. It also provides the necessary means to bring a structured world into view in the first place. Thus consider the perception of sentence structure during speech processing. Here too (see, e.g., Poeppel & Monahan, 2011) we may rely upon stored knowledge to guide a set of guesses about the shape and content of the present sound stream: guesses that are constantly compared to the incoming signal, allowing residual errors to decide between competing guesses and (where necessary) to reject one set of guesses and replace it with another. Such extensive use of existing knowledge (driving the guessing) has, as we have seen, many advantages. It enables us to hear what is said despite noisy surroundings, to adjudicate between alternate possibilities each consistent with the bare sound stream, and so on. It is plausibly only due to the deployment of a rich probabilistic generative model that a hearer can recover semantic and syntactic constituents from the impinging sound stream. Would that mean that perceived sentence structure is 'an inferred fantasy about what lies behind the veil of input'? Surely not. In recovering the right set of interacting distal causes (subjects, objects, meanings, verb-clauses, etc.) we see through the brute sound stream to the multilayered structure and complex purposes of the linguistic environment itself.

We must tread carefully though. When we (as native speakers) encounter such a sound stream, we hear a sequence of words, separated by gaps. The sound stream itself, however, is perfectly continuous, as a spectrogram quite dramatically reveals. Those gaps are added by the listener. What we encounter in perception is in that sense a construct. But it is a construct that tracks real structure in the signal source (other agents producing strings of distinct meaningful words). The predictive brain here lets us see through the noisy, sensory signal to uncover the humanly relevant aspects of the world giving rise to the waves of sensory stimulation. This may be a rather good picture of what perception, on the PP model, quite generally does. If so, then the world we encounter in perception is no more (and no less) a virtual reality or fantasy than the structures of words we hear in an uttered sentence spoken in our native tongue.

Predictive processing here allows us to see through the sensory signal to the human-relevant aspects of the distal world. Seen in this light, the predictive processing story shares much (or so it seems to me) with so-called 'direct' (e.g., Gibson, 1979) views of perception. For it delivers a genuine form—perhaps the only genuine form that is naturally possible—of 'openness to the world'. Against this, however, it must be conceded that extensive reliance on the top-down cascade sometimes makes veridical perception quite heavily dependent upon prior knowledge.

I shall not attempt further to adjudicate this delicate issue here (see Crane, 2005). But if a label is required, it has been suggested that the implied metaphysical perspective may most safely be dubbed 'not-indirect perception'.[21] Perception of this stripe is 'not-indirect' since *what* we perceive is not itself a hypothesis (or model, or fantasy, or virtual reality). Instead, what we perceive is (when all is going well) the structured external world itself. But this is not the world 'as it is', where that implies the problematic notion (see also 9.10) of a world represented independent of human concerns and human action repertoires. Rather, it is a world parsed according to our organism-specific needs and action repertoire. The world thus revealed may be populated with items such as hidden but tasty prey, poker hands, handwritten digits, and structured, meaningful, sentences.

Nor is there any sense in which the objects of perception are here being treated as anything like 'sense data' (Moore, 1913/1922), where these were conceived as proxies intervening *between* the perceiver and the world. The internal representations at issue function *within* us and are not encountered *by* us. They make it possible for us to encounter the organism-salient world under the ecologically common conditions of noise, uncertainty, and ambiguity. We encounter our world in perception, all this suggests, because brains like ours are statistical engines able to lock on to non-linearly interacting causes whose signatures may sometimes be deeply buried among the sensory noise and energetic flux. The result is that the agent-salient structure of the distal realm becomes reflected in both the large-scale shape and (see chapter 9) the spontaneous activity patterns of the neural architecture itself.[22] What is thus revealed is not, however, a distal realm of some action-neutral kind. Instead, it is a world distilled from the statistics of the sensory barrages induced by specifically human (and individual, see Harmelech & Malach, 2013) forms of action and intervention.

6.10   Hallucination as Uncontrolled Perception

Content fixation in these accounts is (epistemically) externalist in nature. Perceptual states function to estimate organism-salient properties and features of the distal environment (including, for these purposes, states of our own bodies and the mental states of other agents). But such states are individuated by reference to the world actually sampled. To see this, consider the case (Hinton, 2005) of a trained-up neural network whose high-level internal states are 'clamped', that is, forced by the experimenter into some specific configuration. Activity then flows downwards in a generative cascade, resulting in a state of (if you will) experimenter-induced hallucination. But what is the content of that state? What is represented, Hinton argues, is best captured by asking how the *world* would have to be were such a cascade to constitute veridical perception. A perceptual state, as here depicted, is thus nothing but 'the state of a hypothetical world in which a high-level internal representation would constitute veridical perception' (Hinton, 2005, p. 1765).

These considerations suggest a twist upon the notion of perception as 'controlled hallucination'. For it would be better, I suggest, to describe hallucination as a kind of 'uncontrolled (hence mock) perception'. In hallucination, all the machinery of perception is brought to bear, but either without the guidance of sensory prediction error at all, or (see 2.12 and chapter 7) with malfunctioning prediction error circuitry. In such cases the agent really does enter a state of what Smith (2002, p. 224) calls 'mock sensory awareness'.

Finally, notice that perceptual content, as delivered by active, affordance-sensitive prediction, is now inherently organized and outward-looking. By this I mean that it reveals—and cannot help but reveal—a structured (and thus in some weak sense 'conceptualized'[23]) external world. It is an external arena populated by the distal, causally interacting items and forces whose joint action best explains (given prior knowledge) the current suite of sensory stimulation. This delivers just the kind of grip on the world that an intelligent agent must possess if she is to act appropriately. When such an agent sees the world, they see a determinate structure of distal, interacting causes apt for action and intervention by the kind of creature that they are. The so-called 'transparency' of perceptual experience[24]—the fact that, in normal daily perception, we seem to see tables, chairs, and bananas rather than proximal excitations of our sensory surfaces such as the play of light on the retina—falls quite naturally out of such models. We seem to see dogs, cats, goals, tackles, and winning poker hands, because these feature among the interacting, nested, structures of distal causes that matter for human choice and action.

6.11 Optimal Illusions

Of course, things can (and do) sometimes go wrong. The human mind, as Paton et al. (2013, p. 222) eloquently argue, is 'always precariously hostage to the urge to rid itself of prediction error [and this] forces very improbable and fantastical perceptions upon us when the world does not collaborate in its usual, uniform way'. It is surprisingly easy, for example, to induce (even in fully alert, normal adults) the illusion that a rubber hand, placed on the table in front of you, is your own. The illusion is created by ensuring that the subject can see someone tapping the realistic rubber hand, while (just out of sight) their own hand is being tapped in exact synchrony (Botvinick & Cohen, 1998). Ramachandran and Blakeslee (1998) describe a similar illusion, in which a blindfold subject's arm is extended and their finger made to tap the nose of another subject seated just in front of them, while their own nose is tapped in perfect synchrony, using an intermittent rhythm, by the experimenter. Here too, the predictive, Bayesian brain may be fooled into generating a false percept—in this case, that you have a two foot long nose! There are many ways in which such mistakes may come about, involving differing balances between prior expectations and the driving sensory signal (for some nice discussion, see Hohwy, 2013, chapters 1 and 7). But for present purposes, all that matters is that a key role is played (as the experimental manipulations clearly reveal) by the facts concerning temporal synchrony. To 'explain away' prediction error when the sensory signal starts to reveal such unexpected (ecologically rare, hence usually highly informative) synchronies, strange and implausible percepts are generated. What, then, does this tell us about our ordinary, daily, perceptual contact with the world?

In one sense it seems to suggest (as Paton et al. argue), a certain fragility in the routines that the brain uses to track and engage the external world. Those routines can indeed be hijacked and coerced in ways that mislead.[25] A good question to ask, however, is: 'What would be the cost, for some given perceptual error, of avoiding that error?' For it may be that the cost, in many cases, would be vast swathes of error elsewhere in our perceptual (or more generally, in our mental) lives.[26] Weiss et al. (2002), as we noted back in chapter 1, used an optimal Bayesian estimator to show that a wide variety of motion 'illusions' are directly implied by the assumption that human motion perception implements an optimal estimator. They conclude that 'many motion "illusions" are not the result of sloppy computation by various components in the visual system, but rather a result of a coherent computational strategy that is optimal under reasonable assumptions' (Weiss et al., 2002, p. 603). This suggests that sometimes, at least, even 'illusory' perceptual experiences constitute an accurate estimation of the most likely real-world source or property, given noisy sensory evidence and the statistical distribution, within some relevant sample, of real-world causes. A few local anomalies may thus be the price we pay for globally optimized performance (Lupyan, in press).

This is an important finding that has now been repeated in many domains, including the sound-induced flash illusion (Shams et al., 2005), ventriloquism effects (Alais & Burr, 2004), and the impact of figure-ground convexity cues in depth perception (Burge et al., 2010). Additionally, Weiss et al.'s (2002) Bayes-optimal account of a class of static (fixation-dependent) motion illusions has now been extended to account for a much wider set of motion illusions generated in the presence of active eye movements during smooth pursuit (see Freeman et al., 2010, and discussion in Ernst, 2010). Perceptual experience, even in these illusory cases, thus looks to be veridically tracking statistical relations between the sensory data and its most probable real-world sources. This again suggests that the intervening mechanisms introduce no worrisome barrier between mind and world. Going slightly off the rails every now and then is simply the price we pay for mostly getting things right.

Or consider, to take one last, and rather more contentious, case, the 'size-weight illusion'. This has been invoked (Buckingham & Goodale, 2013) as a challenge to the supposed generality of optimal cue integration in human psychophysics. In the size-weight illusion, similar-looking objects appear weight-adjusted so that we judge the smaller one to feel heavier than the larger despite their identical objective weights (a pound of lead feels heavier, indeed, than a pound of feathers). Buckingham and Goodale survey recent work on the size-weight illusion noting that although Bayesian treatments do manage to get a grip on the lifting behaviour itself, they fail to explain the subjective comparison effect which some describe as 'anti-Bayesian' since prior expectancies and sensory information there seem contrasted rather than integrated (Brayanov & Smith, 2010). This provides evidence, they suggest, for a more fractured and firewalled cognitive economy: one displaying 'independent sets of priors for motor control and perceptual/cognitive judgments, which ultimately serve quite different functions' (p. 209).

There is, however, an intriguing (though still highly speculative) alternative. Zhu and Bingham (2011) show that the perception of relative heaviness marches delicately in step with the affordance of maximum-distance throwability. Perhaps, then, what we have simply labelled as the experience of 'heaviness' is, in some deeper ecological sense, the experience of optimal weight-for-size to afford long-distance throwability? If that were true, then the experiences that Buckingham and Goodale describe re-emerge as optimal percepts for throwability, albeit ones that we routinely misconceive as simple but erroneous perceptions of relative object weight. What looks from one perspective to be a fragmented, fragile, and disconnected cognitive economy may thus, on deeper examination, turn out to be a robust, well-integrated (though by no means homogeneous) mechanism adapted *not* to deliver simple action-neutral descriptions of the world but to put us in contact with action-relevant structure in the environment.

6.12   Safer Penetration

Such considerations also help reveal why the rampant 'penetration' of lower level processing by higher level predictions and expectations presents no deep threat to our epistemic situation. The worry here (see Fodor, 1983, 1988) is that what we (think we) perceive may—courtesy of all that top-down influence—become too easily infected by what we expect to perceive, and that this would undermine the basis of scientific investigation itself. We want our observations to be positioned to test our theories and expectations, not to simply fall into line with them! Fortunately for us, Fodor argues, perception is not thus penetrable, as evidenced (Fodor claims) by the persistence of visual illusions even after we learn of their illusory status. For example, the equal lines of the classic version of the Muller-Lyer illusion[27] still look unequal in length, even once we have measured them for ourselves. Fodor takes this as evidence that perception in general is 'cognitively impenetrable', that is, not directly affected by higher level knowledge of any kind (Pylyshyn, 1999).

The correct diagnosis, we can now see, is actually rather different. What we ought to be saying is that perception is penetrable by top-down influence when (and only when) such penetration has earned its keep over a sufficiently wide range of training instances. The deep reason that many illusions persist despite countervailing linguaform knowledge is because the task of the perceptual system is to minimize what Lupyan (in press) usefully describes as 'global prediction error'. Relative to the full set of circumstances that the perceptual system has needed to deal with, the hypothesis that the lines are of unequal length is the best hypothesis (Howe & Purves, 2005). From that more global perspective, our susceptibility to the illusion is not really a cognitive failure at all. For were the system to overturn the many delicately inter-laced layers of intermediate-level processing that deliver this verdict, the result would be failures of veridical perception in many other (more ecologically normal) circumstances.

There is no threat here to our epistemic situation. In general, our per-ceptual systems are well-calibrated as devices for mediating between sensory stimulation and action, and their deliverances (though subject to alteration by extensive re-training) are not simply overthrown by our endorsement of sentences such as 'yes, the two lines are indeed of equal length'. Endorsing such a sentence (see Hohwy, 2013) does not adequately account for the full spectrum of lower level predictions and prediction error signals that construct that particular percept, so it is unable to overturn the long-term learning of the system. Where simple exposure to sentences will most plausibly make a difference to perceptual experience is rather in cases where the sensory evidence is ambiguous. In such cases (and see 9.8) hearing a sentence might tip the system into an interpretation of the scene—an interpretation that genuinely affects how the scene appears to the agent (for an example of this kind, see Siegel, 2012, and discussion in 2.9).

In sum, top-down influences of various kinds may impact process-ing at every lower level, but only when those patterns of impact are globally (not merely locally) productive. The upshot is that:

> Perceptual systems are penetrable to the extent that such penetration minimizes global prediction error. If allowing information from another modality, prior experience, expecta-tions, knowledge, beliefs, etc., lowers global prediction error, then such information will be used to guide processing at the lower levels. For example, if hearing a sound can disambigu-ate an otherwise ambiguous visual input. ... then we should expect sound to influence vision. If knowledge that a particular

collection of lines can be interpreted as a meaningful symbol can improve visual processing, then such knowledge will be brought to bear on lower-level visual processes. (Lupyan, in press, p. 8)

This is good news for science. It enables us to be open to the sensory evidence that might discredit our own theory, while also enabling us to become expert perceivers, able to spot the faint trace that signifies the action of a Higgs boson against a daunting backdrop of noise and ambiguity.

6.13   Who Estimates the Estimators?

Finally, what about severe forms of mental disruption, such as the delusions and hallucinations characteristic of schizophrenia and various other forms of psychosis? In cases such as these, the delicately balanced mechanisms that normally serve to balance sensory input, top-down expectation, and neural plasticity have gone badly awry. If the hypotheses scouted in 2.12 are on track, systemic malfunctions (perhaps rooted in abnormal dopaminergic signalling) here disrupt the production and weighting of the prediction error signal itself. This is an especially challenging form of disruption, since (as we saw) persistent, highly weighted prediction error will appear to signal salient external structure, threats, and opportunities. Unresolved, it will thus drive the system to alter and adapt the generative model, initiating a vicious cycle in which false percepts and false beliefs co-emerge, lending each other spurious support.

Worse still, there is no easy way (as Hohwy 2013, p. 47 rightly notes) for the system itself to assess the reliability of its own precision assignments. For precision-weighting on prediction error already reflects systemic estimations of the reliability or otherwise of signals at every level of processing. Obviously, no system can afford to engage in endless spirals of 'computational self-doubt' in which it attempts to estimate its confidence in its own assignments of confidence, the reliability of its own assessments of reliability, and so on. Moreover, it is unclear what types of evidence a system would need to use to compute such meta-meta-measures, given that what is at issue is now the reliability of both the evidence and of measures of confidence in that evidence.[28]

Problems with precision, we may conclude, will be unusually resistant to any form of rational self-correction. This is, of course, exactly the (otherwise rather baffling) profile found in many forms of psychosis. Disruptions of precision estimation render probabilistic predictive contact with the world both unreliable and extremely hard to correct. Such complex disturbances are the subject matter of the next chapter.

6.14   Gripping Tales

Perception, if the probabilistic prediction machine vision is correct, is an active process involving the rolling (sub-personal) prediction of our own evolving neural states. Such a thoroughly inward-looking process of self-prediction may have seemed initially unpromising as a model of how perception reaches out to the world. If the arguments scouted in the present chapter are correct, however, it is the pressure actively to accommodate our own changing sensory states that delivers our grip upon a structured, organism-salient, external world.

In active animals, that grip is not rooted in some kind of action-neutral image of an objective external reality. Instead, to minimize prediction error is to minimize failures to identify the affordances for action that the world presents. Here, a good strategy is to deliver (at every moment) a partial grip upon a number of competing affordances: an 'affordance competition' that is plausibly resolved only as and when action requires. As this process unfolds, processes of decision and action-preparation are continuously intertwined, as multiple responses are prepared in ways graded by the changing probabilities of their expression. Our perceptual grip on the world, all this suggests, is fundamentally interaction-based: it is a grip forged in the presence of, and dedicated to the service of, world-engaging action.

Such a grip is not perfect. It leaves us vulnerable to illusions, mistakes, and even wholesale disruptions of the kinds characteristic of schizophrenia and other forms of psychosis. Does this mean that even the properly functioning system affords contact with merely a 'virtual reality'? In the end, we should probably not worry too much about the words we use here. But the implication of deep and abiding disconnection is misleading. Rather than spawning some kind of virtual reality rudely interposed between the mind and the world, the well-functioning perceptual system disperses the fog of surface statistics and partial information. What is revealed is a world of salient, meaningful patterns shaped by human needs and possibilities.

7

Expecting Ourselves
(Creeping Up On Consciousness)

7.1   The Space of Human Experience

We have covered a large and varied territory. Our story began with the neat trick of learning about the world by trying to predict our own changing sensory states. We went on to explore the use of that trick (in a multilevel setting) to inform perception, imagination, action, and simulation-based reasoning about the world and about other agents. We saw how ongoing estimations of the relative uncertainty associated with activity in different neural populations could further transform the power and scope of such a story, rendering the flow of processing dynamically reconfigurable and delivering context-sensitivity on a truly grand scale. And we have begun the crucial and continuing task of understanding how active, embodied agents put such resources to use by creating and maintaining perception-action cycles that reflect organismic needs and environmental opportunities. Thus enhanced our story has, I believe, the resources required to illuminate the full spectrum of human thoughts, experiences, and actions.

To make good on such a claim—or perhaps even to make such a claim genuinely intelligible—we now need to bring this quite theoretical, large-scale picture into closer contact with the shape and nature of human experience. We need, if you will, to begin to recognize *ourselves* in the swirl of ongoing, multilevel prediction. At that point, many of the more practical—and humanly significant—aspects of our picture begin to emerge, revealing something of the complex space of human minds. Within that space, a few key principles and balances (involving prediction error and its delicate role in the unfolding of action) may determine the shape and nature of both normal and atypical forms of human experience.

There is no way, of course, that I can fully deliver on this. Sadly, but unsurprisingly, a convincing account of the full spread of human experience and its mechanistic (and sociocultural) roots lies significantly out of reach. But an emerging literature offers some promising hints, a few simplified models, and a smattering of intriguing (but speculative) proposals. What, then, can predictive processing hope to tell us about consciousness, emotion, and the varieties of human experience?

7.2   Warning Lights

As this chapter unfolds, the spotlight falls upon a wide range of cases in which human experience becomes structured, disturbed, or subtly inflected in ways that can be illuminated (or so I shall suggest) by appeal to the distinctive apparatus of predictive processing. In each case, one aspect of the PP apparatus plays a central role. That aspect, once again, is the precision of specific prediction error signals, and hence the estimated reliability of different bodies of evidence: evidence that includes exteroceptive sensory signals, interoceptive and proprioceptive sensory signals, and the whole multilevel spectrum of prior beliefs. Such estimates of reliability (equivalently, of uncertainty) provide, as we have repeatedly seen in previous chapters, a crucial added dimensionality to these accounts, enabling the impact of specific prediction error signals to be altered according to task, context, and background information. More generally still, these estimates of precision constitute a fundamentally metacognitive ploy. Such estimates are metacognitive,[1] since they involve estimates (mostly non-conscious and sub-personal) of the certainty or reliability of our own mental states and processes. But this is a metacognitive ploy that is arguably a fundamental part of the basic apparatus of perception and action rather than something emerging only with advanced, 'high-level', reasoning.

Estimating the reliability (or otherwise) of our own prediction error signals is clearly a delicate and tricky business. For it is the prediction error signal that, as we have frequently noted, gets to 'carry the news'.

Here, however, the brain's task is to settle upon the correct weighting of the prediction error signal itself. Estimating the reliability of some (putative) item of news is never easy, as anyone who has encountered widely differing reports of the same event in different media knows! A common strategy, when confronted with this familiar difficulty, is to privilege some specific news source, such as your favourite paper, channel, or blog. But suppose that, unbeknownst to you, ownership of the source changed hands overnight. Streams of information that you are pre-inclined to take very seriously indeed are now (let's imagine) seriously misleading. That feed from your chosen reliable source is now seriously tainted, and in ways you have never expected. Rather than believe this, you may now choose to explore many otherwise unlikely options ('Martians really have landed: The White House press office says so') that you would otherwise have ignored or immediately rejected. Such, in broad outline, is the distinctive shape of an emerging class of accounts of a variety of atypical mental states, as we shall shortly see. These accounts locate the crucial failures as failures of precision-estimation, hence as failures of the very mechanisms whose task is to estimate the reliability of our own information sources. Such failures (as we shall see) can have very complex and varying effects according to which aspects of the complex economy of priors and sensory evidence are most affected.

To get the general flavour, consider the 'warning lights' scenario[2] described in Adams et al. (2013). I quote the case in full, as it neatly captures several factors that will prove important for our subsequent discussion:

> Imagine the temperature warning light in your car is too sensitive (precise), reporting the slightest fluctuations (prediction errors) above some temperature. You naturally infer that there is something wrong with your car and take it to the garage. However, they find no fault—and yet the warning light continues to flash. Your first instinct may be to suspect the garage has failed to identify the fault—and even to start to question the Good Garage Guide that recommended it. From your point of view, these are all plausible hypotheses that accommodate the evidence available to you. However, from the perspective of somebody who has never seen your warning light, your suspicions would have an irrational and slightly paranoid flavor. This anecdote illustrates how delusional systems may be elaborated as a consequence of imbuing sensory evidence with too much precision. (Adams et al., 2013, p. 2)

Adams et al. add then that:

> The primary pathology here is quintessentially metacognitive in nature: in the sense that it rests on a belief (the warning light reports precise information) about a belief (the engine is overheating). Crucially, there is no necessary impairment in forming predictions or prediction errors—the problem lies in the way they are used to inform inference or hypotheses.

Two brief comments upon all this, before proceeding to some actual cases. First, it will do no obvious good to add layers upon layers of complexity here. Suppose we fitted the car with a further device: a warning light malfunction warning light! All we have done is pushed the problem further back. If both lights flash, we now have to determine which one carries the most reliable news. If just one flashes, the information it conveys may still be reliable or not, for all we know. At some point (though not necessarily the same point for all tasks and at all times) the regress of trusting has to stop. And wherever that is, it may form the starting point for self-reinforcing spirals of false or misleading inference. Second, notice that what precision-weighting provides is essentially a means of sculpting patterns of inference and action, and as such it is strangely neutral concerning the intuitive difference between increasing the precision upon (say) a prior belief or decreasing the precision upon the sensory evidence. What matters is just the relative balance of influence, however that is achieved. For it is that relative balance that determines agentive response.

7.3   The Spiral of Inference and Experience

Recall the PP account (Fletcher & Frith, 2009) of the emergence of delusions and hallucination (the so-called 'positive symptoms') in schizophrenia sketched in 2.12. The basic idea was that both these symptoms might flow from a single underlying cause: falsely generated and highly weighted (high-precision) waves of prediction error. The key disturbance is thus a disturbance in metacognition—for it is the weighting (precision) assigned to these error signals that makes them so functionally potent, positioning them to drive the system into plasticity and learning, forming and recruiting increasingly bizarre hypotheses so as to accommodate the unrelenting waves of (apparently) reliable and salient yet persistently unexplained information. The resulting higher level hypotheses (such as telepathy and alien control) appear bizarre and unfounded to the external observer, yet from within now constitute the best, because the only, explanation available—much like suspicions about the Good Garage Guide in the warning light example rehearsed above. Once such higher level stories take hold, new low-level sensory stimulation may be interpreted falsely. When these new priors dominate, we may thus experience hallucinations that appear to confirm or consolidate them. This is no stranger, at root, than prior expectations making a hollow mask look solidly convex (see 1.17) or white noise sound like 'White Christmas' (see 2.2). At that point (Fletcher & Frith, 2009, p. 348), false inferences supply false percepts that lend spurious support to the theories that gave rise to them, and the whole cycle becomes perniciously self-confirming.

What about the 'obvious' higher level explanation, which a friend or doctor might even suggest to an affected agent, namely, that the agent herself is cognitively compromised? This should indeed constitute an acceptable high-level explanation, yet it is one that severely affected subjects find unconvincing. In this context, it is worth noting that prediction error signals are not objects of (or realizers of) experience. The 'red warning light' in the analogy is thus not an experience of a prediction error signal. The PP suggestion is not that we experience our own prediction error signals (or their associated precisions) as such. Instead, those signals act within us to recruit the apt flows of prediction that reveal a world of distal objects and causes. Persistent unresolved prediction error signals may, however, yield amorphous feelings of 'salient strangeness', in which subjects find themselves powerfully affected by what (to others) seem like mere accidental coincidences, and so forth. Within a hierarchical setting, this amounts (Frith & Friston, 2012) to an ongoing disturbance at the lower levels whose only resolution lies in bizarre, counter-evidence resistant, top-level theorizing. This fits, Frith and Friston suggest, with first-person reports such as those of Chadwick (1993), a trained psychologist who suffered an episode of paranoid schizophrenia. Chadwick recalls that he 'had to make sense, any sense, out of all these uncanny coincidences' and that he 'did it by radically changing [his] conception of reality'. Commenting on this, Frith and Friston write that:

> In our terminology, these uncanny coincidences were false hypotheses engendered by prediction errors with inappropriately high precision or salience. To explain them away Chadwick had to conclude that other people, including radio and television presenters, could see into his mind. This was the radical change he had to make in his conception of reality. (Frith & Friston, 2012, section 8)

7.4 *Schizophrenia and Smooth Pursuit Eye Movements*

Such conjectures are both interesting and plausible. But a major attraction of the PP account is that it also provides a compelling account of a variety of other, less dramatic but equally diagnostic, features. One such feature concerns some anomalies in the 'smooth pursuit eye movements' displayed by schizophrenic subjects. The background to this work is a robust pattern of differences between normal and schizophrenic subjects during the smooth pursuit of temporarily visually occluded targets.

Smooth pursuit eye movements[3] may be contrasted with saccadic eye movements. Human eyes are able to saccade around a visual scene, jumping from target to target in quick bursts. But when a moving object is present, the eyes can 'lock on' to the object, smoothly tracking it through space (unless it is moving too quickly, in which case so-called 'catch-up saccades' are initiated). Smooth pursuit eye movements are able to track slowly moving objects, keeping their image upon the high resolution fovea. In smooth pursuit (see Levy et al., 2010), the eyes move at less than 100 degrees per second and (within those bounds) eye velocity closely matches the velocity of the target. A common example, still in use as a handy neurological indicator during physical examinations, is following the doctor's moving finger with your eyes, without moving your head or body, as she moves it to and fro in front of you. (You can perform the same routine on your own, holding your hand out at arm's length and tracking the tip of your forefinger as you move your hand left and right. If your eyes are jerky under such conditions, you would score low on a 'field sobriety test' and might be suspected of being under the influence of alcohol or, for that matter, ketamine.)

Smooth pursuit eye movements involve two phases: an initiation phase and a maintenance phase (distinguished by open and closed loop feedback, respectively). During the maintenance phase, the quantity known as 'pursuit gain' (or equivalently, as 'maintenance gain') measures the ratio of the eye velocity to the target velocity. The closer to 1.0 this is, the greater the correspondence between the velocity of the target and that of the eye. Under such conditions, the image of the target remains stable on the fovea. When the two diverge, catch-up (or back-up) saccades may occur, bringing the two back into line.

Schizophrenic subjects robustly display a variety of impairments to smooth pursuit (also known as 'eye tracking dysfunctions') especially when the pursued target becomes occluded from view or changes direction. According to the authoritative review by Levy et al. (2010), 'eye tracking dysfunction (ETD) is one of the most widely replicated behavioral deficits in schizophrenia and is over-represented in clinically unaffected first-degree relatives of schizophrenia patients' (Levy et al., 2010, p. 311).

In particular, we will focus (following Adams et al., 2012) on three differences that robustly distinguish the performance of normal and schizophrenic subjects. They are:

1. Impaired tracking during visual occlusion. Schizophrenic subjects produce slower tracking and this is especially marked when the tracked item becomes occluded (obscured from view). Thus, whereas the pursuit gain of a neurotypical subject is around 85%, it averages around 75% in the schizophrenic population. More strikingly still, when a moving target becomes temporarily occluded from view, neurotypical subjects are able to track with a gain of 60–70%, while schizophrenic subjects track at 45–55% (see Hong et al., 2008; Thaker et al., 1999, 2003).

2. Paradoxical improvement. When a target unexpectedly changes direction, schizophrenic subjects briefly outperform neurotypical ones, producing a better matching target/eye velocity for the first 30 ms of the new trajectory (see Hong et al., 2005).

3. Impaired repetition learning. When a target trajectory is repeated several times, neurotypical subjects achieve optimal performance, whereas schizophrenic subjects do not (see Avila et al., 2006).

This whole complex of otherwise puzzling effects (the paradoxical improvement as well as the twin deficits) emerge simultaneously as a result of a single disturbance to an economy of hierarchical prediction and precision-weighted prediction error, as we shall next see.

7.5   Simulating Smooth Pursuit

Adams et al. (2012) review a large swathe of evidence suggesting that the predictive components of smooth pursuit eye movements are the most sensitive to schizotypal disturbance, and hence provide greater insight (and diagnostic potential) than simple measures of maintenance gain per se. For example (Nkam et al., 2010), smooth pursuit of a randomly moving stimulus is indistinguishable between schizotypal and neurotypical subjects. Once motion becomes to some degree predictable, differences begin to appear. But they become increasingly marked as the predictive component increases. When the moving object is temporarily occluded from view, the predictive component is large, and the differences between the two populations are (as we saw earlier) greatest.

To highlight the predictive component, a measure known as 'mean predictive gain' was introduced (Thaker et al., 1999). Mean predictive gain is the average gain during periods of occlusion. Occlusion also results, in all subjects, in a period of deceleration of the eye followed by an increase back towards the target velocity. To allow for this, 'residual predictive gain' measures the mean predictive gain minus that period of general deceleration. In a large sample, spanning both severe and less severe sub-types of schizotypal subjects, all showed diminished residual predictive gain, as did symptom-free schizotypal relatives. By contrast, only severely affected individuals showed diminished maintenance gain in general.

Such evidence reveals strong links between the most distinctive patterns of effect upon schizotypal smooth pursuit and the predictability of the moving stimulus. The more predictively demanding the task, the greater the divergence from neurotypical patterns of response and tracking. In this respect, the evidence concerning smooth pursuit falls neatly into place as part of a larger mosaic of results and conjectures concerning schizotypal responses to certain illusions, the well-known work on 'self-tickling' (chapter 4), and delusions of control. We shall return to all of these topics in subsequent sections.

To explore the possible effects of disturbance to a predictive processing system on smooth pursuit eye movements, Adams et al. (2012) deployed a simplified hierarchical generative model involving linked equations for sensing and the control of motion. Heuristically,[4] the model 'believes' that its gaze and the target object are both attracted to a common point defined in extrinsic coordinates lying on a single (horizontal) dimension. Thus, 'the generative model . . . is based upon the prior belief that the centre of gaze and target are attracted to a common (fictive) attractor in visual space' (Adams et al., 2012, p. 8). Such simple heuristics can support surprisingly complex forms of adaptive response. In the case at hand, the simulated agent, operating under the influence of that heuristic 'belief', displays smooth pursuit even in the presence of occluding objects. Pursuit continues despite the intervening occluding object because the network now acts as if a single hidden cause is simultaneously attracting both eye and target. Importantly, however, the generative model also includes sufficient hierarchical structure to allow the network to represent target motion involving periodic trajectories (i.e., the frequency of periodic motion of the target). Finally (and crucially) each aspect and level of processing involves associated precision expectations encoding the simulated agent's confidence about that element of the evolving signal: either the sensory input itself, or expectations concerning the evolution of the sensory input over time—in this case, expectations concerning periodic motion of the target.

This model, simplified though it is, captures many key aspects of normal smooth pursuit eye movements. In the continued presence of the moving target, the eye tracks smoothly after a short delay. When a target is occluded for the first time, the system loses its grip on the hidden motion after about 100 ms, and must produce a catch-up saccade (which is only approximately modelled) when the target emerges. But when the same sequence is repeated, tracking notably improves. At that point, the second level of the network can anticipate the periodic dynamics of the motion and is able to use that knowledge to provide apt context-fixing information to the level below, in effect making the lack of ongoing sensory stimulation (while the target is occluded) less surprising. These results provide a good qualitative fit with data from human subjects (e.g., Barnes & Bennett, 2003, 2004).

7.6   Disturbing the Network (Smooth Pursuit)

Recall the three distinctive features (7.4) of smooth pursuit eye movements in schizophrenic subjects. These were impaired tracking during visual occlusion, paradoxical improvement with unexpected changes of trajectory, and impaired repetition learning. Each of these effects, Adams et al. (2012) argue, can be traced to a single underlying deficit in a prediction-based inner economy: the same deficit, in fact, that (see 4.2) was invoked to explain schizophrenic performance on force-matching tasks, and the much-remarked improvement in the ability to self-tickle (see, e.g., Blakemore et al., 1999; Frith, 2005; Shergill et al., 2005; and discussion in chapter 4).

Thus suppose that schizophrenia, somewhere near the beginning of a long and complex causal chain, actually involves a weakening (see Adams, Stephan, et al., 2013) of the influence of prior expectations relative to the current sensory evidence. This may strike the reader as odd. Surely, I hear you say, the opposite must be the case, for these subjects appear to allow bizarre high-level beliefs to trump the evidence of their senses! It seems increasingly possible, however, that the arrows of causality move in the other direction. A weakened influence of prior expectations relative to the sensory input may result, as we shall later see, in anomalous sensory experiences in which (for example) self-generated action appears (to the agent) to have been externally caused. This in turn may lead to the formation of increasingly strange higher level theories and explanations (see Adams, Stephan, et al., 2013).

An important factor impacting the crucial balance between sensory evidence and higher level beliefs is an agent's capacities to reduce (attenuate) the precision of sensory evidence during self-produced movements. Such a capacity is (for reasons we shall explore shortly) functionally crucial. Weakening of this capacity (i.e., reduced sensory attenuation[5]) would explain, as remarked in chapter 4, schizophrenic subjects' better-than-normal[6] abilities to self-tickle and to accurately match an experienced force with a self-generated one. In exploring these issues, it is important to bear in mind that it is the *balance* between the precision of lower and higher levels states that is functionally significant, so increasing the precision (hence increasing the influence) of low-level sensory prediction errors and decreasing the precision (hence decreasing the influence) of errors associated with higher level predictions will amount—at least as far as the inferential process is concerned—to the same thing.

In the case of smooth pursuit eye movements, reducing the precision on prediction errors at higher levels (specifically, at the second level in the simple simulation of Adams et al., 2012) of the processing hierarchy results in the specific constellation of effects described earlier. To show this, Adams et al. lowered the precision upon prediction error at the second level of the simulated smooth pursuit network sketched in 7.5. The immediate effect of this was to reduce the impact of prediction errors concerning the periodic motion of the target. At lower speeds, while the moving object is in sight, the two networks show the same behaviour, since the 'reduced higher level precision' network (RHLP-net for short) then relies upon the sensory input to guide the behaviour. But when the object is occluded, such reliance is impossible and the RHLP network is impaired relative to its 'neurotypical' cousin. As the number of cycles increases, this effect becomes increasingly pronounced. This is because impaired precision at the second level results not just in a reduction in the immediate influence of expectations concerning motion relative to that of the sensory input but also in an impaired ability to learn—in this case, an inability to learn, from continued exposure, about the frequency of periodic motion (see Adams et al., 2012, p. 12). Finally, the RHLP net also showed a subtle pattern of 'paradoxical improvement', outperforming the neurotypical net when an unoccluded target unexpectedly changes direction. This whole pattern of effects flows very naturally from the presence of reduced higher level precision, since under such conditions the net will do worse when well-constructed predictions improve performance (e.g., behind the occluder and at higher speeds), better when predictions mislead (e.g., when an expected trajectory is suddenly altered), and will be impaired in learning from experience.

The kind of disturbance modelled here is physiologically (Seamans & Yang, 2004) and pharmacologically (Corlett et al., 2010) plausible. If precision is indeed encoded by mechanisms that affect the gain on error reporting superficial pyramidal cells, and if higher level (visual or ocular) error reporting cells are found especially (as it seems likely) in the frontal eye fields of the prefrontal cortex, then the kinds of dopaminergic, NMDA, and GABAergic receptor abnormalities reported in the literature provide a clear route by which higher level precision, implemented as synaptic gain in PFC, might become impaired.[7] Such abnormalities would selectively impair the acquisition and use of higher level expectations, reducing both the benefits and (under rare conditions) costs associated with the use of contextual information to anticipate sensory input.

7.7   Tickling Redux

The explanatory apparatus that so neatly accounts for the disturbances to smooth pursuit eye movements also suggests important amendments to the standard account of enhanced schizophrenic capacities for self-tickling sketched in chapter 4. The most revealing aspect of these amendments, as we shall see, is that they better connect the sensory effects to both motor impairments and the emergence of delusional beliefs, thus explaining a complex constellation of observed effects using a single mechanism.

Schizophrenic subjects, recall, show enhanced capacities for self-tickling when compared with neurotypical controls. Self-produced tickles, that is to say, are rated as more genuinely ticklish by the schizophrenic subjects than by neurotypical controls (Blakemore et al., 2000). This effect is genuinely at the level of the sensations involved and is not merely some anomaly of verbal reporting, as evidenced by schizophrenic performance on the force-matching task (see 4.2) in which verbal report is replaced by attempting to match a reference force. Here, neurotypical agents, as remarked earlier, 'over-match' the reference force, delivering greater self-generated forces in ways that lead (in multiagent scenarios) to ongoing escalations of applied pressure. This effect is reduced in schizophrenic subjects who perform the task more accurately (Shergill et al., 2005). Here too, then, there is a kind of 'paradoxical improvement' in which the schizotypal percept is more accurate than that of a neurotypical subject. Neurotypical subjects display

sensory attenuation for many forms of self-generated stimuli including the pleasantness and intensity of self-generated touch (rated as less
pleasant and less intense than the same stimulation when provided
by alternative means) and even for self-generated visual and auditory
stimuli (Cardoso-Leite et al., 2010; Desantis et al., 2012). Quite generally, then, self-produced sensation is attenuated (reduced) in the neurotypical case, and this attenuation is *itself* reduced in schizophrenic
subjects.

A possible explanation, and one that simultaneously accounts
for the emergence of characteristic delusional beliefs about agency, is
offered by Brown et al. (2013) (see also Adams et al., 2013; Edwards et al.,
2012). The more standard explanation (the one we met in chapter 4) is
that an accurate forward model normally allows us to anticipate our
own self-applied forces, which seem weaker (attenuated) as a result.
Should such a model be compromised, the effects of our own actions
will (the standard model suggests) seem more surprising, hence more
likely to be attributed to external causes leading to the emergence
of delusions concerning agency and control. Brown et al. note three
important shortfalls of this standard account:

1. The link between successful prediction and reduced *intensity* of
    a percept (e.g., in the force-matching or tickling tasks) is unclear.
    Well-predicted elements of a signal, as we saw in chapters 1–3, are
    'explained away' and hence exert no pressure to select a new or
    different hypothesis. But this says nothing about the intensity or
    otherwise of the perceptual experience that the current winning
    hypothesis delivers.
2. Manipulating the predictability of a self-generated sensation
    does not seem to impact the degree of sensory attenuation expe-
    rienced (Baess et al., 2008). In other words, the magnitude of pre-
    diction error looks unrelated to the degree of sensory attenuation
    experienced.
3. Most significantly, sensory attenuation occurs even for stimuli that
    are *externally generated* (e.g., by the experimenter) as long as they
    are applied to a body-part that is either undergoing self-generated
    motion or that the agent expects to move (Voss et al., 2008). Such
    attenuation in respect of externally applied stimulations cannot
    be explained, Voss et al. note, by the normal apparatus of forward
    models and efference copy. Instead, they provide 'evidence for
    predictive sensory attenuation based on higher-level motor prepa-
    ration alone, excluding explanations based on both motor com-
    mand and (re-)afferent mechanisms' (Voss et al., 2008, p. 4).

To accommodate these findings , Brown et al. first draw our attention to a somewhat perplexing complication for the PP account of action described in chapter 4. Movement ensues, if that story is correct, when the sensory (proprioceptive) consequences of an action are strongly predicted. Since those consequences (specified as a temporal trajectory of proprioceptive sensations) are not yet actual, prediction error occurs, which is then quashed by the unfolding of the action. This is 'active inference' in the sense of Friston (2009) and Friston, Daunizeau, et al. (2010). But notice that movement will only occur if the body alters in line with the proprioceptive predictions rather than allowing the brain to alter its predictions to conform to the current proprioceptive state (which might signal e.g that the arm is currently resting on the table). In such cases there is an apparent tension between the recipe for perception (alter sensory predictions to match signals from the world) and the recipe for action (alter the body/world to match sensory predictions)

This may seem surprising, given that PP claimed to offer an attractively unified account of perception and action. But, in fact, it is this very unity that now makes trouble. For action, this account suggests, is under the control of perception, at least insofar as bodily movements are specified not by distinct high-level 'motor commands' but implicitly—by the trajectory of proprioceptive signals that would characterize some desired action. The shape of our movements is thus determined, PP here suggests, by predictions concerning the flow of proprioceptive sensations as movements unfold (see Friston, Daunizeau, et al., 2010; Edwards et al., 2012). Those predicted proprioceptive consequences are then brought about by a nested series of unpackings culminating in simple 'reflex arcs'—fluid routines that progressively resolve the high-level specification into apt muscle commands.

The tension between action and perception is now revealed. For another way to quash proprioceptive prediction error is by altering the predictions to conform to the actual sensory input (input that is currently specifying 'hand resting on table') rather than by bringing the predicted proprioceptive flow into being by moving the body. To avoid immobility, the agent needs to ensure that action, contingent upon the predicted proprioceptive states associated with (say) reaching for the beer mug, wins out over veridical perception (signalling that the hand is currently immobile).

There are two (functionally equivalent) ways this might be achieved. Either the precision associated with the current sensory input (specifying that the hand is immobile on table) needs to be reduced, or the precision associated with the higher level representation (specifying the trajectory to the beer mug) needs to be increased. As long as the *balance* between these is correct, movement (and mug grasping) will ensue. In the next two sections, we consider what happens if that balance is altered or disturbed.

7.8   *Less Sense, More Action?*

Brown, Adams, et al. (2013) offer a series of simulations that (just as in the experiments reported in 7.6) explore the consequences of altering the precision-modulated balance between sensory input and higher level prediction. The basic scenario here is one in which a given somatosensory input (e.g., one involving a sensation of touch) is generated ambiguously and could be the result of a self-generated force, an externally imposed force, or some mixture of the two. To identify the origin of the somatosensory stimulation, the system (in this simplified model) must use proprioceptive information (information about muscle tensions, joint pressures, and so on) to distinguish between self-generated and externally generated inputs. Proprioceptive predictions originating from higher levels of processing are (in the usual manner of active inference) positioned to bring about movement. Finally, variable precision-weighting of sensory prediction error enables the system to attend to current sensory input to a greater or lesser degree, flexibly balancing reliance upon (or confidence in) the input with reliance upon (or confidence in) its own higher level predictions.

Such a system (for the full implementation, see Brown, Adams, et al., 2013) is able to generate a bodily movement when (but only when) the balance between reliance upon current sensory input and reliance upon higher level predictions is correct. At the limit, errors associated with the higher level proprioceptive predictions (specifying the desired trajectory) would be accorded a very high weighting, while those associated with current proprioceptive input (specifying the current position of the limb or effector) would be low-weighted. This would deliver extreme attenuation of the current sensory information, allowing errors concerning the predicted proprioceptive signals to enjoy functional primacy, becoming a self-fulfilling prophecy as the system moves so as to quash those highly weighted errors.

As sensory attenuation is reduced, however, the situation changes dramatically. At the opposite extreme, when sensory precision is much higher than that associated with higher level prediction, there is no attenuation of the current sensory input and no movement can ensue. Brown et al. explored this balance using many different runs of the simulation, showing (as would now be expected) that 'as the prior precision increases in relation to sensory precision, prior beliefs are gradually able to incite more confident movement' (p. 11). In the active inference setting, then, 'sensory attenuation is necessary if prior beliefs are to supervene over sensory evidence, during self-generated behavior' (p. 11). This is already an interesting result, since it provides a fundamental reason for the kinds of sensory attenuation noted in 7.7, including attenuation, during self-generated movement, in respect even of externally generated inputs (the case most resistant to explanation by the standard forward-model-based account).

Importantly, less confidence in sensory prediction error means less confidence in beliefs about the causes of such error. Brown, Adams, et al. (2013, p. 11) describe this state as one of 'transient uncertainty' due to a 'temporary suspension of attention [recall that attention, in PP is implemented by increased precision-weighting of prediction error] to sensory input'. The upshot is that externally generated sensations will in general be registered much more forcefully than internally generated ones. In the context of self-generated movements, higher level predictions are able to entrain movements only courtesy of the attenuation (reduced precision) of current sensory inputs. A somatosensory state, when externally produced, will thus appear more intense (less attenuated) than the very same state when produced by means of self-generated action (see Cardoso-Leite et al., 2010). If a subject is then asked to match an externally generated force with an internally generated one (as in the force-matching task rehearsed earlier), force escalation will immediately follow (for some compelling simulation studies of this effect, using the apparatus of active inference described above, see Adams, Stephan et al., 2013).

In sum, action (under active inference) requires a kind of targeted dis-attention in which current sensory input is attenuated so as to allow predicted sensory (proprioceptive) states to entrain movement. At first sight, this is a rather baroque (Heath Robinson / Rube Goldberg –like) mechanism[8] involving an implausible kind of self-deception. According to this story, it is only by downplaying genuine sensory information specifying how our bodily parts are *actually* currently arrayed in space that the brain can 'take seriously' the *predicted* proprioceptive information that determines movement, allowing those predictions to act (as we saw in chapter 4) directly as motor commands. Whether this part of the PP story is correct, it seems to me, is one of the larger open questions hereabouts. On the plus side, however, such a model helps make sense of familiar (but otherwise puzzling) phenomena, such as the impairment of fluent motor action by deliberate acts of attention ('choking'), and a variety of somatic delusions and disorders of movement, as we shall now see.

7.9   Disturbing the Network (Sensory Attenuation)

Assuming (for the sake of argument) that the story just rehearsed is correct, we can now ask ourselves what would happen if this capacity for targeted dis-attention is impaired or damaged? Such a system would be unable to attenuate the impact of ascending sensory prediction errors. Impaired capacities for attenuation will tend (we saw) to prevent self-generated movement. The situation is nicely summarized by Edwards et al. who note that:

> If the precision of high-level representations supervenes, then proprioceptive prediction errors will be resolved through classical reflex arcs and movement will ensue. However, if proprioceptive precision is higher, then proprioceptive prediction errors may well be resolved by changing top-down predictions to accommodate the fact that no movement is sensed. In short, not only does precision determine the delicate balance between sensory evidence and prior beliefs in perception, through exactly the same mechanisms, it can also determine whether we act or not. (Edwards et al., 2012, p. 4)

If sensory attenuation is impaired, the higher level predictions that would normally result in movement may indeed be formed, but will now enjoy reduced precision relative to the sensory input, rendering them functionally inert or (at the very least) severely compromised.[9]

This pattern of effects, Brown, Adams, et al. (2013, p. 11) argue, might also underlie the everyday experience of 'choking' while engaged in some sport or delicate (but well-practiced) physical activity (see Maxwell et al., 2006). In such cases, the deployment of deliberate attention to the movement seems to interfere with our own capacities to produce it with fluency and ease. The problem may be that attending to the movement increases the precision of current sensory information with a consequent decrease in the influence of the higher level proprioceptive predictions that would otherwise entrain fluid movement.

At high levels of impairment (of the normal process of sensory attenuation), movement becomes impossible and the system—although biomechanically sound—is incapable of movement. This was demonstrated by Brown et al. using a simple simulation in which systemic confidence or certainty about sensory prediction error was varied.

Movement required the precision of higher level proprioceptive predictions to be high relative to that of the sensory evidence. When the
reverse was the case, movement was blocked. Under such conditions,
the only way to restore movement is to artificially inflate the precision
of the higher level states (i.e., to increase the precision of prediction
errors at the higher level). Weakened sensory attenuation is now overcome and movement enabled. This is because the higher level predictions (that unpack into a trajectory of proprioceptive states implied by
some target action) now enjoy increased precision relative to that of
the (still unattenuated) current sensory states. At a certain point (as
demonstrated in the simulation studies by Adams, Stephan, et al.,
2013) this will allow movement to occur yet abolish the force-matching
illusion (and presumably enable self-tickling, were that part of the
simulation!)—the combination characteristic of schizophrenic subjects.

   This remedy, however, brings with it a cost. For the system, though
now able to self-generate movements, becomes prone to a variety of
'somatic delusions'. This is because those over-precise (unattenuated)
sensory prediction errors still need to be explained. To do so, the simulated agents studied by Adams, Stephan, et al. (2013; and by Brown,
Adams, et al., 2013) infer an additional external force—a 'hidden external cause' for what is, in fact, a purely self-generated pattern of sensory stimulation. This agent 'believes that when it presses its finger on
its hand, something also pushes its hand against its finger' (Brown,
Adams, et al., 2013, p. 14). We 'expect' the sensed consequences of our
own actions to be attenuated relative to similar sensory consequences
when induced by external forces. But now (despite being, in fact, the
originator of the action) the simulated agent fails to attenuate those sensory consequences, unleashing a flow of prediction error that recruits a
new—but delusional—hypothesis. This establishes a fundamental link
between the observed failures of sensory attenuation in schizophrenia
and the emergence of false beliefs concerning agency.

7.10   'Psychogenic Disorders' and Placebo Effects

A very similar pattern of disturbed inference, again consequent upon
alterations to the delicate economy of precision-weighting, may explain
certain forms of 'functional motor and sensory symptoms'. This names
a constellation of so-called 'psychogenic' disorders in which there are
abnormal movements or sensations, yet no apparent 'organic' or physiological cause. Following Edwards et al. (2012), I use the term 'functional motor and sensory symptoms' to cover such cases: cases that are

sometimes described as 'psychogenic', 'non-organic', 'unexplained', or even (in older parlance) 'hysterical'.[10] The suggestions that follow are equally applicable (though they are there associated with more positive outcomes) to an understanding of the potency and scope of 'placebo effects' (see Büchel et al., 2014; Atlas & Wager 2012; Anchisi and Zanon 2015).

Functional motor and sensory symptoms are surprisingly common and are diagnosed in around 16% of neurological patients (Stone et al., 2005). Examples included organically unexplained cases of 'anaesthesia, blindness, deafness, pain, sensorimotor aspects of fatigue, weakness, aphonia, abnormal gait, tremor, dystonia and seizures' (Edwards et al., 2012, p. 2). Strikingly, the contours of the problems that afflict these patients often follow 'folk' notions of the demarcation of bodily parts (e.g., where a paralysed hand stops and an unparalysed arm begins[11]) or of the visual field. Another example is:

> 'tubular' visual field defect, where patients with a functional loss of their central visual field report a defect of the same diameter, whether it is mapped close to them or far away. This defies the laws of optics, but may fit with (lay) beliefs about the nature of vision. (Edwards et al., 2012, p. 5)

Similarly, so-called 'whiplash injury' following motor accidents turns out to be very rare in countries where the general population is unaware of the anticipated 'shape' of this injury (Ferrari et al., 2001). But where the injury is well-publicized, Edwards et al. (2012, p. 6) note 'the expectation in population surveys of the medical consequences of minor traffic accidents mirrors the incidence of whiplash symptoms'.

The role of expectations and prior beliefs in the etiology of such (genuinely physically experienced) effects is further evidenced by their manipulability. Thus:

> In a related study of low back pain after minor injury in Australia, a state-wide campaign to change expectations regarding the consequences of such injury led to a sustained and significant reduction in the incidence and severity of chronic back pain (Buchbinder and Jolley, 2005). (Edwards et al., 2012, p. 6)

One route by which prior beliefs might impact both sensory and motor performances is via the distribution of attention. Functional motor and sensory symptoms are already associated, in a long and compelling literature, with alterations in the flow and distribution of bodily attention and more specifically with introspective tendencies and a kind of 'body-focused attentional bias' (see Robbins & Kirmayer, 1991, and reviews by Brown, 2004, and Kirmayer & Tailefer, 1997). Attempting to tie this large literature together, Brown identifies, as a leading thread, 'the repetitive reallocation of high-level attention on to symptoms'. It is natural to suppose that the allocation of attention, in such cases, is an effect rather than a cause. However, both the tendency to 'track' folk notions of sensory and motor physiology and the diagnostic signs used to identify cases of functional motor and sensory symptoms speak against this. For example, 'if a patient with functional leg weakness is asked to flex their unaffected hip, their unattended "paralysed" hip will automatically extend; this is known as Hoover's sign (Ziv et al., 1998)' (Edwards et al., 2012, p. 6). In a wide range of cases, functional sensory and motor symptoms are thus 'masked' when subjects are not attending to the affected element.

Such linkages between functional motor and sensory symptoms and abnormalities in the allocation of attention are especially suggestive when considered within the predictive processing framework. Within that framework, attention corresponds, as we have noted on many occasions, to the weighting of prediction error signals at various processing levels according to their estimated precision (inverse variance). This weighting determines the balance between top-down expectation and bottom-up sensory evidence. That same balance, if the class of models we have been pursuing is on track, determines what is perceived and how we act. This opens up a space in which to explore a unified model of the etiology of functional symptoms in both the sensory and motor domain.

7.11   Disturbing the Network ('Psychogenic' Effects)

The fundamental problem leading to functional motor and sensory symptoms, Edward et al. suggest, may be a disturbance to the mechanisms of precision-weighting at (in the first instance) intermediate[12] levels of sensorimotor processing. Such a disturbance (itself as ultimately biological as any other physiological malfunction) would consist in the overweighting of prediction error at that intermediate level, leading to a kind of systemic overconfidence in that specific set of probabilistic expectations, and hence in any bottom-up sensory inputs that seem to conform to them.

Suppose this were to occur against the backdrop of some salient physical event, such as an injury or a viral infection. Such events frequently (but not always, see below) precede the onset of functional motor or sensory symptoms (Stone et al., 2012). Under such conditions:

> salient sensory data arising from these precipitating events are afforded excessive precision (weight) . . . this instantiates an abnormal prior belief at an intermediate level in the cortical hierarchy trying to explain or predict those sensations—and that abnormal belief or expectation is rendered resistant to extinction through the unusually high levels of precision (synaptic gain) enjoyed during its formation. (Edwards et al., 2012, p. 6)

Precipitating events are not, however, a necessary condition (given the model) for functional motor and sensory symptoms. Thus suppose that, for whatever reason, some sub-personal, intermediate-level expectation of a sensation or bodily movement (or equally, some expectation of a *lack* of sensation or bodily movement) is formed. That intermediate-level prediction now enjoys enhanced status, due to the disturbed (inflated) precision of prediction error reporting at that level. Now, even random noise (fluctuations within normal bounds) may be interpreted as signal, and the stimulus (or lack of stimulus) 'detected'. This is simply the 'White Christmas' effect that we have now encountered many times in the text. In other words, from the predictive processing perspective 'there might only be a quantitative—not qualitative—difference between "somatic amplification" and the generation of completely false perceptions' (Edwards et al., 2012, p. 7).

To complete the picture, notice that the precise prediction errors that select and 'confirm' the intermediate-level hypotheses serve to reinforce the intermediate-level prior, hence self-stabilizing the misleading pattern of somatic inference. At the same time, higher level networks must try to make sense of these apparently confirmed, but actually pathologically self-produced, patterns of stimulation (or lack of stimulation). No higher level explanation, in terms of, for example, some expected percept or sensation, or a systemic decision to move or to not move, is available. The higher levels, one might say, were not predicting the movement or sensation, even though it originated from the system itself. To make sense of this, new causes—such as basic illness or neurological injury—are inferred. In short, there occurs what Edwards et al. (2012, p. 14) describe as a 'misattribution of agency, where experiences that are usually generated in a voluntary way are perceived as involuntary'. The self-produced sensations are now classed as symptoms of some elusive biological dysfunction. And indeed they are: but the dysfunction might also, and perhaps more properly, be thought of as cybernetic: as an imbalance in the complex inner economy of evidence, inference, and control.[13]

The same broad story applies, as mentioned earlier, to so-called 'placebo effects'. Recent decades have seen an increasing appreciation of the power and scope of such effects (for reviews, see Benedetti, 2013; Tracey, 2010). Expectancy, quite general, demonstrably affects the behavioural, physiological, and neural outcomes of treatment and does so both in the context of inert (classic placebo) treatments and in the context of real treatments (Bingel et al., 2011; Schenk et al., 2014). In a recent review article on 'placebo analgesia' (though the authors prefer to speak of 'placebo hypoalgesia', thus stressing expectancy-based pain reduction rather than pain elimination), it is suggested that:

> the ascending and descending pain system resembles a recurrent system that allows for the implementation of predictive coding—meaning that the brain is not passively waiting for nociceptive [painful] stimuli to impinge upon it but is actively making inferences based on prior experience and expectations. (Buchel et al., 2014, p. 1223)

The suggestion is that top-down predictions of pain relief are combined, at multiple levels of the neural hierarchy, with bottom-up signals, in a way modulated (as always) by their estimated precision—the certainty or reliability assigned to the predictions. This provides a very natural account of the documented impact of complex rituals, visibly sophisticated interventions, and patient confidence in doctors, practitioners, and treatments.[14]

7.12   Autism, Noise, and Signal

Disturbances to that same complex economy of evidence, inference, and expectation might (Pellicano & Burr, 2012) help explain the origination of the so-called 'non-social symptoms' of autism. These are symptoms manifest in the sensory rather than the social domain. The social symptoms include the well-known difficulties in the recognition of other agents' emotions and intentions and aversion to many forms of social interaction. Non-social symptoms include hypersensitivity to sensory—especially unexpected sensory—stimulation, repetitive behaviours and highly regimented, restricted interests and activities. For a sketch of the whole constellation of social and non-social elements, see Frith (2008).

A key finding in the perceptual domain (Shah & Frith, 1983) was the enhanced capacity of autistic subjects to find an element (such as a triangle) when it occurs 'hidden' within the context of a larger mean-ingful figure (e.g., a picture of a pram). The capacity consistently to out-perform neurotypical subjects on this 'embedded figures' task led to the suggestion (Frith, 1989; Happé & Frith, 2006) that autistic subjects display 'weak central coherence', that is, a processing style that fore-grounds parts and detail at the expense of an easy grip upon the larger context in which they occur. The hypothesis of a significant perceptual processing difference between autistic and neurotypical populations is further supported, Pellicano and Burr note, by studies showing autistic subjects to be less susceptible to some visual illusions (e.g., the Kanizsa triangle illusion, the hollow mask illusion, which we met in chapter 1,[15] and the tabletop illusion, see Figure 7.1). Autistic subjects are also more likely to possess absolute pitch, are better at many forms of visual dis-crimination (see Happé, 1996; Joseph et al., 2009; Miller, 1999; Plaisted et al., 1998a,b), and are less susceptible to the hollow mask illusion (Dima et al., 2009).

Given this body of evidence, some authors (Mottron et al., 2006; Plaisted, 2001) have explored the idea that autism involves abnormally strengthened or enhanced sensory experience. Such accounts have been presented as alternatives to the notion of weak central coher-ence, or weakened influence of top-down expectations. Notice however that from a broadly Bayesian perspective, this apparent opposition

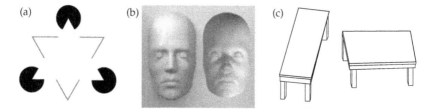

FIGURE 7.1   Autistic Subjects Are Less Susceptible to Illusions in Which Prior Knowledge is Used to Interpret Ambiguous Sensory Information
Examples of such illusions include (a) the Kanizsa triangle. The edges of the triangle are not really there, but would be for the most probable physical structure: a white triangle overlaying three regular circles. (b) The hollow-face illusion. A strong bias (or 'prior') for natural concave faces offsets competing information (such as shadows) and causes one to perceive a concave, hollow mask (right) as a normal convex face (left). (c) Shepard's table illusion. The 2D images of the parallelograms are in fact identical. However, the image is consis-tent with many 3D shapes, the most probable being real tables slanting at about 458: to be consistent with the identical 2D images, the table-tops need to be of very different dimensions.

Source: Pellicano & Burr, 2012.

loses some of its force since what really matters (see Brock, 2012) is the achieved balance between top-down and bottom-up modes of influence.

Taking the Bayesian perspective, Pellicano and Burr depict autistic perception as involving a disturbance to systemic abilities to deal with sensory uncertainty due to an attenuated influence of prior knowledge.[16] The upshot of such weakened influence is a positive capacity to treat more incoming stuff as signal and less as noise (leading to the enhanced capacities to spot hidden figures and to recognize the true contours of the sensory data). But this means, in turn, that huge amounts of incoming information are treated as salient and worthy of attention, thus increasing effortful processing and incurring significant emotional costs. For example, where a neurotypical child learns to recognize objects under a wide variety of lighting conditions and can use the shadows cast by objects as a source of useful information, such situations prove challenging to autistic subjects (Becchio et al., 2010). Instead of falling into place as a predictable pattern of sensory stimulation associated, in current context, with the presence of a certain object, shadows may be treated as sensory data in need of further explanation. In other words, the influence of top-down predictions (priors) may usually serve—exactly as the predictive processing model suggests—to strip the sensory signal of much of its 'newsworthiness'. Weakened influence of this kind (described by Pellicano and Burr as 'hypo-priors'[17]) would result in a constant barrage of information demanding further processing and might plausibly engender severe emotional costs and contribute to the emergence of a variety of self-protective strategies involving repetition, insulation, and narrowing of focus.

Such an account, it seems to me, holds out promise not just as a means of accommodating the 'non-social symptoms' of autism but also as a potential bridge between those symptoms and disturbances to fluid social engagement and interpersonal understanding. The more complex the domain, one might reasonably suspect, the greater the impact of attenuated priors upon inference and (hence) upon performance and response. The social domain is highly complex (frequently involving the appreciation of perspectives upon perspectives, as when we know that John suspects that Mary is not telling the truth). It is, moreover, a domain in which context (as every soap opera fan knows) is everything and in which the meaning of small verbal and non-verbal signs must be interpreted against a rich backdrop of prior knowledge. The kind of signal/noise imbalance described earlier might thus result in especially marked difficulties with both social interaction and (as a result) social learning. In just this vein, Van de Cruys et al. (2013) suggest that:

> The taxing experience in autism (cf. sensory overload) may result from a perceptual system that continuously signals prediction errors, indicating that there always remains something to be learnt still and that attentional resources are needed. The accompanying negative feelings could cause these patients to avoid the most variable or unpredictable situations where context-dependent high-level predictions are more important than concrete perceptual details. This may be the case for social interaction in particular. The overwhelming prediction errors cause these patients (or their caregivers) to externalize and enforce predictability through exact routines and patterns in their daily activities. (Van de Cruys et al., 2013, p. 96)

Van de Cruys et al. suggest, however, that rather than simply thinking in terms of attenuated priors, it might be fruitful to focus upon the mechanisms by which the impact of priors at different levels are modulated. This corresponds, within the predictive processing framework, to the modulation of precision according to the demands of task and context. In support of this proposal, the authors cite various evidence showing that autistic subjects can construct and deploy strong priors but may have difficulties applying them. This might follow if those priors were constructed to fit a signal that, from a neurotypical perspective at least, actually includes a lot of noise but is being treated as precise. There is, however, no deep conflict between this account and the more general sketch by Pellicano and Burr, since the assignment of precision to prediction errors at various levels of processing itself requires estimations of precision. It is the weakened influence of these estimations (technically, these are hyperpriors) that then explains the gamut of effects rehearsed above (see Friston, Lawson, & Frith, 2013). Both autism and schizophrenia may thus involve (different but related) disturbances to this complex neuromodulatory economy, impacting experience, learning, and affective response.

In sum, variations in the (precision-modulated) tendency to treat more or less of the incoming sensory information as 'news', and more generally in the ability flexibly to modify the balance between top-down and bottom-up information at various stages of processing, will play a major role in determining the nature and contents of perceptual experience. Some variation along these dimensions may also be expected in the general population also and might contribute to differences of learning style and of preferred environment. We thus glimpse a rich, multidimensional space in which to begin to capture both the wide variation seen amongst autistic subjects and within the neurotypical population.

7.13   Conscious Presence

The accounts of schizophrenia, autism, and functional motor and sensory symptoms just rehearsed move seamlessly between computational, neuroscientific, and phenomenological description. This fluid spanning of levels is, we have seen, one of the hallmarks of the predictive processing stable of models. Can we use this apparatus to shed light on other aspects of human experience?

One such aspect is the feeling of 'conscious presence'.[18] Using hierarchical predictive processing as a theoretical framework, Seth et al. (2011) sketch a preliminary theoretical account of this feeling, which may be glossed as the feeling of being truly present in some real-world setting. The account, though speculative, is consistent with a wide variety of pre-existing theory and evidence (for a summary, see Seth et al., 2011; for some important developments, see Seth, 2014; and for a review, Seth, 2013).

Alteration or loss of the sense of reality of the world is known as 'derealization' and of the self, 'depersonalization', and the occurrence of either or both symptoms is labelled Depersonalization Disorder (DPD) (see Phillips et al., 2001; Sierra & David, 2011). DPD patients may describe the world as seeming to be cut off from them, as if they were seeing it in a mirror or behind glass, and symptoms of DPD often occur during the early (prodromal) stages of psychoses such as schizophrenia, where a general feeling of 'strangeness or unreality' may precede the onset of positive symptoms such as delusions or hallucinations (Moller & Husby, 2000).

The feeling of presence results, Seth et al. suggest, from the successful suppression (by successful top-down prediction) of interoceptive sensory signals. Interoceptive sensory signals are signals (as the name suggests) concerning the current inner state and condition of the body—they thus constitute a form of 'inner sensing' whose targets include states of the viscera, the vasomotor system, muscular and air-supply systems, and many more. From a subjective viewpoint, interoceptive awareness manifests as a differentiated array of feelings including those of 'pain, temperature, itch, sensual touch, muscular and visceral sensations . . . hunger, thirst, and "air hunger" ' (Craig, 2003, p. 500). The interoceptive system is thus mostly concerned with pain, hunger, and the states of various inner organs, and is distinct from both the exteroceptive system which includes vision, touch, and audition, and from the proprioceptive system[19] that carries information about relative limb positions, effort, and force. Finally, it is thought that anterior insular cortex (AIC) plays a special role in the integration and use of interoceptive information, and (more generally) in the construction of emotional awareness—perhaps by encoding what Craig (2003, p. 500) describes as 'a meta-representation of the primary interoceptive activity'.

Seth et al. invoke two interacting sub-mechanisms, one concerned with 'agency' and implicating the sensorimotor system, and the other with 'presence' and implicating autonomic and motivational systems (see Figure 7.2). The agency component here will be familiar from some of our earlier discussions as it is based upon the original (Blakemore et al., 2000; see also Fletcher & Frith, 2009) model of the disturbed sense of agency in schizophrenia. That account (see 4.2) invoked a weakened capacity to predict (with sufficient precision) the sensory consequences of our actions as a prime component in the origination of feelings of alien control and so on. But the account is compatible with the recent refinements (7.7–7.9) suggesting that the primary pathology may actually be a failure to attenuate the impact of ascending sensory prediction errors. The compatibility (for present purposes) is assured since what matters functionally speaking is the balance between the precision assigned to downwards-flowing prediction and to upward-flowing sensory information—a balance that could be disturbed either by overestimating the precision of certain lower level signals (hence failing to attenuate the impact of the current sensory state), or by underestimating the precision of relevant higher level predictions.

The sense of presence arises, Seth et al. suggest, from the interaction of the systems involved in explaining away exteroceptive and proprioceptive error and systems involved in another type of prediction: prediction of our own complex interoceptive states. A key site here, Seth et al. speculate, may be the AIC since this area (as noted above) is thought to integrate various bodies of interoceptive and exteroceptive information (see Craig, 2002; Critchley et al., 2004; Gu et al., 2013). The AIC is also known to participate in the prediction of painful or affect-laden stimulations (see Lovero et al., 2009; Seymour et al., 2004; and recall the discussion in 7.9). AIC is also activated by seeing movies of people scratching, and its level of activation correlates with the extent of 'itch contagion' experienced by the viewers (Holle et al., 2012), suggesting that interoceptive inference can be socially as well as physiologically driven (see Frith & Frith, 2012).

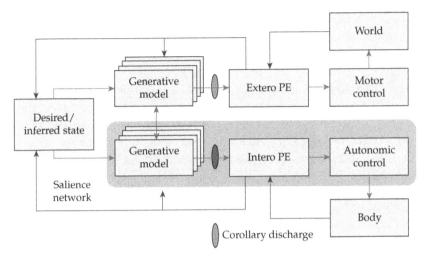

FIGURE 7.2   Seth's Model of Interoceptive Inference
In the model, emotional responses depend on continually updated predictions of the causes of interoceptive input. Starting with a desired or inferred physiological state (which is itself subject to update based on higher level motivational and goal-directed factors), generative models are engaged which predict interoceptive (and exteroceptive) signals via corollary discharge. Applying active inference, prediction errors (PEs) are transcribed into actions via engagement of classical reflex arcs (motor control) and autonomic reflexes (autonomic control). The resulting prediction error signals are used to update the (functionally coupled) generative models and the inferred/desired state of the organism. (At high hierarchical levels these generative models merge into a single multimodal model.) Interoceptive predictions are proposed to be generated, compared, and updated within a 'salience network' (shaded) anchored on the anterior insular and anterior cingulate cortices (AIC, ACC) that engage brainstem regions as targets for visceromotor control and relays of afferent interoceptive signals. Sympathetic and parasympathetic outflow from the AIC and ACC are in the form of interoceptive predictions that enslave autonomic reflexes (e.g., heart/respiratory rate, smooth muscle behaviour), just as proprioceptive predictions enslave classical motor reflexes in PP formulations of motor control This process depends on the transient attenuation of the precision of interoceptive (and proprioceptive) PE signals. Lightly/darkly shaded arrows signify top-down/bottom-up connections.

Source: Seth, 2013.

The suppression of AIC activity by successful top-down predictions of the ebb and flow of interoceptive states results, Seth et al. suggest, in the sense of presence (or at least, in the absence of a sense of non-presence, see note 18). Whereas DPD results, they argue, from pathologically imprecise interoceptive predictions. Such imprecise (hence functionally emaciated) downward-flowing predictions will fail to explain away the incoming streams of interoceptive information, leading to the generation of persistent (but ill-founded) flurries of prediction error. This may manifest subjectively as a hard-to-explain sense of strangeness arising at the meeting point between exteroceptive and interoceptive expectations. Eventually, in severe cases, the ongoing attempt to explain away such persistent error signals may lead to the emergence of new but bizarre explanatory schemas (delusional beliefs concerning our own embodiment and agency). The Seth et al. account is thus structurally isomorphic to the account of Fletcher and Frith (2009), as described in chapter 2.

There is increasing evidence, moreover, for an interoceptive-inference-based account of the more general experience of body ownership (EBO), where this just means the experience of 'owning and identifying with a particular body' (Seth, 2013, p. 565). Here too, the suggestion is that EBO may be the result of an inferential process involving 'multisensory integration of self-related signals across interoceptive and exteroceptive domains' (Seth, 2013, pp. 565–566). Clearly, our own body is a hugely important part of the world upon which we must maintain some kind of grip if we are to survive and flourish. We must build and maintain a grip upon our own bodily position (where we are), our bodily morphology (current shape and composition), and our internal physiological condition (as indexed by states of hunger, thirst, pain, and arousal). To do so, Seth (2013) argues, we must learn and deploy a generative model that isolates 'the causes of those signals "most likely to be me" across interoceptive and exteroceptive domains'. This is not as hard as it sounds, for our own body is uniquely positioned to generate a variety of time-locked multimodal signals as we move, sense, and act in the world. These include both exteroceptive and interoceptive signals, which alter together in ways that are closely determined by our own movements. Thus:

> Among all physical objects in the world, it is only our body that will evoke (i.e., predicts) this kind of multisensory sensation—[a] congruence of multisensory input that has ... been called 'self-specifying' (Botvinick, 2004). (Limanowski & Blankenburg, 2013, p. 4)

The importance of bodily sensations in this constructive process is evidenced in a number of well-known studies involving the so-called 'rubber hand illusion' (Botvinick & Cohen, 1998) mentioned in 6.11. Recall that in these studies a visible artificial hand is stroked in time with a subject's real hand. Attending to the visually presented artificial hand induces a transient sense of ownership of the hand—one that translates into genuine fear when the hand is suddenly menaced with a hammer. Our experience of our own body, all this suggests, is the ongoing product of a generative model that infers bodily location and composition from the time-locked barrage of multimodal sensory information. Given the ecological implausibility of feeling a delicately timed sequence of touches on a visible but non-owned hand, we downgrade some elements of the signal (those specifying the precise spatial location of the actual hand) so as to arrive at a best overall hypothesis—one that now incorporates the rubber hand as a bodily part. Such effects, Seth notes, are remarkably robust and have since been extended into face perception and whole-body ownership (Ehrsson, 2007; Lenggenhager et al., 2007; Sforza et al., 2010).

Extending these studies to incorporate interoceptive (rather than simply tactile) sensory evidence, Suzuki et al. (2013) used a virtual reality headset to make a displayed rubber hand 'pulse' (by changing colour) in time or out-of-time with subjects' own heartbeats. Synchrony between the interocepted cardiac rhythm and the visual pulse increased the sense of rubber-hand ownership (see Figure 7.3). This exciting result provides the first clear-cut evidence that:

> statistical correlations between interoceptive (e.g., cardiac) and exteroceptive (e.g., visual) signals can lead to updating of predictive models of self-related signals through minimization of prediction error, just as may happen for purely exteroceptive multisensory conflicts in the classic RHI [Rubber Hand Illusion]. (Seth, 2013, p. 6)

Our ongoing sense of our own embodiment, all this suggests, depends upon accommodating the full (interoceptive and exteroceptive) sensory barrage using a generative model whose dimensions crucially track aspects of *ourselves*—our bodily array, our spatial location, and our own internal physiological condition.

7.14 Emotion

These same resources may be deployed as the starting point for a promising account of emotion. At this point, the proposal draws (with a twist) upon the well-known James-Lange model of emotional states as arising from the perception of our own bodily responses to external stimuli and events (James, 1884; Lange, 1885). The idea there, in a nutshell, was that our emotional 'feelings' are nothing but the

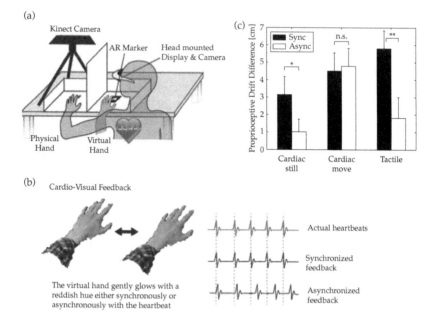

FIGURE 7.3 Interoceptive Rubber-Hand Illusion
(a) Participants sat facing a desk so that their physical (left) hand was out
of sight. A 3D model of the real hand was captured by Microsoft Kinect
and used to generate a real-time virtual hand that was projected into the
head-mounted display (HMD) at the location of the augmented-reality (AR)
marker. Subjects wore a front-facing camera connected to the HMD, so they
saw the camera image superimposed with the virtual hand. They also wore a
pulse-oximeter to measure heartbeat timings and they used their right hand
to make behavioural responses. (b) Cardio-visual feedback (left) was implemented by changing the colour of the virtual hand from its natural colour
towards red and back, over 500 ms either synchronously or asynchronously
with the heartbeat. Tactile feedback (middle) was given by a paintbrush,
which was rendered into the AR environment. A 'proprioceptive drift' (PD)
test (right), adapted for the AR environment, objectively measured perceived
virtual hand position by implementing a virtual measure and cursor.
The PD test measures the perceived position of the real (hidden) hand by asking the participant to move a cursor to its estimated location (c) The experiment consisted of three blocks of four trials each. Each trial consisted of two
PD tests flanking an induction period, during which either cardio-visual or
tactile-visual feedback was provided (120 s). Each trial ended with a questionnaire presented in the HMD. (D) PD differences (PDD, post-induction minus
pre-induction) were significantly larger for synchronous versus asynchronous cardio-visual feedback in the 'cardiac still' (without finger movements),
but not the 'cardiac move' condition (with finger movements). PDDs were

perceptions of our own varying physiological responses. According to James:

> *the bodily changes follow directly the perception of the exciting fact, and ... our feeling of the same changes as they occur is the emotion.* Common sense says, we lose our fortune, are sorry and weep; we meet a bear, are frightened and run; we are insulted by a rival, become angry and strike. The hypothesis here to be defended says that this order of sequence is incorrect ... and that the more rational statement is that we feel sorry because we cry, angry because we strike, afraid because we tremble ... Without the bodily states following on the perception, the latter would be purely cognitive in form, pale, colorless, destitute of emotional warmth. We might then see the bear, and judge it best to run, receive the insult and deem it right to strike, but we should not actually feel afraid or angry. (James, 1890/1950, p. 449)

In other words, it is our interoceptive perception of the bodily changes characteristic of fear (sweating, trembling, etc.) that, for James, constitutes the very feeling of fear, giving it its distinctive psychological flavour. The feeling of fear, if James is right, is essentially the detection of a physiological signature that has already been induced by exposure to the threatening situation.

Such an account is promising, but far from adequate as it stands. For it seems to require a one-to-one mapping between distinct emotional states and distinctive 'brute-physiological' signatures, and it seems to suggest that whenever the physiological state is induced and detected, the same emotional feeling should arise. Neither of these implications (see Critchley, 2005) is borne out by observation and experiment. The basic James-Lange story has, however, been extended and refined in important work such as Critchley (2005), Craig (2002, 2009), Damasio (1999, 2010), and Prinz (2005). Recent work by Seth (2013) and by Pezzulo (2013) continues this trajectory of improvement, adding an important 'predictive twist'. A neglected core component, Seth and

---

also significantly larger for synchronous versus asynchronous tactile-visual feedback ('tactile' condition), replicating the classical RHI. Each bar shows the across-participant average and standard error. (E) Subjective questionnaire responses that probed experience of ownership showed the same pattern as PDDs, whereas control questions showed no effect of cardio-visual or tactile-visual synchrony.

Source: Adapted from Seth (2013) by permission.

Pezzulo each suggest, is the match (or mismatch) between a cascading series of top-down predictions of our own interoceptive states, and the forward-flowing information contained in (interoceptive) sensory prediction error. Such interoceptive predictions, this story suggests 'arise from multiple hierarchical levels, with higher levels integrating interoceptive, proprioceptive, and exteroceptive cues in formulating descending predictions' (Seth 2013, p. 567).

These interoceptive, proprioceptive, and exteroceptive predictions are constructed differently in different contexts, and each provides ongoing guidance to the other. A single inferential process here integrates all these sources of information, generating a context-reflecting amalgam that is experienced as emotion. Felt emotions thus integrate basic information (e.g., about bodily arousal) with higher-level predictions of probable causes and preparations for possible actions. In this way: "the close interplay between interoceptive and exteroceptive inference implies that emotional responses are inevitably shaped by cognitive and exteroceptive context, and that perceptual scenes that evoke interoceptive predictions will always be affectively coloured" (Seth 2013, p. 563).

The Anterior Insular Cortex is—as remarked earlier—remarkably well-positioned to play a major role in such a process. Emotion and subjective feeling states arise, this story suggests, as the result of multilevel inferences that combine sensory (interoceptive, proprioceptive, and exteroceptive) signals with top-down predictions to generate a sense of how things are for us and of what we might be about to do. Such a sense of 'action-ready being' encompasses our background physiological condition, estimations of current potentials for action, and the perceived state of the wider world.

This provides a new and natural way of accommodating large bodies of experimental results suggesting that the character of our emotional experience depends both on the interoception of brute bodily signals and higher level 'cognitive appraisals' (see Critchley & Harrison, 2013; Dolan, 2002; Gendron & Barrett, 2009; Prinz, 2004). An example of a brute bodily signal is generic arousal as induced by—to take the classic example from Schachter and Singer (1962)—an injection of adrenaline. Such brute signals combine with contextually induced 'cognitive appraisals' leading us to interpret the very same bodily 'evidence' as either elation, anger, or lust according to our framing expectations. Those experiments proved hard to replicate,[20] but better evidence comes from recent studies that subtly manipulate interoceptive feedback—for example, studies showing that false cardiac feedback can enhance subjective ratings of emotional stimuli (see Valins 1966; Gray et al., 2007; and discussion in Seth 2013).

The 'predictive twist' thus allows us to combine a core insight of the James-Lange theory (the idea that interoceptive self-monitoring is a key component in the construction of emotional experience) with a fully integrated account of the role of other factors, such as context and expectation. Previous attempts to combine these insights have taken the form of so-called 'two-factor' theories, where these depict subjective feeling states as essentially hybrid states involving two components—a bodily feeling and a 'cognitive' interpretation. It is worth stressing that the emerging predictive processing account of emotion is not a 'two-factor' theory as such. Instead, the claim is that a single, highly flexible process fluidly combines top-down predictions with all manner of bottom-up sensory information, and that subjective feeling states (along with the full range of exteroceptive perceptual experiences) are determined by the ongoing unfolding of this single process.[21]

Such a process will involve distributed patterns of neural activity across multiple regions. Those patterns will themselves change and alter according to task and context, along with the relative balances between top-down and bottom-up influence (see especially chapters 2 and 5). Importantly, that same process determines not just the flow of perception and emotion, but the flow of action too (chapters 4–6). PP thus posits a single, distributed, constantly self-reconfiguring, prediction-driven regime as the common basis for perception, emotion, reason, choice, and action. The PP account of emotion thus belongs, it seems to me, in the same broad camp as so-called 'enactivist' accounts (see Colombetti, 2014; Colombetti & Thompson, 2008; and discussion in chapter 9) that reject any fundamental cognition/emotion divide and that stress continuous reciprocal interactions between brain, body, and world.

7.15   Fear in the Night

Pezzulo (2013) develops an account that is in many ways complementary to those of Seth (2013), and Seth et al. (2011). Pezzulo's target is the apparently irrational experience of 'fear in the night'. Here is the vignette with which Pezzulo opens his treatment:

> It's a windy night. You go to sleep a bit shocked because, say, you had a small car accident or just watched a shark attack horror movie. During the night, you hear a window squeaking. In normal conditions, you would attribute this noise to the windy night. But this night the idea that a thief or even a killer is entering your house jumps into your mind. Normally you

would have immediately dismissed this hypothesis, but now it seems quite believable despite the fact that there have been no thefts in your town in the last few years; and you suddenly find yourself expecting a thief coming out from the shadows. How is this possible? (Pezzulo, 2013, p. 902)

The explanation, Pezzulo argues, once again involves interoceptive prediction. Thus suppose we consider only the exteroceptive sensory evidence. Given our priors, the wind hypothesis then provides the best way of 'explaining away' the sensory data. And even if we add some small biasing or priming effects stemming from seeing the accident or from viewing the movie, this alone seems unlikely to alter that outcome. The sounds of creaking doors and the sight of moving shadows are surely still best accommodated by the simple hypothesis of a windy but otherwise safe and normal situation.

Things alter, however, once we add the effects of interoceptive prediction to the mix. For now we have two sets of sensory evidence in need of explanation. One set comprises the current sights and sounds just mentioned. Another set, however, comprises the kinds of complex multidimensional interoceptive information (including motivational information, in the form of interoceptive states registering hunger, thirst, etc.) described in 7.13. Let's assume that viewing the accident or horror movie—and perhaps recalling it just before bed—results in altered bodily states such as increased heart rate and galvanic skin response, and other internal signs of generalized arousal. There are now two co-occurring streams of sensory evidence to be 'explained away'. Furthermore (and this, it seems to me, is the crucial move in Pezzulo's account), one of those streams of evidence—the interoceptive stream—is typically known with great certainty. The streams of interoceptive evidence that reveal our own bodily states (such as hunger, thirst, and generalized arousal) are normally accorded high reliability, so prediction errors associated with those states will enjoy high precision and great functional efficacy.[22] At this point, the Bayesian balance tilts, Pezzulo argues, more strongly towards the alternative (initially seemingly implausible) hypothesis of a thief in the night. For this hypothesis explains both sets of data and is highly influenced by the interoceptive data—the data that is estimated as highly reliable.[23]

This account thus offers—like that of Seth (2013)—a kind of Bayesian gloss on the James-Lange model according to which aspects of felt emotion involve the perception of our own bodily (visceral, interoceptive) states. Adding the predictive dimension now allows us to link this independently attractive proposal to the full explanatory apparatus of hierarchical predictive processing. The relevant aspects of felt emotion, Seth and Pezzulo each suggest, depend upon the combination of our own interoceptive and exteroceptive expectations and the incoming interoceptive and exteroceptive sensory streams. The various checks and balances that this involves are, moreover, themselves determined by ongoing estimations of (1) the relative reliability of the various types of sensory signal, and (2) the relative reliability of top-down expectations and bottom-up sensory information. All this is occurring (if the account in chapter 6 is on the mark) within an economy that is fundamentally action-oriented, involving estimations of multiple probabilistic affordances—multiple graded potentials for action and intervention. Such affordances, we may now speculate, will be selected and nuanced in part by interoceptive signals, enabling what Lowe and Ziemke (2011) call 'action-tendency prediction-feedback loops': looping interactions in which emotional responses reflect, select, and regulate bodily states and actions. The upshot is a hugely complex cognitive-emotional-action-oriented economy whose fundamental guiding principles are simple and consistent: the multilevel, multi-area, flow of prediction, inflected at every stage by changing estimations of our own uncertainty.

7.16   A Nip of the Hard Stuff

Reflections upon uncertainty, prediction, and action are essential, I believe, if we are to begin to bridge the daunting gap between the world of lived human experience and a cognitive scientific understanding of the inner (and outer) machinery of mind and reason. To be sure, the uncertainty-based discussions of schizophrenia, autism, functional sensory and motor systems, DPD, emotion, and 'fear in the night' reported in the present chapter are at best tentative and preliminary. But they begin to suggest, in broad outline, ways to connect our neurophysiological understandings, via computational and 'systems level' theorizing, to the shape and nature of human experience. Perhaps most significantly of all, they do all this in a way that begins to bring together (perhaps for the very first time) an understanding of the perceptual, motoric, emotional, and cognitive dimensions of various neuropsychological disturbances—superficially distinct elements that are now bound together in a single regime.

The picture that emerges is one that sits extremely well with lived human experience. It does so, I suggest, precisely *because* it binds together many of the elements (perceptual, cognitive, emotional, and motoric) that previous cognitive scientific theorizing has tended to pull apart. In our lived experience what we encounter is first and foremost a world worth acting in: a world of objects, events, and persons, presented as apt for engagement, permeated by affect, desire, and the rich web of conscious and non-conscious expectations.[24] To understand how this complex economy actually operates, how it responds to various disturbances, and how it supports large individual variations even within 'neurotypical' experience, a key tool is the realization that this complex flow is tempered at every level by estimated uncertainty. Here, PP suggests, systems encoding the estimated precision or reliability of prediction error signals play a crucial, and surprisingly unified, role.[25]

Such models leave many important questions unresolved. For example, is the primary pathology in the case of schizophrenic subjects really a failure to attenuate the impact of sensory prediction error, or is it some causally antecedent weakening of the influence of top-down expectations? From a Bayesian perspective, the results are indistinguishable since what matters (as we have now frequently remarked) is rather the balance between top-down expectation and bottom-up sensing. But from a clinical perspective, such options are importantly distinct, implicating different aspects of the neural implementation. Moreover, it was also suggested that one result of failures of low-level sensory attenuation might actually be artificially *inflated* precision at higher levels, so as to enable movement (but at the cost of increased exposure to various delusions of agency and control). The delicate system of uncertainty-based checks and balances may thus be disturbed in many different ways, some of them hard to associate with distinct behavioural outcomes.

Exploring the many ways to alter or disturb that delicate system of check and balances offers, however, a golden opportunity to account for a wide variety of conditions (including the large variation in 'neurotypical' response) using a single theoretical apparatus and a single bridging notion: hierarchical action-oriented predictive processing with disturbances to estimations of uncertainty. We may thus be entering (or at least spotting on the not-too-distant horizon) a golden age of 'computational psychiatry' (Montague et al., 2012) in which superficially different sets of symptoms may be explained by subtly different disturbances to core mechanisms implicated in perception, emotion, inference, and action. Such disturbances, PP suggests, are mostly disturbances of (multiple and varied) mechanisms of attention and targeted dis-attention. Foregrounding attention in all its varieties hints at future bridges with many existing forms of therapy and intervention, ranging from Cognitive Behavioural Therapy, to meditation, and the surprisingly potent role of patients' own outcome expectations.

Using this integrated apparatus might we, inch-by-inch and phenomenon-by-phenomenon, begin to solve the so-called 'hard problem' of conscious experience itself—the mystery (Chalmers, 1996; Levine, 1983; Nagel, 1974) of why it feels *like this* (or indeed, like anything at all) to be a human agent immersed in a world of sights, sounds, and feelings? It is far too early to say, but it feels like progress.[26] Much of that progress, we saw, depends upon a swathe of recent empirically informed conjecture concerning the role of 'interoceptive inference'—roughly, the prediction and accommodation of our own internal bodily states. Taken together, and mixed liberally with the rich PP account of prediction, action, and imagination, these deliver a startlingly familiar vision: the vision of a creature whose own bodily needs, condition, and sense of physical presence forms the pivot-point for knowing, active encounters with a structured and inherently meaningful external world. This multilayered texture, in which a world of external causes and opportunities for organism-salient action is presented to a creature in a way constantly intermingled with a grip upon its own bodily condition may lie at the very heart of that ever-elusive, and ever-familiar, beast that we call 'conscious experience'.

The world thus revealed is a world tailored for action, structured by complex, multilevel patterns of interoceptive, proprioceptive, and exteroceptive expectation, and nuanced by targeted attention and estimated uncertainty. This is a world in which unexpected absences are every bit as salient (as newsworthy relative to our best multilevel prediction) as that which is real and present. It is a world of structure and opportunity, constantly inflected by external and internal (bodily) context. By bringing this familiar world back into view, PP offers a unique and promising approach to understanding agency, experience, and human mattering.

Part III

SCAFFOLDING PREDICTION

8

The Lazy Predictive Brain

8.1   Surface Tensions

'Fast, Cheap, and Out of Control' was the name of a 1997 documentary by Errol Morris, part of which was devoted to work in what was (at that time) the fairly new discipline of behaviour-based robotics. The movie took its name from the title of a famous 1989 paper[1] in which Rodney Brooks and Anita Flynn reviewed many of the emerging principles of work in this field: work that aimed to address the thorny problems confronting mobile autonomous (or semi-autonomous) robots. What was most striking about this new body of work was its radical departure from many deeply entrenched assumptions about the inner roots of adaptive response. In particular, Brooks and others were attacking what might be dubbed 'symbolic, model-heavy' approaches in which successful behaviour depends upon the acquisition and deployment of large bodies of symbolically coded knowledge concerning the nature of the operating environment. Instead, Brooks' robots got by using a number of simpler tricks, ploys, and stratagems whose combined effect (in the environments in which they were to operate) was to support fast, robust, computationally inexpensive forms of online response.

The most extreme versions of Brooks' approach proved intrinsically limited and did not (perhaps unsurprisingly) scale up well to confront truly complex, multidimensional problem spaces (for some discussion, see Pfeifer & Scheier, 1999, chapter 7). Nonetheless, Brooks' work was part of the vanguard of hugely productive and important waves of work addressing the many ways in which intelligent agents might make the most of the many opportunities made available by their own bodily forms, actions, and the persisting, manipulable structure of the environment itself (see Clark, 1997; Clark, 2008; Pfeifer & Bongard, 2008).

This poses something of a puzzle. For on first encounter, work on hierarchical predictive processing can look rather different—it can seem to be stressing the burgeoning multilevel complexity of stored knowledge *rather* than the delicate, opportunistic dance of brain, body, and world. Such a diagnosis would be deeply misguided. It would be misguided because what is on offer is, first and foremost, a story about efficient, self-organizing routes to adaptive success. It is a story, moreover, in which those efficient routes may—and frequently do— involve complex patterns of body- and world-exploiting action and intervention. Properly viewed, PP thus emerges as a new and powerful tool for making organized (and neurocomputationally sound) sense of the ubiquity and power of the efficient problem-solving ploys celebrated by work on the embodied mind. Strikingly, PP offers a systematic means of *combining* those fast, cheap modes of response with more costly, effortful strategies, revealing these as simply extreme poles on a continuum of self-organizing dynamics. As a kind of happy side-effect, attention to the many ways PP embeds and illuminates the full spectrum of embodied response also helps expose the fundamental flaw in some common worries (the ominous-sounding 'darkened room' objections) concerning the overarching vision of a prediction-driven brain.

8.2   Productive Laziness

A recurrent theme in work on the embodied, environmentally situated mind has been the value of 'productive laziness'. I owe this phrase to Aaron Sloman, but the general idea goes back at least to Herbert Simon's (1956) explorations of economical but effective strategies and heuristics: problem-solving recipes that are not (in any absolute sense) optimal or guaranteed to work under all conditions, but that are 'good enough' to meet a need while respecting limitations of time and processing power. For example, rather than attempt a full examination of reviews and menus for every restaurant within a five-mile radius, we might very well choose one that a trustworthy friend mentioned yesterday instead. We do so reasonably confident that it will be good enough, and thereby save the temporal and energetic costs of taking further information into account.

The associated notion of adaptive organisms as 'satisficers' rather than absolute optimizers led to important work in the area of 'bounded rationality' (Gigerenzer & Selton, 2002; Gigerenzer et al., 1999), exploring the unexpected potency of simple heuristics that may lead us astray at times but that also deliver quick verdicts using minimal processing resources.[2] The undoubted role of simple heuristics in the genesis of many human judgments and responses has also been amply demonstrated in large bodies of work displaying the sometimes distortive role of stereotypic scenarios and associated biases in human reasoning (e.g., Tversky & Kahneman, 1973, and for a lovely integrative treatment, Kahneman, 2011). Nonetheless, we humans are also clearly capable of slower, more careful modes of reasoning that can, for limited periods at least, keep some of the errors at bay. To accommodate this, some theorists (see e.g., Stanovich & West, 2000) have suggested a 'two systems' view that posits two different cognitive modes, one ('system 1') associated with fast, automatic, 'habitual' response, and the other ('system 2') with slow, effortful, deliberative reasoning. The PP perspective offers, as we shall see, a flexible means of accommodating such multiple modes and the context-dependent use of fast, heuristic strategies within a single overarching processing regime.

8.3   Ecological Balance and Baseball

Fast, heuristically governed strategies for reasoning are, however, only one part of the rich mosaic of 'productive laziness'. Another part (the focus of much of my own previous work in this area, see Clark, 1997, 2008) involves what might be thought of as ecologically efficient uses of sensing, and the distribution of labour between brain, body, and world. For example, there are circumstances, as Sloman (2013) points out, in which the best way to get through an open door is to rely upon a simple servo-control, or bump-and-swerve, mechanism.

Or consider the task of two-legged locomotion. Some bipedal robots (Honda's flagship 'Asimo' is perhaps the best-known example) walk by means of very precise, and energy-intensive, joint-angle control systems. Biological walking agents, by contrast, make maximal use of the mass properties and biomechanical couplings present in the overall musculoskeletal system and walking apparatus itself. Nature's own bipedal walkers thus make extensive use of so-called 'passive dynamics', the kinematics and organization inhering in the physical device alone (McGeer, 1990). It is such passive dynamics that enable some quite simple toys, that have no on-board power source, to stroll fluently down a gentle incline. Such toys have minimal actuation and no control system. Their walking is a consequence not of complex joint movement planning and actuating, but of their basic morphology (the shape of the body, the distribution of linkages and weights of components, etc.). Locomotion, as nicely noted by Collins et al. (2001, p. 608), is thus 'a natural motion of legged mechanisms, just as swinging is a natural motion of pendulums'.

Passive walkers (and their elegant powered counterparts, see Collins et al., 2001) conform to what Pfeifer and Bongard (2006) describe as a 'Principle of Ecological Balance'. This principle states:

> first . . . that given a certain task environment there has to be a match between the complexities of the agent's sensory, motor, and neural systems . . . second. . . . that there is a certain balance or task-distribution between morphology, materials, control, and environment. (Pfeifer & Bongard, 2006, p. 123)

This principle reflects one of the big lessons of contemporary robotics, which is that the co-evolution of morphology (which can include sensor placement, body-plan, and even the choice of basic building materials, etc.) and control yields a golden opportunity to spread the problem-solving load between brain, body, and world. Robotics thus rediscovers many ideas explicit in the continuing tradition of J. J. Gibson and of 'ecological psychology' (see Gibson, 1979; Turvey & Carello, 1986; Warren, 2006). Thus William Warren, commenting on a quote from Gibson (1979), suggests that:

> biology capitalizes on the regularities of the entire system as a means of ordering behavior. Specifically, the structure and physics of the environment, the biomechanics of the body, perceptual information about the state of the agent-environment system, and the demands of the task all serve to constrain the behavioral outcome. (Warren, 2006, p. 358)

Another Gibsonian theme concerns the role of sensing in action. According to a familiar (more classical) vision, the role of sensing is to get as much information into the system as is needed to solve the problem. These are the 're-constructive' approaches that we met back in chapter 6. For example, a planning agent might scan the environment so as to build up a problem-sufficient model of what is out there and where it is located, at which point the reasoning engine can effectively throw away the world and operate instead upon the inner model, planning and then executing a response (perhaps checking now and then during execution to be sure that nothing has changed). Alternative approaches (see, e.g., Beer, 2000, 2003; Chemero, 2009; Gibson, 1979; Lee & Reddish, 1981; Warren, 2005) depict sensing as a channel productively coupling agent and environment, sidestepping where possible the need to convert world-originating signals into a persisting inner model of the external scene.

Thus consider once again the 'outfielder's problem' as described in chapter 6. This was the problem of running so as to catch a 'fly ball' in baseball. Giving perception its standard role, we might have assumed that the job of the visual system is to transduce information about the current position of the ball so as to allow a distinct 'reasoning system' to project its future trajectory. Nature, however, looks to have found a more elegant and efficient solution. The solution, a version of which was first proposed in Chapman (1968), involves running in a way that seems to keep the ball moving at a constant speed through the visual field. As long as the fielder's own movements cancel any apparent changes in the ball's optical acceleration, she will end up in the location where the ball is going to hit the ground. This solution, Optical Acceleration Cancellation (OAC), explains why fielders, when asked to stand still and simply predict where the ball will land, typically do rather badly. They are unable to predict the landing spot because OAC is a strategy that works by means of moment-by-moment self-corrections that crucially involve the agent's own movements. The suggestion that we rely on such a strategy is also confirmed by some interesting virtual reality experiments in which the ball's trajectory is suddenly altered in flight, in ways that could not happen in the real world (see Fink, Foo, & Warren, 2009). OAC is a nice case of fast, economical problem-solving. The canny use of data freely available in the optic flow enables the catcher to sidestep the need to deploy a rich inner model to calculate the forward trajectory of the ball.[3]

Such strategies are suggestive, as we also noted in chapter 6 (see also Maturana, 1980) of a rather different role for the perceptual coupling itself. Instead of using sensing to get enough information inside, past the visual bottleneck, so as to allow the reasoning system to 'throw away the world' and solve the problem wholly internally, they use the sensor as *an open conduit allowing environmental magnitudes to exert a constant influence on behaviour*. Sensing is thus depicted as the opening of a channel, with successful whole-system behaviour emerging when activity in this channel is kept within a certain range. In such cases, as Randall Beer puts it, 'the focus shifts from accurately representing an environment to continuously engaging that environment with a body so as to stabilize appropriate co-ordinated patterns of behavior' (Beer, 2000, p. 97).

Finally, embodied agents are also able to act on their worlds in ways that actively generate cognitively and computationally potent time-locked patterns of sensory stimulation. For example (and for a fuller discussion, see Clark, 2008), Fitzpatrick et al. (2003) (see also Metta & Fitzpatrick, 2003) show how active object manipulation (pushing and touching objects in view) can help generate information about object boundaries. Their 'baby robot' learns about the boundaries by poking and shoving. It uses motion detection to see its own hand/arm moving, but when the hand encounters (and pushes) an object there is a sudden spread of motion activity. This cheap signature picks out the object from the rest of the environment. In human infants, grasping, poking, pulling, sucking, and shoving creates a rich flow of time-locked *multimodal* sensory stimulation. Such multimodal input streams have been shown (Lungarella & Sporns, 2005) to aid category learning and concept formation. The key to all such capabilities is the robot or infant's capacity to maintain coordinated sensorimotor engagement with its environment. Self-generated motor activity, such work suggests, acts as a 'complement to neural information-processing' (Lungarella & Sporns, 2005, p. 25) in that:

> The agent's control architecture (e.g. nervous system) attends to and processes streams of sensory stimulation, and ultimately generates sequences of motor actions which in turn guide the further production and selection of sensory information. [In this way] 'information structuring' by motor activity and 'information processing' by the neural system are continuously linked to each other through sensorimotor loops. (Lungarella & Sporns, 2005, p. 25)

One major strand of work in robotics and artificial life thus stresses the importance of the distribution of the problem-solving load across the brain, the active body, and the manipulable structures of the local environment. This distribution allows the productively lazy brain to do as little as possible while still solving (or rather, while the whole embodied, environmentally located system solves) the problem.

8.4   Embodied Flow

Work on embodied cognition also calls into question the idea that there is a sequential flow of processing whose stages neatly correspond to perceiving, thinking, and acting. When we engage the world in daily behaviour, we often do not do it by first passively taking in lots of information, then making a full plan, then implementing the plan courtesy of some sequence of motor commands. Instead, sensing, thinking, and acting conspire, overlap, and start to merge together as whole perceptuo-motor systems engage the world.

Examples of such merging and interweaving include work on interactive vision (Churchland et al., 1994), dynamic field theory (Thelen et al., 2001), and 'deictic pointers' (Ballard et al., 1997) (for some reviews, see Clark, 1997, 2008). By way of illustration, consider the task studied by Ballard et al. (1997). In this task, a subject is given a model pattern of coloured blocks and asked to copy the pattern by moving similar blocks, one at a time, from a reserve area to a new workspace. The task is performed by drag and drop using a mouse and monitor, and as you perform, eye tracker technology monitors exactly where and when you are looking as you tackle the problem. What subjects did *not* do, Ballard et al. discovered, was to look at the target, decide on the colour and position of the next block to be added, then execute their mini-plan by moving a block from the reserve area. Instead, repeated rapid saccades to the model were used during the performance of the task—many more saccades than you might expect. For example, the model is consulted *both before and after* picking up a block, suggesting that when glancing at the model, the subject stores only one small piece of information: either the colour or the position of the next block to be copied, but not both. Even when repeated saccades are made to the same site, very minimal information looked to be retained. Instead, repeated fixations seem to be providing specific items of information 'just in time' for use.[4] Repeated saccades to the physical model thus allowed the subjects to deploy what Ballard et al. dub 'minimal memory strategies' to solve the problem. The idea is that the brain creates its programs so as to minimize the amount of working memory that is required, and that eye motions are here recruited to place a new piece of information into memory. By altering the task demands, Ballard et al. were also able to systematically alter the particular mixes of biological memory and active, embodied retrieval recruited to solve different versions of the problem, concluding that in this task 'eye movements, head movements, and memory load trade off against each other in a flexible way' (p. 732). This is another now-familiar (but still important) lesson from embodied cognition. Eye movements here allow the subject to use the external world itself, where appropriate, as a kind of storage buffer (for lots more on this kind of strategy, see Clark, 2008; Wilson, 2004).

Putting all this together already suggests a much more integrated model of perception, cognition, and action. Perception is here tangled up with possibilities for action and is continuously influenced by cognitive, contextual, and motor factors. This is also the picture suggested earlier by Pfeifer et al.'s (2007) notion of the 'self-structuring of information flows' (8.3). Action serves to deliver fragments of information 'just in time' for use, and that information guides action, in an ongoing circular causal embrace. Perception thus construed need not yield a rich, detailed, and action-neutral inner model awaiting the services of 'central cognition' to deduce appropriate actions. In fact, these distinctions (between perception, cognition, and action) now seem to obscure, rather than illuminate, the true flow of effect. In a certain sense, the brain is revealed not as (primarily) an engine of reason or quiet deliberation, but as an organ for the environmentally situated control of action. Cheap, fast, world-exploiting action, rather than the pursuit of truth, optimality, or deductive inference, is now the key organizing principle. Embodied, situated agents, all this suggests, are masters of 'soft assembly', building, dissolving, and rebuilding temporary ensembles that exploit whatever is available, creating shifting problem-solving wholes that effortlessly span brain, body, and world.

8.5   Frugal Action-Oriented Prediction Machines

Superficially, these 'lessons from embodiment' can seem to point in a rather different direction to work on prediction-driven processing. Prediction-driven processing is often described as combining evidence (the sensory input), prior knowledge (the generative model yielding the predictions), and estimations of uncertainty (via the precision-weighting upon prediction error) to generate a multiscale best guess at how the world is. But this, as we have previously remarked, is subtly misleading. For what real-world prediction is all about is the selection and control of world-engaging action. Insofar as such agents do try to 'guess the world', that guessing is always and everywhere inflected in ways apt to support cycles of action and intervention. At the most fundamental level, this is simply because the whole apparatus (of prediction-based processing) exists only in order to help animals achieve their goals while avoiding fatally surprising encounters with the world. Action, we might say, is where the predictive rubber meets the adaptive road. And once we consider the role of prediction in the genesis and unfolding of action, the picture alters dramatically.

The shape of the new picture was visible in our earlier discussion (6.5) of Cisek's Affordance Competition hypothesis. Predictive processing was there shown to implement a strong version of 'affordance competition' in which the brain continuously computes multiple probabilistically inflected possibilities for action, and does so using an architecture in which perception, planning, and action are continuously intermingled, supported by highly overlapping resources, and executed using the same basic computational strategy. PP here results in the creation and deployment of what Cisek and Kalaska (2011) called 'pragmatic' representations: representations tailored to the production of good online control rather than aiming for rich mirroring of an action-independent world. Those representations simultaneously serve epistemic functions, sampling the world in ways designed to test our hypotheses and to yield better information for the control of action itself. The upshot was a picture of neural processing as fundamentally action-oriented, representing the world as an evolving matrix of parallel, partially computed possibilities for action and intervention. The picture of embodied flow presented in the previous section is thus echoed, almost point-for-point, by work on action-oriented predictive processing.

To complete the reconciliation, however, we must leverage one final ingredient. That ingredient is the capacity to use prediction error minimization and variable precision-weighting to sculpt patterns of connectivity within the brain selecting, at various timescales, the simplest circuits that can reliably drive a target behaviour. This too is a feature that we have encountered earlier (see chapter 5). But the resulting circuits, as we shall now see, neatly encompass the simple, frugal, 'sensing-for-coupling' solutions suggested by Gibson, Beer, Warren, and others. Better yet, they accommodate those 'model-sparse' solutions within the larger context of a fluid, reconfigurable inner economy in which richly knowledge-based strategies and fast, frugal solutions are merely different points on a single scale. Such points reflect the recruitment of different ensembles of inner and outer resources: ensembles that form and dissolve in ways determined by external context, current needs and bodily state, and ongoing estimations of our own uncertainty. This process of recruitment is itself constantly modulated, courtesy of the circular causal dance of perceptuo-motor response, by the evolving state of the external environment. At that point (I shall argue) all the key insights from work on embodiment and situated, world-exploiting action are fully realized using the distinctive apparatus of action-oriented predictive processing.

8.6   Mix 'n' Match Strategy Selection

To see how this might work in practice, it helps to start with some examples from a different (but in fact quite closely related) literature. This is the extensive literature concerning choice and decision-making. Within that literature, it is common to distinguish between 'model-based' and 'model-free' approaches (see, e.g., Dayan, 2012; Dayan & Daw, 2008; Wolpert, Doya, & Kawato, 2003). Model-based strategies rely, as the name suggests, on a model of the domain that includes information about how various states (worldly situations) are connected, thus allowing a kind of principled estimation (given some cost function) of the value of a putative action. Such approaches involve the acquisition and the (computationally challenging) deployment of fairly rich bodies of information concerning the structure of the task-domain. Model-free strategies, by contrast, are said to 'learn action values directly, by trial and error, without building an explicit model of the environment, and thus retain no explicit estimate of the probabilities that govern state transitions' (Gläscher et al., 2010, p. 585). Such approaches implement pre-computed 'policies' that associate actions directly with rewards, and that typically exploit simple cues and regularities while nonetheless delivering fluent, often rapid, response.

Model-free learning has been associated with a 'habitual' system for the automatic control of choice and action, whose neural underpinnings include the midbrain dopamine system and its projections to the striatum, while model-based learning has been more closely associated with the action of cortical (parietal and frontal) regions (see Gläscher et al., 2010). Learning in these systems has been thought to be driven by different forms of prediction error signal—affectively salient 'reward prediction error' (see, e.g., Hollerman & Schultz, 1998; Montague et al., 1996; Schultz, 1999; Schultz et al., 1997) for the model-free case, and more affectively neutral 'state prediction error' (e.g., in ventromedial prefrontal cortex) for the model-based case. These relatively crude distinctions are, however, now giving way to a much more integrated story (see, e.g., Daw et al., 2011; Gershman & Daw, 2012) as we shall see.

How should we conceive the relations between PP and such 'model-free' learning? One interesting possibility is that an onboard process of reliability estimation might select strategies according to context. If we suppose that there exist multiple, competing neural resources capable of addressing some current problem, there needs to be some mechanism that arbitrates between them. With this in mind, Daw et al. (2005) describe a broadly Bayesian 'principle of arbitration' whereby estimations of the relative uncertainty associated with distinct 'neural controllers' (e.g., 'model-based' versus 'model-free' controllers) allows the most accurate controller, in the current circumstances, to determine action and choice. Within the PP framework this would be implemented using the familiar mechanisms of precision estimation and precision-weighting. Each resource would compute a course of action, but only the most reliable resource (the one associated with the least uncertainty when deployed in the current context) would get to determine high-precision prediction errors of the kind needed to drive action and choice. In other words, a kind of meta-model (one rich in precision expectations) would be used to determine and deploy whatever resource is best in the current situation, toggling between them when the need arises.

Such a story is, however, almost certainly over-simplistic. Granted, the 'model-based / model-free' distinction is intuitive and resonates with old (but increasingly discredited) dichotomies between habit and reason, and between emotion and analytic evaluation. But it seems likely that the image of parallel, functionally independent, neural sub-systems will not stand the test of time. For example, a recent fMRI study (Daw, Gershman, et al., 2011) suggests that rather than thinking in terms of distinct (functionally isolated) model-based and model-free learning systems, we may need to posit a single 'more integrated computational architecture' (p. 1204) in which the different brain areas most commonly associated with model-based and model-free learning (pre-frontal cortex and dorsolateral striatum, respectively) *each* trade in both model-free and model-based modes of evaluations and do so 'in proportions matching those that determine choice behavior' (p. 1209). One way to think about this, from within the PP perspective, is by associating 'model-free' responses with processing dominated ('bottom-up') by the sensory flow, while 'model-based' responses are those that involve greater and more widespread kinds of 'top-down' influence.[5] The context-dependent balancing between these two sources of information, achieved by adjusting the precision-weighting of prediction error, then allows for whatever admixtures of strategy task and circumstances dictate.

Support for this notion of a more integrated inner economy was provided by a decision task (Daw, Gershman et al., 2011) in which experimenters were able to distinguish between apparently model-based and apparently model-free influences on subsequent choice and action. This is possible because model-free response is inherently backwards-looking, associating specific actions with previously encountered rewards. Animals exhibiting only model-free responses are, in that sense, condemned to repeat the past, releasing previously reinforced actions when circumstances dictate. A model-based system, by contrast, is able to evaluate potential actions using (as the name suggests) some kind of inner surrogate of the external arena in which actions are to be performed and choices made—such systems may, for example, deploy mental simulations to determine whether or not one action is to be preferred over another. Animals that deploy a model-based system are thus able, in the terms of Seligman et al. (2013), to 'navigate into the future' rather than remaining 'driven by the past'.

Most animals, it now seems clear, are capable of both forms of response and combine dense enabling webs of habit with sporadic bursts of genuine prospection. According to the standard picture, recall, there exist distinct neural valuation systems and distinct forms of prediction error signal supporting each type of learning and response. Using a sequential choice task, Daw et al. were able to create conditions under which the computations of one or other of these neural valuation systems should dissociate from behaviour, revealing the presence of independent computations (in different, previously identified, brain areas) of value by a model-free and a model-based system. Instead they found neural correlates of apparently model-free and apparently model-based responses in both areas. Strikingly, this means that even striatally computed 'reward prediction errors' do not simply reflect learning using a truly model-free system. Instead, recorded activity in the striatum 'reflected a mixture of model-free and model-based evaluations' (Daw et al., 2011, p. 1209) and 'even the signal most associated with model-free RL [reinforcement learning], the striatal RPE [reward prediction error], reflects both types of valuation, combined in a way that matches their observed contributions to choice behavior' (Daw et al., 2011, p. 1210). Top-down information, Daw et al. (2011) suggest, might here control the way different strategies are combined in differing contexts for action and choice. Greater integration between model-based and model-free valuations might also, they speculate, flow from the action of some kind of hybrid learning routine in which a model-based resource may train and tune the responses of a (quicker, in context more efficient) model-free resource.[6]

At a more general level, such results add to a growing literature (for a review, see Gershman & Daw, 2012) that suggests the need for a deep reworking of the standard decision-theoretic model. Where that model posits distinct representations of utility and probability, associated with the activity of more-or-less independent neural sub-systems, we may actually confront a more deeply integrated architecture in which 'perception, action, and utility are ensnared in a tangled skein [involving] a richer ensemble of dynamical interactions between perceptual and motivational systems' (Gershman & Daw, 2012, p. 308). The larger picture scouted in this section here makes good functional sense, allowing 'model-free' modes to use model-based schemes to teach them how to respond. Within the PP framework, this results in a hierarchical embedding of the (shallow) 'model-free' responses in a (deeper) model-based economy. This has many advantages, since model-based schemes are (chapter 5 above) profoundly context-sensitive, whereas model-free or habitual schemes—once in place—are fixed, bound to the details of previous contexts of successful action. By delicately combining the two modes within an overarching economy, adaptive agents may identify the appropriate contexts in which to deploy the model-free ('habitual') schemes. 'Model-based' and 'model-free' modes of valuation and response, if this is correct, simply name extremes along a single continuum and may appear in many mixtures and combinations determined by the task at hand.

8.7   Balancing Accuracy and Complexity

We can now locate these insights within a larger probabilistic framework. Fitzgerald, Dolan, and Friston (2014, p. 1) note that 'Bayes optimal agents seek both to maximize the *accuracy* of their predictions and to minimize the *complexity* of the models they use to generate those predictions'. Maximizing accuracy corresponds to maximizing how well the model predicts the observed data. Minimizing complexity, on the other hand, requires reducing computational costs as far as possible, consistent with performing the task at hand. Formally, this can be achieved by incorporating a complexity-penalizing factor—sometimes called an Occam factor, after the thirteenth-century philosopher William of Occam who famously cautioned us not to 'multiply entities beyond necessity'. Overall 'model evidence' is then a kind of composite quantity reflecting a delicate (and context-variable) accuracy/complexity trade-off. Fitzgerald, Dolan, and Friston go on to outline a specific scheme (involving 'Bayesian model averaging'[7]) in which 'models are weighted or chosen according to their evidence [i.e., their overall model evidence as just defined] rather than simply their accuracy' (Fitzgerald et al., 2014, p. 7). Within PP, variations in the precision-weighting of select prediction errors provide one mechanism capable of implementing just such task- and context-sensitive competition between different models, while synaptic pruning (see 3.9 and 9.3) serves complexity reduction on longer timescales.

All this suggests a possible reworking of the popular suggestion (8.2) that human reasoning involves the operation of two functionally distinct systems, one for fast, automatic, 'habitual' response and the other dedicated to slow, effortful, deliberative reasoning. Instead of a truly dichotomous inner organization, we may benefit from a richer form of organization in which fast, habitual, or heuristically based modes of response are often the default, but within which a large variety of possible strategies may be available. The balance between these strategies is then determined by variable precision-weightings, hence (in effect) by various forms of endogenous and exogenous attention (Carrasco, 2011). Humans and other animals would thus deploy multiple—rich, frugal, and all points in between—strategies defined across a fundamentally unified web of neural resources (for some preliminary exploration of this kind of more integrated space, see Pezzulo et al., 2013, and 8.8).

Nor, finally, is there any fixed limit to the complexities of the possible strategic embeddings that might occur even within a single more integrated system. We might, for example, use some quick-and-dirty heuristic strategy to identify a context in which to use a richer one, or use intensive model-exploring strategies to identify a context in which a simpler one will do. The most efficient strategy is simply the (active) inference that minimizes overall complexity costs. From this emerging vantage point the very distinction between model-based and model-free response (and indeed between system 1 and system 2, insofar as these are conceived as distinct systems rather than modes[8]) looks increasingly shallow. These are now just convenient labels for different admixtures of resource and influence, each of which is recruited in the same general way as circumstances dictate.

8.8 Back to Baseball

Now let's return to the outfielder's problem described earlier. Here too, already-active neural predictions and simple, rapidly-processed perceptual cues must work together (if PP is correct) to determine a pattern of precision-weightings for different prediction error signals. This creates (recall chapter 5) a transient web of effective connectivity (a temporary distributed circuit) and, within that circuit, it sets the balance between top-down and bottom-up modes of influence. In the case at hand, however, efficiency demands selecting a circuit in which sensing plays the non-reconstructive role described in chapter 6 and 8.3. The temporary task of visual sensing, in this context, becomes that of cancelling the optical acceleration of the fly ball. That means giving high weighting to the prediction errors associated with cancelling the vertical acceleration of the ball's optical projection, and (to put it bluntly) not attending very much to anything else.

Apt precision weightings thus select a pre-learnt, fast, low-cost strategy for solving the problem. Contextually recruited patterns of precision weighting here accomplish a form of set-selection or strategy switching.[9] This assumes that slower processes of learning and adaptive plasticity have already sculpted patterns of neural connectivity in ways that make the low-cost strategy available. But this is unproblematic. It can be motivated in general terms by the drive towards minimizing complexity (which is indistinguishable, under plausible constraints, from the drive towards 'satisficing'). The required learning can thus be accomplished using prediction error minimization operating at many timescales. Such processes range all the way from the slow learning of the child baseball player, to the faster online adaptation of the pro-player factoring in (during a match) changing specifics of the wind conditions and the play of opposing batters.

The upshot is a complex but rewarding picture in which bedrock processes of predictive learning slowly install models that include precision expectations allowing patterns of effective connectivity to be built and re-built 'on the fly'. This enables fast, knowledge-sparse modes of response to be recruited and nuanced according to current context. The resulting compatibility of 'productively lazy' and model-based approaches should come as no surprise. To see this, we need only reflect that the model or model fragment that underlies any given behaviour can be a simple, easily computed, heuristic (a simplified 'rule-of-thumb') just as easily as something with a more complex causal structure. Such low-cost models will in many cases rely upon action, exploiting patterns of circular causal commerce (between perceptual inputs and motor actions) to deliver task-relevant information 'just in time' for use.

Fast, automatic, over-learnt behaviours are especially good candidates for control by models taking a more heuristic form. The role of context-reflecting precision assignments is then to select and enable the low-cost procedural model that has proven able to support the target behaviour. Such low-cost models—OAC is a nice example—will in many cases rely upon the self-structuring of our own information flows, exploiting patterns of circular causal commerce (between perceptual inputs and motor actions) to deliver task-relevant information 'just in time' for use.

More complex (intuitively more 'model-rich', though this is now just another location along a continuum) strategies may also involve simplifications and approximations. A nice example is work by Battaglia et al. (2013) on 'intuitive physics'. Human agents are able to make rapid inferences about the physical behaviour of ordinary objects. Such inferences might include spotting that the pile of books or washing-up is unstable and at risk of toppling over, or that a lightly brushed object is going to fall and hit some other object. Underlying that capacity, Battaglia et al. suggest, may be a probabilistic scene simulator (a probabilistic generative model) able to deliver rapid verdicts on the basis of partial, noisy information. Such a simulator does not rely upon propositional rules but rather upon 'quantitative aspects and uncertainties of object's geometry, motions, and force dynamics' (p. 18327). Battaglia et al. describe and test just such a model, showing that it fits data from many different psychophysical tasks. Importantly, the Battaglia et al. model delivers robustness and speed by simulating the physical world using approximations to the behaviour of real objects. In this way it 'trades precision and veridicality for speed, generality, and the ability to make predictions that are good enough for the purposes of everyday activities' (Battaglia et al., 2013, p. 18328).

The 'intuitive physics engine'—or generative model by any other name—here produces simplified probabilistic simulations that are nonetheless able to predict key aspects of the ebb and flow of the physical world. Such an 'intuitive physics engine' is able to infer key facts about the likely behaviours of objects in the kinds of scene shown in Figure 8.1—facts such as which object in fix 1C, will fall first, in what direction, and with what kinds of knock-on effect. Reliance upon approximations and the estimation of uncertainty also explains the existence of illusions (such as the stability illusion in Figure 8.1F) and errors in reasoning about the physical world. Our daily approximations, that is to say, may not readily 'comprehend' the delicate structure of balances that makes the tower of rocks stable. A model that was able to do so would in some circumstances be more accurate, but at some temporal cost (so perhaps we would not spot the instability of the washing-up pile in time to prevent a catastrophic state-transition).

Approximate solutions such as these reflect what Gershman and Daw (2012, p. 307) describe as a kind of 'meta-optimization over the costs (e.g., extra computation) of maintaining [a] full representation relative to its benefits'. The deepest explanation for the neural intermingling of perception, action, and utility may, Gershman and Daw

FIGURE 8.1   Some Scenes That Evoke Physical Intuitions
Everyday scenes, activities, and art that evoke strong physical intuitions.
(a) A cluttered workshop that exhibits many nuanced physical properties.
(b) A 3D object-based representation of the scene in A that can support physical inferences based on simulation. (c) A precarious stack of dishes looks like
an accident waiting to happen. (d) A child exercises his physical reasoning by
stacking blocks. (e) Jenga puts players' physical intuitions to the test. (f) 'Stone
balancing' exploits our powerful physical expectations (photo and stone
balance by Heiko Brinkmann).

Source: Battaglia et al., 2013.

(2012, p. 308) suggest, lie right there, in adaptive pressure to find and
deploy representational forms and statistical approximations that 'concentrate their density in regions of high utility'. The upshot is a kind
of meta-Bayesian determination of what to represent, and of when,
and how, to represent it. Implausible implications of pervasive brute
optimality are thus abandoned in favour of strategies that deliver some
combination of efficacy, reliability, and energetic efficiency. Agents
like this will use the most efficient strategy that is good enough to do
the job, and that is currently available for soft-assembly within the
reconfigurable flow.

Dealing with a complex time-pressured world thus demands the
use of many strategies, ranging from very simple heuristics to more
complex structures of interacting approximations. That diverse landscape may, however, form part of an overarching uncertainty-based cognitive eco-system—an eco-system within which these many strategies

emerge, dissolve, and interact. Within the PP framework, strategies of many different stripes may be selected moment-by-moment by changing estimations of precision. Such estimations alter patterns of effective connectivity, enabling different webs of inner (and outer, see below) circuitry to control behaviour at different times.[10]

8.9   Extended Predictive Minds

All this suggests a very natural model of 'extended cognition' (Clark, 2008; Clark & Chalmers, 1998), where this is simply the idea that bio-external structures and operations may sometimes form integral parts of an agent's cognitive routines. Nothing in the PP framework materially alters, as far as I can tell, the arguments previously presented, both pro and con, regarding the possibility of genuinely extended cognitive systems.[11] What PP does offer, however, is a specific, and highly 'extension-friendly', proposal concerning the shape of the specifically neural contribution to cognitive success.

To see this, reflect that known external (e.g., environmental) operations provide—by partly constituting—additional strategies apt for the kind of 'meta-model-based' selection described in the previous sections. This is because actions that engage and exploit specific external resources will now be selected in just the same manner as the inner coalitions of neural resources themselves. For example, when performing the block-placing task (Ballard et al., 1997) described in 8.4, the brain must assign high precision to the predictions that underlie the various actions that are allowing us to 'use the world as its own best model' while performing the task. Such world-engaging actions are determined, in turn, by the acquired estimation that reliable, salient (task-relevant) information is available at such-and-such a location and at such-and-such a time. Or consider the case where salient high-precision information is available by the use of some bio-external device, such as a laptop or smartphone. The core routine that selects actions to reduce prediction error will now select actions that invoke the bio-external resource. Invoking a bio-external resource, and moving our own effectors and sensors to yield high-quality task-relevant information are here expressions of the same underlying strategy, reflecting our brain's best estimates of where and when reliable, task-relevant information is available. The strategies thus selected are typically, just as Ballard et al. suggested, minimal-internal-memory strategies whose success conditions require both organismic action and the cooperation of the external environment. Such strategies again highlight the importance of distributed resource-webs spanning brain, body, and world.

As a simple illustration, consider work by Pezzulo, Rigoli, and Chersi, (2013). Here, a so-called 'Mixed Instrumental Controller' determines whether to choose an action based upon a set of simple, pre-computed ('cached') values, or by running a mental simulation enabling a more flexible, model-based assessment of the desirability, or otherwise, of actually performing the action. The mixed controller computes the 'value of information' selecting the more informative (but costly) model-based option only when that value is sufficiently high. Mental simulation, in those cases, then produces new reward expectancies that can determine current action by updating the values used to determine choice. We can think of this as a mechanism that, moment-by-moment, determines (as discussed in previous sections) whether to exploit simple, already-cached routines or to explore a richer set of possibilities using some form of mental simulation. It is easy to imagine a version of the mixed controller that determines (on the basis of past experience) the value of the information that it believes would be made available by means of some kind of bio-external apparatus, such as the manipulation of an abacus, an iPhone, or a physical model. Deploying a simple cached strategy, a more costly mental simulation, or exploiting the environment itself as a cognitive resource are thus all strategies apt for context-sensitive recruitment using the PP apparatus.

Seen from this perspective, the recruitment of task-specific inner neural coalitions within an interaction-dominated PP econ-omy is entirely on a par with the recruitment of task-specific neural-bodily-worldly ensembles. The formation and dissolution of extended (brain-body-world) problem-solving ensembles here obeys many of the same basic rules and principles (balancing efficacy and efficiency, and reflecting complex ongoing estimations of uncer-tainty) as does the recruitment of temporary *inner* coalitions bound by effective connectivity. In each case, what is selected is a tempo-rary problem-solving ensemble (a 'temporary task-specific device', see Anderson, Richardson, & Chemero, 2012) recruited as a function of context-varying estimations of uncertainty. This is simply the embod-ied, environmentally embedded version of the emergence of 'tran-siently assembled local neural subsystems' described in 5.5.

Such temporary ensembles emerge and are deployed within the empowering contexts that we have described (8.4) as 'embodied flow'. Within such flows, perceptuo-motor routines deliver new inputs that recruit new transient ensembles of resources. It is these rolling cycles that most clearly characterize human cognition in the wild. Within these rolling cycles, arbitrarily complex amounts of 'leaning on the world' may become progressively folded in, expanding our practical cognitive capacities by offloading work from brain to (non-neural) body, and from organism to (physical, social, and technological) world. What PP makes unusually clear is that it is these rolling cycles that the neural economy constantly (and not just in the special cases involving mind-extending tools and technologies) serves. As such cycles unfold, no inner homunculus oversees the repeated soft-assembly of the distributed problem-solving ensembles that result. Instead, such ensembles emerge and dissolve in ways determined by the progressive reduction, in environmental context, of precise, high-quality, prediction error. Organismically salient (high precision) prediction error may thus be the all-purpose adhesive that, via its expressions in action, binds elements from brain, body, and world into temporary problem-solving wholes.

8.10   Escape from the Darkened Room

Prediction error minimization is consistent, then, with a very large range of strategies for adaptive response. But there is one vibrant thread in the tapestry of such responses that can seem especially resistant to reconstruction using the resources on offer. That vibrant thread concerns play, exploration, and the attractions of novelty. The cognitive imperative of prediction error minimization, it is sometimes feared, is congenitally unable to accommodate such phenomena, offering instead a prescription for quietism, deliberate cognitive diminishment, and (perhaps) even fatal inactivity! The hapless prediction-driven organism, the worry goes, should simply seek out states that are easily predicted, such as an empty darkened room in which to spend the remainder of its increasingly hungry, thirsty, and depressing days. This is the so-called 'Darkened Room Puzzle' (Friston, Thornton, & Clark, 2012).

This worry (though important) is multiply misguided. It is misguided at the most basic biological level, where it is presented as a threat to the integrity and persistence of the organism. And it is misguided at the more rarefied level of 'human flourishing', where it is seen (see, e.g., Froese & Ikegami, 2013) as militating against play, exploration, and the deliberate search for novelty and new experiences. In each of these cases the solution to the puzzle is to notice the important role of the evolutionary and cultural backdrops against which processes of moment-by-moment prediction error minimization emerge and unfold.

Prediction-error-based neural processing is, we have seen, part of a potent recipe for multiscale self-organization. Such multiscale self-organization does not occur in a vacuum. Instead, it operates only against the backdrop of an evolved organismic (neural and gross-bodily) form, and (as we will see in chapter 9) an equally transformative backdrop of slowly accumulated material structure and cultural practices: the socio-technological legacy of generation upon generation of human learning and experience.

To start to bring this larger picture into focus, the first point to notice is that explicit, fast timescale processes of prediction error minimization must answer to the needs and projects of evolved, embodied, and environmentally embedded agents. The very existence of such agents (see Friston, 2011b, 2012c) thus already implies a huge range of structurally implicit creature-specific 'expectations'. Such creatures are built to seek mates, to avoid hunger and thirst, and to engage (even when not hungry or thirsty) in the kinds of sporadic environmental exploration that will help prepare them for unexpected environmental shifts, resource scarcities, new competitors, and so on. On a moment-by-moment basis, then, prediction error is minimized only against the backdrop of this complex set of creature-defining 'expectations'.

The scare quotes flag what seems to me to be an important difference between expectations that are acquired on the basis of lifetime experience and those that are, one way or another, *structurally implicit*. We are built to breathe air through our lungs, hence we embody a kind of structural 'expectation' of staying (mostly) above water—unlike (say) an octopus. Some of our action tendencies are likewise built-in. The reflexive response to touching a hot plate is to draw away. This reflex amounts to a kind of bedrock 'expectation' of avoiding tissue damage. In this attenuated sense every embodied agent (even a bacterium) is, just as Friston (2012c) claims, already a kind of surprise-minimizing model of its environment. Thus we read that:

> biological systems can distil structural regularities from environmental fluctuations (like changing concentrations of chemical attractants or sensory signals) and embody them in their form and internal dynamics. In essence, they become models of causal structure in their local environment, enabling them to predict what will happen next and counter surprising violations of those predictions. (Friston, 2012c, p. 2101)

Another simple example is the information made available by our species-specific array of sensory receptors, and their placement at specific bodily locations. This (at least until the invention of night-vision aids and other sensory augmentations) selects and constrains the space within which sensory prediction error can be actively minimized. But there is more to it than this. As evolved creatures we also 'expect' (still with my scare quotes) to remain warm, well-fed, and healthy, and sensed deviations from these ingrained norms will yield prediction errors capable of driving short-term response and adaptation. Such agents (when normally functioning) simply do not feel the pull of the darkened room. Creature-defining 'expectations' of this kind are not subject to revision even by long-term life experiences (such as enduring a famine).

The first thing to do when confronting the Darkened Room puzzle is thus to view things from a rather more cosmic (long timescale) perspective. At such timescales, 'surprisal' (see 1.7) is reduced by any form of adaptation or change whose effect is to help the organism to resist dissolution and disorder, minimizing 'free energy' (Appendix 2) in its exchanges with the environment. Considered over these longer timescales, we may say that this amounts to providing them with a kind of overarching set of structurally implicit 'beliefs' or 'expectations'—still with those important scare quotes—that condition and constrain our moment-by-moment processes of explicit prediction error minimization. Relative to the full set of 'expectations' that in this way define an evolved agent, a darkened room usually[12] holds no lure at all. Typical evolved agents strongly 'expect', as Friston (2012c) suggests, not to spend very long at all in such unrewarding environments. This means that the Darkened Room holds no allure for creatures like us.

Friston's way of expressing this important fact is, however, potentially problematic—hence my use of all those scare quotes. For it threatens to conflate the various ways in which surprisal may be minimized—for example, by details of gross bodily form and neuro-anatomy, and by the more explicit, generative-model-based issuing of top-down probabilistic predictions to meet the incoming sensory stream. If my skin heals after a cut, it would be misleading to say that in some structural, embodied fashion I 'predict' an unbroken membrane. Yet it is only in this strained sense that, to take another example, the shape of the fish could be said to embody expectations concerning the hydrodynamics of seawater.[13] Perhaps we should allow that in some very broad sense, fish-y 'surprisal' is indeed partially determined by such morphological factors. Our focus, however, has been on suites of entwined predictions issued by a neurally encoded generative model—the kind of process implemented, if PP is correct, by iterated exchanges of prediction and prediction error signaling in asymmetric bidirectional cascades of neuronal processing. Consequently, I do not think we ought properly (without scare quotes) to speak of all these bedrock adaptive states and responses as themselves amounting to structurally sedimented (Friston says 'embodied') predictions or expectations. Better, I think, to say that healing (along with a swathe of other neural and bodily mechanisms ensuring survival and success) *sets the scene* against which our predictive models of the world can take shape. Prediction error minimization here emerges as just one process among many—but one that (I have argued) plays a very special role in allowing agents like us to encounter, in perception and action, a structured world of interacting distal causes, rather than simply (like plants or very simple life-forms) running routines that keep us viable.

The 'creature-defining backdrop' is thus best understood—at least for our purposes—as setting the scene for the deployment (sometimes, in some animals) of more explicit prediction error minimizing strategies of learning and response. Nonetheless, the creature-defining backdrop is hugely important and influences both what we (in the rich sense) predict and, crucially, *what we do not need*, in that full sense, to predict—because, for example, it is already taken care of by basic biomechanical features, such as passive dynamics and the inbuilt synergies of muscles and tendons. It is only against that hugely empowering backdrop that online computations of prediction error can explain our complex, fluid forms of behavioural success.

8.11   *Play, Novelty, and Self-Organized Instability*

The Darkened Room Puzzle has another—slightly more subtle—dimension, nicely captured in the following passage:

> If our main objective is to minimize surprise over the states and outcomes we encounter, how can this explain complex human behavior such as novelty seeking, exploration, and, furthermore, higher level aspirations such as art, music, poetry, or humor? Should we not, in accordance with the principle, prefer living in a highly predictable and un-stimulating environment where we could minimize our long-term surprise? Shouldn't we be aversive to novel stimuli? As it stands, this seems highly implausible; novel stimuli are sometimes aversive, but often quite the opposite. The challenge here is to reconcile the fundamental imperative that underlies self-organized behavior with the fact that we avoid monotonous environments and actively explore in order to seek novel and stimulating inputs. (Schwartenbeck et al., 2013, p. 2)

In just this vein Froese and Ikegami (2013) suggest that good ways of minimizing surprisal will include 'stereotypic self-stimulation, catatonic withdrawal from the world, and autistic withdrawal from others'. The worry here is not (quite) that we will seek out some darkened room death trap. That worry was already dealt with by the observations concerning bedrock structure and native 'expectations'. The worry, rather, is that the PP story can seem strangely silent with respect to the more *positive* attractions of novelty and exploration. It seems strangely silent, that is to say, regarding 'why we actively aspire (to a certain extent) to novel, complex states' (Schwartenbeck et al., 2013). It is thus silent about, for example, much of the huge industry of entertainment, art, and culture.

This is a large and challenging topic that I cannot hope to address in a few short comments. But part of the solution may itself involve (in a kind of bootstrapping way) forms of culturally-mediated lifetime learning that install global policies that actively favour increasingly complex forms of novelty-seeking and exploration. A global policy, in this sense, is just a rather general action selection rule—one that entails whole varieties of actions rather than a single act. The simplest such policy relevant to play and exploration is one that reduces the value of a state the longer that state is occupied. In worlds where resources are unevenly distributed in space and time, this may be an adaptively valuable policy.

It may be useful to give this kind of policy a dynamical spin. As our trajectories though space and time unfold, potentially stable stopping points (attractors, in the language of dynamical systems) constantly arise and dissolve, often under the influence of our own evolving inner states and actions. Some systems, however, have a tendency to destroy their own fixed points, actively inducing instabilities in ways that result in what Friston, Breakspear, & Deco (2012) call 'peripatetic or itinerant (wandering) dynamics'. Such systems would appear to pursue change and novelty 'for their own sake'.

An entertaining illustration involves what may well be the first 'urban myth' of developmental robotics. According to this story, a robot had been set up to minimize prediction error in a toy environment. But having done that, instead of simply ceasing to behave, the robot began to spin around and around, creating a variety of optical artefacts that it then proceeded to model and predict. The story (which I heard in connection with work by Meeden et al., 2009) turns out to be not quite true, though it is based upon some interesting robot behaviour that was indeed actually exhibited.[14] But a creature genuinely disposed to destroy its own fixed points, finding itself trapped in a highly restricted environment, might indeed be driven to seek out new horizons by any means available. In a similar vein, Lauwereyns (2012) reports a study[15] showing that:

> Human beings confined in a dark room with a minimum of stimulation will press buttons to make patterns of colored spots of light appear, preferring those sequences of pattern that offer the most variety and unpredictability. (Berlyne, 1966, p. 32, quoted in Lauwereyns, 2012, p. 28)

More recently, Kidd et al. (2012) conducted a series of experiments with 7- and 8-month-old infants measuring attention to sequences of events of varying (and well-controlled) complexity. Infant attention, they found, was characterized by what they dub a 'Goldilocks Effect', focusing upon events presenting an intermediate degree of predictability—neither too easily predictable, nor too hard to predict. The probability of an infant looking away was thus greatest when complexity (calculated as negative log probability) was either very high or very low. The functional upshot, Kidd et al. suggest, is that 'infants implicitly seek to maintain intermediate rates of information absorption and avoid wasting cognitive resources on overly simple or overly complex events' (Kidd et al., 2012, p. 1).

Such tendencies to seek out 'just-novel-enough' situations are a good candidate for some form of innate specification, since they would cause active agents to self-structure the flow of information in ways ideally suited to the incremental acquisition and tuning of an informative generative model of their environment. More generally still, agents that inhabit complex, changing worlds would be well-served by a variety of policies that drive them to explore those worlds, even when no immediate gains or rewards are visible. Such agents would actively perturb their own trajectories through space and time in ways that enforce a certain amount of exploration.[16] The resulting 'itinerant' trajectories (Friston, 2010; Friston et al., 2009) provide adaptively valuable gateways to new learning and discovery.[17]

Extending this perspective, Schwartenbeck et al. (2013) suggest that certain agents may acquire policies that positively value the opportunity to visit many new states. For such agents, the value of some current state is partially determined by the number of possible other states that it allows them to visit. The complex human-built environments of art, literature, and science look like nice examples of domains structured to support and encourage just such open-ended forms of exploration and novelty-seeking. Predictive agents immersed in these kinds of designer environment will learn to expect (hence demand and actively seek out) those characteristic kinds of novelty and change. In structuring our cultural and social worlds we may thus be structuring *ourselves* in ways that promote increasingly rarefied patterns of exploration and novelty-seeking. This incremental cultural self-scaffolding (the culmination of humanity's escape from the darkened room) is the topic of the next, and final, chapter.

8.12   *Fast, Cheap, and Flexible Too*

We live in changing and challenging worlds. Such worlds demand the use of many strategies, including fast, efficient modes of perception-action coupling and slower, effortful processes of reasoning and mental simulation. To stay ahead of such worlds, we must use what we know both to anticipate, and actively to sculpt, the sensory barrage. In so doing, we do not simply engage the world. Instead we select, moment-by-moment, the very strategies (the neural and extra-neural circuits and activities) by which we will do so. Those strategies range from the quick and dirty to the slow and accurate, from those dominated by bottom-up sensory flow to those more reliant upon top-down contextual modulation, and all points and admixtures in between. They range too from the highly exploratory to the deeply conservative, enabling fluent switching whenever the value of gaining information and experience starts to be outweighed by the costs and risks involved in obtaining it. These strategic switches balance expected temporal, energetic, and computational costs against possible benefits.

Creatures like us are thus built to be persistently active, productively lazy, and occasionally exploratory and playful. We are built to maximize success while minimizing effort, both intellectual and physical. We do this, in large part, by deploying strategies that are fundamentally action-oriented. Minds like ours are not in the business of representing the world in some passive, descriptive manner. Instead, they engage it in complex rolling cycles in which actions determine percepts that select actions, evoking and exploiting all manner of environmental structures and opportunities along the way.

The worry that predictive processing organizations might overemphasize computationally expensive, representation-heavy strategies over other (quicker, dirtier, more 'embodied') ones is thus fully and satisfyingly resolved. The ever-active predictive brain is now revealed as a lazy brain: a brain vigilant for any opportunity to achieve more by doing less.

9

Being Human

9.1   Putting Prediction in Its Place

Our neural economy exists to serve the needs of embodied action. It does so, we saw, by initiating and sustaining complex circular causal flows in which actions and perceptions are co-determined and co-determining. These circular causal flows enact structural couplings that keep the organism within its own window of viability. In this way, the vision of the ever-active predictive brain dovetails elegantly with work on the embodied and situated mind. We have seen evidence of this already, as we explored the circular causal webs uniting perception and action, the use of low-cost strategies making the most of body and world, and the complex continuous interweaving of perceiving, deciding, and acting. To complete the picture, however, we must now explore the many ways in which nested webs of social and environmental structure inform, and are informed by, these unfolding processes of embodied neural prediction.

At the core lie multi-timescale processes of self-organization. Prediction error minimization provides a plausible and powerful mechanism for self-organization—a mechanism capable of yielding nested dynamical regimes of great complexity. But that complexity, in the rather special case of human agents, now involves a potent and labile sociocultural envelope. We humans—uniquely in the terrestrial natural order—build, and repeatedly rebuild, the social, linguistic, and technological worlds whose regularities then become reflected in the generative models making the predictions. It is because the brain itself is such a potent organ of unsupervised self-organization that our sociocultural immersions can be as efficacious as they are. But it is only in the many complex and ill-understood interactions *between* these two fundamental forces (between complex self-organizing neural dynamics and the evolving swirl of social and material influence) that minds like ours emerge from the material flux. We must thus confront the ever-active predictive brain in its proper setting—inextricably intertwined with an empowering backdrop of material, linguistic, and sociocultural scaffolding. What follows is a preliminary gesture towards that large and important task.

9.2   *Reprise: Self-Organizing around Prediction Error*

Prediction error provides an organismically computable quantity apt to drive neural self-organization in many ways and at many temporal scales. We have seen this principle in action many times in previous chapters, but it is worth pausing to admire the potent sweep of self-organization that results. At the heart of the process lies a probabilistic generative model that progressively alters so as better to predict the plays of sensory data that impinge upon a biological organism or artificial agent. This results in learning that can separate out interacting bodily and environmental causes operating at varying scales of space and time. Such approaches describe a potent mechanism for self-organized, grounded, structural learning. Learning is now grounded because distal causes are uncovered only as a means of predicting the play of sensory data (a play that also reflects the organism's own actions and interventions upon the world). Such learning is structure-revealing, unearthing complex patterns of interdependencies among causes operating at different scales of space and time. All this provides a kind of palette of predictive routines that can be combined in novel ways to deal with new situations.

Such systems are *self-organizing* because they are not aiming at any specific input-output mapping. Instead, they must discover the patterns of cascading regularity that best accommodate their own (partially self-induced) flows of sensory information. This is liberating because it means that such systems can deliver ways of knowing that are not tied to the performance of specific tasks (although the plays of sensory data to be accommodated are themselves constrained by the broad forms of human activity).

Such systems are also deeply context-sensitive. This is because systemic response in any area or at any level is now answerable to the full downwards (and lateral) cascade of context-fixing information. This non-linear dynamical picture increases still further in complexity because the flow of influence is itself reconfigurable, as changing precision estimations alter moment-by-moment patterns of effective connectivity.

By self-organizing around prediction error, these architectures thus deliver a multiscale grip upon the organism-salient features of the world—a grip whose signature is the capacity to engage that world in ongoing cycles in which perception and action work together to quash high-precision prediction error.

9.3   Efficiency and 'The Lord's Prior'

An important point to notice is that such systems do not simply cease to change and alter just because sensory prediction error has been successfully minimized. For there is, as we saw in chapter 8, another (less frequently highlighted) factor that can still drive change and learning. That factor is efficiency. Efficiency (see, e.g., Barlow, 1961; Olshausen & Field, 1996) is intuitively the opposite of redundancy and excess. A scheme or strategy is efficient if it uses only the minimal resources necessary to do the job. A generative model that is rich enough to maintain an organismic grip upon the regularities important for selecting behaviour, but that does so using minimal energetic or representational resources (for example, using few parameters) is efficient in this sense. By contrast, a system that uses a large number of parameters to accommodate or respond to the same data is not therby rendered a 'more accurate' modeller of its world. On the contrary, the result will often be 'over-fitting' the observed data, some of which turns out to be merely 'noise' or random fluctuations around the informative signal.

The Optical Acceleration Cancellation procedure described in chapter 8 is a nice example of a model that combines low complexity (few parameters) with high behavioural leverage. At the most general level, the drive towards efficiency is simply part and parcel of the overall imperative to minimize the sum of sensory prediction errors. This involves finding the most parsimonious model that successfully *engages* the sensory flow. For the deep functional role of the prediction error signal, or so I have argued, is not to recruit new and better hypotheses about the world, so much as to leverage sensory information so as to guide fluent engagements with those aspects of the world relevant to our current needs and projects.[1]

All this is nicely dramatized in Feldman's (2013, p. 15) discussion of the 'Lord's Prior' where this rather mischievously names the misleading idea that 'the optimal Bayesian observer is correctly tuned when its priors match those objectively in force in the environment'. The deep problems with such a notion emerge as soon as we reflect that active agents are not, at root, simply trying to model the data so much as to come up with recipes for acting appropriately in the world. This will mean separating agent-salient signal from noise, selectively ignoring much of what the sensory signal makes available. Moreover, 'one would be unwise to fit one's prior too closely to any finite set of observations about how the world behaves, because inevitably the observations are a mixture of reliable and ephemeral factors' (Feldman, 2013, p. 25).

There is no guarantee that online predictive learning will correctly separate out signal from noise in the efficient way that that this requires. But all is not lost. For efficiency can be increased (complexity reduced) even in the absence of ongoing data-driven learning. One way to do this is to 'prune' synaptic connectivity (perhaps, as speculated in chapter 3, during sleep) by removing connections that are weak or redundant. The 'skeletonization' algorithm[2] in connectionism (see Mozer & Smolensky, 1990, and discussion in Clark, 1993) and the aptly named wake-sleep algorithm (Hinton et al., 1995) are early examples of such procedures, each aiming to deliver robust performance while systematically reducing representational excess. The major benefit of such pruning is improved generalization—an improved ability to use what you know in a wide range of superficially distinct (but fundamentally similar) cases. Synaptic pruning provides a plausible mechanism for improving efficiency and reducing model complexity—an effect that may most frequently occur when exteroceptive sensory systems are dampened or shut down as occurs during sleep (see, e.g., Gilestro, Tononi, & Cirelli, 2009; Tononi & Cirelli, 2006).

9.4   Chaos and Spontaneous Cortical Activity

Synaptic pruning provides an endogenous means of improving our grip upon the world. It enables us to improve the grip of our models and strategies by eliminating spurious information and associations, and thus avoiding—or at least repairing—the kind of 'overfitting' that occurs when a system uses valuable resources to track accidental or unimportant features of the training data. Synaptic pruning of this kind is best seen as a mechanism for improving the models that we already, in some rough sense, command. But we routinely do much more than that. For we are capable of a kind of deliberate imaginative exploration of our own mental space. The rudiments of this capacity come for free (as we saw in chapter 3) with the use of hierarchical neural prediction as a means of driving learning, perception, and action. Creatures deploying that kind of strategy turned out to be natural imaginars, able to drive their own sensorimotor systems 'from the top down'. Such creatures can benefit from the use of mental simulations that automatically respect the interlocking constraints implied by the generative model. Such simulations provide a means of getting the most out of the generative model that we already command, while synaptic pruning helps improve that model from within.

But all this can still sound somewhat conservative, as if we are doomed (until new experiences are constructed or intervene) to stay, broadly speaking, within the limits of our achieved world view. To glimpse the possibility of more radical forms of endogenous cognitive exploration, recall the account of spontaneous cortical activity briefly sketched in 6.6. According to that account (see Berkes et al., 2011; see also Sporns, 2010 chapter 8), such spontaneous activity is not 'mere neural noise'. Instead, it reflects a creature's overall model of the world. Evoked activity (the activity resulting from a specific external stimulus) then reflects that model as it is applied to a specific sensory input.

What this and other work (see Sadaghiani et al., 2010) suggests is that spontaneous cortical activity is an expression (a kind of gross signature) of the specific generative model underlying perception and action. According to such an account, 'ongoing activity patterns reflect a historically informed internal model of causal dynamics in the world (that serves to generate predictions of future sensory input)' (Sadaghiani et al., 2010, p. 10). Combining this picture of spontaneous cortical activity with the suggestions (8.11) regarding self-organizing instability opens up an intriguing possibility for more radical explorations of cognitive space.

Suppose that our acquired world model is implemented by a dynamical regime that is never quite stable, most likely due (see, e.g., Van Leeuwen, 2008) to various chaos-style effects. Under such conditions, the model itself (where this is nothing but the constellations of structured neural activity ready to guide perception and action) is constantly 'flittering', exploring the edges of its own territory. Variations in such activity would determine subtly different responses to the encountered sensory stimuli. Even in the absence of compelling sensory inputs, that activity will not stop. Instead, it will continue to occur yielding ongoing forms of stimulus-detached exploration around the edges of the acquired model—explorations that, we may speculate, might suddenly result in a new or more imaginative (and often more parsimonious, see 9.3) solution to a problem or puzzle that has been occupying our attention. In addition, work by Coste et al. (2011) suggests that some spontaneous cortical activity is related to fluctuations in precision optimizations.[3] Perhaps such fluctuations allow us to explore the edges of our own 'meta-model'—our own estimates of context-relative reliability.

Might all this be at least part of the solution to deep and abiding puzzles concerning the origins of new ideas and creative problem-solving? Sadaghiani et al. (2010) link their account to some recent work in machine learning and robotics (Namikawa & Tani, 2010; Tsuda, 2001) in which such mental 'wanderings' are indeed the primary source of new forms of behaviour. Such wanderings might themselves be mandated by implicit hyperpriors that depict the world itself as changing and unstable, hence as no suitable place for systems that would rest on their cognitive laurels. Instead, we would be driven continuously to explore the edges of our own knowledge spaces, subtly altering our predictions and expectations (including our precision expectations) from moment to moment even in the absence of new information and experience.

In an interesting extension of these themes, Namikawa et al. (2011) explored the relationship between complex hierarchical structure and self-organizing instabilities (deterministic chaos) using neuro-robotic simulations. In this work, a generative model with multi-timescale dynamics enables a set of motor behaviours. In these simulations (just as in the PP models to which they are formally closely related):

> Action per se, was a result of movements that conformed to the proprioceptive predictions of ... joint angles [and] perception and action were both trying to minimize prediction errors throughout the hierarchy, where movement minimized the prediction errors at the level of proprioceptive sensations. (Namikawa et al., 2011, p. 4)

In the simulations, deterministic chaos affecting slower timescale (higher level) network dynamics was found to enable new spontaneous transitions among primitive actions (the basic repertoire of the agent). This organization was shown to be both emergent and functionally crucial. It was emergent insofar as the concentration of chaotic dynamics in the higher level network occurred naturally as long as the time constant of the higher level was significantly larger than that of the other regions (for the numerical details, see Namikawa et al., 2011, p. 3). And this partial segregation of the chaotic dynamics was functionally crucial, since by restricting the impact of self-organized chaos to the higher level (slower timescale) networks, the robots were able to explore the useful, well-constrained space of possible action sequences without simultaneously undermining the stable, reusable elements of the action repertoire itself. They were thus able to generate new, spontaneous action transitions without disturbing the faster timescale dynamics (in lower level networks) that rendered their actions robust and reliably reproducible 'on demand'.

Only the networks whose timescale dynamics were sufficiently spread out in this way proved able to display 'both itinerant behaviors with accompanying spontaneous transitions of behavior primitives *and* intentional fixed behaviors (repeatedly executable) [using] the same dynamic mechanism' (Namikawa et al., 2011, p. 3, italics added). By contrast, if the timescale dynamics of the higher level network were reduced (becoming faster, hence closer to those of the lower level networks), robot behaviour became unstable and unreliable, leading the authors to conclude that 'hierarchical timescale differences … are essential for achieving the two functions of freely combining actions in a compositional manner and generating them stably in a physical environment' (Namikawa et al., 2011, p. 9). Such results, preliminary though they are, begin to suggest something of the deep functional role of multiple timescale dynamics—dynamics that occur naturally as a result of hierarchical predictive processing and that are plausibly realized by the spread of labour between neural structures with varying temporal response characteristics.[4]

9.5   Designer Environments and Cultural Practices

There is nothing specifically human, however, about any of the mechanisms for improving and exploring mental space just scouted. Prediction-driven learning, imagination, limited forms of simulation, and the canny exploitation of multi-timescale dynamics are all plausibly displayed, albeit to varying degrees, by other mammals. The most basic elements of the predictive processing story, as Roepstorff (2013, p. 224) correctly notes, may thus be found in many types of organism and model system. The neocortex (the layered structure housing cortical columns that provides the most compelling neural implementation for predictive processing machinery) displays some dramatic variations in size but is common to all mammals. Core features of the PP model may also be supported in other species using other structures (e.g., the so-called 'mushroom bodies' found in insect brains are conjectured to provide a means of implementing forward models used for prediction, see Li & Strausfeld, 1999, and discussion in Webb, 2004).

What, then, makes us (superficially at least) so very different? What is it that allows us—unlike dogs, chimps, or dolphins—to latch on to distal causes that include not just food, mates, and relative social rankings but also neurons, predictive processing, Higgs bosons, and black holes? One possibility (Conway & Christiansen, 2001) is that adaptations of the human neural apparatus have somehow conspired to create, in us, an even more complex and context-flexible hierarchical learning system than is found in other animals. Insofar as the PP framework allows for rampant context-dependent influence within the distributed system, the same basic operating principles might (given a few new opportunities of routing and influence) result in the emergence of qualitatively novel forms of behaviour and control. Such changes might explain why human agents display what Spivey (2007, p. 169) nicely describes as an 'exceptional sensitivity to hierarchical structure in *any* time-dependent signal'.

Another (possibly linked and certainly highly complementary) possibility involves a potent complex of features of human life, especially our abilities of temporally co-ordinated social interaction (see Roepstorff, 2013) and our abilities to construct artefacts, and designer environments. Some of these ingredients have emerged in other species too. But in the human case the whole mosaic comes together under the influence of flexible structured symbolic language (this was the target of the Conway and Christiansen treatment mentioned above) and an almost obsessive drive (Tomasello et al., 2005) to engage in shared cultural practices. We are thus enabled repeatedly to redeploy our core cognitive skills in the transformative context of exposure to what Roepstorff et al. (2010) call 'patterned sociocultural practices'. These include the use of symbolic inscriptions (encountered as 'material symbols', see Clark, 2006) embedded in complex practices and social routines (Hutchins, 1995, 2014). Such environments and practices include those of mathematics, reading,[5] writing, structured discussion, and schooling. The succession and tuning of such designer environments then constitutes the complex and ill-understood process that Sterelny (2003) describes as 'incremental downstream epistemic engineering'.

What are the potential effects of such stacked and transmissible structures (designer environments and practices) upon prediction-driven learning in neural systems? Prediction-driven learning routines make human minds permeable, at multiple spatial and temporal scales, to the statistical structure of the action-ready, organism-salient world, as reflected in the training signals. But those training signals are now delivered as part of a complex developmental web that gradually comes to include all the complex regularities embodied in the web of statistical relations among the symbols and other forms of sociocultural scaffolding in which we are immersed. We thus self-construct a kind of rolling 'cognitive niche' able to induce the acquisition of generative models whose reach and depth far exceeds their apparent base in simple forms of sensory contact with the world.

To see how this might work, recall that the way to construct a new idea or concept (assuming the resources of PP) is to encounter a new sensory pattern that results in highly weighted (organism-salient) prediction error. Highly weighted errors, if the system is unable to explain them away by recruiting some model that it already commands, result in increased plasticity and (if all goes well) the acquisition of new knowledge about the shape and nature of the distal causes responsible for the surprising sensory inputs. But we humans are also expert at deliberately manipulating our physical and social worlds so that they provide new and ever-more-challenging patterns that will drive new learning. A very simple example is the way that learning to perform mental arithmetic has been scaffolded, in some cultures, by the deliberate use of an abacus. Experience with the sensory patterns thus made available helps to install appreciation of many complex arithmetical operations and relations (for discussion, see Stigler et al., 1986). The specific example does not matter very much, but the general strategy does. We structure (and repeatedly restructure) our physical and social environments in ways that make available new knowledge and skills (for some lovely explorations, see Goldstone, Landy, & Brunel, 2011; Landy & Goldstone, 2005; and, for an information-theoretic twist, Salge, Glackin, & Polani, 2014). Prediction-hungry brains, exposed in the course of embodied action to novel patterns of sensory stimulation, may thus acquire forms of knowledge that were genuinely out-of-reach prior to such physical-manipulation-based retuning of the generative model.

Such retuning and enhancement is now served by a huge variety of symbol-mediated loops into material and social culture: loops that involve (see Clark, 2003, 2008) notebooks, sketchpads, smartphones, and also (see Pickering & Garrod, 2007) written and spoken conversations with other agents.[6] Such loops are effectively enabling new forms of re-entrant processing. They take a 'first-order' cognitive product (such as the visual experience of seeing a new purple skyscraper) clothe it in public symbols (turning it into the written or spoken sequence, "I saw a new purple skyscraper today") and launch it into the world so that it can re-enter our own cognitive system, and the cognitive systems of other agents, as a new kind of concrete perceptible—the percept of a written or spoken sentence (Clark 2006, 2008). Those new perceptibles bear highly informative statistical relations to other such linguaform perceptibles. Once externalized, an idea or thought is thus able to participate in brand new webs of higher order and more abstract statistical correlation. The signature of such correlations is that words predict the occurrence of other words, tokens of mathematical symbols and operators predict the occurrence of other such tokens, and so on.

We glimpse the power of the complex internal statistical relationships enshrined in human languages in Landauer and colleagues' fascinating work on 'latent semantic analysis' (LSA). This work reveals the vast amount of information now embodied in statistical (but deep, not first order) relations between words and the larger contexts (sentences and texts) in which they occur (see Landauer & Dumais, 1997; Landauer et al., 2007). For example, deep statistical relations among words were here shown to contain information that could help predict the grade-score of essays in specific subject areas. More generally (for LSA is a very specific technique with strict limitations) the rich symbolic world we humans immerse ourselves in is now demonstrably chock-full of information about meaning relations *in itself*. Those meaning relations are reflected in our patterns of use (hence in patterns of occurrence) and they can be identified and exploited regardless of the many more fundamental hooks that link words and symbols to practical actions and the (rest of our) sensory world. Some of those meaning relations, moreover, obtain in realms whose core constructs are now far, far removed from any simple sensory signatures, visible only in the internal relations proper to the arcane worlds of quantum theory, higher mathematics, philosophy, art, and politics (to name but a few).

Our best takes on the world are thus given material form and made available (in that new guise) as publically perceptible object— words, sentences, equations. An important side-effect of this is that our own thoughts and ideas now become available, to ourselves and others, as potential objects for deliberate processes of attention. This opens the door to a whole array of knowledge-improvement and knowledge-testing techniques, ranging from simple conversations in which we ask for reasons, to the complex practices of testing, dissemination, and peer-review characteristic of contemporary science. Courtesy of all that material public vehicling in spoken words, written text, diagrams, and pictures, *our* best predictive models of the world (unlike those of other creatures) have thus become stable, rein-spectable objects apt for public critique and systematic, multi-agent, multi-generational test and refinement. Our best models of the world are thus able to serve as the basis for cumulative, communally distrib-uted reasoning, rather than just providing the *means* by which indi-vidual thoughts occur. The same potent predictive processing regimes, now targeting these brand new types of statistically pregnant 'designer inputs', are then enabled to discover and refine new generative mod-els, latching onto (and at times actively creating) ever more abstract structure in the world. The upshot is that the human-built (material and sociocultural) environment becomes a potent source of new trans-missible structure that trains, triggers, and repeatedly transforms the activity of the prediction-hungry biological brain.[7]

In sum, our human-built worlds are not merely the arenas in which we live, work, and play. They also structure the life-long statistical immersions that build and rebuild the generative models that inform each agent's repertoire for perception, action, and reason. By construct-ing a succession of designer environments, such as the human-built worlds of education, structured play, art, and science, we repeatedly restructure our own minds. These designer environments have slowly become tailored to creatures like us, and they 'know' us as well as we know them. As a species, we refine them again and again, generation by generation. It is this iterative re-structuring, and not sheer process-ing power, memory, mobility, or even the learning algorithms them-selves, that completes the human mental mosaic.

9.6   White Lines

To further appreciate the power and scope of such culturally-mediated reshaping, recall the main moral of chapter 8. The moral was that the predictive brain is not doomed to deploy high-cost, model-rich strate-gies moment-by-moment in a demanding and time-pressured world. Instead, action and environmental structuring can both be called upon to reduce complexity. In such cases, PP delivers and deploys low-cost strategies that make the most of body, world, and action. In the simple case of running to catch a fly ball, the problem to be solved was 'posed' by the very ball whose in-flight optical properties made available the low-cost solution itself. In such cases, we did not need to actively struc-ture our world so as to make the low-cost strategy available, or cue its use. In other cases, however, the cultural snowball has enabled us to structure our worlds in ways that *both cue and help constitute* low-cost routes to behavioural or cognitive success.

A maximally simple example is painting white lines along the edges of a winding cliff-top road. Such environmental alterations allow the driver to solve the complex problem of keeping the car on the road by (in part) predicting the ebb and flow of various simpler optical features and cues (see, e.g., Land, 2001). In such cases, we are building a better world to predict in, while simultaneously structuring the world to cue that strategy at the right time. In other words, we build worlds that cue simpler strategies that are only available because of the way we have altered the world in the first place. Other examples include the use of posted prices in supermarkets (Satz & Ferejohn, 1994), wearing the colours of our favourite football team, or displaying the distinctive clothing styles of our chosen subculture.

The full potential of the prediction error minimization model of how cortical processing most fundamentally operates may thus emerge only when that story is paired with an appreciation of what immersion in a huge variety of sociocultural designer environments can do (for some early steps in this direction, see Roepstorff et al., 2010). Such a combined approach would implement a version of 'neuroconstructivism' (Mareschal et al., 2007), a view according to which

> The architecture of the brain ... and the statistics of the environment, [are] not fixed. Rather, brain-connectivity is subject to a broad spectrum of input-, experience-, and activity-dependent processes which shape and structure its patterning and strengths. ... These changes, in turn, result in altered interactions with the environment, exerting causal influences on what is experienced and sensed in the future. (Sporns, 2007, p. 179)

Much of what is distinctive about human thought and reason may thus be best explained by the operation of what Hutchins (2014, p. 35) describes as 'cultural ecosystems operating at large spatial and temporal scales'. Within such ecosystems slowly evolved culturally transmitted practices sculpt the very worlds within which neural prediction error minimization occurs. Those cultural practices may themselves be usefully understood, Hutchins conjectures, as entropy (surprise) minimization devices operating at extended spatial and temporal scales. Action and perception then work together to reduce prediction error only against the more slowly evolving backdrop of a culturally distributed process that spawns a succession of practices and designer environments whose impact on the development (e.g., Smith & Gasser, 2005) and unfolding of human thought and reason can hardly be overestimated.

There is a downside, of course. The downside is that these culturally mediated processes may also incur costs in the form of various kinds of path-dependence (Arthur, 1994) in which later solutions build on earlier ones. Sub-optimal path-based idiosyncrasies may then become frozen (perhaps like the much-discussed QWERTY keyboard or Betamax video format) into our material artefacts, institutions, notations, measuring tools, and cultural practices. But these costs are easy to bear. For it is those very same trajectory-sensitive cultural processes that deliver the vast cognitive profits that flow from the slow, multigenerational development of designer environments—environments that help human minds go where other animal minds do not.

9.7   Innovating for Innovation

Adding further fuel to this sociocultural-technological fire, it may even be the case, as elegantly argued by Heyes (2012), that many of our *capacities for cultural learning* are *themselves* cultural innovations, acquired by social interactions, rather than flowing directly from fundamental biological adaptations. The idea here is that:

> the specialized features of cultural learning—the features that make cultural learning especially good at enabling the social transmission of information—are acquired in the course of development through social interaction. . . . They are products as well as producers of cultural evolution. (Heyes, 2012, p. 2182)

Cultural learning, to borrow Heyes own analogy, would not merely be a producer of more and more 'grist' (transmissible facts about the world) but a source of 'mills'—the 'psychological processes that enable us to learn the grist from others' (Heyes, 2012, p. 2182).

The most obvious example is reading and writing, a matched pair of cultural practices that seem to have emerged far too recently to be a result of genetic adaptations. The practice of reading is known to cause widespread changes in human neural organization (Dehaene et al., 2010; Paulesu et al., 2000). The resulting new organization exploits what Anderson (2010) describes as a fundamental principle of 'neural reuse' in which pre-existing elements are recruited and repurposed. In this way:

> learning to read takes old parts and remodels them into a new system. The old parts are computational processes and cortical

regions originally adapted, genetically and culturally, for object recognition and spoken language, but it is an ontogenetic, cultural process— literacy training—that makes them into a new system specialized for cultural learning. (Heyes, 2012, p. 2182)

Reading is thus a nice example of a culturally inherited mill—a product of cultural evolution that feeds and fuels the process of cultural evolution itself. Other examples, Heyes argues, may include key mechanisms of social learning (learning by observing other agents in action) and imitation. If Heyes is right, then *culture itself* may be responsible for many of the sub-mechanisms that give the cultural snowball the means and momentum to deliver minds like ours.

9.8   Words as Tools for Manipulating Precision

Words and phrases enjoy a double life. They function as communicative vehicles, but they also seem to play a role in the unfolding and development of our own thoughts and ideas. This latter role is sometimes referred to as the supra-communicative dimension of language (see Clark, 1998; Dennett, 1991; Jackendoff, 1996). This supra-communicative role can seem rather mysterious. What cognitive advantage could possibly accrue to an agent simply in virtue of expressing a thought (one that, you might insist, she already has) using language? The answer, presumably, is that we are wrong to depict the case in quite that way. Rather than merely expressing a thought we already have, such acts must somehow alter, impact, or transform the thinking itself. But just how might this work?

Consider, from the PP perspective, the likely effects of encountered, self-produced, or conversationally co-constructed words or phrases upon individual processing and problem-solving. In such cases we, either alone or as part of a collective, are creating 'artificial input streams' that may be peculiarly well-adapted to alter and nuance the flows of inner processing that help determine perception, experience, and action.

In a bare-bones exploration of such ideas, Lupyan and Ward (2013) conducted an experiment using a technique called Continuous Flash Suppression (CFS).[8] In CFS an image continuously presented to one eye is suppressed when a changing stream of other images is presented to the other eye. This is another example of bi-stable perception, related to the binocular rivalry case that we explored way back in chapter 1.[9] Lupyan and Ward found that an object that is masked from awareness by CFS can be unsuppressed (consciously detected) if the right word—the word 'zebra', if the suppressed object was a zebra—is heard before the trial begins. Hearing the right word increased the 'hit rate' for detecting the object and shortened reaction times too. The explanation, the authors suggest, is that 'when information associated with verbal labels matches incoming (bottom-up) activity, language provides a top-down boost to perception, propelling an otherwise invisible image into awareness' (Ward & Lupyan, 2013, p. 14196). In this experiment the verbal enhancement was externally provided. But related effects, in which no external cueing is provided, have also been demonstrated for conscious recognition. Thus, Melloni et al. (2011, and discussion in 3.6) showed that the onset time required to form a reportable conscious percept varies substantially (by around 100 ms) according to the presence or absence of apt expectations, even when those expectations emerge naturally as the subject performs a task. Putting these two effects together suggests that exposure to words functions to alter or nuance the active expectations that help construct our ongoing experience.

In some ways, this seems obvious enough. Words make a difference! But there is emerging evidence that the expectations induced by exposure to words and phrases are especially strong, focused, and targeted. Lupyan and Thompson-Schill (2012) found that hearing the word 'dog' is better than simply hearing a barking sound as a means of improving performance in a related discrimination task. There is also intriguing evidence (see Çukur et al., 2013, and discussion in Kim & Kasstner, 2013) that category-based attention (as when we are told covertly to attend to 'vehicles' or to 'humans' when watching a movie or video clip) temporarily alters the tuning of neuronal populations, shifting the category sensitivity of neurons or of neuronal ensembles in the direction of the attended content.

Such transient instruction-induced alterations of cortical representations could be cashed out by the suite of mechanisms that alter the precision-weighting of specific prediction error signals. This is suggestive. A potent feature of structured language is its ability to cheaply and very flexibly target highly specific aspects of our own understanding or of our understanding of another agent. One way in which this could work, within the context of a PP-style cognitive architecture, is thus by impacting our ongoing estimations of precision, hence the relative uncertainty assigned to different aspects of ongoing neural activity. Recent work by Yuval-Greenberg and Heeger (2013, p. 9365) suggests that 'CFS is based on modulating the gain of neural responses, akin to reducing target contrast'. The PP mechanism for modulating such gain is, of course, the precision-weighting of prediction error. Language, it may be conjectured, provides a finely tuned means of artificially manipulating the precision (hence of temporarily modifying the impact) of prediction error at different levels of neural processing. Such transient, targeted, subtle manipulations of precision could selectively enhance or mute the influence of any aspect of our own or another agent's world model. Self-produced (or mentally rehearsed) language would then emerge as a potent means of exploring and exploiting the full potential of our own acquired generative model, providing a kind of *artificial second system* for manipulating the precision-weighting of our own prediction errors—hence a 'neat trick' (Dennett, 1991) for artificially manipulating our estimations of our own uncertainty enabling us to make fully flexible use of what we know.

Words, we might say, are (for us language users) a metabolically cheap and flexible source of 'artificial contexts' (Lupyan & Clark, in press). Viewed from the PP perspective, the impact of strings of words upon neural processing is thus flexibly to modify both what top-down information is brought to bear, and how much influence it has at every level of processing (see Figure 9.1). Such a powerful tool for targeted

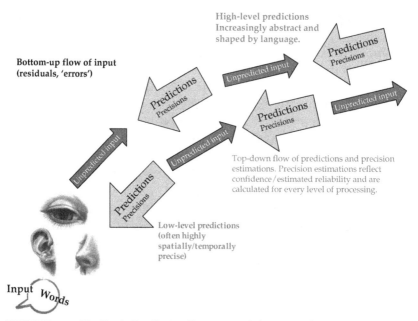

FIGURE 9.1   The Basic Predictive Processing Schema, with Language as an Additional Input

Source: Adapted from Lupyan & Clark, in press.

self-manipulation will provide a huge boost to intelligence, improving performance in ways that go far beyond those associated with linguistic performance alone.[10] It is a tool, moreover, whose overall cognitive impact would be expected to vary in proportion to the subtlety and range of the linguistic repertoire of the agent.

This is a tempting picture indeed. But exactly how public lingua-form encodings interact with the kinds of structured probabilistic knowledge representation posited by PP remains largely unknown. Such interactions lie at the heart of the processes of cultural construction described earlier and must constitute a crucial target for future research.

9.9   Predicting with Others

In the social world, many of the tricks and ploys we have just sketched come together in a mutually supportive mix. Other agents are (recall chapter 5) often apt for prediction using the same generative model that gives rise to our own actions. But other agents also provide a unique form of 'external scaffolding', since their actions and responses can be exploited to reduce our own individual processing loads. Finally, other agents are *themselves* predictors, and this opens up an interesting space for mutually beneficial (or sometimes destructive—recall 2.9) processes of 'continuous reciprocal prediction'.

A nice example, explored in some detail by Pickering and Garrod (2007, 2013) is the co-construction of a conversation. In conversation, Pickering and Garrod suggest, each person uses their own language production system (hence the generative model underlying their own behaviour) to help predict the other's utterances, while also using the output of the other as a kind of external scaffolding for their own ongoing productions. These predictions (just as PP would suggest) are probabilistic, and span multiple different levels from phonology to syntax and semantics. As conversation proceeds, multiple predictions are thus continuously co-computed with their associated probabilities (see also Cisek & Kalaska, 2011; Spivey, 2007). Each party to such a process is, in the typical case, in the business of matching, or attempting to match, their behaviour and expectations to those of the other. As conversation proceeds, words, grammar, intonation, gesture, and eye movements may all be overtly copied or covertly imitated (for a handy review of the linguistic and behavioural evidence, see Pickering & Garrod, 2004). Overt copying, in particular, helps support mutual prediction and mutual understanding since 'if B overtly imitates A, then

A's comprehension of B's utterance is facilitated by A's memory for A's previous utterance' (Pickering & Garrod, 2007, p. 109). The upshot is that 'prediction and imitation can jointly explain why conversation tends to be easy, even though it involves constant task-switching and the need to determine when to speak and what to say' (p. 109).

Such piggybacking is not, of course, restricted to our conversational interactions. Instead, in one form or another it seems to characterize many forms of human joint action ranging from team sports to changing the bed linen with a partner (Sebanz & Knoblich, 2009). Individual agents may also actively constrain their own behaviour so as to make themselves more easily predictable by other agents. Thus, we might artificially stabilize our own public personas so as to encourage others to enter into economic or emotional arrangements with us (Ross, 2004). On an even grander scale, Colombo (in press) depicts social norms (the mostly unwritten 'rules' of daily social behaviour, such as leaving a tip in a restaurant) as devices whose role is to reduce mutual uncertainty by creating structures or schemas within which behaviour becomes more mutually predictable. Social norms, Colombo argues, are entropy-minimizing devices, represented as probability distributions, that serve to make social behaviour predictable. Expectations about our own behaviour are thus simultaneously descriptive and prescriptive in nature.

This dual nature is also evident (Hirsh et al., 2013) in the cognitive role of personal narratives: the stories we tell, to ourselves and to others, about the flow and meaning of our lives. Such narratives function as high-level elements in the models that structure our own self-predictions, and thus inform our own future actions and choices. But personal narratives are often co-constructed with others, and thus tend to feed the structures and expectations of society back in so that they become reflected in the models that an individual uses to make sense of her own acts and choices. Personal narratives may thus be considered as another species of communal uncertainty-reducing device.

Roepstorff and Frith (2004) note that many cases of human interaction involve a kind of top-level 'script-sharing' in which the highest-level processes that control one agent's action may originate in the brain of another agent. The case they examine in detail is the construction of a sufficient understanding of an experimental situation to allow a subject to participate in a specific psychological experiment. In such cases, human agents can often achieve the (sometimes quite demanding) understanding needed to participate simply by means of a bout of verbal instruction in which high-level understandings are communicated directly from experimenter to subject. This is a case of what

Roepstorff and Frith engagingly dub 'top-top control of action', in which elements of the experimenter's high-level understanding become positioned, courtesy of linguistic exchange, to control patterns of response in another agent. Such a situation may be contrasted with the long and arduous training process needed to install sufficient understanding in a monkey. The especially challenging example that Roepstorff and Frith describe involved performing a simplified version of the Wisconsin Card Sorting Task and required, before the monkeys were able to act as suitable subjects, a full year of operant conditioning (see Nakahara et al., 2002). Following this training, Nakahara et al. found anatomically similar brain activations in both monkeys and human subjects as they performed the task, suggesting that, as planned, the monkeys had indeed learnt the same 'cognitive set' (the same guiding recipe for action and choice) as the human subjects. But despite this end-point similarity, the process was, clearly, radically different, since:

> whereas the human participant receives this script directly from the experimenter in a 'top-top' exchange, the monkey has to reconstruct this script solely via the concrete stimuli and rewards offered to it. It happens as the monkey, based on the previous understandings of the situation, reacts to the reward responses that the experimenter dispenses. (Roepstorff & Frith, 2004, p. 193)

In the case of the monkey, script-synchronization required the experimenters' top-level understanding to be recreated via a truly bottom-up process of learning, whereas in the case of the human subjects, this arduous route could be avoided by the judicious use of language and pre-existing shared understandings. Among human subjects already possessing significant shared understanding, language thus provides a kind of cheap, readily available 'top-top' route for the control of action. Looping linguaform interactions can thus help create what Hasson et al. (2012, p. 114) describe as systems of 'brain-to-brain coupling' in which 'the perceptual system of one brain [is] coupled to the motor system of another' in ways that enable the emergence of new forms of joint behaviour—for example, when one agent shouts commands to another while moving a grand piano up a flight of stairs.

Language also provides a means for whole groups of human agents to collectively negotiate complex representational spaces. In particular, it provides a means (see Clark, 1998) of taming 'path-dependent' learning. Path dependency, in its most familiar form, is the rationale for structured education and training. This is necessary because certain ideas can be understood only once others are in place. Such 'cognitive path dependency' is nicely explained (see, e.g., Elman, 1993) by treating intellectual progress as involving something like a process of computational search in a large and complex space. Previous learning inclines the system to try out certain locations in the space and not others. When the prior learning is appropriate, the job of discovering some new regularity is made tractable: the prior learning acts as a filter on the space of options to be explored. The hierarchical nature of the prediction-based approaches we have been exploring makes them especially well-suited as inner mechanisms capable of supporting complex patterns of path-dependent learning in which later achievements build on earlier ones. At the same time, however, prior learning makes certain other regularities harder (at times impossible) to spot. Prior knowledge is thus always both constraining and enabling.

When confronting agents that exhibit path-dependent learning, the mundane observation that language allows ideas to be preserved and (in some sense) to migrate between individuals takes on a new force. For we can now appreciate how such migrations may allow the communal construction of extremely delicate and difficult intellectual trajectories and progressions. An idea which only Joe's experience makes available, but which can flourish and realize its full potential only in the intellectual niche currently provided by the brain of Mary, can now realize its full potential by journeying between those agents. Different agents (and the same agent at different times) constitute different 'filters', and groups of such agents make available trajectories of learning and discovery that no single agent could comprehend. The variety of intellectual niches available within a linguistically linked community thus provides a stunning matrix of group-level multi-agent trajectories. In sum, socially interacting agents benefit from nested and self-reinforcing cycles of ongoing mutual prediction. This kind of joint piggy-backing emerges naturally when groups of interacting, predictive agents construct a shared social world and may be a fundamental source of low-cost computational strategies for human interaction. Inter-agent exchanges thus create new paths through the space of possible understandings, allowing webs of communicating agents communally to explore intellectual trajectories that would rapidly defeat any individual agent.

9.10   Enacting Our Worlds

The combined effects of action, cultural learning, reciprocal prediction, the canny use of language, and the many forms of socio-technological scaffolding are transformative. It is the ill-understood alchemy between the predictive brain and this whole raft of mutually supportive tricks and ploys that makes us distinctively human. An immediate implication of our larger story is thus that there is a very real sense in which human agents help construct the very worlds they model and inhabit. That process of construction corresponds rather closely to the mysterious-sounding notion of 'enacting a world', at least as that notion appears in Varela et al. (1991).[11]

Varela et al. write that:

> The overall concern of an enactive approach to perception is not to determine how some perceiver-independent world is to be recovered; it is, rather, to determine the common principles or lawful linkages between sensory and motor systems that explain how action can be perceptually-guided in a perceiver-dependent world. (Varela et al., 1991, p. 173)

Such an approach to perception is prefigured, Varela et al. report, in the work of Merleau-Ponty (1945/1962). There, Merleau-Ponty stresses the important degree to which perception itself is structured by human action. Thus, we often think of perception as simply the source of information that is then used for the guidance of action. But expand the temporal window a little and it becomes clear that we might equally well think of action as the selector of the perceptual stimulations themselves. In the words of Merleau-Ponty:

> since all the stimulations which the organism receives have in turn been possible only by its preceding movements which have culminated in exposing the receptor organ to external influences, one could also say that behavior is the first cause of all the stimulations. (Merleau-Ponty, 1945/1962, p. 13)

In a striking image, Merleau-Ponty then compares the active organism to a keyboard which moves itself around so as to offer different keys to the 'in itself monotonous action of an external hammer' (p. 13).[12] The message that the world 'types onto the perceiver' is thus largely created (or so the image suggests) by the nature and action of the perceiver herself: the way she offers herself to the world. The upshot, according to Varela et al. (1991, p. 174) is that 'the organism and environment [are] bound together in reciprocal specification and selection'.

This kind of relation is described by Varela et al. as one of 'structural coupling' in which 'the species brings forth and specifies its own domain of problems' (p. 198) and in that sense 'enacts' or brings forth (p. 205) its own world. In discussing these matters, Varela et al. are also concerned to stress that the relevant histories of structural coupling may select what they describe as 'non-optimal' features, traits, and behaviours: ones that involve 'satisficing' (see Simon, 1956, and chapter 8) where that means settling for whatever 'good enough' solution or structure 'has sufficient integrity to persist' (Varela et al., 1991, p. 196). PP has the resources to cash all these 'enactivist' cheques, depicting the organism and the organism-salient world as bound together in a process of mutual specification in which the simplest approximations apt to support a history of viable interaction are the ones that are learnt, selected, and maintained.[13]

The simplest way in which a predictive-processing enabled agent might be said to actively construct its world is by sampling. Action here serves perception by moving the body and sense organs around in ways that aim to 'serve up' predicted patterns of stimulation. In particular, they aim (chapter 2) to serve up predicted sequences of high-reliability, task-relevant information. This is a very clear case, it seems to me, of the kind of 'active keyboard' effect imagined by Merleau-Ponty—the organism selectively moves its body and receptors to try to discover the very stimuli that it predicts. In this way, different organisms and individuals may selectively sample in ways that both actively construct and continuously confirm the existence of different 'worlds'. It is in this sense that, as Friston, Adams, and Montague (2012, p. 22) comment, our implicit and explicit models might be said to 'create their own data'.

Such a process repeats at several organizational scales. Thus, we humans do not merely sample some natural environment. We also structure that environment in (as we just saw) a wide variety of potent, interacting, and often cumulative ways. We do this by building material artefacts (from homes to highways), creating cultural practices and institutions, and trading in all manner of symbolic and notational props, aids, and scaffoldings. Some of our practices and institutions are also designed to train us to sample and exploit our human-built environment more effectively—examples would include sports practice, training in the use of specific tools and software, learning to speed-read, and many, many more. Finally, some of our technological infrastructure is now self-altering in ways that are designed to reduce the load on the predictive agent, learning from our past behaviours and searches so as to serve up the right options at the right time. In all these ways, and at all these interacting scales of space and time, we build and selectively sample the very worlds that—in iterated bouts of statistically sensitive interaction—install the generative models that we bring to bear upon them.

The task of the generative model in all these settings is to capture the simplest approximations that will support the actions required to do the job—that (as we saw in chapter 8) means taking into account whatever work can be done by a creature's morphology, physical actions, and socio-technological surroundings. PP thus harmonizes fully with work that stresses frugality, satisficing, and the ubiquity of simple but adequate solutions that make the most of brain, body, and world. Brain, body, and the partially self-constructed environment stand revealed as 'mutually embedded systems' (Varela et al., 2001, p. 423) working together in the service of situated success.

9.11   Representations: Breaking Good?

There remains, however, at least one famously vexed issue upon which PP and enactivism (at least if history is any guide) seem doomed to disagree. That is the issue of 'internal representation'. Thus Varela et al. are explicit that on the enactivist conception 'cognition is no longer seen as problem solving on the basis of representations' (p. 205). PP, however, deals extensively in internal models—rich, frugal, and all points in-between—whose role is to control action by predicting complex plays of sensory data. This, the enactivist might fear, is where our promising story about neural processing 'breaks bad'. Why not simply ditch the talk of inner models and internal representations and stay on the true path of enactivist virtue?

This issue requires a lot more discussion than I shall (perhaps mercifully) attempt here.[14] Nonetheless, the remaining distance between PP and enactivism may not be as great as that bald opposition suggests. We can begin by recalling that PP, although it trades heavily in talk of inner models and representations, invokes representations that are probabilistic and action-oriented through and through. These are representations that (see chapters 5–8) are *fundamentally* in the business of serving action within the context of rolling sensorimotor cycles. Such representations aim to *engage* the world, rather than to depict it in some action-neutral fashion. They remain, moreover, firmly rooted in the patterns of organism-environment interaction that served up the structured sensory stimulations reflected in the mature probabilistic generative model. The role of that generative model is to deliver an efficient, context-sensitive grip upon a world of multiple competing affordances for action.

The shape of that grip is well captured by Itay Shani who writes that:

> Actual sensory systems are not concerned with truth and accuracy as such but rather, with action and the need to maintain the functional stability of the organisms in which they are embedded. They do not report, or register, what is where like an idealized scientific observer but, rather, help organisms to cope with changing conditions in their external, and internal (somatic), environments. (Shani, 2006, p. 90)

This is exactly the role played, if PP is correct, by the multilevel probabilistic generative models that guide perception and action.[15]

What are the *contents* of the states governed by these multilevel action-oriented probabilistic generative models? The generative model issues predictions that estimate various identifiable worldly states (including states of the body and the mental states of other agents).[16] But it is also necessary, as we have repeatedly seen, to estimate the context-variable reliability (precision) of the neural estimations themselves. Some of these precision-weighted estimates drive action, and it is action that then samples the scene, delivering percepts that select more actions. Such looping complexities will make it hard (perhaps impossible) adequately to capture the contents or the cognitive roles of many key inner states and processes using the terms and vocabulary of ordinary daily speech. That vocabulary is 'designed' for communication (though it may also enable various forms of cognitive self-stimulation). The probabilistic generative model, by contrast, is designed to engage the world in rolling, uncertainty-modulated, cycles of perception and action. The representations thus constructed are 'not actual re-presentations or duplicates of objects in the world but ... incomplete, abstract code that makes predictions about the world and revises its predictions on the basis of interaction with the world' (Lauwereyns, 2012, p. 74). Within PP, high-level states (of the generative model) target large-scale, increasingly invariant patterns in space and time. Such states help us to keep track of specific individuals, properties, and events despite large moment-by-moment variations in the stream of sensory stimulation. Unpacked via cascades of descending prediction, such higher level states simultaneously inform both perception and action, locking them into continuous circular causal flows. Instead of simply describing 'how the world is', these models—even when considered at the 'higher' more abstract levels—are geared to engaging those aspects of the world that matter to us. They are delivering a grip on the *patterns that matter* for the *interactions that matter*.

This suggests a recipe for peace in the disputes concerning internal representation. Varela et al. (1991) strongly reject appeals to 'internal representation'. But for them, this notion implies the 'action-neutral' capture of what they call a 'pregiven world'. Organism and world, they argued, are instead co-defined by a history of structural coupling: a kind of active 'fitting' of each to the other, rather than a passive 'mirroring'. PP, I have tried to show, fully respects this intuition. It posits a hierarchical generative model that helps maintain the integrity and viability of a system by enabling it to minimize prediction errors and thus avoid compromising (possibly fatal) encounters with the environment. That distributed inner model is itself the result of self-organizing dynamics operating at multiple temporal scales, and it functions selectively to expose the agent to the patterns of stimulation that it predicts. The generative model thus functions—just as an enactivist might insist—to enable and maintain structural couplings that serve our needs and that keep us viable.

Could we perhaps have told our story in entirely non-representational terms, without invoking the concept of a hierarchical probabilistic generative model at all? One should always beware of sweeping assertions about what might, one day, be explanatorily possible! But as things stand, I simply do not see how this is to be achieved.[17] For it is surely that very depiction that allows us to understand how it is that these looping dynamical regimes arise and enable such spectacular results. The regimes arise and succeed because the system self-organizes so as to capture patterns in the (partially self-created) input stream. These patterns specify bodily and worldly causes operating at varying scales of space and time. Subtract this guiding vision and what remains is just a picture of complex looping dynamics spanning brain, body, and world. Such a vision is surely correct, as far as it goes. But it does not explain (does not render intelligible) the emergence of a structured meaningful realm apt for perception, thought, imagination, and action.

Consider those same looping dynamics from the explanatory perspective afforded by PP, however, and many things fall naturally into place. With that schema in mind, we comprehend perception, imagination, and simulation-based reasoning as co-emergent from a single cognitive architecture; we see how that architecture simultaneously supports perception and action, locking them together in a circular causal embrace; we see why, and exactly how, perception and action are themselves co-constructed and co-determining; we see how, at longer timescales, statistically driven learning can unearth interacting distal and bodily causes in the first place, revealing a structured world of human-sized opportunities for action; and we understand how it is that unexpected omissions and absences can be every bit as salient and perceptually striking as the most concrete of ordinary perceptibles. We appreciate all this, moreover, from a perspective that both accommodates and unifies impressive swathes of work in machine learning, in psychophysics, in cognitive and computational neuroscience and (increasingly) in computational neuropsychiatry. This is surely encouraging. Perhaps models in this broad ballpark offer our first glimpse of the shape of a fundamental and unified science of the embodied mind?

9.12   Prediction in the Wild

Our neural economy exists to serve the needs of embodied action. It does so by initiating and sustaining complex circular causal flows in which actions and perceptions are co-determined and co-determining. These flows enact structural couplings that serve our needs while keeping the organism within its own specialized window of viability. All this is orchestrated, or so our story suggests, by a multilevel generative model tuned to predict task-salient aspects of the current sensory signal.

Is this an inner economy bloated with representations, detached from the world? Not at all. This is an inner economy geared for action that aims to lock embodied agents onto opportunities in their worlds. Dynamically speaking, the whole embodied, active system here self-organizes around the organismically-computable quantity 'prediction error'. This is what delivers that multi-level, multi-area grip on the evolving sensory barrage—a grip that must span multiple spatial and temporal scales. Such a grip simultaneously determines perception and action, and it selects (enacts) the ongoing stream of sensory bombardment itself. The generative model that here issues sensory predictions is thus nothing but that multi-level, multi-area, multi-scale, body-and-action involving grip on the unfolding sensory stream. To achieve that grip is to know the structured and meaningful world that we encounter in experience and action.

That grip, in the somewhat special case of the human mind, is further enriched and transformed by layer upon layer of sociocultural structures and practices. Steeped in such practices, our predictive brains are empowered to redeploy their basic skills in new and transformative ways. Understanding the resulting interplay between culture, technology, action, and cascading neural prediction is surely one of the major tasks confronting twenty-first-century cognitive science.

10

Conclusions

The Future of Prediction

> Remember that all models are wrong; the practical question is how wrong do they have to be to not be useful.
>
> —Box & Draper, 1987

10.1   Embodied Prediction Machines

Predictive processing (PP) offers a vision of the brain that dovetails perfectly (or so I have argued) with work on the embodied and environmentally situated mind. This is a fit forged by action and by the circular causal flows that bind acting and perceiving. It is a fit that reveals perception, understanding, reason, and imagination as co-emergent, and restless itinerant dynamics as the signature of the embodied mind. Within this ever-active, self-organizing flow, neural sub-assemblies form and dissolve in ways determined by changing estimations of relative uncertainty. These temporary circuits recruit, and are recruited by, shifting webs of bodily and extra-bodily structure and resources. The resulting transient wholes are the true (frugal, efficient) vehicles of adaptive and behavioural success. The predictive brain is thus not an insulated inference engine "in the head" so much as an action-oriented engagement engine, delivering a rolling grip on task-salient opportunities.

Sculpting and maintaining that rolling grip are the deep cognitive engines of downwards (and lateral) flowing prediction. It is those deep cognitive engines (multilevel probabilistic generative models) that enable us to encounter, in perception and action, a world parsed for human needs and purposes. Sprinkled liberally with estimations of the precision (the variance or uncertainty) of our own prediction errors, this provides a potent toolkit for surfing the waves of sensory uncertainty. Creatures thus equipped are nature's experts at separating the signal from the noise, discerning the salient interacting causes that are structuring the constant energetic pummelling of their sensory surfaces.

Perception and action here emerge as two sides of a single computational coin. Rooted in multilevel prediction-error minimizing routines, perception and action are locked in a complex circular causal flow. Within that flow, actions select sensory stimulations that both test and respond to the bodily and environmental causes identified by the multilevel cascade. Percepts and action-recipes here co-emerge, combining motor prescriptions with continuous efforts at understanding our world. Perception and action are thus similarly and simultaneously constructed, and intimately entwined.

Systems such as these are knowledge-driven, courtesy of the structured probabilistic know-how encoded in complex multilevel generative models. But they are also fast and frugal, able to use that know-how to help select the most cost-efficient strategy for a given task and context. Many of those cost-efficient strategies trade the use of action and of bodily and environmental structure (and intervention) against the use of expensive forms of on-board computation. Working alongside the full gamut of strategies and ploys installed by slower processes of evolutionary adaptation, this enables the flexible and intelligent selection of low-cost efficient strategies whenever task and context allows.

The fit with embodied and situated cognitive science is thus fully realized. Perception-action loops are fundamental; low-cost, representationally efficient options are preferred; and the continuous stream of error-minimizing action allows for the recruitment and use of arbitrarily complex suites of external resources—resources that are now simply swept up in the ongoing circular causal flow.

The world thus encountered is a world structured, in large part, by the affordances for action that it presents. As our affordance-based exploration of this world proceeds, interoceptive and exteroceptive information are constantly combined as environmental causes are identified and behaviours entrained. This provides a rich new entry point for accounts of experience, emotion, and affect: accounts that do not compartmentalize cognition and emotion, but reveal them as (at most) distinctive threads in a single inferential weave. In this dense, ongoing, multilayer exchange, interoceptive, proprioceptive, and exteroceptive information work constantly together, and the flow of human experience emerges as a continuous construct at the meeting point of diverse systemic expectations and the self-structured sensory flow.

There are hints here of a new understanding of what it means to encounter the world in perception.[1] This will be an understanding in which experience, expectation, estimated uncertainty, and action are inextricably intertwined, together delivering a grip upon—and a trajectory within—a world whose organism-salient features are continuously disclosed (and in some cases, continuously created) as a result of our own activity. The fit between mind and world, if this is correct, is a fit forged not by some form of passive 'apt description' but by action itself: action that continuously selects the stimuli to which we respond. Key to this process of continual sensorimotor flow is the use of precision-weighting to control not just the relative influence of prior knowledge (hence predictions) at every level but also the large-scale flows of information that constitute the transient-but-unified processing regimes that form and disperse as we move from task to task and from context to context.

By self-organizing around prediction error, and by learning a generative rather than a merely discriminative (i.e., pattern-classifying) model, these approaches realize many of the dreams of previous work in artificial neural networks, robotics, dynamical systems theory, and classical cognitive science. They perform unsupervised learning using a multilevel architecture and acquire a satisfying grip—courtesy of the problem decompositions enabled by their hierarchical form—upon structural relations within a domain. They do this, moreover, in ways that remain firmly grounded in the patterns of sensorimotor experience that structure learning, using continuous, non-linguaform, inner encodings (probability density functions and probabilistic inference). Courtesy of precision-based restructuring of patterns of effective connectivity, those same approaches nest simplicity within complexity and make as much (or as little) use of body and world as task and context dictate.

10.2   Problems, Puzzles, and Pitfalls

All this hints at the shape of a truly fundamental and deeply unified science of the embodied mind. In the present text, it is this bigger picture that I have tried to bring into focus. This meant concentrating on that positive, integrative story—a strategy that seems warranted, at least while the science of the predictive mind is still in its infancy. But there remain a raft of problems, pitfalls, and shortfalls that need to be addressed. Among the key puzzles and problems, four stand out as especially challenging and important.

The first concerns the urgent need to explore a larger space of approximations and of possible representational forms. Complex real-world problems demand the use of approximations to truly optimal forms of probabilistic inference, and there are many ways in which neuronal populations might represent probabilities and many ways to perform probabilistic inference (see, e.g., Beck et al., 2012; Kwisthout & van Rooij, 2013; Pouget, Beck, et al., 2013). Much more work is thus required to discover which approximations the brain actually deploys. Moreover, the form of such preferred approximations will interact with the kinds of representation used and will reflect the availability of domain-knowledge that could be used to shrink the search space. Addressing these issues, both in simulation (Thornton, ms), using behavioural metrics (Houlsby et al., 2013) and by probing biological brains (Bastos et al., 2012; Egner & Summerfield, 2013; Iglesias, Mathys, et al., 2013; Penny, 2012) is essential if relatively abstract theoretical models (such as PP) are to be tested and transformed into plausible accounts of human cognition.

A second issue concerns the need to explore multiple variant architectures. The present text focused mostly upon one possible architectural schema: a schema requiring functionally distinct neural populations coding for representation (prediction) and for prediction error, and in which predictions flow backwards (and laterally) through the neural hierarchy while information concerning residual prediction error flows forwards (and laterally). But that schema represents just one point in the large and complex space of probabilistic generative-model based approaches, and there are many possible architectures, and possible ways of combining top-down predictions and bottom-up sensory information, in the general vicinity. For example, the foundational work by Hinton and colleagues on deep belief networks (Hinton, Osindero, & Tey, 2006; Hinton & Salakhutdinov, 2006) differs (chapter 1, note 13) despite sharing an emphasis upon probabilistic generative models; McClelland (2013) and Zorzi et al. (2013) bring work on deep unsupervised learning into alignment with work on Bayesian models of contextual effects and with neural network models such as the connectionist interactive activation model; Spratling (2010, 2011, 2014) has proposed an alternative predictive coding model, PC/BC, standing for predictive coding/biased competition, that implements the key principles of predictive coding using a different flow of prediction and error, and that is described by a variant mathematical framework; Dura-Bernal, Wennekers et al. (2011, 2012) develop a variant of the Spratling PC/BC architecture that extends the well-known HMAX (Riesenhuber & Poggio, 1999; Serre et al., 2007) feedforward model of object recognition, accommodating strong top-down effects (such as the perception of illusory contours) while reproducing many of the computational efficiencies of the feedforward approach; Wacongne et al. (2012) develop a detailed neuronal model implementing predictive coding (for auditory cortex) using layered networks of spiking neurons; O'Reilly, Wyatte, and Rohrlich (ms; see also Kachergis et al., 2014) offer a rich neuro-computational account of predictive learning in which the very same layer encodes expectations and outcomes (at differing temporal stages of processing) and in which input is often only partially predicted; Phillips and Silverstein (2013) develop a broader, computationally rich perspective on context-sensitive gain control; den Ouden, Kok, and de Lange (2012) survey the many ways in which the brain seems to code prediction error signals, and the varying functional roles of such signals in different brain regions; Pickering and Garrod (2013) present a rich cognitive psychological account of language production and comprehension using the apparatus of mutual prediction and forward models; and roboticists such as Tani (2007), Saegusa et al. (2008), Park et al. (2012), Pezzulo (2007), and Mohan, Morasso, et al. (2011), Martius, Der, and Ay (2013) are exploring the use of a variety of prediction-based learning routines as a means of grounding higher cognitive functions in the solid bedrock of sensorimotor engagements with the world.

This remarkable efflorescence of work on prediction-based learning and response is both encouraging and vital. For it is only by considering the full space of possible prediction-and-generative-model based architectures and strategies that we can start to ask truly pointed experimental questions of the brain and of biological organisms: questions that might one day favour one of these models (or, more likely, one coherent sub-set of models[2]) over the rest, or else may reveal deep faults and failings among their substantial common foundations. Only then will we find out, to echo the laudably dour sentiments of Box and Draper, just how wrong, or how useful, these models actually are.

The third set of challenges concerns the extension of these accounts into the intuitively 'higher level' domains of long-term planning, cognitive control, social cognition, conscious experience,[3] and explicit, linguistically inflected, reasoning. Here, the present text ventured at least a smattering of hints and suggestions—for example, linking planning and social cognition to varying kinds of generative-model-based simulation; control to context-sensitive gating routines; conscious experience to delicate mixtures of interoceptive and exteroceptive predictions; and linguistically inflected reasoning to the artificial self-manipulation of precision-weightings. But despite these tentative footsteps, the extension of these accounts into such domains remains murky at best. (For some discussion, see Fitzgerald, Dolan, & Friston, 2014; Harrison, Bestmann, Rosa, et al., 2011; Hobson & Friston, 2014; Hohwy, 2013, chapters 9–12; Jiang, Heller, & Egner, 2014; King & Dehaene, 2014; Limanowski & Blankenburg, 2013; Moutoussis et al., 2014; Panichello, Cheung, & Bar, 2012; and Seth, 2014). Most challenging of all, perhaps, will be the implied reconstruction of motivation, value, and desire in terms of more fundamental processes of prediction, Bayesian inference, and self-estimated uncertainty (see Friston, Shiner, et al., 2012; Gershman & Daw 2012; Bach & Dolan 2012; Solway & Botvinick 2012; Schwartenbeck et al., 2014).

The fourth and final batch of issues is more strategic and conceptual. Does the picture of extensive reliance upon multilevel generative models and top-down prediction somehow over-intellectualize the mind? Are we back-sliding towards an outmoded 'Cartesian' view in which the mind is an insulated inner arena, teeming with internal representations yet somehow estranged from the multiple problem-simplifying opportunities provided by body and world? Nothing, or so I have argued, could be further from the truth. Instead we have seen how the use of prediction-driven learning and multilevel generative models directly serve the twin pillars of perception and action, enabling fast, fluent forms of context-sensitive response. The predictive brain, I have tried to show, is an *action-oriented engagement machine*, adept at finding efficient embodied solutions that make the most of body and world. Brains now emerge as complex nodes in a constant two-way flux in which the inner (neural) organization is open to constant reconfiguration by external (bodily and environmental) factors and forces, and vice versa. Inner and outer here become locked in constant co-determining patterns of exchange, as predictive agents continuously select the stimulations that they receive. This pattern repeats at more extended scales of space and time, as we structure (and repeatedly restructure) the social and material worlds that slowly but surely structure us.

The brain thus revealed is a restless, pro-active organ locked in dense, continuous exchange with body and world. Thus equipped we encounter, through the play of self-predicted sensory stimulation, a world of meaning, structure, and opportunity: a world parsed for action, pregnant with future, and patterned by the past.

Appendix 1

Bare Bayes

Bayes theorem delivers an optimal way of altering existing beliefs in response to new information or evidence. In the case of sensory evidence, it shows how to update belief in some hypothesis (e.g., that there is a cat on the mat) as a function of how well the sensory data (e.g., plays of light on the retina, or more realistically, the unfolding plays of light resulting from active exploration of the scene) are predicted by the hypothesis. In so doing, it assumes a prior state of belief of some kind and then specifies how to alter that belief in the light of the new evidence. This allows continual, rational updating of our background model (the source of the prior states of belief) as more and more new evidence arrives.

For our—admittedly rather limited—purposes, the mathematics here does not matter (though for a lovely primer, see Doya & Ishii, 2007; for something more informal, see Bram, 2013, chapter 3; and for discussion of applications to human cognition, see Jacobs & Kruschke, 2010). But what the mathematics achieves is something rather wonderful. It allows us to adjust the impact of some incoming sensory data according to background information about (1) the chances of getting that sensory data if the world was, indeed, in such-and-such a state (that is, 'the probability of the data given the hypothesis', i.e., how well the data are predicted by the hypothesis) and (2) the prior probability of the hypothesis (the chances, regardless of the sensory data, of the cat being on the mat). Crunching all that together in the right way yields the correct estimation (given what you know) of the revised (posterior) probability of the hypothesis given the new sensory evidence.[1] The nice thing here is that once you have updated your prior belief to a posterior belief, the posterior belief can serve as the prior for the next observation.

The crunching is important, since failures to take account of background information can badly skew assessments of the impact of new evidence. Classic examples include how to assess your chances of having some medical condition given a positive result using an accurate test, or assessing the chances that a defendant is guilty given some forensic (e.g., DNA) evidence. In each case, the proper impact of the evidence turns out to depend much more strongly than we intuitively imagine upon the prior chances of having the condition (or being guilty of the crime) anyway, independently of that specific evidence. In essence, Bayes rule is thus a device for combining prior knowledge (about base rates, for example) with what Kahneman (2011, p. 154) calls the 'diagnosticity of the evidence'—the degree to which the evidence favours one hypothesis over another. A direct implication is that—as the cosmologist Carl Sagan famously put it—'extraordinary claims need extraordinary evidence'.

The 'predictive processing' models discussed in the text implement just such a process of 'rational impact adjustment'. They do so by meeting the incoming sensory signal with a set of top-down probabilistic predictions based on what the system knows about the world and what it knows about the context-varying reliability of its own sensing and processing. There is a reformulation of Bayes's rule that makes especially clear its relation to such prediction-based models of perception. The reformulation (as translated into prose by Joyce, 2008) says that:

> The ratio of probabilities for two hypotheses conditional on a body of data is equal to the ratio of their unconditional [baseline] probabilities multiplied by the degree to which the first hypothesis surpasses the second as a predictor of the data.

The drawback, you might think, is that all this will only work when you know all that stuff about unconditional probabilities (the priors and 'statistical background conditions') already. That is where so-called 'empirical Bayes' (Robbins, 1956) gets to make a special contribution. For within a hierarchical scheme, the required priors can themselves be estimated from the data, using the estimates at one level to provide the priors (the background beliefs) for the level below. In predictive processing architectures, the presence of multilevel structure induces such 'empirical priors' in the form of the constraints that one level in the hierarchy places on the level below. These constraints can be progressively tuned, using standard gradient descent methods, by the sensory input itself. Such multilevel learning procedures look neuronally implementable courtesy of the hierarchical and reciprocally connected structure and wiring of cortex (see Bastos et al., 2012; Friston, 2005; Lee & Mumford, 2003).

Some words of caution however. The notion that the brain performs some form of approximate Bayesian inference is increasingly popular. In its broadest form, this need only mean that the brain uses a generative model (a model, that is, embodying background knowledge about the statistical structure of the task) to compute its best guess (the 'posterior distribution') about the world, given the current sensory evidence. Such methods need not deliver good results or optimal inference. The generative model might be wrong, coarse, or incomplete, either because the training environment was too limited or skewed, or because the true distributions were too hard to learn or impossible to implement using available neural circuitry. Such conditions force the use of approximations. The moral is that 'all optimal inference is Bayesian, but not all Bayesian inference is optimal' (Ma, 2012, p. 513). In other words, there is a large space hereabouts, and it needs careful handling. For a useful survey, see Ma (2012).

Appendix 2

The Free-Energy Formulation

Free-energy formulations originate in statistical physics and were introduced into the machine-learning literature in seminal treatments that include Hinton and von Camp (1993), Hinton and Zemel (1994), MacKay (1995), and Neal and Hinton (1998). Such formulations can arguably be used (e.g., Friston, 2010) to display the prediction error minimization strategy as *itself* a manifestation of a more fundamental mandate to minimize an information-theoretic isomorph of thermodynamic free energy in a system's exchanges with the environment.

Thermodynamic free energy is a measure of the energy available to do useful work. Transposed to the cognitive/informational domain, it emerges as the difference between the way the world is represented (modelled) as being and the way it actually is. Care is needed here, though, as that notion of 'the way the world is represented as being' is a slippery beast and must not be read as implying a kind of passive ('mirror of nature', see Rorty, 1979) story about the implied fit between model and world. For the test of a good model, as we see at some length in the present text, is how well it enables the organism to engage the world in a rolling cycle of actions that maintain it within a window of viability. The better the engagements, the lower the information-theoretic free energy (this is intuitive, since more of the system's resources are being put to 'effective work' in modelling the world). Prediction error reports this information-theoretic free energy, which is mathematically constructed so as always to be greater than 'surprisal' (where this names the sub-personally computed implausibility of some sensory state given a model of the world, see Tribus, 1961). Entropy, in this information-theoretic rendition, is the long-term average of surprisal, and reducing information-theoretic free energy amounts to improving the world model so as to reduce prediction errors, hence reducing surprisal (better models make better predictions). The overarching rationale is that good models (by definition) are those that help us successfully engage the world and hence help us to maintain our structure and organization so that we appear—over extended but finite timescales—to resist increases in entropy and (hence) the second law of thermodynamics.

The 'free-energy principle' itself then states that 'all the quantities that can change; i.e. that are part of the system, will change to minimize free-energy' (Friston & Stephan, 2007, p. 427). Notice that, thus formulated, this is a claim about all elements of systemic organization (from gross morphology to the entire organization of the brain) and not just about cortical information processing. Using a series of elegant mathematical formulations, Friston (2009, 2010) suggests that this principle, when applied to various elements of neural functioning, leads to the generation of efficient internal representational schemes and reveals the deepest rationale behind the links between perception, inference, memory, attention, and action explored in the present text. Morphology, action tendencies (including the active structuring of environmental niches), and gross neural architecture are all expressions, if this story is correct, of this single principle operating at varying timescales.

The free-energy account is of great independent interest. It represents a kind of 'maximal version' of the claims concerning the computational intimacy of perception and action, and it is at least suggestive of a general framework that might accommodate the growing interest (see, e.g., Thompson, 2010) in understanding the complex relations between life and mind. Essentially, the hope is thus to illuminate the very *possibility* of self-organization in biological systems (see, e.g., Friston, 2009, p. 293, and discussion in chapter 9).

A full assessment of the free-energy principle and its potential applications to understanding life and mind is, however, far beyond the scope of the present treatment.

Notes

INTRODUCTION

1. Hermann von Helmholtz (1860) depicts perception as involving probabilistic inference. James (1890), who studied under Helmholtz, also depicts perception as drawing upon prior knowledge to help deal with imperfect or ambiguous inputs. These insights informed the 'analysis-by-synthesis' paradigm within psychology (see Gregory, 1980; MacKay, 1956; Neisser, 1967; for a review, see Yuille & Kersten, 2006). Helmholtz's insight was also pursued (as we shall see in chapter 1) in an important body of computational and neuroscientific work. Crucial to this lineage were seminal advances in machine learning that began with pioneering connectionist work on backpropagation learning (McClelland et al., 1986; Rumelhart et al., 1986) and continued with work on the aptly named 'Helmholz Machine' (Dayan et al., 1995; Dayan & Hinton, 1996; see also Hinton & Zemel, 1994). For useful reviews, see Brown & Brüne, 2012; Bubic et al., 2010; Kveraga et al., 2007. See also Bar et al., 2006; Churchland et al., 1994; Gilbert and Sigman, 2007; Grossberg, 1980; Raichle, 2010.
2. Barney was at that time working with Dennett at the Curricular Software Studio, which Dennett co-founded at Tufts in 1985. The project advisor was Tufts geologist Bert Reuss.

3. The remark is made during an interview with Danny Scott ('Racing to the Bottom of the World') published in the *Sunday Times Magazine*, 27 November 2011, p. 82.

4. These are cases that are sometimes described as 'psychogenic', 'non-organic', 'unexplained' or even (in older parlance) 'hysterical'. I borrow the term 'functional motor and sensory symptoms' from Edwards et al. (2012).

CHAPTER 1

1. Examples include Biederman, 1987; Hubel & Wiesel, 1965; and Marr, 1982.

2. I will sometimes write, as a kind of shorthand, that predictions flow downwards (from higher areas towards the sensory peripheries) in these systems. This is correct, but importantly incomplete. It highlights the fact that predictions, at least in standard implementations of PP, flow from each higher level to the level immediately below. But a great deal of predictive information is also passed laterally within levels. Talk of downward-flowing prediction should thus be read as indicating 'downward and lateral flowing' prediction. Thanks to Bill Phillips for suggesting that I clarify this at the outset.

3. I have seen this dictum variously attributed to the machine-learning pioneer Max Clowes, and to the neuroscientists Rodolfo Llinas and Ramesh Jain. The 'controlled hallucination' spin can, however, make it seem as if our perceptual grip on reality is fragile and disturbingly indirect. On the contrary, it seems to me—though the arguments for this must wait until later—that this view of perception shows, in detail, just how perception (or better, perception-action loops) puts us in genuine cognitive contact with the salient aspects of our environment. It might thus be better, or so I will later (chapter 6) suggest, to regard hallucination as a form of 'uncontrolled perception'.

4. In practice, simple back-propagation networks starting with random assignments of weights and non-problem-specific architectures tended to learn very slowly and often got stuck in so-called local minima.

5. Famous victims of this temptation include Chomsky, Fodor, and to a lesser extent, Pinker (see his 1997).

6. By this I mean, in forms that multiplied the layers of so-called 'hidden units' intervening between input and output. For a nice discussion of these difficulties, see Hinton, 2007a.

7. There are echoes here both of Husserl and of Merleau-Ponty. For some nice discussion, see Van de Cruys & Wagemans, 2011.

8. 'Analysis by synthesis' is a processing strategy in which the brain does not build its current model of worldly causes by accumulating, bottom-up, a mass of low-level cues. Instead, the brain tries to predict the current suite of sensory cues from its best models of interacting worldly causes (see Chater & Manning, 2006; Neisser, 1967; Yuille & Kersten, 2006).

9. For a nice account, defending a prediction-based model, see Poeppel & Monahan, 2011.

10. This was a computationally tractable approximation to 'maximum likelihood learning' as used in the expectation-maximization (EM) algorithm of Dempster et al. (1977).

11. Readers unfamiliar with this notion might want to revisit the informal example of SLICE presented in the Introduction.

12. You can see the network in action on Hinton's website at: http://www.cs.toronto.edu/~hinton/digits.html.

13. The differences mostly concern the kinds of message passing schemes that are, and are not, allowed, and the precise ways that top-down and bottom-up influences are used and combined during both learning and online performance. In Hinton's digit-recognition work, for example, generative-model based prediction plays a key role during learning. But what that learning delivers are simpler (purely feedforward) strategies for use in rapid online discrimination. We shall later see (in Part III) how PP systems might fluidly and flexibly accommodate the use of such simple, low-cost strategies. What all these approaches share, however, is a core emphasis, at least during learning, on the use of generative models within a multilevel setting. For a useful introduction to Hinton and colleagues (often more 'engineering-driven') work on 'deep learning' systems, see Hinton, 2007a; Salakhutdinov & Hinton, 2009.

14. For a sustained discussion of these failings, and the attractions of connectionist (and post-connectionist) alternatives, see Bermúdez, 2005; Clark, 1989, 1997; Pfeifer & Bongard, 2006.

15. See Kveraga, Ghuman, & Bar, 2007.

16. For a selection of pointers to this important, and much larger, space, see chapter 10.

17. The basic story just rehearsed is, as far as I can tell, still considered correct. But for some complications, see Nirenberg et al., 2010.

18. See essays in Alais & Blake, 2005, and the review article by Leopold & Logothetis, 1999. For an excellent introduction, see Schwartz et al., 2012.

19. Such methods use their own target data sets to estimate the prior distribution: a kind of bootstrapping that exploits the statistical independencies that characterize hierarchical models.

20. For further discussion, see Hohwy, 2013.

21. This is not 'explaining away' in the sense of Pearl (1988), where that names the effect by which confirming one cause reduces the need to invoke alternative causes (as Hypothesis 1 increases its posterior probability, Hypothesis 2 will decrease its, even if they were independent before the evidence arrived). Nor is it 'explaining away' in the sense associated with the elimination of unnecessary entities from an ontology. Rather, the idea is simply that well-predicted sensory signals are not treated as newsworthy, since their implications are already accounted for in systemic response. Thanks to Jakob Hohwy for pointing this out.

22. Notice, however, that the obvious efficiencies in forward processing are here bought at the cost of the multilevel generative machinery itself: machinery whose implementation and operation requires a whole set of additional connections to realize the downward swoop of the bidirectional cascade.

23. The consistency of selective sharpening and dampening also makes it harder—though not impossible—to tease apart the empirical implications of predictive coding and 'evidence accumulation' accounts such as Gold and Shadlen's (2001). For a review, see Smith & Ratcliff, 2004. For an attempt to do so, see Hesselmann et al., 2010.

24. The most minimal suggestion might be that the separation is essentially temporal, implicating the very same units at diffferent processing stages. Such proposals would, however, be required to resolve a host of technical problems that do not afflict more standard suggestions (such as Friston's).

25. Experimental tests have also recently been proposed (Maloney & Mamassian, 2009; Maloney & Zhang, 2010) which aim to 'operationalize' the claim that a target system is (genuinely) computing its outputs using a Bayesian scheme, rather than merely behaving 'as if' it did so. This, however, is an area that warrants a great deal of further thought and investigation (for some nice discussion, see Colombo & Seriès, 2012).

26. Potter et al. (2014) show that the minimum viewing time needed for comprehension of the conceptual gist of a visually presented scene (e.g., 'smiling couple' or 'picnic' or 'harbour with boats') can be as low as 13ms. This is too fast to allow new feedforward-feedback loops ('re-entrant loops') to become established. Moreover, the results do not depend upon the subjects being told the target labels *before* seeing the images (thus controlling for specific top-down expectations that might already be in place before presentation of the image). This suggests that gists of these kinds can indeed be extracted (as Barrett and Bar suggest) by an ultra-rapid feedforward sweep.

27. This means that we need to be very careful when generalizing from ecologically strange laboratory conditions that effectively deprive us of such ongoing context. For some recent discussion, see Barrett & Bar, 2009; Fabre-Thorpe, 2011; Kveriga et al., 2007.

28. Such effects have long been known in the literature, where they first emerged in work on sensory habituation, and most prominently in Eugene Sokolov's pioneering (1960) studies of the orienting reflex. More on this in chapter 3.,

29. For an excellent discussion of this recent work, see de-Wit et al., 2010.

30. Possible alternative implementations are discussed in Spratling and Johnson (2006) and in Engel et al. (2001).

31. This is a measure of relative neural activity ('brain activation') as indexed by changes in blood flow and blood oxygen level. The assumption is that neural activity incurs a metabolic cost that this signal reflects. It is

widely acknowledged (see, e.g., Heeger & Ross, 2002) to be a rather indirect, assumption-laden, and 'blunt' measure compared to, say, single cell recording. Nonetheless, new forms of multivariate pattern analysis are able to overcome some of the limitations of earlier work using this technique.

32. This could, the authors note, be due to some fundamental metabolic difference in processing cost between representing and error detection, or it may be that for other reasons the BOLD signal tracks top-down inputs to a region more than bottom-up ones (see Egner at al., 2010, p. 16607).

33. These views stress the pro-active elicitation of task-relevant information 'just-in-time' for use. Examples include Ballard, 1991; Ballard et al., 1997; Churchland et al., 1994. For discussion, see Clark, 1997, 2008. We return to these topics in chapters 4 through 9.

34. For windows onto this large literature, see Raichle, 2009; Raichle & Snyder, 2007; Sporns, 2010, chapter 8; Smith, Vidaurre, et al., 2013. See also the discussions of spontaneous neural activity in chapters 8 and 9.

35. Such economy and preparedness is biologically attractive, and neatly sidesteps many of the processing bottlenecks (see Brooks, 1991) associated with more passive models of the flow of information. In predictive processing, the downward flow of prediction does most of the computational 'heavy-lifting', allowing moment-by-moment processing to focus only on the newsworthy departures signified by salient (high-precision, see chapter 2) prediction errors. We take up these issues in chapters 4 to 9.

CHAPTER 2

1. For another new one, that involves movement and requires viewing using a web browser, try http://www.michaelbach.de/ot/cog-hiddenBird/index.html.

2. 'Beliefs' thus construed are best understood as induced by 'probability density functions' (PDFs), where these describe the relative likelihood that some continuous random variable assumes a given value. A random variable simply assigns a number to an outcome or state and may be discrete (if the possible values are at different points) or continuous (if they are defined over an interval).

3. This flexible computation of sensory uncertainty is common ground between predictive processing and 'Kalman filtering' (see Friston, 2002; Grush, 2004; Rao & Ballard, 1999).

4. Recall that in these models, error units receive signals from representation-units at their own level, and from representation-units at the level above, while representation units (sometimes called 'state units') are driven by error units at the same level and at the level below. See Friston, 2009, Box 3, p. 297.

5. So-called 'synchronous gain' (in which synchronized pre-synaptic inputs modify post-synaptic gain; see Chawla, Lumer, & Friston, 1999) may also be a contributor here. There is also recent speculation, as Friston (2012a) points out, concerning a possible role for fast (gamma) and slow (beta) frequency oscillations in conveying bottom-up sensory information and top-down predictions, respectively. This affords a nice mapping to the activity of superficial and deep pyramidal cells. Investigations of these interesting dynamic possibilities remain in their infancy, but see Bastos et al., 2012; Friston, Bastos, et al., 2015; Buffalo et al., 2011; and the more general discussion in Engel, Fries, & Singer, 2001. See also Sedley & Cunningham, 2013, p. 9.

6. Hohwy (2012) offers a wonderful quotation from Helmholtz' 1860 *Treatise on Physiological Optics* that captures this experience well. The quotation (as translated by Hohwy) reads:

> The natural unforced state of our attention is to wander around to ever new things, so that when the interest of an object is exhausted, when we cannot perceive anything new, then attention against our will goes to something else. . . . If we want attention to stick to an object we have to keep finding something new in it, especially if other strong sensations seek to decouple it. (Helmholtz, 1860, p. 770; translated by JH)

7. Here too, such assignments may sometimes mislead, and plausible accounts of phenomena such as change blindness and inattentional blindness can be constructed that turn upon variations of precision-weighting across different types and channels of information, see Hohwy (2012).

8. Such cases may also involve another kind of prediction, associated with emotions (in this case, fear and arousal)—interoceptive predictions concerning our own physiological state. These further dimensions are discussed in chapter 7.

9. I here concentrate on vision, but the points should apply equally well to other modalities (consider, e.g., the way we explore a familiar object by touch).

10. Despite this core commonality with PP-style approaches, important differences (especially concerning the roles of reward and reinforcement learning) separate these accounts. See the discussion in Friston, 2011a; and in chapter 4.

11. It is thus not a 'conspicuity' based map of the kind rejected by Tatler, Hayhoe et al. (2011).

12. The simulation captures only the direct effects of the winning hypothesis on the pattern of saccades. A more complex model would need to include the effects of neural estimations of precision, driving the simulated agent to probe the scene according to where the most reliable (not just most distinctive) sensory information is expected.

13. For example, the suggestion of purchases that reflect previous choices may lead to cycles of new purchasing (and consequently adjusted

recommendations) that progressively cement and narrow the scope of our own interests, making us victims of our own predictability. For some discussion, see Clark, 2003, chapter 7.

14. Indeed, stimulus contrast can be used as a proxy to manipulate precision. An example of this is the empirical evidence for changes in post-synaptic gain—of the sort seen during attentional modulation—induced by changing luminance contrast. See Brown et al., 2013.

15. For a similar example, see Friston, Adams, et al., 2012, p. 4.

16. A much better understanding of such multiple interacting mechanisms (various slow neuromodulators perhaps acting in complex concert with neural synchronization) is now needed, along with a thorough examination of the various ways and levels at which the flow of prediction and the modulating effects of the weighting of prediction error (precision) may be manifest (see Corlett et al., 2010; Friston & Kiebel, 2009; Friston, Bastos et al., 2015). See also Phillips & Silverstein (2013); Phillips, Clark, & Silverstein (2015).

17. Intriguingly, the authors are also able to apply the model to one non-pharmacological intervention: sensory deprivation.

18. Feldman and Friston (2010) point out that precision behaves as if it were itself a limited resource, in that turning up the precision on some prediction error units requires reducing it on others. They also comment, intriguinly (op cit p. 11) that "The reason that precision behaves like a resource is that the generative model contains prior beliefs that log-precision is redistributed over sensory channels in a context-sensitive fashion but is conserved over all channels." Clearly, such 'beliefs' will in no way be explicitly encoded but must instead be somehow inherent in the basic structure of the system. This raises important issues (concerning what is and is not explicitly encoded in the generative model) that we return to in chapter 8.

CHAPTER 3

1. See also DeWolf & Eliasmith, 2011, section 3.2. It is interesting to notice that key signature elements are preserved even when physical motion is minimized, as in the use of surgical micro-tools as non-standard implements for signing one's name. Experienced micro-surgeons succeed at the first attempt and show the same handwriting style as their normal writing (except that at 40X magnification, they can become tangled in the individual fibres of the paper!); see Allard & Starkes, 1991, p. 148. Such feats attest to our remarkable capacity to construct new skilled performances using existing elements and knowledge.

2. Sokolov, 1960; see also Bindra, 1959; Pribram, 1980; and Sachs, 1967.

3. See Sutton et al., 1965; Polich, 2003, 2007.

4. I remain deliberately uncommitted as to the correct neuronal interpretation of this essentially functional notion of layers or levels. But for some speculations, see Bastos et al., 2012.

5. Though they do not, of course, recognize them under those descriptions!

6. I make no attempt to specify which animals fall under this broad umbrella, but the presence of bidirectional neocortical circuitry (or—and this is obviously harder to establish—functional analogues of such circuitry) should provide a good clue.

7. A voxel is a 'volumetric pixel'. Each voxel tracks activity in a circumscribed three-dimensional space. A single fMRI voxel typically represents a fairly large volume (typically 27 cubic mm within a 3mm x 3mm x 3mm cube).

8. Actually, the experimenter's task is harder, as the raw fMRI data provides at best a coarse shadow (built from hemodynamic response) of the underlying neural activity itself.

9. Recall, however, that each voxel covers a substantial volume (around 27 cubic mm) of neural tissue.

10. Thanks to Bill Phillips for suggesting this (personal communication).

11. There may also be scope hereabouts for some illuminating discussion of 'disjunctivism'—the idea, roughly, that veridical percepts and hallucinations share no common kind. Much turns, of course, on just how the disjunctivist claim is to be unpacked. For a pretty comprehensive sampling of possible formulations, see the essays in Haddock & Macpherson, 2008, and in Byrne & Logue, 2009.

12. This paragraph condenses, and slightly oversimplifies, the views found in Hobson (2001) and Blackmore (2004). See also Roberts, Robbins, & Weiskrantz, 1998; and Siegel, 2003.

13. Just such a two-stage process, as Hobson and Friston note, lay at the heart of Hinton et al.'s aptly named wake-sleep algorithm (see Hinton et al., 1995, and discussion in chapter 1).

14. See chapter 2 and further discussion in chapters 5 and 8.

15. This second-order ('meta-memory') component is necessary to account for the feeling of familiarity-without-episodic-recall. (Think, for example, of recognizing a face as familiar, despite having no episodic memory of any specific encounter with that individual.)

16. For another attempt to tackle memory using predictive-processing-style resources, see Brigard, 2012. For a different strategy, see Gershman, Moore, et al., 2012.

17. For another example of this kind of account, see van Kesteren et al., 2012.

18. For example some model-elements must account for small variations in the sensory signals that accompany bodily movement and that help to specify a perspective upon a scene, while others track more invariant items, such as the identity and category of the perceived object. But it is the precision-modulated interactions between these levels, often mediated (see Part II) by ongoing motor action of one kind or another, that now emerges as the heart of intelligent, adaptive response.

CHAPTER 4

1. James, 1890, vol. 2, p. 527.
2. The perceived opposition is apparent in treatments including Anderson and Chemero (2013), Chemero (2009), Froese and Ikegami (2013). More ecumenical views are defended in treatments including Clark (1997, 2008).
3. See also Weiskrantz, Elliot, and Darlington (1971), who there introduce what has rather charmingly become known as the 'standard tickle apparatus' allowing easy experimental comparisons between self- and other-induced tickling.
4. See Decety, 1996; Jeannerod, 1997; Wolpert, 1997; Wolpert, Ghahramani, & Jordan, 1995; Wolpert, Miall, & Kawato, 1998.
5. A related (but simpler and more general) explanation of such effects is made available by the absorption of the standard accounts into the more general framework of prediction-based processing. According to this account, the reason we do not see the world as moving simply because we move our eyes is that the sensory flow thus induced is best predicted using an internal model whose highest levels depict a stable world available for motoric sampling.
6. In that more complete account, descending precision expectations during self-made acts turn down the volume or gain of prediction errors reporting the sensory consequences of those acts. In effect, we thus temporarily suspend our attention to many of the sensory perturbations that we ourselves cause (see Brown et al., 2013; and further discussion in chapter 7).
7. These are cost functions that address bodily dynamics, systemic noise, and required accuracy of outcome. See Todorov, 2004; Todorov & Jordan, 2002.
8. See Adams, Shipp, & Friston, 2012; Brown et al., 2011; Friston, Samothrakis, & Montague, 2012.
9. For the full story, see Shipp et al., 2013. Compactly, 'the descending projections from motor cortex share many features with top-down or backward connections in visual cortex; for example, corticospinal projections originate in infragranular layers, are highly divergent and (along with descending cortico-cortical projections) target cells expressing NMDA receptors' (Shipp et al., 2013, p. 1).
10. Anscombe's target was the distinction between desire and belief, but her observations about direction of fit generalize (as Shea, 2013, nicely notes) to the case of actions, here conceived as the motoric outcomes of certain forms of desire.
11. Two commonly cited costs are thus 'noise' and 'effort'—fluent action seems to depend upon the minimization of each of these factors. See Harris & Wolpert, 1998; Faisal, Selen, & Wolpert, 2008; O'Sullivan, Burdet, & Diedrichsen, 2009.

12. Recall that the term 'belief' is here used to cover any of the contents of the generative models that guide perception and action. Such beliefs need not be agent-accessible and, as previously noted, are usually understood as expressions of probability density functions describing the relative likelihood that some continuous random variable assumes a given value. In the context of action selection, for example, a PDF might specify, in a continuous fashion, the current probability of the transition to some successor state.

13. What this all amounts to, in the end, is a combination of active construction, selective sampling, and selective representing. The full picture here will not emerge until Part III of our text. But when all those factors conspire, the knowing agent locks on to the organism-relevant structure of the surrounding (social, physical, and technological) environment, achieving a delicate and life-sustaining balancing act between building a world and being constrained by a world. This is the same balancing act highlighted by Varela, Thompson, and Rosch in their classic (1991) treatment, *The Embodied Mind*.

14. I borrow this phrase from one of my favourite philosophers, Willard van Orman Quine, who used it when commenting on a rather bloated ontology, writing that 'Wyman's overpopulated universe is in many ways unlovely. It offends the aesthetic sense of us who have a taste for desert landscapes' (Quine, 1988, p. 4).

15. For some critical concerns about this general strategy, see Gershman & Daw, 2012. Gershman and Daw worry, in effect, that collapsing costs and utilities into expectations delivers too blunt a tool, since it makes it hard to see how unexpected events (such as winning the lottery) could be treated as valuable. This kind of worry underestimates the resources available to the fans of prediction and expectation. Adaptive agents should expect to be able, at times, to benefit from surprises and environmental change. This suggests that the two approaches may not be as conceptually distinct as they might at first appear. They may even be inter-translatable, since everything that one side might wish to express using talk of utility and value, the other may express using talk of higher level (more abstract and flexible) expectations. For more on these and related issues, see Part III.

16. See Friston, 2011a; Mohan & Morasso, 2011.

17. For some discussion, see Friston, 2009, p. 295.

18. The apparent radicalism of this view depends mostly upon the contrast with work that posits multiple paired forward and inverse models as the substrate of fluent, flexible motor behaviour. As we saw, alternative approaches (such as Feldman, 2009; Feldman & Levin, 2009) that posit, e.g., equilibrium or reference points as their core organizing principle provide a very natural fit with the proprioceptive prediction-based process model (for further discussion, see Friston, 2011a; Pickering & Clark, 2014; Shipp et al., 2013).

19. For the most part (but see Mohan & Morasso, 2011; Mohan, Morasso, et al., 2013) work in Cognitive Developmental Robotics (CDR) has retained the classical structure of paired forward/inverse models, efference copy, and value and reward signals. The CDR experiments are suggestive, however, insofar as they show that prediction-error-based encodings can structure motor actions in ways that open the door to imitation learning.

20. Predictive processing is, I think, ideally positioned to satisfy this remit, since it combines powerful learning routines with a fully unified perspective encompassing perception and action.

21. In the work by Park et al., this kind of early learning was enabled using a self-organizing feature map (Kohonen, 1989, 2001). This is closely related to Hebbian learning, but it adds a 'forgetting term' to restrict the potential explosion of learned associations. Another approach to such learning deploys a modified recurrent neural network (a 'recurrent neural network with parametric biases', see Tani et al., 2004).

22. Dynamic Anthropomorphic Robot with Intelligence—Open Platform, from the Virginia Tech Robotics and Mechanisms Lab. See http://www.romela.org/main/DARwIn_OP:_Open_Platform_Humanoid_Robot_for_Research_and_Education.

CHAPTER 5

1. Of course, they may also be treated simply as further phenomena requiring the development of brand new models—a less efficient strategy that may be mandated by encounters with the alien and exotic, or perhaps (see Pellicano & Burr, 2012, and comments by Friston, Lawson, & Frith 2013) by malfunctions of the context/prediction machinery itself. See also chapter 7.

2. See McClelland & Rumelhart, 1981, and for an updated 'multinomial interactive activation' model, see Khaitan & McClelland, 2010; McClelland, Mirman, et al., 2014.

3. There are deep connections between this form of connectionism and work in the PP paradigm. For some explorations, see McClelland, 2013, and Zorzi et al., 2013.

4. For an alternative implementation, that nonetheless preserves key features of the PP model, and that also implements a functional hierarchy, see Spratling (2010, 2012).

5. Recall that empirical priors are the probabilistic densities or 'beliefs' associated with intermediate levels in a hierarchical model.

6. See Aertsen et al., 1987; Friston, 1995; Horwitz, 2003; Sporns, 2010.

7. Sporns (2010, p. 9) suggests that structural connectivity remains stable 'on a scale of seconds to minutes', while changes in effective connectivity may occur on the order of hundreds of milliseconds.

8. For useful introductions to these approaches, see Stephan, Harrison, et al., 2007, and Sporns, 2010.

9. Context-reflecting expectations about reliability and salience are thus acquired in just the same way as knowledge about other worldly or bodily properties and states of affairs. Estimations of reliability and salience are themselves determined by the current interaction of sensory data with the overall generative model, giving rise to the increasingly intractable problem of 'estimating the reliability of one's own estimates of reliability' (for some nice discussion, see Hohwy, 2013, chapter 5).

10. As achieved, for example, using various forms of network analysis (for a rich and comprehensive review, see Sporns, 2002) able to reveal patterns of functional and effective connectivity between neurons and between neuronal populations. See also Colombo, 2013.

11. The brain thus construed is 'labile' and comprises 'an ensemble of functionally specialized areas that are coupled in a nonlinear fashion by effective connections' (Friston & Price, 2001, p. 277). Except that where Friston and Price speak of 'functionallly specialized' areas, I think it would be better to follow Anderson (2014, pp. 52–53) and speak of 'functionally differentiated' ones.

12. Such accounts share core commitments with several related proposals (for reviews, see Arbib, Metta, et al., 2008, section 62.4, and Oztop et al., 2013). The HMOSAIC model (Wolpert et al., 2003) exploits the same kind of hierarchical prediction-driven multilevel model as a means of supporting action imitation, and Wolpert et al. further suggest that that approach might likewise address issues concerning action understanding and the 'extraction of intentions'.

13. For ease of exposition, I will sometimes speak as if we commanded distinct generative models for different domains. Mathematically, however, this can always be couched as further tuning of a single, overall generative model. This is clear in the various treatments by Friston and colleagues, see, e.g., Friston, 2003.

14. The suggestion here is not that our somatosensory areas themselves are rendered inactive during action observation. Indeed, there is considerable evidence (reviewed in Keysers et al., 2010) that such areas are indeed active during passive viewing. Rather, it is that the forward flowing influence of (the relevant aspects of) proprioceptive prediction error now becomes muted, rendering such error unable to impact higher levels of somatosensory processing. Just such a pattern (of lower level activity combined with higher level inactivity) was found by Keysers et al. (2010). See also Friston, Mattout, et al., 2011, p. 156.

15. This, as Jakob Hohwy (personal communication) nicely notes, is not a lucky or ad hoc trick. It is simply another manifestation of learning the best ways to estimate precision so as to minimize prediction errors.

16. There is large and complex literature on this topic, see Vignemont & Fourneret, 2004, for a useful review, and some important fine-tuning of the basic notion. See also Hohwy, 2007b.

17. See, e.g., Friston, 2012b; Frith, 2005; Ford & Mathalon, 2012.

18. See Barsalou, 1999, 2009; Grush, 2004; Pezzulo, 2008; Pezzulo et al., 2013; see also Colder, 2011; Hesslow, 2002.

19. In this work, an ambiguous figure (the famous face-vase figure) is seen as either a face or a vase in ways that co-varied with spontaneous pre-stimulus activity in the fusiform face area (FFA). As the authors note, however 'it is unclear whether the variations in the ongoing activity of FFA signals reported here are akin to slow fluctuations as they have been described in the form of resting state networks' (Hesselmann et al., 2008, p. 10986).

20. Some sleeping states and perhaps some practices (such as meditation and chanting) may provide exceptions to this rule.

21. Such estimates of our own uncertainty play a central role in a wide variety of recent computational and neuroscientific work. See, e.g., Daw, Niv, & Dayan, 2005; Dayan & Daw, 2008; Knill & Pouget, 2004; Yu & Dayan, 2005; Daw, Niv, & Dayan 2005; Dayan & Daw, 2008; Ma, 2012; van den Berg et al., 2012; Yu & Dayan, 2005.

CHAPTER 6

1. As noted in chapter 1, the phrase 'perception as controlled hallucination' has been variously attributed to Ramesh Jain, Rodolfo Llinas, and Max Clowes. It is also quoted by Rick Grush in his work on the 'emulation theory of representation' (e.g., Grush, 2004).

2. Given the standard implementation of the predictive processing story—for an alternative implementation, see Spratling, 2008.

3. Though recall the discussion (in 1.13) of the surprising power of an ultra-rapid feedforward pass to uncover the conceptual gist of a visually presented scene (Potter et al., 2013).

4. For an example of this, see 6.9.

5. The notion of an affordance is widely used and widely interpreted. In the hands of its originator, J. J. Gibson, affordances were agent-relative possibilities for action present (though not necessarily recognized by the agent) in the distal environment (see Gibson, 1977, 1979). For a careful, nuanced discussion, see Chemero, 2009, chapter 7.

6. See also Kemp et al., 2007.

7. The process level here corresponds to what Marr (1982) described as the level of the algorithm.

8. The classic critique is that of Fodor and Pylyshyn (1988), but related points were made by more ecumenical theorists, such as Smolensky (1988) whose later work on optimality theory and harmonic grammar (Smolensky & Legendre, 2006) likewise accommodates both generative

structure and statistical learning. For further discussion of this important issue, see Christiansen & Chater, 2003.

9. For an excellent discussion of this attractive feature of hierarchical Bayesian approaches, see Tenenbaum et al., 2011. Caution is still required, however, since the mere fact that multiple forms of knowledge representation *can* co-exist within such models does not show us, in any detail, how such various forms may effectively be combined in unified problem-solving episodes.

10. For a review, see Tenenbaum et al., 2011. But for an important critique of some of the claims as applied to higher-level cognition, see Marcus & Davis, 2013.

11. As Karl Friston (personal communication) has suggested.

12. For example, a system might start with a set of so-called 'perceptual input analyzers' (Carey, 2009) whose effect is to make a few input features more salient for learning. For discussion of the combined effects of HBM learning and such simple biases, see Goodman et al., in press.

13. This 'action-oriented' paradigm is associated with insights from developmental psychology (Smith & Gasser, 2005; Thelen et al., 2001), ecological psychology (Chemero, 2009; Gibson, 1979; Turvey & Shaw, 1999), dynamical systems theory (Beer, 2000), cognitive philosophy (Clark, 1997; Hurley, 1998; Wheeler, 2005), and real-world robotics (Pfeifer & Bongard, 2006). For a useful sampling of many of these themes, see the essays in Núñez & Freeman, 1999.

14. There is a nice discussion of this issue in Wiese (2014).

15. Such appeals to powerful (and often quite abstract) hyperpriors will clearly form an essential part of any larger, broadly Bayesian, story about the shape of human experience. Despite this, no special story needs to be told about either the very *presence* or the *mode of action* of such hyperpriors. Instead, they arise quite naturally within hierarchical models of the kind we have been considering where they may be innate (giving them an almost Kantian feel) or acquired in the manner of empirical (hierarchical) Bayes.

16. See Ballard (1991), Churchland et al., (1994), Warren (2005), Anderson (2014), pp. 163-172.

17. Thus Hohwy et al. (2008) note that 'Terms like "predictions" and "hypotheses" sound rather intellectualist when it comes to basic perceptual inference. But at its heart the only processing aim of the system is simply to minimize prediction error or free energy, and indeed, the talk of hypotheses and predictions can be translated into such a less anthropomorphic framework [and] implemented using relatively simple neuronal infrastructures' (Hohwy et al., 2008, pp. 688–690).

18. One might even deny that evil demon style manipulations actually deceive us. Instead, they merely suggest an alternate substrate for the same old veridical knowledge about an external reality: a world built

of tables, chairs, baseball games, and the like. For this kind of response, see Chalmers (2005).

19. Typically, these rich inner models involved symbolic encodings that described states of affairs using complex language-like knowledge structures. Nothing like this is implied by PP.

20. A versions of this misplaced worry also appears in Froese & Ikegami, 2013.

21. Thanks to Michael Rescorla for this helpful terminological suggestion.

22. Thus Friston, in a passage already quoted back in chapter 1, suggests that 'the hierarchical structure of the real world literally comes to be "reflected" by the hierarchical architectures trying to minimize prediction error, not just at the level of sensory input but at all levels of the hierarchy' (Friston, 2002, p. 238).

23. It is a weak sense because there is no guarantee that the potential thinkings of beings deploying this strategy will form the kind of closed set (encompassing all possible combinations of the component grasps) required by the so-called Generality Constraint (Evans, 1982).

24. See, e.g., Moore, 1903/1922; Harman, 1990.

25. In this case we are perceptually misled even though we, as reflective agents know better. In more severe cases (cases of delusions and hallucinations) we may be misled at every level.

26. It is not inconceivable, for example, that a broader ecological perspective might reveal the rubber hand illusion and its ilk as the inescapable price of being a labile biological system whose parts may grow, change, and suffer various forms of unexpected damage and/or augmentation.

27. For a nice introduction to this illusion, with accompanying graphics, see http://psychology.about.com/od/sensationandperception/ss/muller-lyer-illusion.htm.

28. Advanced agents may manage a step or two into these murky metawaters. See, e.g., Daunizeau, den Ouden, et al., 2010a, b.

CHAPTER 7

1. For an excellent discussion of many general issues concerning metacognition and prediction error, see Shea (2013). That discussion is couched in terms of 'reward prediction error' but all the key claims apply, as far as I can tell, to the more general case of sensory prediction error discussed in the present text.

2. This illustration first appeared in Frith and Friston (2012).

3. For a review of some of the recent literature, see Schütz et al., 2011.

4. For the equations, see Adams et al., 2012, pp. 8–9. Note that the equations on those pages specify first, the process *generating* the sensory inputs that the agent receives (exteroceptive retinal input concerning the target location, in an intrinsic (retinal) frame of reference, and proprioceptive input reporting angular displacement of the eye) then second, the

generative model that the agent brings to bear upon those inputs. Only the latter is described (informally) in the present text.

5. There is a kind of double negation here that can be a little confusing. The picture is one in which the standard (neurotypical) state involves an attenuation (i.e., a reduction) of the sensory consequences of self-produced actions. When this attenuation is itself reduced (abolished or lessened), such sensory consequences are—in one sense at least—experienced more veridically. They are experienced as being of the same intensity as the same event (a certain pressure on the hand, say) externally generated. But this, as we shall see, is not always a good thing and may also lead to the emergence of various illusions of agency and control.

6. All subjects underestimate their own applied forces but that underestimation is much reduced in the case of the schizophrenic subjects (see Shergill et al., 2005).

7. See Adams et al., 2012, pp. 13–14; Feldman & Friston, 2010; Seamans & Yang, 2004; see also Braver et al., 1999.

8. Heath Robinson, was a British cartoonist whose work, rather like that of Rube Goldberg in the USA, often depicted weird and complex machinery for the achievement of simple goals—for example, a long arrangement of chains, pulley, levers, and cuckoo-clocks to butter a slice of bread or deliver a cup of tea at a pre-arranged time.

9. It is worth repeating that what matters in all these cases is really just the relative balance between the precision of prediction errors computed at various levels. It does not matter, functionally speaking, whether high-level precision is decreased or low-level precision increased. This is not to say that such differences are unimportant, as they concern patterns of causality that may have clinical implications concerning etiology and treatment.

10. The label 'functional motor and sensory symptoms', unlike many of these older locutions, is considered acceptable by patients (see Stone et al., 2002).

11. The influence of folk-physiological expectations has also been noted when hypnotized patients are told that their hand is paralysed. Here, as in cases of so-called 'hysterical paralysis', the boundaries of the paralysis reflect our commonsense ideas about the borders of the hand rather than the true physiology of the hand as a moveable unit (see Boden, 1970).

12. E.g., insular cortex (in the case of functional pain symptoms) or premotor cortex or supplementary motor area (in the case of functional motor symptoms).

13. For an interesting application of this kind of framework to the special case of phantom limb pain, see De Ridder, Vanneste, & Freeman, 2012.

14. For reviews, see Benedetti, 2013; Enck et al., 2013; Price et al., 2008. Buchel et al. also speculate (2014, pp. 1227–1229) that administered

opioids might similarly play a (somewhat more direct and 'mechanical') role in modulating the precision of top-down predictions. For an intriguing evolutionary account that seems broadly compatible with the PP model, see Humphrey, 2011.

15. It is enlightening to visit the online discussion forum 'wrongplanet. com' and search for 'hollow mask illusion'. On one thread, a variety of autistic subjects report initially failing to see the hollow mask illusion (instead seeing it as it really is, i.e., as an inverted concave mask rather than as a convex face-shape). But many subjects were able to learn to see it in the neurotypical way, and those same subjects then found themselves unable to experience the inverted mask as concave. This is very much like the neurotypical experience of sine-wave speech (see 2.2).

16. There is emerging empirical support for this story (see Skewes et al., 2014).

17. This is probably not the best term here, as it invites a false parallel with the technical notion of a hyper-prior (see Friston, Lawson, & Frith, 2013).

18. In exploring the so-called 'sense of presence', it is not clear whether the experiential target is some nebulous but positive sense of presence, or simply the normal absence of a sense of non-presence, unreality or disconnection. The model that Seth et al. propose is deliberately agnostic on this subtle but potentially quite illuminating issue. Instead, their target is whatever (a feeling of presence, or the absence of a feeling of absence) is impaired in so-called 'dissociative psychiatric disorders': disorders where the sense of reality of the world, or of the self, is altered or lost.

19. Sometimes proprioception is counted as part of exteroception. Seth et al. themselves carve the cake in this manner. Nothing in the present treatment turns upon this terminological choice, but it is worth bearing in mind when viewing Figure 7.2

20. For criticisms and complexities, see Marshall and Zimbardo (1979), Maslach (1979), and LeDoux (1995).

21. There is resonance here with the complex and subtle work of Nick Humphrey, who argues (Humphrey, 2006) that sensation always involves something pro-active—the ongoing attempt to meet the incoming signal with an active (predictive processing would say, 'anticipatory') response.

22. Towards the end of his treatment, Pezzulo adds a further (and I think important) twist, arguing (2013, p. 18) that 'interoceptive information is part and parcel of the representation of entities such as "wind", "thief", and many others'. The idea here is that the internal states that become active in the presence of specific external states of affairs are always richly contextually inflected, and that this inflection now seamlessly combines 'objective' and 'subjective' (e.g., emotional and body-related) elements.

23. An additional factor (Pezzulo, 2013, p. 14) might be the greater simplicity or parsimony of the single model (thief in the night) as against the

complex model involving two co-occurring but causally unrelated factors. We shall have more to say about this kind of factor in chapters 8
and 9.

24. For a lovely rendition of this kind of picture, see Barrett & Bar, 2009.

25. Consistent with this single crucial role, insults or disturbances impacting distinct neural populations, or selectively impacting tonic or phasic
dopaminergic response, will often have very different behavioural and
experiential effects (see Friston, Shiner, et al. 2012).

26. It will only feel like progress, of course, if you are already somewhat
sceptical about the way the 'hard problem' is typically presented in the
literature. True believers in the hard problem will say that all we can
make progress with using these new-fangled resources is the familiar
project of explaining patterns of response and judgement, and not the
very existence of experience itself. Those of a more optimistic nature
will think that explaining enough of that just *is* explaining why there
is experience at all. For a start on this project, as it takes shape within
the broadly Bayesian framework on offer, see Dennett, 2013.

CHAPTER 8

1. The full title was 'Fast, Cheap, and Out of Control: A Robot Invasion
of the Solar System'—this alluded to parts of the paper mooting the
idea of sending hundreds of tiny, cheap robots into space. See Brooks &
Flynn, 1989.

2. For example, if asked to judge which of a pair of towns has the highest population, we will often choose the one whose name we find most
familiar. In many cases this familiarity contest (or 'recognition heuristic') will indeed track population size. For a balanced review, see
Gigerenzer and Goldstein (2011).

3. There are related accounts of how dogs catch Frisbees, a rather more
demanding task due to occasional dramatic fluctuations in the flight
path (see Shaffer et al., 2004).

4. To test this hypothesis, Ballard et al. used a computer program to alter
the colour of a block while the subject was looking elsewhere. For most
of these interventions, subjects did not notice the changes even for
blocks and locations that had been visited many times before, or that
were the focus of the current action.

5. Thanks to Jakob Hohwy (personal communication) for this helpful
suggestion.

6. This might be implemented as an adapted version of the so-called
'actor-critic' account (see Barto, 1995; Barto et al. 1983) but one in which
a model-free 'actor' is trained by a model-based 'critic' (see Daw et al.,
2011, p. 1210).

7. In essence, this involves creating a weighted average of the predictions made by different models. Bayesian model selection, by contrast,

involves selecting one model over others (see, e.g., Stephan et al., 2009). The reader may note that for most of the present chapter, I frame my own discussion in terms of model selection. Nonetheless, model averaging, under some (high sensitivity) conditions, can deliver outright model selection. Agents able to vary the sensitivity of their own model comparisons would benefit from increased flexibility though it is not yet clear which procedure provides the best fit with behavioural and neural evidence. For further discussion, see Fitzgerald, Dolan, & Friston, 2014.

8. Weaker versions of the 'dual systems' view, such as those recently defended by Evans (2010) and Stanovich (2011) are, however, potentially consistent with the more integrated PP account. See also Frankish, forthcoming.

9. Such an effect has been demonstrated in some simple simulations of cued reaching under the influence of changing tonic levels of dopamine firing—see Friston, Shiner, et al., (2012).

10. This kind of approach, in which simple, efficient models are gated and enabled within the larger context of a hierarchical Bayesian system, is by no means unique to predictive processing. It is present, for example, in the MOSAIC framework due to Haruno, Wolpert, & Kawato, 2003. In general, this kind of strategy will be available wherever estimations of our own uncertainty are available to gate and nuance online response.

11. For a thorough rehearsal of the positive arguments, see Clark, 2008. For critiques, see Adams & Aizawa, 2008; Rupert, 2004, 2009. For a rich sampling of the ongoing debate, see the essays in Menary, 2010.

12. Except at bed time! I use the term 'darkened room' to mean the scenario in which we retire to a dark chamber and remain there, without food, water, or amusements until we die—this is the kind of 'predictable but deadly' circumstance that the critics have in mind.

13. This example occurs in Campbell, 1974.

14. This was confirmed by Lisa Meeden (personal communication). Meeden thinks the story might originate with a learning robot (Lee et al., 2009) designed to seek out learnable (but as yet unlearnt) sensory states. One such 'curiosity-bot' (or 'intrinsically motivated controller'), instead of simply learning the easiest stuff first, seemed to challenge itself by trying to learn a hard thing alongside an easier one. This behaviour was not one that the experimenters had anticipated and resulted in the robot displaying oscillating back-and-forth viewing routine. Commenting on the mythological spinning behaviour, Meeden (personal communication) notes that 'it would be interesting to see what would happen with a curiosity-based learning robot placed into a fairly simple environment for a long period of time. Would it begin to create new experiences for itself by trying new combinations of movements?' For more on robotics and intrinsic motivations, see Oudeyer et al., 2007.

15. The original study was that of Jones, Wilkinson, and Braden (1961).

16. For more on this 'exploration/exploitation' trade-off, see Cohen, McClure, & Yu, 2007.

17. In the case of perception, another fundamental pay-off for such 'self-organized instability' may be avoiding overconfidence, thus always leaving room to explore other possibilities.

CHAPTER 9

1. As noted earlier (4.5) I do not mean to suggest that all prediction errors can be quashed by action. What seems right, however, is that even in the case where the error cannot itself be resolved by action, the error-minimizing routine is still trying to deliver a grip upon the world that is apt for the selection of action. Salient unexplained errors, even in the 'purely perceptual' case, are thus geared to select percepts that are fundamentally designed to help us select actions.

2. This routine (Mozer & Smolensky, 1990) removed the least necessary hidden units from a trained-up network and thus improved both efficiency and generalization. Similarly, in computer graphics, skeletonization routines remove the least necessary pixels from an image. For some discussion, see Clark (1993).

3. Thanks to Jakob Hohwy for drawing this work to my attention.

4. In the work by Namikawa et al., the neural structures thus implicated were prefrontal cortex, supplementary motor area, and primary motor cortex (see Namikawa et al., 2011, pp. 1–3).

5. The potency and the complexity of such effects are nicely illustrated in Dehaene's (2004) 'neuronal re-cycling' account of the complex interplay between neural precursors, cultural developments, and the neural effects of those cultural developments, as manifest in the key cognitive domains of reading and writing (see 9.7 following).

6. For some intriguing speculations concerning the initial emergence of all those discrete symbols in predictive, probabilistic contexts, see König & Krüger, 2006.

7. See, e.g., Anderson, 2010; Griffiths & Gray, 2001; Dehaene et al., 2010; Hutchins, 2014; Oyama, 1999; Oyama et al., 2001; Sterelny, 2003; Stotz, 2010; Wheeler & Clark, 2008. For a useful review, see Ansari, 2011.

8. For some discussion, see Tsuchiya & Koch, 2005.

9. Exposure to words does not, however, appear to work in the case of binocular rivalry, although priming with other (image-congruent) sounds does, see Chen, Yeh, & Spence, 2012.

10. This would go some way towards explaining why simple language-based measures (such as vocabulary size) are good predictors of performance on non-verbal intelligence tests. See Cunningham & Stanovich, 1997. See also Baldo et al., 2010.

11. There is now a large, and not altogether unified, literature on enaction. For our purposes, however, it will suffice to consider only the classic

statement by Varela et al. (1991). Important contributions to the larger space of enactivist, and enactivist-inspired, theorizing include Froese and Di Paolo (2011), Noë (2004, 2010), and Thompson (2010). The edited volume by Stewart et al. (2010) provides an excellent window onto much of this larger space.

12. Part of this image is misleading, insofar as it suggests that the external world is merely a source of undifferentiated perturbations (the repeated striking of a monotonous hammer). What seems correct is that the agent, by exposing herself to the varied stimulations predicted by the generative model, actively contributes to the world as sampled. Since it is only the world as sampled that the model needs to accommodate and explain, this delivers a very real sense in which (subject to the overarching constraint of structural self-maintenance, i.e., persistence and survival) we do indeed build or 'enact' our individual and species-specific worlds.

13. Variants of such a process may be found at several organizational scales, perhaps down to the level of dendrites of single cells. In just this vein, Kiebel and Friston (2011) suggest that one can understand intra-cellular processes as minimizing 'free energy' (see Appendix 2).

14. I have engaged such arguments at length elsewhere (see Clark, 1989, 1997, 2008, 2012). For sustained arguments *against* the explanatory appeal to internal representation, see Chemero, 2009; Hutto & Myin, 2013; Ramsey, 2007. For some useful discussion, see Gallagher, Hutto, Slaby, & Cole, 2013; Sprevak, 2010, 2013.

15. It is also the role more broadly played by what Engel et al. (2013) describe as 'dynamic directives'—dispositions towards action that are rooted in emergent ensembles that can include multiple neural and bodily structures.

16. Bayesian perceptual and sensorimotor psychology already has much to say about just what worldly and bodily states these may be. See e.g., Körding & Wolpert, 2006; Rescorla, 2013, In Press.

17. For a wonderful attempt, see Orlandi (2013). Orlandi's provocative but closely argued claim is that vision is not a cognitive activity and does not involve trading in internal representations (although it may sometimes generate mental representations as a kind of end-product). The argument is restricted in scope, however, as it targets only the processes involved in online visual perception.

CHAPTER 10

1. Such an understanding may have social and political consequences too. For at the very heart of human experience, PP suggests, lie the massed strata of our own (mostly unconscious) expectations. This means that we must carefully consider the shape of the worlds to which we (and our children) are exposed. If PP is correct, our percepts may be deeply

informed by non-conscious expectations acquired through the statistical lens of our own past experience. So if (to take just the glaringly obvious examples) the world that tunes those expectations is thoroughly sexist or racist, that will structure the subterranean prediction machinery that actively constructs our own future perceptions—a potent recipe for tainted 'evidence', unjust reactions, and self-fulfilling negative prophecies.

2. One such subset is, of course, the set of hierarchical dynamic models (see Friston, 2008).

3. Conscious experience is something of an outlier in this set, since it may well be a rather basic feature of animal cognition. This is suggested, in fact, by recent work (reviewed in chapter 7) associating conscious experience with interoceptive prediction: prediction of our own physiological states.

APPENDIX 1

1. The posterior probability of the hypothesis given some new data (or sensory evidence) is proportional to the probability of the data given the hypothesis, multiplied by the prior probability of the hypothesis.

References

Adams, F., & Aizawa, K. (2001). The bounds of cognition. *Philosophical Psychology, 14*(1), 43–64.

Adams, R. A., Perrinet, L. U., & Friston, K. (2012). Smooth pursuit and visual occlusion: Active inference and oculomotor control in schizophrenia. *PLoS One, 7*(10), e47502. doi:10.1371/journal.pone. 0047502.

Adams, R. A., Shipp, S., & Friston, K. J. (2013). Predictions not commands: Active inference in the motor system. *Brain Struct. Funct., 218*(3), 611–643.

Adams, R. A., Stephan, K. E., Brown, H. R., Frith, C. D., & Friston, K. J. (2013). The computational anatomy of psychosis. *Front. Psychiatry, 30*(4), 47. 1–26.

Addis, D. R., Wong, A., & Schacter, D. L. (2007). Remembering the past and imagining the future: Common and distinct neural substrates during event construction and elaboration. *Neuropsychologia, 45*, 1363–1377.

Addis, D. R., Wong, A., & Schacter, D. L. (2008). Age-related changes in the episodic simulation of future events. *Psychological Science, 19*, 33–41.

Aertsen, A., Bonhöffer, T., & Krüger, J. (1987). Coherent activity in neuronal populations: Analysis and interpretation. In E. R. Caianiello (Ed.), *Physics of cognitive processes* (pp. 1-3400–00). Singapore World Scientific Publishing.

Aertsen, A., and Preißl, H. (1991). Dynamics of activity and connectivity in physiological neuronal networks. In H. G. Schuster (Ed.), *Non linear dynamics and neuronal networks* (pp. 281–302). New York: VCH Publishers.

Alais, D., & Blake, R. (Eds.). (2005). *Binocular rivalry*. Cambridge, MA: MIT Press.

Alais, D., & Burr, D. (2004). The ventriloquist effect results from near-optimal bimodal integration. *Current Biology, 14,* 257–262.

Alink, A., Schwiedrzik, C. M., Kohler, A., Singer, W., & Muckli, L. (2010). Stimulus predictability reduces responses in primary visual cortex. *J. Neurosci., 30,* 2960–2966.

Allard, F., & Starkes, J. (1991). Motor skill experts in sports, dance and other domains. In K. Ericsson & J. Smith (Eds.), *Towards a general theory of expertise: Prospects and limits* (pp. 126–152). New York: Cambridge University Press.

Anchisi, D., & Zanon, M. (2015). A Bayesian perspective on sensory and cognitive integration in pain perception and placebo analgesia. *Plos One, 10,* e0117270. doi:10.1371/journal.pone.0117270.

Andersen, R. A., & Buneo, C. A. (2003). Sensorimotor integration in posterior parietal cortex. *Adv. Neurol., 93,* 159–177.

Anderson, M. L. (2010). Neural reuse: A fundamental organizational principle of the brain. *Behavioral and Brain Sciences, 33,* 245–313.

Anderson, M. L. (2014). *After phrenology: Neural reuse and the interactive brain* Cambridge, MA: MIT Press.

Anderson, M. L., & Chemero, A. (2013). The problem with brain GUTs: Conflation of different senses of 'prediction' threatens metaphysical disaster. *Behavioral and Brain Sciences, 36*(3), 204–205.

Anderson, M. L., Richardson, M., & Chemero, A. (2012). Eroding the boundaries of cognition: Implications of embodiment. *Topics in Cognitive Science,* 4(4), 717–730.

Ansari, D. (2011). Culture and education: New frontiers in brain plasticity. *Trends in Cognitive Sciences, 16*(2), 93–95.

Anscombe, G. E. M. (1957). *Intention.* Oxford: Basil Blackwell.

Arbib, M., Metta, G., & Van der Smagt, P. (2008). Neurorobotics: From vision to action. In B. Siciliano & K. Oussama (Eds.), *Handbook of robotics.* New York: Springer.

Arthur, B. (1994). *Increasing returns and path dependence in the economy.* Ann Arbor: University of Michigan Press.

Asada, M., MacDorman, K., Ishiguro, H., & Kuniyoshi, Y. (2001). Cognitive developmental robotics as a new paradigm for the design of humanoid robots. *Robotics and Autonomous Systems, 37,* 185–193.

Asada, M., MacDorman, K., Ishiguro, H., & Kuniyoshi, Y. (2009). Cognitive developmental robotics: A survey. *IEEE Trans. Autonomous Mental Development, 1*(1), 12–34.

Atlas, L. Y., & Wager, T. D. (2012). How expectations shape pain. *Neuroscience Letters, 520,* 140–148. doi:10.1016/j.neulet.2012.03.039.

Avila, M. T., Hong, L. E., Moates, A., Turano, K. A., & Thaker, G. K. (2006). Role of anticipation in schizophrenia-related pursuit initiation deficits. *J. Neurophysiol., 95*(2), 593–601.

Bach, D. R., & Dolan, R. J. (2012). Knowing how much you don't know: a neural organization of uncertainty estimates. *Nature Reviews Neuroscience, 13*(8), 572–586. doi: 10.1038/nrn3289.

Baess, P., Jacobsen, T., & Schroger, E. (2008). Suppression of the auditory N1 event-related potential component with unpredictable self-initiated tones: Evidence for internal forward models with dynamic stimulation. *Int. J. Psychophysiol., 70*, 137–143.

Baldo, J. V., Bunge, S. A., Wilson, S. M., & Dronkers, N. F. (2010). Is relational reasoning dependent on language? A voxel-based lesion symptom mapping study. *Brain and Language, 113*(2), 59–64. doi:10.1016/j.bandl.2010.01.004.

Ballard, D. (1991). Animate vision. *Artificial Intelligence, 48*, 57–86.

Ballard, D. H., & Hayhoe, M. M. (2009). Modeling the role of task in the control of gaze. *Visual Cognition, 17*, 1185–1204.

Ballard, D., Hayhoe, M., Pook, P., & Rao, R. (1997). Deictic codes for the embodiment of cognition. *Behavioral and Brain Sciences, 20*, 4. 723–767.

Bar, M. (2004). Visual objects in context. *Nat. Rev. Neurosci. 5*, 617–629.

Bar, M. (2007). The proactive brain: Using analogies and associations to generate predictions. *Trends in Cognitive Sciences, 11*(7), 280–289.

Bar, M. (2009). The proactive brain: Memory for predictions. Theme issue: Predictions in the brain: Using our past to generate a future (M. Bar, Ed.). *Philosophical Transactions of the Royal Society B, 364*, 1235–1243.

Bar, M., Kassam, K. S., Ghuman, A. S., Boshyan, J., Schmidt, A. M., Dale, A. M., Hamalainen, M. S., Marinkovic, K., Schacter, D. L., Rosen, B. R., & Halgren, E. (2006). Top-down facilitation of visual recognition. *Proceedings of the National Academy of Science, 103*(2), 449–454.

Bargh, J. A. (2006). What have we been priming all these years? On the development, mechanisms, and ecology of nonconscious social behavior. *European Journal of Social Psychology, 36*, 147–168.

Bargh, J. A., Chen, M., & Burrows, L. (1996). Automaticity of social behavior: Direct effects of trait construct and stereotype activation on action. *Journal of Personality and Social Psychology, 71*, 230–244.

Barlow, H. B. (1961). The coding of sensory messages. In W. H. Thorpe & O. L. Zangwill (Eds.), *Current problems in animal behaviour* (pp. 330–360). Cambridge: Cambridge University Press.

Barnes, G. R., & Bennett, S. J. (2003). Human ocular pursuit during the transient disappearance of a visual target. *Journal of Neurophysiology, 90*(4), 2504–2520.

Barnes, G. R., & Bennett, S. J. (2004). Predictive smooth ocular pursuit during the transient disappearance of a visual target. *Journal of Neurophysiology, 92*(1), 578–590.

Barone, P., Batardiere, A., Knoblauch, K., & Kennedy, H. (2000). Laminar distribution of neurons in extrastriate areas projecting to visual areas V1 and V4 correlates with the hierarchical rank and indicates the operation of a distance rule. *J. Neurosci., 20*, 3263–3281. pmid: 10777791.

Barrett, H. C., & Kurzban, R. (2006). Modularity in cognition: Framing the debate. *Psychological Review, 113*(3), 628–647.

Barrett, L. F., & Bar, M. (2009). See it with feeling: Affective predictions in the human brain. *Royal Society Phil. Trans. B, 364*, 1325–1334.

Barsalou, L. (1999). Perceptual symbol systems. *Behav. Brain Sci., 22*, 577–660.

Barsalou, L. (2003). Abstraction in perceptual symbol systems. *Philosophical Transactions of the Royal Society of London: Biological Science, 358*, 1177–1187.

Barsalou, L. (2009). Simulation, situated conceptualization, and prediction. *Philosophical Transactions of the Royal Society of London: Biological Sciences, 364*, 1281–1289.

Barto, A., Sutton, R., & Anderson, C. (1983). Neuronlike adaptive elements that can solve difficult learning control problems. *IEEE Trans. Syst. Man Cybern., 13*, 834–846.

Barto, A. G. (1995). Adaptive critics and the basal ganglia. In J. L. Davis, J. C. Houk, & D. G. Beiser (Eds.), *Models of information processing in the basal ganglia* (pp. 215–232). Cambridge, MA: MIT Press.

Bastian, A. (2006). Learning to predict the future: The cerebellum adapts feedforward movement control. *Current Opinion in Neurobiology, 16*(6), 645–649.

Bastos, A. M., Usrey, W. M., Adams, R. A., Mangun, G. R., Fries, P., & Friston, K. J. (2012). Canonical microcircuits for predictive coding. *Neuron, 76*, 695–711.

Bastos, A. M., Vezoli, J., Bosman, C. A., Schoffelen, J.-M., Oostenveld, R., Dowdall, J. R., De Weerd, P., Kennedy, H., and Fries, P. (2015). Visual areas exert feedforward and feedback influences through distinct frequency channels. *Neuron*, 1–12. doi:10.1016/j.neuron.2014.12.018.

Battaglia, P. W., Hamrick, J. B., & Tenenbaum, J. B. (2013). Simulation as an engine of physical scene understanding. *Proceedings of the National Academy of Sciences of the United States of America, 110*(45), 18327–18332. doi:10.1073/pnas.1306572110.

Becchio, C., et al. (2010). Perception of shadows in children with autism spectrum disorders. *PLoS One, 5*, e10582. doi:10.1371/journal.pone.0010582.

Beck, D. M., & Kastner, S. (2005). Stimulus context modulates competition in human extrastriate cortex. *Nature Neuroscience, 8*, 1110–1116.

Beck, D. M., & Kastner, S. (2008). Top-down and bottom-up mechanisms in biasing competition in the human brain. *Vision Research, 49*, 1154–1165.

Beck, J. M., Ma, W. J., Pitkow, X., Latham, P. E., & Pouget, A. (2012, April 12). Not noisy, just wrong: The role of suboptimal inference in behavioral variability. *Neuron, 74*(1), 30–39. doi:10.1016/j.neuron.2012.03.016.

Beer, R. (2000). Dynamical approaches to cognitive science. *Trends in Cognitive Sciences, 4*(3), 91–99.

Beer, R. (2003). The dynamics of active categorical perception in an evolved model agent. *Adaptive Behavior, 11*, 209–243.

Bell, C. C., Han, V., & Sawtell, N. B. (2008). Cerebellum-like structures and their implications for cerebellar function. *Annu. Rev. Neurosci., 31*, 1–24.

Benedetti, F. (2013). Placebo and the new physiology of the doctor–patient relationship. *Physiol. Rev., 93*, 1207–1246.

Bengio, Y. (2009). Learning deep architectures for AI. *Foundations and Trends in Machine Learning, 2*(1):, 1–127.

Bengio, Y., & Le Cun, Y. (2007). Scaling learning algorithms towards AI. In Bottou L., Chapelle O., DeCoste D. and Weston J. (Eds.), *Large scale kernel machines* (pp. 321–360). Cambridge, MA: MIT Press.

Berkes, P., Orban, G., Lengyel, M., & Fiser, J. (2011). Spontaneous cortical activity reveals hallmarks of an optimal internal model of the environment. *Science, 331*, 83–87.

Berlyne, D. (1966). Curiosity and exploration. *Science, 153*(3731), 25–33.

Bermúdez, J. (2005). *Philosophy of psychology: A contemporary introduction*. New York: Routledge.

Berniker, M., & Körding, K. P. (2008). Estimating the sources of motor errors for adaptation and generalization. *Nature Neuroscience, 11*, 1454–1461.

Betsch, B. Y., Einhäuser, W., Körding, K. P., & König, P. (2004). The world from a cat's perspective: Statistics of natural videos. *Biological Cybernetics, 90*, 41–50.

Biederman, I. (1987). Recognition-by-components: A theory of human image understanding. *Psychological Review, 94*, 115–147.

Bindra, D. (1959). Stimulus change, reactions to novelty, and response decrement. *Psychological Review, 66*, 96–103.

Bingel, U., Wanigasekera, V., Wiech, K., Ni Mhuircheartaigh, R., Lee, M. C., Ploner, M., & Tracey, I. (2011). The effect of treatment expectation on drug efficacy: Imaging the analgesic benefit of the opioid remifentanil. *Sci. Transl. Med., 3*, 70ra14. 1–9 doi:10.1126/scitranslmed.3001244.

Bissom, T. (1991). Alien/Nation. *Omni. (Science fiction magazine)*

Blackmore, S. (2004). *Consciousness: An introduction*. New York: Oxford University Press.

Blakemore, S.-J., Frith, C. D., & Wolpert, D. W. (1999). Spatiotemporal prediction modulates the perception of self-produced stimuli. *Journal of Cognitive Neuroscience, 11*(5), 551–559.

Blakemore, S.-J., Wolpert, D. M., & Frith, C. D. (1998). Central cancellation of self-produced tickle sensation. *Nature Neuroscience, 1*(7), 635–640.

Blakemore S. J., Wolpert D., Frith C. (2000). Why can't you tickle yourself? *Neuroreport 11*, R11–16.

Blakemore, S.-J., Wolpert, D. M., & Frith, C. D. (2002). Abnormalities in the awareness of action. *Trends in Cognitive Sciences, 6*, 237–242.

Block, N., & Siegel, S. (2013). Attention and perceptual adaptation. *Behavioral and Brain Sciences, 36*(4), 205–206.

Boden, M. (1970). Intentionality and physical systems. *Philosophy of Science, 37*, 200–214.

Botvinick, M. (2004). Probing the neural basis of body ownership. *Science, 305*, 782–783. doi:10.1126/science. 1101836.

Botvinick, M., & Cohen, J. (1998). Rubber hands 'feel' touch that eyes see. *Nature*, *391*, 756. doi:10. 1038/35784.

Bowman, H., Filetti, M., Wyble, B., & Olivers, C. (2013). Attention is more than prediction precision. *Behav. Brain Sci.*, *36*(3), 233–253.

Box, G. P., & Draper, N. R. (1987). *Empirical model-building and response surfaces.* NJ Wiley.

Boynton, G. M. (2005). Attention and visual perception. *Curr. Opin. Neurobiol.*, *15*, 465–469. doi:10.1016/j.conb.2005. 06.009.

Brainard, D. (2009). Bayesian approaches to color vision. In M. Gazzaniga (Ed.), *The visual neurosciences* (4th ed.). Cambridge, MA: MIT Press.

Bram, U. (2013). *Thinking statistically.* San Francisco: Capara Books.

Braver, T. S., Barch, D. M., & Cohen, J. D. (1999). Cognition and control in schizophrenia: A computational model of dopamine and prefrontal function. *Biological Psychiatry*, *46*(3), 312–328.

Brayanov, J. B., & Smith, M. A. (2010). Bayesian and "anti-Bayesian" biases in sensory integration for action and perception in the size–weight illusion. *Journal of Neurophysiology*, *103*(3), 1518–1531.

Brock, J. (2012, November 2). Alternative Bayesian accounts of autistic perception: Comment on Pellicano and Burr. *Trends in Cognitive Sciences*, *16*(12), 573–574. doi:10.1016/j.tics.2012.10.005.

Brooks, R., & Flynn, A(1989). Fast, cheap, and out of control: A robot invasion of the solar system. *J. Brit. Interplanetary Soc.*, *42*(10), 478–485.

Brown, E. C., & Brüne, M. (2012). The role of prediction in social neuroscience. *Front. Hum. Neurosci.*, *6*, 147. doi:10.3389/fnhum.2012.00147.

Brown, H., Adams, R. A., Parees, I., Edwards, M., & Friston, K. (2013). Active inference, sensory attenuation and illusions. *Cogn. Process.* 14 (4), 411–427.

Brown, H., & Friston, K. (2012). Free-energy and illusions: The Cornsweet effect. *Frontiers in Psychology*, *3*, 43. doi:10.3389/fpsyg.2012.00043.

Brown, H., Friston, K., & Bestmann, S. (2011). Active inference, attention, and motor preparation. *Frontiers in Psychology*, *2*, 218. doi:10.3389/fpsyg.2011.00218.

Brown, R. J. (2004). Psychological mechanisms of medically unexplained symptoms: An integrative conceptual model. *Psychol. Bull.*, *130*, 793–812.

Bubic, A., von Cramon, D. Y., & Schubotz, R. I. (2010). Prediction, cognition and the brain. *Front. Hum. Neurosci.*, *4*, 25. doi:10.3389/fnhum.2010.00025.

Buchbinder, R., & Jolley, D. (2005). Effects of a media campaign on back beliefs is sustained 3 years after its cessation. *Spine*, *30*, 1323–1330.

Büchel, C., Geuter, S., Sprenger, C., & Eippert, F., et al. (2014). Placebo analgesia: A predictive coding perspective. *Neuron*, *81*(6), 1223–1239.

Buckingham, G., & Goodale, M. (2013). When the predictive brain gets it really wrong. *Behavioral and Brain Sciences*, *36*(3), 208–209.

Buffalo, E. A., Fries, P., Landman, R., Buschman, T. J., & Desimone, R. (2011). Laminar differences in gamma and alpha coherence in the ventral stream.

Proceedings of the National Academy of Sciences of the United States of America,
   108(27), 11262–11267. doi.org/10.1073/pnas.1011284108.

Burge, J., Fowlkes, C., & Banks, M. (2010). Natural-scene statistics predict how the
   figure–ground cue of convexity affects human depth perception. *Journal of
   Neuroscience, 30*(21), 7269–7280. doi:10.1523/JNEUROSCI.5551-09.2010.

Burge, T. (2010). *Origins of objectivity.* New York: Oxford University Press.

Byrne, A., & Logue, H. (Eds.). (2009). *Disjunctivism: Contemporary readings.*
   Cambridge, MA: MIT Press.

Caligiore, D., Ferrauto, T., Parisi, D., Accornero, N., Capozza, M., & Baldassarre,
   G. (2008). Using motor babbling and Hebb rules for modeling the develop-
   ment of reaching with obstacles and grasping. In *CogSys2008—International
   Conference on Cognitive Systems* (E 1–8. Cambridge, MA: MIT Press.

Campbell, D. T. (1974). Evolutionary epistemology. In P. A. Schlipp (Ed.), *The
   philosophy of Karl Popper* (pp. 413–463). LaSalle, IL: Open Court.

Cardoso-Leite, P., Mamassian, P., Schütz-Bosbach, S., & Waszak, F. (2010).
   A new look at sensory attenuation: Action-effect anticipation affects
   sensitivity, not response bias. *Psychological Science, 21,* 1740–1745.
   doi:10.1177/0956797610389187.

Carey, S. (2009). *The origin of concepts.* New York: Oxford University Press.

Carrasco, M. (2011). Visual attention: The past 25 years. *Vision Res., 51*(13),
   1484–1525. doi:10.1016/j.visres.2011.04.012.

Carrasco, M., Ling, S., & Read, S. (2004). Attention alters appearance. *Nature
   Neuroscience, 7,* 308–313.

Carruthers, P. (2009). Invertebrate concepts confront the generality constraint
   (and win). In Robert W. Lurz (Ed.), *The philosophy of animal minds* (pp.
   89–107). Cambridge: Cambridge University Press.

Castiello, U. (1999). Mechanisms of selection for the control of hand action.
   Trends in Cognitive Sciences, 3(7), 264–271.

Chadwick, P. K. (1993). The step ladder to the impossible: A first hand phenomenological account of a schizo-affective psychotic crisis. *Journal of Mental
   Health, 2,* 239–250.

Chalmers, D. (1996). *The conscious mind.* Oxford: Oxford University Press.

Chalmers, D. (2005). The matrix as metaphysics. In R. Grau (Ed.), *Philosophers
   explore the matrix.* New York: Oxford University Press.

Chapman, S. (1968). Catching a baseball. *American Journal of Physics, 36,* 868–870.

Chater, N., & Manning, C. (2006). Probabilistic models of language processing
   and acquisition. *Trends in Cognitive Sciences, 10*(7), 335–344.

Chawla, D., Friston, K., & Lumer, E. (1999). Zero-lag synchronous dynamics in
   triplets of interconnected cortical areas. *Neural Networks, 14*(6–7) 727–735.

Chemero, A. (2009). *Radical embodied cognitive science.* Cambridge,
   MA: MIT Press.

Chen, C. C., Henson, R. N., Stephan, K. E., Kilner, J. M., & Friston, K. J. (2009).
   Forward and backward connections in the brain: A DCM study of functional asymmetries. *Neuroimage, 45*(2), 453–462.

Chen, Yi-Chuan, Su-Ling Yeh, & Spence, C. (2011). Crossmodal constraints on human perceptual awareness: Auditory semantic modulation of binocular rivalry. *Frontiers in Psychology, 2,* 212. doi:10.3389/fpsyg.2011.00212.

Christiansen, M., & Chater, N. (2003). Constituency and recursion in language. In M. A. Arbib (Ed.), *The handbook of brain theory and neural networks* (pp. 267–271). Cambridge, MA: MIT Press.

Churchland, P. M. (1989). *The neurocomputational perspective.* Cambridge, MA: MIT/Bradford Books.

Churchland, P. M. (2012). *Plato's camera: How the physical brain captures a landscape of abstract universals.* Cambridge, MA: MIT Press.

Churchland, P. S. (2013). *Touching a nerve: The self as brain.* W. W. Norton.

Churchland, P. S., Ramachandran, V., & Sejnowski, T. (1994). A critique of pure vision. In C. Koch & J. Davis (Eds.), *Large-scale neuronal theories of the brain* (pp. 23–61). Cambridge, MA: MIT Press.

Cisek, P. (2007). Cortical mechanisms of action selection: The affordance competition hypothesis. *Philosophical Transactions of the Royal Society B, 362,* 1585–1599.

Cisek, P., & Kalaska, J. F. (2005). Neural correlates of reaching decisions in dorsal premotor cortex: Specification of multiple direction choices and final selection of action. *Neuron, 45*(5), 801–814.

Cisek, P., & Kalaska, J. F. (2011). Neural mechanisms for interacting with a world full of action choices. *Annual Review of Neuroscience, 33,* 269–298.

Clark, A. (1989). *Microcognition: Philosophy, cognitive science and parallel distributed processing.* Cambridge, MA: MIT Press/Bradford Books.

Clark, A. (1993). *Associative engines: Connectionism, concepts and representational change.* Cambridge, MA: MIT Press, Bradford Books.

Clark, A. (1997). *Being there: Putting brain, body and world together again.* Cambridge, MA: MIT Press.

Clark, A. (1998). Magic words: How language augments human computation. In P. Carruthers & J. Boucher (Eds.), *Language and thought: Interdisciplinary themes* (pp. 162–183). Cambridge: Cambridge University Press.

Clark, A. (2003). *Natural-born cyborgs: Minds, technologies, and the future of human intelligence.* New York: Oxford University Press.

Clark, A. (2006). Language, embodiment and the cognitive niche. *Trends in Cognitive Sciences, 10*(8), 370–374.

Clark, A. (2008). *Supersizing the mind: Action, embodiment, and cognitive extension* New York: Oxford University Press.

Clark, A. (2012). Dreaming the whole cat: Generative models, predictive processing, and the enactivist conception of perceptual experience. *Mind, 121*(483), 753–771. doi:10.1093/mind/fzs106.

Clark, A. (2013). Whatever next? Predictive brains, situated agents, and the future of cognitive science. *Behavioral and Brain Sciences, 36*(3), 181–204.

Clark, A. (2014). Perceiving as predicting. In M. Mohan, S. Biggs, & D. Stokes (Eds.), *Perception and its modalities.* New York: Oxford University Press, 23–43.

Clark, A., & Chalmers, D. (1998). The extended mind. *Analysis, 58*(1), 7–19.

Cocchi, L., Zalesky, A., Fornito, A., & Mattingley, J. (2013). Dynamic cooperation and competition between brain systems during cognitive control. *Trends in Cognitive Sciences, 17,* 493–501.

Coe, B., Tomihara, K., Matsuzawa, M., & Hikosaka, O. (2002). Visual and anticipatory bias in three cortical eye fields of the monkey during an adaptive decision-making task. *J. Neurosci., 22*(12), 5081–5090.

Cohen, J. D., McClure, S. M., & Yu, A. J. (2007). Should I stay or should I go? How the human brain manages the trade-off between exploitation and exploration. *Philosophical Transactions of the Royal Society London B: Biological Sciences, 29*(362), 933–942. doi:10.1098/rstb.2007.2098.

Colder, B. (2011). Emulation as an integrating principle for cognition. *Front. Hum. Neurosci., 5,* 54. doi:10.3389/fnhum.2011.00054.

Cole, M. W., Anticevic, A., Repovs, G., and Barch, D. (2011). Variable global dysconnectivity and individual differences in schizophrenia. *Biological Psychiatry, 70,* 43–50.

Collins, S. H., Wisse, M., & Ruina, A. (2001). A 3-D passive dynamic walking robot with two legs and knees. *International Journal of Robotics Research, 20*(7), 607–615.

Colombetti, G. (2014). *The feeling body.* Cambridge, MA: MIT Press.

Colombetti, G., & Thompson, E. (2008). The feeling body: Towards an enactive approach to emotion. In W. F. Overton, U. Muller, & J. L. Newman (Eds.), *Developmental perspectives on embodiment and consciousness* (pp. 45–68). New York: Lawrence Erlbaum Assoc.

Colombo, M. (2013). Moving forward (and beyond) the modularity debate: A network perspective. *Philosophy of Science, 80,* 356–377.

Colombo, M. (in press). Explaining social norm compliance: A plea for neural representations. *Phenomenology and the Cognitive Sciences.*

Coltheart, M. (2007). Cognitive neuropsychiatry and delusional belief (The 33rd Sir Frederick Bartlett Lecture). *Quarterly Journal of Experimental Psychology, 60*(8), 1041–1062.

Conway, C., & Christiansen, M. (2001). Sequential learning in non-human primates. *Trends in Cognitive Sciences, 5*(12), 539–546.

Corlett, P. R., Frith, C. D., & Fletcher, P. C. (2009). From drugs to deprivation: A Bayesian framework for understanding models of psychosis. *Psychopharmacology (Berl), 206*(4), 515–530.

Corlett, P. R., Krystal, J. K., Taylor, J. R., & Fletcher, P. C. (2009). Why do delusions persist? *Front. Hum. Neurosci., 3,* 12. doi:10.3389/neuro.09.012.2009.

Corlett, P. R., Taylor, J. R., Wang, X. J., Fletcher, P. C., & Krystal, J. H. (2010). Toward a neurobiology of delusions. *Progress in Neurobiology, 92*(3), 345–369.

Coste, C. P., Sadaghiani, S., Friston, K. J., & Kleinschmidt, A. (2011). Ongoing brain activity fluctuations directly account for intertrial and indirectly for intersubject variability in Stroop task performance. *Cereb. Cortex, 21,* 2612–2619.

Craig, A. D. (2002). How do you feel? Interoception: The sense of the physiological condition of the body. *Nat. Rev. Neurosci., 3,* 655–666.

Craig, A. D. (2003). Interoception: The sense of the physiological condition of the body. *Curr. Opin. Neurobiol.*, *13*, 500–505.

Craig, A. D. (2009). How do you feel—now? The anterior insula and human awareness. *Nat. Rev. Neurosci.*, *10*, 59–70.

Crane, T. (2005). What is the problem of perception? *Synthesis Philosophica*, *40*(2), 237–264.

Crick, F. (1984). Function of the thalamic reticular complex: The searchlight hypothesis. *Proceedings of the National Academy of Sciences of the United States of America*, *81*, 4586–4590.

Critchley, H. D. (2005). Neural mechanisms of autonomic, affective, and cognitive integration. *Journal of Comparative Neurology*, *493*(1), 154–166. doi:10.1002/cne.20749.

Critchley, H. D., & Harrison, N. A. (2013). Visceral influences on brain and behavior. *Neuron*, *77*, 624–638.

Critchley, H. D., et al. (2004). Neural systems supporting interoceptive awareness. *Nat. Neurosci.*, *7*, 189–195.

Crowe, S., Barot, J., Caldow, S., D'Aspromonte, J., Dell'Orso, J., Di Clemente, A., Hanson, K., Kellett, M., Makhlota, S., McIvor, B., McKenzie, L., Norman, R., Thiru, A., Twyerould, M., & Sapega, S. (2011). The effect of caffeine and stress on auditory hallucinations in a nonclinical sample. *Personality and Individual Difference*, *50*(5), 626–630.

Cui, X., Jeter, C. B., Yang, D., Montague, P. R., and Eagleman, D. M. (2007). Vividness of mental imagery: Individual variability can be measured objectively. *Vision Res.*, *47*, 474–478.

Çukur, T., Nishimoto, S., Huth, A. G., & Gallant, J. L. (2013). Attention during natural vision warps semantic representation across the human brain. *Nature Neuroscience*, *16*(6), 763–770. doi:10.1038/nn.3381.

Cunningham, A. E., & Stanovich, K. E. (1997). Early reading acquisition and its relation to reading experience and ability 10 years later. *Developmental Psychology*, *33*(6), 934–945.

Damasio, A. (1999). *The feeling of what happens*. New York: Harcourt, Brace & Co.

Damasio, A. (2010). *Self comes to mind: Constructing the conscious brain*. Toronto Pantheon.

Damasio, A., & Damasio, H. (1994). Cortical systems for retrieval of concrete knowledge: The convergence zone framework. In C. Koch (Ed.), *Large-scale neuronal theories of the brain* (pp. 61–74). Cambridge, MA: MIT Press.

Daunizeau, J., Den Ouden, H., Pessiglione, M., Stephan, K., Kiebel, S., & Friston, K. (2010a). Observing the observer (I): Meta-Bayesian models of learning and decision-making. *PLoS One*, *5*(12), e15554.

Daunizeau, J., Den Ouden, H., Pessiglione, M., Stephan, K., Kiebel, S., & Friston, K. (2010b). Observing the observer (II): Deciding when to decide. *PLoS One*, *5*(12), e15555.

Davis, M. H., & Johnsrude, I. S. (2007). Hearing speech sounds: Top-down influences on the interface between audition and speech perception. *Hearing Research*, *229*(1–2), 132–147.

Daw, N., Niv, Y., & Dayan, P. (2005). Uncertainty-based competition between prefrontal l and dorsolateral striatal systems for behavioral control. *Nature Neuroscience, 8*(12), 1704–1711.

Daw, N. D., Gershman, S. J., Seymour, B., Dayan, P., & Dolan, R. J. (2011). Model-based influences on humans' choices and striatal prediction errors. *Neuron, 69*, 1204–1215.

Dayan, P. (1997). Recognition in hierarchical models. In F. Cucker & M. Shub (Eds.), *Foundations of computational mathematics* (pp. 79–87). Berlin, Germany: Springer.

Dayan, P. (2012). How to set the switches on this thing. *Curr. Opin. Neurobiol., 22*, 1068–1074.

Dayan, P., & Daw, N. D. (2008). Decision theory, reinforcement learning, and the brain. *Cognitive, Affective & Behavioral Neuroscience, 8*, 429–453.

Dayan, P., & Hinton, G. (1996). Varieties of Helmholtz machine. *Neural Networks, 9*, 1385–1403.

Dayan, P., Hinton, G. E., & Neal, R. M. (1995). The Helmholtz machine. *Neural Computation, 7*, 889–904.

De Brigard, F. (2012). Predictive memory and the surprising gap. *Frontiers in Psychology, 3*, 420. doi:10.3389/fpsyg.2012.00420.

De Ridder, D., Vanneste, S., & Freeman, W. (2012). The Bayesian brain: Phantom percepts resolve sensory uncertainty. *Neurosci. Biobehav. Rev.* http://dx.doi.org/10.1016/j.neubiorev.2012.04.001.

de Vignemont, F., & Fourneret, P. (2004). The sense of agency: A philosophical and empirical review of the Who system. *Consciousness and Cognition, 13*, 1–19.

de-Wit, L., Machilsen, B., & Putzeys, T. (2010). Predictive coding and the neural response to predictable stimuli. *J. Neurosci., 30*, 8702–8703.

den Ouden, H. E. M., Daunizeau, J., Roiser, J., Friston, K., & Stephan, K. (2010). Striatal prediction error modulates cortical coupling. *J. Neurosci., 30*, 3210–3219.

den Ouden, H. E. M., Kok, P. P., & de Lange, F. P. F. (2012). How prediction errors shape perception, attention, and motivation. *Front. Psychol., 3*, 548. doi:10.3389/fpsyg.2012.00548.

Decety, J. (1996). Neural representation for action. *Rev. Neurosci., 7*, 285–297.

Dehaene, S. (2004). Evolution of human cortical circuits for reading and arithmetic: The 'neuronal recycling' hypothesis. In S. Dehaene, J. Duhamel, M. Hauser, & G. Rizzolatti (Eds.), *From monkey brain to human brain* (pp.133–158). Cambridge, MA: MIT Press.

Dehaene, S., Pegado, F., Braga, L., Ventura, P., Nunes G., Jobert, A., Dehaene-Lambertz, G., Kolinsky, R., Morais, J., & Cohen, L. (2010). How learning to read changes the cortical networks for vision and language. *Science, 330*(6009), 1359–1364. doi:10.1126/science.1194140.

Demiris, Y., & Meltzoff, A. (2008). The robot in the crib: A developmental analysis of imitation skills in infants and robots. *Infant and Child Development, 17*, 43–58.

Dempster, A. P., Laird, N. M., & Rubin, D. B. (1977). Maximum likelihood from incomplete data via the EM algorithm. *Journal of the Royal Statistical Society Series B, 39*, 1–38.

Deneve, S. (2008). Bayesian spiking neurons I: inference. *Neural Comput., 20*, 91–117.

Dennett, D. (1982). Beyond belief. In A. Woodfield (Ed.), *Thought and object* (pp.74–98). Oxford: Clarendon Press.

Dennett, D. (1991). *Consciousness explained*. Boston: Little Brown.

Dennett, D. (2013). Expecting ourselves to expect: The Bayesian brain as a projector. *Behavioral and Brain Sciences, 36*(3), 209–210.

Desantis, A., Hughes, G., & Waszak, F. (2012). Intentional binding is driven by the mere presence of an action and not by motor prediction. *PLoS One, 7*, e29557. doi:10.1371/journal.pone.0029557.

Desimone, R. (1996). Neural mechanisms for visual memory and their role in attention. *Proc. Natl. Acad. Sci. USA, 93*(24), 13494–13499.

Desimone, R., & Duncan, J. (1995). Neural mechanisms of selective visual attention. *Annu. Rev. Neurosci., 18*, 193–222.

Dewey, J. (1896). The reflex arc concept in psychology. *Psychological Review, 3*, 357–370.

DeWolf, T., & Eliasmith, C. (2011). The neural optimal control hierarchy for motor control. *Journal of Neural Engineering, 8*(6), 21. doi:10.1088/1741-2560/8/6/065009.

DeYoe, E. A., & Van Essen, D. C. (1988). Concurrent processing streams in monkey visual cortex. *Trends in Neuroscience, 11*, 219–226.

Diana, R. A., Yonelinas, A. P., & Ranganath, C. (2007). Imaging recollection and familiarity in the medial temporal lobe: A three-component model. *Trends in Cognitive Sciences, 11*, 379–386.

Dima, D., Roiser, J., Dietrich, D., Bonnemann, C., Lanfermann, H., Emrich, H., & Dillo, W. (2009). Understanding why patients with schizophrenia do not perceive the hollow-mask illusion using dynamic causal modelling. *NeuroImage, 46*(4), 1180–1186.

Dolan, R. J. (2002). Emotion, cognition, and behavior. *Science, 298*, 1191–1194.

Dorris, M. C., & Glimcher, P. W. (2004). Activity in posterior parietal cortex is correlated with the relative subjective desirability of action. *Neuron, 44*(2), 365–378.

Doya, K., & Ishii, S. (2007). A probability primer. In K. Doya, S. Ishii, A. Pouget, & R. Rao (Eds.), *Bayesian brain: Probabilistic approaches to neural coding* (pp. 3–15). Cambridge, MA: MIT Press.

Doya, K., Ishii, S., Pouget, A., & Rao, R. (Eds.). (2007). *Bayesian brain: Probabilistic approaches to neural coding*. Cambridge, MA: MIT Press.

Dura-Bernal, S., Wennekers, T., & Denham, S. (2011). The role of feedback in a hierarchical model of object perception. *Advances in Experimental Medicine and Biology, 718*, 165–179. doi:10.1007/978-1-4614-0164-3_14.

Dura-Bernal, S., Wennekers, T., & Denham, S. (2012). Top-down feedback in an HMAX-like cortical model of object perception based on hierarchical Bayesian networks and belief propagation. *PloS One*, *7*(11), e48216. doi:10.1371/journal.pone.0048216.

Edelman, G. (1987). *Neural Darwinism: The theory of neuronal group selection.* New York: Basic Books.

Edelman, G., & Mountcastle, V. (1978). *The mindful brain: Cortical organization and the group-selective theory of higher brain function.* Cambridge, MA: MIT Press.

Edwards, M. J., Adams, R. A., Brown, H., Pareés, I., & Friston, K. (2012). A Bayesian account of 'hysteria'. *Brain*, *135*(Pt 11), 3495–3512.

Egner, T., Monti, J. M., & Summerfield, C. (2010). Expectation and surprise determine neural population responses in the ventral visual stream. *Journal of Neuroscience*, *30*(49), 16601–16608.

Egner, T., & Summerfield, C. (2013). Grounding predictive coding models in empirical neuroscience research. *Behavioral and Brain Sciences*, *36*, 210–211.

Ehrsson, H. H. (2007). The experimental induction of out-of-body experiences. *Science*, *317*, 1048.

Einhäuser, W., Kruse, W., Hoffmann, K. P., & König, P. (2006). Differences of monkey and human overt attention under natural conditions. *Vision Res.*, *46*, 1194–1209.

Eliasmith, C. (2005). A new perspective on representational problems. *Journal of Cognitive Science*, *6*, 97–123.

Eliasmith, C. (2007). How to build a brain: From function to implementation. *Synthese*, *153*(3), 373–388.

Elman, J. L. (1993). Learning and development in neural networks: The importance of starting small. *Cognition*, *48*, 71–99.

Enck, P., Bingel, U., Schedlowski, M., & Rief, W. (2013). The placebo response in medicine: Minimize, maximize or personalize? *Nat. Rev. Drug Discov.*, *12*, 191–204.

Engel, A., Maye, A., Kurthen, M., & König, P. (2013). Where's the action? The pragmatic turn in cognitive science. *Trends in Cognitive Sciences*, *17*(5), 202–209. doi:10.1016/j.tics.2013.03.006.

Engel, A. K., Fries, P., & Singer, W. (2001). Dynamic predictions: Oscillations and synchrony in top-down processing. *Nature Reviews*, *2*, 704–716.

Ernst, M. O. (2010). Eye movements: Illusions in slow motion. *Current Biology*, *20*(8), R357–R359.

Ernst, M. O., & Banks, M. S. (2002). Humans integrate visual and haptic information in a statistically optimal fashion. *Nature*, *415*, 429–433.

Evans, G. (1982). *The varieties of reference.* Oxford: Oxford University Press.

Evans, J. St. B. T. (2010). *Thinking twice: Two minds in one brain.* Oxford: Oxford University Press.

Fabre-Thorpe, M. (2011). The characteristics and limits of rapid visual categorization. *Frontiers in Psychology*, *2*(243). doi:10.3389/fpsyg.2011.00243.

Fadiga, L., Craighero, L., Buccino, G., & Rizzolatti, G. (2002). Speech listening specifically modulates the excitability of tongue muscles: A TMS study. *Eur. J. Neurosci.*, *15*(2), 399–402.

Fair, D. (1979). Causation and the flow of energy. *Erkenntnis*, *14*, 219–250.

Faisal, A. A., Selen, L. P. J., & Wolpert, D. M. (2008). Noise in the nervous system. *Nature Rev. Neurosci.*, *9*, 292–303. doi:10.1038/nrn2258.

Fecteau, J. H., & Munoz, D. P. (2006). Salience, relevance, and firing: A priority map for target selection. *Trends in Cognitive Sciences*, *10*, 382–390.

Feldman, A. G. (2009). New insights into action-perception coupling. *Experimental Brain Research*, *194*(1), 39–58.

Feldman, A. G., & Levin, M. F. (2009). The equilibrium-point hypothesis—past, present and future. *Advances in Experimental Medicine and Biology*, *629*, 699–726.

Feldman, H., & Friston, K. (2010). Attention, uncertainty, and free-energy. *Frontiers in Human Neuroscience*, *2*(4), 215. doi:10.3389/fnhum.2010.00215.

Feldman, J. (2010). Cognitive science should be unified: Comment on Griffiths et al. and McClelland et al. *Trends in Cognitive Sciences*, *14*(8), 341. doi:10.1016/j.tics.2010.05.008.

Feldman, J. (2013). Tuning your priors to the world. *Topics in Cognitive Science*, *5*(1), 13–34. doi:10.1111/tops.12003.

Felleman, D. J., & Van Essen, D. C. (1991). Distributed hierarchical processing in primate cerebral cortex. *Cerebral Cortex*, *1*, 1–47.

Fernandes, H. L., Stevenson, I. H., Phillips, A. N., Segraves, M. A., & Kording, K. P. (2014). Saliency and saccade encoding in the frontal eye field during natural scene search. *Cerebral Cortex*, *24*(12), 3232–3245.

Fernyhough, C. (2012). *Pieces of light: The new science of memory*. London: Profile Books.

Ferrari, PF et al. (2003). Mirror neurons responding to the observation of ingestive and communicative mouth actions in the ventral premotor cortex. *European Journal of Neuroscience*, *17*(8), 1703–1714.

Ferrari, R., Obelieniene, D., Russell, A. S., Darlington, P., Gervais, R., & Green, P. (2001). Symptom expectation after minor head injury: A comparative study between Canada and Lithuania. *Clin. Neurol. Neurosurg.*, *103*, 184–190.

Fink, P. W., Foo, P. S., & Warren, W. H. (2009). Catching fly balls in virtual reality: A critical test of the outfielder problem. *Journal of Vision*, *9*(13):14, 1–8.

FitzGerald, T., Dolan, R., & Friston, K. (2014). Model averaging, optimal inference, and habit formation. *Frontiers in Human Neuroscience*, *8*, 1–11. doi:10.3389/fnhum.2014.00457.

Fitzhugh, R. (1958). A statistical analyzer for optic nerve messages. *Journal of General Physiology*, *41*, 675–692.

Fitzpatrick, P., Metta, G., Natale, L., Rao, S., & Sandini, G. (2003). Learning about objects through action: Initial steps towards artificial cognition. *IEEE International Conference on Robotics and Automation (ICRA)*, 12–17 May, Taipei, Taiwan.

Flash, T., & Hogan, N. (1985). The coordination of arm movements: An experimentally confirmed mathematical model. *J. Neurosci.*, *5*, 1688–1703.

Fletcher, P., & Frith, C. (2009). Perceiving is believing: A Bayesian approach to explaining the positive symptoms of schizophrenia. *Nature Reviews: Neuroscience, 10,* 48–58.

Fodor, J. (1983). *The modularity of mind.* Cambridge, MA: MIT Press.

Fodor, J. (1988). A Reply to Churchland's 'Perceptual plasticity and theoretical neutrality'. *Philosophy of Science, 55,* 188–198.

Fodor, J., & Pylyshyn, Z. (1988). Connectionism and cognitive architecture: A critical analysis. *Cognition, 28*(1–2), 3–71.

Fogassi, L., Ferrari, P. F., Gesierich, B., Rozzi, S., Chersi, F., & Rizzolatti, G. (2005). Parietal lobe: From action organization to intention understanding. *Science, 308,* 662–667. doi:10.1126/science.1106138.

Fogassi, L., Gallese, V., Fadiga, L., & Rizzolatti, G. (1998). Neurons responding to the sight of goal directed hand/arm actions in the parietal area PF (7b) of the macaque monkey. *Soc. Neurosci. Abstr., 24,* 257.

Ford, J., & Mathalon, D. (2012). Anticipating the future: Automatic prediction failures in schizophrenia. *International Journal of Psychophysiology, 83,* 232–239.

Fornito, A., Zalesky, A., Pantelis, C., & Bullmore, E. T. (2012). Schizophrenia, neuroimaging and connectomics. *Neuroimage, 62,* 2296–2314.

Frankish, K. (in press). Dennett's dual-process theory of reasoning. In C. Muñoz-Suárez and F. De Brigard, F. (Eds.), *Content and consciousness revisited.* New York: Springer.

Franklin, D. W., & Wolpert, D. M. (2011). Computational mechanisms of sensorimotor control. *Neuron, 72,* 425–442.

Freeman, T. C. A., Champion, R. A., & Warren, P. A. (2010). A Bayesian model of perceived head-centred velocity during smooth pursuit eye movement. *Current Biology, 20,* 757–762.

Friston, K. (1995). Functional and effective connectivity in neuroimaging: A synthesis. *Hum. Brain Mapp., 2,* 56–78.

Friston, K. (2002). Beyond phrenology: What can neuroimaging tell us about distributed circuitry? *Annu. Rev. Neurosci., 25,* 221–250.

Friston, K. (2003). Learning and inference in the brain. *Neural Networks, 16*(9), 1325–1352.

Friston, K. (2005). A theory of cortical responses. *Philos. Trans. R. Soc. Lond. B Biol. Sci., 360*(1456), 815–836.

Friston, K. (2008). Hierarchical models in the brain. *PLoS Computational Biology, 4*(11), e1000211.

Friston, K. (2009). The free-energy principle: A rough guide to the brain? *Trends in Cognitive Sciences, 13,* 293–301.

Friston, K. (2010). The free-energy principle: A unified brain theory? *Nat. Rev. Neurosci., 11*(2), 127–138.

Friston, K. (2011a). What is optimal about motor control? *Neuron, 72,* 488–498.

Friston, K. (2011b). Embodied inference: or 'I think therefore I am, if I am what I think'. In W. Tschacher & C. Bergomi (Eds.), *The implications of embodiment (cognition and communication)* (pp. 89–125). Exeter, UK: Imprint Academic.

Friston, K. (2011c). Functional and effective connectivity: A review. *Brain Connectivity, 1*(1), 13–36. doi:10.1089/brain.2011.0008.

Friston, K. (2012a). Predictive coding, precision and synchrony. *Cognitive Neuroscience, 3*(3–4), 238–239.

Friston, K. (2012b). Prediction, perception and agency. *Int. J. Psychophysiol., 83*, 248–252.

Friston, K. (2012c). A free energy principle for biological systems. *Entropy, 14*, 2100–2121. doi:10.3390/e14112100.

Friston, K. (2013). Active inference and free energy. *Behavioral and Brain Sciences, 36*(3), 212–213.

Friston, K., Adams, R., & Montague, R. (2012). What is value-accumulated reward or evidence? *Frontiers in Neurorobotics, 6*, 11. doi:10.3389/fnbot.2012.00011.

Friston, K., Adams, R. A., Perrinet, L., & Breakspear, M. (2012). Perceptions as hypotheses: Saccades as experiments. *Front. Psychol., 3*, 151. doi:10.3389/fpsyg.2012.00151.

Friston, K., & Ao, P. (2012). Free-energy, value and attractors. *Computational and Mathematical Methods in Medicine.* Article ID 937860.

Friston, K. J., Bastos, A. M., Pinotsis, D., & Litvak, V. (2015). LFP and oscillations-what do they tell us? *Current Opinion in Neurobiology, 31*, 1–6. doi:10.1016/j.conb.2014.05.004

Friston, K., Breakspear, M., & Deco, G. (2012). Perception and self-organized instability. *Front. Comput. Neurosci., 6*, 44. doi:10.3389/fncom.2012.00044.

Friston, K., Daunizeau, J., & Kiebel, S. J. (2009, July 29). Reinforcement learning or active inference? *PLoS One, 4*(7), e6421.

Friston, K., Daunizeau, J., Kilner, J., & Kiebel, S. J. (2010). Action and behavior: A free-energy formulation. *Biol Cybern., 102*(3), 227–260.

Friston, K., Harrison, L., & Penny, W. (2003). Dynamic causal modelling. *Neuroimage, 19*, 1273–1302.

Friston, K., & Kiebel, S. (2009). Cortical circuits for perceptual inference. *Neural Networks, 22*, 1093–1104.

Friston, K., Lawson, R., & Frith, C. D. (2013). On hyperpriors and hypopriors: Comment on Pellicano and Burr. *Trends in Cognitive. Sciences, 17*, 1. doi:10.1016/j.tics.2012.11.003.

Friston, K., Mattout, J., & Kilner, J. (2011). Action understanding and active inference. *Biol. Cybern., 104*, 137–160.

Friston, K., & Penny, W. (2011). Post hoc Bayesian model selection. *Neuroimage, 56*(4), 2089–2099.

Friston, K., & Price, C. J. (2001). Dynamic representations and generative models of brain function. *Brain Res. Bull., 54*(3), 275–285.

Friston, K., Samothrakis, S., & Montague, R. (2012). Active inference and agency: Optimal control without cost functions. *Biol. Cybern., 106*(8–9), 523–541.

Friston, K., Shiner, T., FitzGerald, T., Galea, J. M., Adams, R., et al. (2012). Dopamine, affordance and active inference. *PLoS Comput. Biol., 8*(1), e1002327. doi:10.1371/journal.pcbi.1002327.

Friston, K., & Stephan, K. (2007). Free energy and the brain. *Synthese, 159*(3), 417–458.

Friston, K., Thornton, C., & Clark, A. (2012). Free-energy minimization and the dark-room problem. *Frontiers in Psychology, 3*, 1–7. doi:10.3389/fpsyg.2012.00130.

Frith, C. (2005). The self in action: Lessons from delusions of control. *Consciousness and Cognition, 14*(4), 752–770.

Frith, C. (2007). *Making up the mind: How the brain creates our mental world.* Oxford: Blackwell.

Frith, C., & Friston, K. (2012). False perceptions and false beliefs: Understanding schizophrenia. In *Working Group on Neurosciences and the Human Person: New perspectives on human activities, the Pontifical Academy of Sciences,* 8–10 November 2012, Casina PioIV.

Frith, C., & Frith, U. (2012). Mechanisms of social cognition. *Annu. Rev. Psychol., 63,* 287–313.

Frith, C., Perry, R., & Lumer, E. (1999). The neural correlates of conscious experience: An experimental framework. *Trends in Cognitive Sciences, 3*(3), 105–114.

Frith, U. (1989). *Autism: Explaining the enigma.* Oxford: Blackwell.

Frith, U. (2008). *Autism: A very short introduction.* New York: Oxford University Press.

Froese, T., & Di Paolo, E. A. (2011). The enactive approach: Theoretical sketches from cell to society. *Pragmatics and Cognition, 19,* 1–36.

Froese, T., & Ikegami, T. (2013). The brain is not an isolated 'black box' nor is its goal to become one. *Behavioral and Brain Sciences, 36*(3), 33–34.

Gallagher, S., Hutto, D., Slaby, J., & Cole, J. (2013). The brain as part of an enactive system. *Behavioral and Brain Sciences, 36*(4), 421–422.

Gallese, V., Fadiga, L., Fogassi, L., & Rizzolatti, G. (1996). Action recognition in the premotor cortex. *Brain, 119,* 593–609.

Gallese, V., Keysers, C., & Rizzolatti, G. (2004). A unifying view of the basis of social cognition. *Trends in Cognitive Sciences, 8*(9), 396–403.

Ganis, G., Thompson, W. L., & Kosslyn, S. M. (2004). Brain areas underlying visual mental imagery and visual perception: An fMRI study. *Brain Res. Cogn. Brain Res., 20,* 226–241.

Garrod, S., & Pickering, M. (2004). Why is conversation so easy? *Trends in Cognitive Sciences, 8*(1), 8–11.

Gazzola, V., & Keysers, C. (2009). The observation and execution of actions share motor and somatosensory voxels in all tested subjects: Single-subject analyses of unsmoothed fMRI data. *Cerebral Cortex, 19*(6), 1239–1255.

Gendron, M., & Barrett, L. F. (2009). Reconstructing the past: A century of ideas about emotion in psychology. *Emot. Rev., 1,* 316–339.

Gerrans, P. (2007). Mechanisms of madness: Evolutionary psychiatry without evolutionary psychology. *Biology and Philosophy, 22,* 35–56.

Gershman, S. J., & Daw, N. D. (2012). Perception, action and utility: The tangled skein. In M. Rabinovich, M., K. Friston, & P. Varona (Eds.), *Principles of brain dynamics: Global state interactions* (pp. 293–312). Cambridge, MA: MIT Press.

Gershman, S. J., Moore, C. D., Todd, M. T., Norman, K. N., & Sederberg, P. B. (2012). The successor representation and temporal context. *Neural Computation, 24,* 1–16.

Gibson, J. J. (1977). The theory of affordances. In R. Shaw & J. Bransford (Eds.), *Perceiving, acting, and knowing* (pp. 66–82). Hillsdale, NJ.

Gibson, J. J. (1979). *The ecological approach to visual perception.* Boston: Houghton-Mifflin.

Gigernzer, G. & Goldstein, D. (2011). The recognition heuristic: A decade of research. *Judgment and Decision Making 6*: 1: 100–121.

Gigerenzer, G., & Selten, R. (2002). *Bounded rationality.* Cambridge, MA: MIT Press.

Gigerenzer, G., Todd, P. M., & the ABC Research Group. (1999). *Simple heuristics that make us smart.* New York: Oxford University Press.

Gilbert, C., & Sigman, M. (2007). Brain states: Top-down influences in sensory processing. *Neuron, 54*(5), 677–696.

Gilbert, D., & Wilson, T. (2009, May 12). Why the brain talks to itself sources of error in emotional prediction. *Philosophical Transactions of the Royal Society of London, Series B, Biological Sciences, 364*(1521), 1335–1341. doi:10.1098/rstb.2008.0305.

Gilestro, G. F., Tononi, G., & Cirelli, C. (2009). Widespread changes in synaptic markers as a function of sleep and wakefulness in Drosophila. *Science, 324*(5923), 109–112.

Glascher, J., Daw, N. D., Dayan, P., & O'Doherty, J. P. (2010). States versus rewards: Dissociable neural prediction error signals underlying model-based and model-free reinforcement learning. *Neuron, 66*(4):585–95 doi:10.1016/j.neuron.2010.04.016.

Gold, J. N., & Shadlen, M. N. (2001). Neural computations that underlie decisions about sensory stimuli. *Trends in Cognitive Sciences, 5*:1: pp. 10–16.

Goldstone, R. L. (1994). Influences of categorization on perceptual discrimination. *Journal of Experimental Psychology: General, 123,* 178–200.

Goldstone, R. L., & Hendrickson, A. T. (2010). Categorical perception. *Interdisciplinary Reviews: Cognitive Science, 1,* 65–78.

Goldstone, R. L., Landy, D., & Brunel, L. (2011) Improving perception to make distant connections closer. *Frontiers in Psychology, 2,* 385. doi:10.3389/fpsyg.2011.00385.

Goldwater, S., Griffiths, T. L., & Johnson, M. (2009). A Bayesian framework for word segmentation: Exploring the effects of context. *Cognition, 112,* 21–54.

Goodman, N., Ullman, T., & Tenenbaum, J. (2011). Learning a theory of causality. *Psychological Review.* 118.1: 110–119.

Gregory, R. (2001). The Medawar Lecture 2001: Knowledge for vision: Vision for knowledge. *Philosophical Transactions B, 360.* 1458: 1231–1251.

Gregory, R. (1980). Perceptions as hypotheses. *Phil. Trans. R. Soc. Lond., Series B, Biological Sciences, 290*(1038), 181–197.

Griffiths, P. E., & Gray, R. D. (2001). Darwinism and developmental systems. In S. Oyama, P. E. Griffiths, & R. D. Gray (Eds.), *Cycles of contingency: Developmental systems and evolution* (pp. 195–218). Cambridge, MA: MIT Press.

Griffiths, T., Chater, N., Kemp, C., Perfors, A., & Tenenbaum, J. B. (2010). Probabilistic models of cognition: Exploring representations and inductive biases. *Trends in Cognitive Sciences, 14*(8), 357–364.

Griffiths, T. L., Sanborn, A. N., Canini, K. R., & Navarro, D. J. (2008). Categorization as nonparametric Bayesian density estimation. In M. Oaksford & N. Chater (Eds.), *The probabilistic mind: Prospects for rational models of cognition* 303-350. Oxford: Oxford University Press.

Grill-Spector, K., Henson, R., & Martin, A. (2006). Repetition and the brain: Neural models of stimulus-specific effects. *Trends in Cognitive Sciences, 10*(1), 14–23.

Grossberg, S. (1980). How does a brain build a cognitive code? *Psychological Review, 87*(1), 1–51.

Grush, R. (2004). The emulation theory of representation: Motor control, imagery, and perception. *Behavioral and Brain Sciences, 27*, 377–442.

Gu, X., et al. (2013). Anterior insular cortex and emotional awareness. *J. Comp. Neurol., 521*, 3371–3388.

Haddock, A., & Macpherson, F. (Eds.). (2008). *Disjunctivism: Perception, action, and knowledge.* Oxford: Oxford University Press.

Happe, F., & Frith, U. (2006). The weak coherence account: Detail focused cognitive style in autism spectrum disorders. *J. Autism Dev. Disord., 36*, 5–25.

Happe, F. G. (1996). Studying weak central coherence at low levels: Children with autism do not succumb to visual illusions. A research note. *J. Child Psychol. Psychiatry, 37*, 873–877.

Harman, G. (1990). The intrinsic quality of experience. In J. Tomberlin (Ed.), *Philosophical Perspectives 4* (pp. 64–82). Atascadero, CA: Ridgeview Press.

Harmelech, T., & Malach, R. 2013 Neurocognitive biases and the patterns of spontaneous correlations in the human cortex. *Trends in Cognitive Sciences, 17*(12), 606–615.

Harris, C. M., & Wolpert, D. M. (1998). Signal-dependent noise determines motor planning. *Nature, 394*, 780–784. doi:10.1038/29528.

Harris, C. M., & Wolpert, D. M. (2006). The main sequence of saccades optimizes speed-accuracy trade-off. *Biological Cybernetics, 95*(1), 21–29.

Harrison, L., Bestmann, S., Rosa, M., Penny, W., & Green, G. (2011). Time scales of representation in the human brain: Weighing past information to predict future events. *Frontiers in Human Neuroscience, 5*, 37. doi:10.3389/fnhum.2011.00037.

Haruno, M., Wolpert, D. M., & Kawato, M. (2003). Hierarchical mosaic for movement generation. *International Congress Series, 1250*, 575–590.

Hassabis, D., Kumaran, D., Vann, S. D., & Maguire, E. A. (2007). Patients with hippocampal amnesia cannot imagine new experiences. *Proc. Natl Acad. Sci. USA, 104*, 1726–1731. doi:10.1073/pnas.0610561104.

Hassabis, D., & Maguire, E. A. (2009). The construction system of the brain. *Phil. Trans. R. Soc. B, 364*, 1263–1271. doi:10.1098/rstb.2008.0296.

Hasson, U., Ghazanfar, A. A., Galantucci, B., Garrod, S., & Keysers, C. (2012). Brain-to-brain coupling: A mechanism for creating and sharing a social world. *Trends in Cognitive Sciences, 16*(2), 114–121.

Hawkins, J., & Blakeslee, S. (2004). *On intelligence.* New York: Owl Books.

Haxby, J. V., Gobbini, M. I., Furey, M. L., Ishai, A., Schouten, J. L., & Pietrini, P. (2001). Distributed and overlapping representations of faces and objects in ventral temporal cortex. *Science, 293*, 2425–2430.

Hayhoe, M. M., Shrivastava, A., Mruczek, R., & Pelz, J. B. (2003). Visual memory and motor planning in a natural task. *Journal of Vision, 3*(1), 49–63.

Hebb, D. O. (1949). *The organization of behavior.* New York: Wiley & Sons.

Heeger, D., & Ress, D. (2002). What does fMRI tell us about neuronal activity? *Nature Reviews/Neuroscience, 3*, 142–151.

Helmholtz, H. (1860/1962). *Handbuch der physiologischen optik* (J. P. C. Southall, Ed., English trans., Vol. 3). New York: Dover.

Henson, R. (2003). Neuroimaging studies of priming. *Progress in Neurobiology, 70*, 53–81.

Henson, R., & Gagnepain, P. (2010). Predictive, interactive multiple memory systems. *Hippocampus, 20*(11), 1315–1326.

Herzfeld, D., & Shadmehr, R. (2014). Cerebellum estimates the sensory state of the body. *Trends in Cognitive Neurosciences, 18*, 66–67.

Hesselmann, G., Kell, C., Eger, E., & Kleinschmidt, A. (2008). Spontaneous local variations in ongoing neural activity bias perceptual decisions. *Proceedings of the National Academy of Sciences, 105*(31), 10984–10989.

Hesselmann, G., Sadaghiani, S., Friston, K. J., & Kleinschmidt, A. (2010). Predictive coding or evidence accumulation? False inference and neuronal fluctuations. *PLoS One, 5*(3), e9926.

Hesslow, G. (2002). Conscious thought as simulation of behaviour and perception. *Trends in Cognitive Sciences, 6*(6), 242–247.

Heyes, C. (2001). Causes and consequences of imitation. *Trends in Cognitive Sciences, 5*, 253–261. doi:10.1016/S1364-6613(00)01661-2.

Heyes, C. (2005). Imitation by association. In S. Hurley & N. Chater (Eds.), *Perspectives on imitation: From mirror neurons to memes* (pp. 157–176). Cambridge, MA: MIT Press.

Heyes, C. (2010). Where do mirror neurons come from? *Neuroscience and Biobehavioral Reviews, 34*, 575–583.

Heyes, C. (2012). New thinking: The evolution of human cognition. *Phil. Trans. R. Soc. B 367*, 2091–2096.

Hilgetag, C., Burns, G., O'Neill, M., Scannell, J., & Young, M. (2000). Anatomical connectivity defines the organization of clusters of cortical areas in the macaque monkey and the cat. *Philos. Trans. R. Soc. Lond. B Biol. Sci., 355*, 91–110. doi:10.1098/rstb.2000.0551; pmid: 10703046.

Hilgetag, C., O'Neill, M., & Young, M. (1996). Indeterminate organization of the visual system. *Science, 271*, 776–777. doi:10.1126/science.271.5250.776; pmid: 8628990.

Hinton, G. E. (1990). Mapping part–whole hierarchies into connectionist networks *Artificial Intelligence, 46,* 47–75.

Hinton, G. E. (2005). What kind of a graphical model is the brain? *International Joint Conference on Artificial Intelligence,* Edinburgh.

Hinton, G. E. (2007a). Learning multiple layers of representation. *Trends in Cognitive Sciences, 11,* 428–434.

Hinton, G. E. (2007b). To recognize shapes, first learn to generate images. In P. Cisek, T. Drew & J. Kalaska (Eds.), *Computational neuroscience: Theoretical insights into brain function* (pp. 535–548). Amsterdam: Elsevier.

Hinton, G. E., Dayan, P., Frey, B. J., & Neal, R. M. (1995). The wake-sleep algorithm for unsupervised neural networks. *Science, 268,* 1158–1160.

Hinton, G. E., & Ghahramani, Z. (1997). Generative models for discovering sparse distributed representations. *Philosophical Transactions Royal Society B, 352,* 1177–1190.

Hinton, G. E., & Nair, V. (2006). Inferring motor programs from images of handwritten digits. In Y. Weiss (Ed.), *Advances in neural information processing systems,* 18 (pp. 515–522). Cambridge, MA: MIT Press.

Hinton, G. E., Osindero, S., & Teh, Y. (2006). A fast learning algorithm for deep belief nets. *Neural Computation, 18,* 1527–1554.

Hinton, G. E., & Salakhutdinov, R. R. (2006). Reducing the dimensionality of data with neural networks. *Science, 313*(5786), 504–507.

Hinton, G. E., & von Camp, D. (1993). Keeping neural networks simple by minimizing the description length of weights. *Proceedings of COLT-93,* 5–13.

Hinton, G. E., & Zemel, R. S. (1994). Autoencoders, minimum description length and Helmholtz free energy. In J. Cowan, G. Tesauro, & J. Alspector (Eds.), *Advances in neural information processing systems,* 6. San Mateo, CA: Morgan Kaufmann.

Hipp, J. F., Engel, A. K., & Siegel, M. (2011). Oscillatory synchronization in large-scale cortical networks predicts perception. *Neuron, 69,* 387–396.

Hirschberg, L. (2003). Drawn to narrative. *New York Times Magazine,* November 9.

Hobson, J., & Friston, K. (2012). Waking and dreaming consciousness: Neurobiological and functional considerations. *Prog. Neurobiol.,* 98(1), 82–98.

Hobson, J., & Friston, K. (2014). Consciousness, dreams, and inference. *Journal of Consciousness Studies, 21*(1–2), 6–32.

Hobson, J. A. (2001). *The dream drugstore: Chemically altered states of consciousness.* Cambridge, MA: MIT Press.

Hochstein, S., & Ahissar, M. (2002). View from the top: Hierarchies and reverse hierarchies in the visual system. *Neuron, 36*(5), 791–804.

Hohwy, J. (2007a). Functional integration and the mind. *Synthese, 159*(3), 315–328.

Hohwy, J. (2007b). The sense of self in the phenomenology of agency and perception. *Psyche, 13*(1) 1-20 (Susanna Siegel, Ed.).

Hohwy, J. (2012). Attention and conscious perception in the hypothesis testing brain. *Frontiers in Psychology, 3,* 96. doi:10.3389/fpsyg.2012.00096. 2012.

Hohwy, J. (2013). *The predictive mind.* New York: Oxford University Press.

Hohwy, J. (2014). The self-evidencing brain. *Noûs.* 1–27 doi: 10.1111/nous.12062.

Hohwy, J., Roepstorff, A., & Friston, K. (2008). Predictive coding explains binocular rivalry: An epistemological review. *Cognition, 108*(3), 687–701.

Holle, H., et al. (2012). Neural basis of contagious itch and why some people are more prone to it. *Proc. Natl. Acad. Sci. USA, 109*, 19816–19821.

Hollerman, J. R., & Schultz, W. (1998). Dopamine neurons report an error in the temporal prediction of reward during learning. *Nat. Neurosci., 1*, 304–309.

Hong, L. E., Avila, M. T., & Thaker, G. K. (2005). Response to unexpected target changes during sustained visual tracking in schizophrenic patients. *Exp. Brain Res., 165*, 125–131. PubMed: 15883805.

Hong, L. E., Turano, K. A., O'Neill, J., Hao, L. I. W., McMahon, R. P., Elliott, A., & Thaker, G. K. (2008). Refining the predictive pursuit endophenotype in schizophrenia. *Biol. Psychiatry, 63*, 458–464. PubMed: 17662963.

Horwitz, B. (2003). The elusive concept of brain connectivity. *Neuroimage, 19*, 466–470.

Hoshi, E., & Tanji, J. (2007). Distinctions between dorsal and ventral premotor areas: Anatomical connectivity and functional properties. *Curr. Opin. Neurobiol., 17*(2), 234–242.

Hosoya, T., Baccus, S. A., & Meister, M. (2005). Dynamic predictive coding by the retina. *Nature, 436*(7), 71–77.

Houlsby, N. M. T., Huszár, F., Ghassemi, M. M., Orbán, G., Wolpert, D. M., & Lengyel, M. (2013). Cognitive tomography reveals complex, task-independent mental representations. *Curr. Biol., 23*, 2169–2175.

Howe, C. Q., & Purves, D. (2005). The Müller-Lyer illusion explained by the statistics of image–source relationships. *Proceedings of the National Academy of Sciences of the United States of America, 102*(4), 1234–1239. doi:10.1073/pnas.0409314102.

Huang, Y., & Rao, R. (2011). Predictive coding. *Wiley Interdisciplinary Reviews: Cognitive Science, 2*, 580–593.

Hubel, D. H., & Wiesel, T. N. (1965). Receptive fields and functional architecture in two nonstriate visual areas (18 and 19) of the cat. *Journal of Neurophysiology, 28*, 229–289.

Hughes, H. C., Darcey, T. M., Barkan, H. I., Williamson, P. D., Roberts, D. W., & Aslin, C. H. (2001). Responses of human auditory association cortex to the omission of an expected acoustic event. *Neuroimage, 13*, 1073–1089.

Humphrey, N. (2000). How to solve the mind–body problem. *Journal of Consciousness Studies, 7*, 5–20.

Humphrey, N. (2006). *Seeing red: A study in consciousness.* Cambridge, MA: Harvard University Press.

Humphrey, N. (2011). *Soul dust: The magic of consciousness.* Princeton, NJ: Princeton University Press.

Humphreys, G. W., & Riddoch, J. M. (2000). One more cup of coffee for the road: Object-action assemblies, response blocking and response capture after frontal lobe damage. *Exp. Brain Res., 133*, 81–93.

Hupé, J. M., James, A. C., Payne, B. R., Lomber, S. G., Girard, P., & Bullier, J. (1998). Cortical feedback improves discrimination between figure and background by V1, V2 and V3 neurons. *Nature, 394,* 784–787.

Hurley, S. (1998). *Consciousness in action.* Cambridge, MA: Harvard University Press.

Hutchins, E. (1995). *Cognition in the wild.* Cambridge, MA: MIT Press.

Hutchins, E. (2014). The cultural ecosystem of human cognition. *Philosophical Psychology, 27*(1), 34–49.

Hutto, D. D., & Myin, E. (2013). *Radicalizing enactivism: Basic minds without content.*

Iacoboni, M. (2009). Imitation, empathy, and mirror neurons. *Annu. Rev. Psychol., 60,* 653–670.

Iacoboni, M., Molnar-Szakacs, I., Gallese, V., Buccino, G., Mazziotta, J. C., & Rizzolatti, G. (2005). Grasping the intentions of others with one's own mirror neuron system. *PLoS Biology, 3,* e79.

Iacoboni, M., Woods, R. P., Brass, M., Bekkering, H., Mazziotta, J. C., & Rizzolatti, G. (1999). Cortical mechanisms of human imitation. *Science, 286*(5449), 2526–2528.

Iglesias, S., Mathys, C., Brodersen, K. H., Kasper, L., Piccirelli, M., den Ouden, H. E., & Stephan, K. E. (2013). Hierarchical prediction errors in midbrain and basal forebrain during sensory learning. *Neuron, 80*(2), 519–530. doi:10.1016/j.neuron.2013.09.009.

Ingvar, D. H. (1985). 'Memory of the future': An essay on the temporal organization of conscious awareness. *Human Neurobiology, 4,* 127–136.

Ito, M., & Gilbert, C. D. (1999). Attention modulates contextual influences in the primary visual cortex of alert monkeys. *Neuron, 22,* 593–604.

Jackendoff, R. (1996). How language helps us think. *Pragmatics and Cognition, 4*(1), 1–34.

Jackson, F. (1977). *Perception: A representative theory.* Cambridge: Cambridge University Press.

Jacob, B., Hirsh, R., Mar, A., & Peterson, J. B. (2013). Personal narratives as the highest level of cognitive integration. *Behavioral and Brain Sciences, 36,* 216–217. doi:10.1017/S0140525X12002269.

Jacob, P., & Jeannerod, M. (2003). *Ways of seeing: The scope and limits of visual cognition.* Oxford: Oxford University Press.

Jacobs, R. A., & Kruschke, J. K. (2010). Bayesian learning theory applied to human cognition. *Wiley Interdisciplinary Reviews: Cognitive Science, 2,* 8–21. doi:10.1002/wcs.80.

Jacoby, L. L., & Dallas, M. (1981). On the relationship between autobiographical memory and perceptual learning. *J. Exp. Psychol. Gen., 110,* 306–340.

James, W. (1890/1950). *The principles of psychology,* Vols. I, II. Cambridge, MA: Harvard University Press.

Jeannerod, M. (1997). *The cognitive neuroscience of action.* Cambridge, MA: Blackwell.

Jeannerod, M. (2006). *Motor cognition: What actions tell the Self.* Oxford: Oxford University Press.

Jehee, J. F. M., & Ballard, D. H. (2009). Predictive feedback can account for biphasic responses in the lateral geniculate nucleus. *PLoS Comput. Biol.,* 5(5), e1000373.

Jiang, J., Heller, K., & Egner, T. (2014). Bayesian modeling of flexible cognitive control. *Neuroscience and Biobehavioral Reviews, 46,* 30–34.

Johnson, J. D., McDuff, S. G. R., Rugg, M. D., & Norman, K. A. (2009). Recollection, familiarity, and cortical reinstatement: A multivoxel pattern analysis. *Neuron, 63,* 697–708.

Johnson-Laird, P. N. (1988). *The computer and the mind: An introduction to cognitive science.* Cambridge, MA: Harvard University Press.

Jones, A., Wilkinson, H. J., & Braden, I. (1961). Information deprivation as a motivational variable. *Journal of Experimental Psychology, 62,* 310–311.

Joseph, R. M., et al. (2009). Why is visual search superior in autism spectrum disorder? *Dev. Sci., 12,* 1083–1096.

Joutsiniemi, S. L., & Hari, R. (1989) Omissions of auditory stimuli may activate frontal cortex. *Eur. J. Neurosci., 1,* 524–528.

Jovancevic, J., Sullivan, B., & Hayhoe, M. (2006). Control of attention and gaze in complex environments. *Journal of Vision,* 6(12):9, 1431–1450. http://www.journalofvision.org/content/6/12/9, doi:10.1167/6.12.9.

Jovancevic-Misic, J., & Hayhoe, M. (2009). Adaptive gaze control in natural environments. *Journal of Neuroscience, 29,* 6234–6238.

Joyce, J. (2008). Bayes' Theorem. *Stanford Encyclopedia of Philosophy* (2008).

Kachergis, G., Wyatte, D., O'Reilly, R. C., de Kleijn, R., & Hommel, B. (2014). A continuous time neural model for sequential action. Phil. Trans. R. Soc. B 369: 20130623.

Kahneman, D. (2011). *Thinking fast and slow.* London: Allen Lane.

Kahneman, D., & Tversky, A. (1972). Subjective probability:A judgment of representativeness. *Cognitive Psychology* 3 (3), 430–454. doi:10.1016/0010-0285(72)90016-3

Kahneman, D., Krueger, A. B., Schkade, D., Schwarz, N., & Stone, A. A. (2006). Would you be happier if you were richer? A focusing illusion. *Science, 312,* 1908–1910.

Kaipa, K. N., Bongard, J. C., & Meltzoff, A. N. (2010). Self discovery enables robot social cognition: Are you my teacher? *Neural Networks, 23,* 1113–1124.

Kamitani, Y., & Tong, F. (2005). Decoding the visual and subjective contents of the human brain. *Nat. Neurosci., 8,* 679–685.

Kanwisher, N. G., McDermott, J., & Chun, M. M. (1997). The fusiform face area: A module in human extrastriate cortex specialized for face perception. *Journal of Neuroscience, 17,* 4302–4311.

Kaplan, E. (2004). The M, P and K pathways of the primate visual system. In J. S. Werner & L. M. Chalupa (Eds.), *The visual neurosciences* (pp. 481–493). Cambridge, MA: MIT Press.

Kawato, M. (1999). Internal models for motor control and trajectory planning. *Current Opinion in Neurobiology, 9*, 718–727.

Kawato, M., Hayakama, H., & Inui, T. (1993). A forward-inverse optics model of reciprocal connections between visual cortical areas. *Network, 4*, 415–422.

Kay, K. N., Naselaris, T., Prenger, R. J., & Gallant, J. L. (2008). Identifying natural images from human brain activity. *Nature, 452*, 352–355.

Keele, S. W. (1968). Movement control in skilled motor performance. *Psychol. Bull., 70*, 387–403. doi:10.1037/ h0026739.

Kemp, C., Perfors, A., & Tenenbaum, J. B. (2007). Learning overhypotheses with hierarchical Bayesian models. *Developmental Science, 10*(3), 307–321.

Keysers, C., Kaas, J. H., & Gazzola, V. (2010). Somatosensation in social perception. *Nature Reviews Neuroscience, 11*(6), 417–428.

Khaitan, P., & McClelland, J. L. (2010). Matching exact posterior probabilities in the Multinomial Interactive Activation Model. In S. Ohlsson & R. Catrambone (Eds.), *Proceedings of the 32nd Annual Meeting of the Cognitive Science Society* (p. 623). Austin, TX: Cognitive Science Society.

Kidd, C., Piantadosi, S., & Aslin, R. (2012). The Goldilocks effect: Human infants allocate attention to visual sequences that are neither too simple nor too complex. *PLoS One, 7*(5), e36399. doi:10.1371/journal.pone.0036399.

Kiebel, S. J., & Friston K. J. (2011) Free energy and dendritic self-organization. *Frontiers in Systems Neurosci. 5*(80), 1–13.

Kiebel, S. J., Daunizeau, J., & Friston, K. J. (2009). Perception and hierarchical dynamics. *Front. Neuroinform., 3*, 20.

Kiebel, S. J., Garrido, M. I., Moran, R., Chen, C., & Friston, K. J. (2009). Dynamic causal modeling for EEG and MEG. *Human Brain Mapping, 30*(6), 1866–1876.

Kilner, J. M., Friston, K. J., & Frith, C. D. (2007). Predictive coding: An account of the mirror neuron system. *Cogn. Process., 8*, 159–166.

Kim, J. G., & Kastner, S. (2013). Attention flexibility alters tuning for object categories. *Trends in Cognitive Sciences, 17*(8), 368–370.

King, J., & Dehaene, S. (2014). A model of subjective report and objective discrimination as categorical decisions in a vast representational space. *Phil. Trans. R. Soc. B, 369*.

Kirmayer, L. J., & Taillefer, S. (1997). Somatoform disorders. In S. M. Turner & M. Hersen (Eds.), *Adult psychopathology and diagnosis* (3rd edn.) (pp. 333–383). New York: Wiley.

Kluzik, J., Diedrichsen, J., Shadmehr, R., & Bastian, A. J. (2008). Reach adaptation: What determines whether we learn an internal model of the tool or adapt the model of our arm? *J. Neurophysiol., 100*, 1455–1464.

Knill, D., & Pouget, A. (2004). The Bayesian brain: The role of uncertainty in neural coding and computation. *Trends in Neurosciences, 27*(12), 712–719.

Koch, C., & Poggio, T. (1999). Predicting the visual world: Silence is golden. *Nature Neuroscience, 2*(1), 79–87.

Koch, C., & Ullman, S. (1985). Shifts in selective visual attention: Towards the underlying neural circuitry. *Human Neurobiology, 4*, 219–227.

Kohonen, T. (1989). *Self-organization and associative memory*. Berlin: Springer-Verlag.

Kohonen, T. (2001). *Self-organizing maps* (3rd, extended edn.). Berlin: Springer.

Kok, P., Brouwer, G. J., van Gerven, M. A. J., & de Lange, F. P. (2013). Prior expectations bias sensory representations in visual cortex. *Journal of Neuroscience. 33*(41): 16275–16284; doi: 10.1523/JNEUROSCI.0742-13.2013.

Kok, P., Jehee, J. F. M., & de Lange, F. P. (2012). Less is more: Expectation sharpens representations in the primary visual cortex. *Neuron, 75*, 265–270.

Kolossa, A., Fingscheidt, T., Wessel, K., & Kopp, B. (2013). A model-based approach to trial-by-trial P300 amplitude fluctuations. *Frontiers in Human Neuroscience, 6*(359), 1–18. doi:10.3389/fnhum.2012.00359.

Kolossa, A., Kopp, B., & Fingscheidt, T. (2015). A computational analysis of the neural bases of Bayesian inference. *NeuroImage, 106*, 222–237. doi:10.1016/j.neuroimage.2014.11.007.

König, P., & Krüger, N. (2006). Symbols as self-emergent entities in an optimization process of feature extraction and predictions. *Biological Cybernetics, 94*(4), 325–334.

König, P., Wilming, N., Kaspar, K., Nagel, S. K., & Onat, S. (2013). Predictions in the light of your own action repertoire as a general computational principle. *Behavioral and Brain Sciences, 36*, 219–220.

Körding, K., & Wolpert, D. (2006). Bayesian decision theory in sensorimotor control. *Trends in Cognitive Sciences, 10*(7), 319–326. doi:10.1016/j.tics.2006.05.003.

Körding, K. P., Tenenbaum, J. B., & Shadmehr, R. (2007). The dynamics of memory as a consequence of optimal adaptation to a changing body. *Nature Neuroscience, 10*, 779–786.

Kosslyn, S. M., Thompson, W. L., Kim, I. J., & Alpert, N. M. (1995). Topographical representations of mental images in primary visual cortex. *Nature, 378*, 496–498.

Koster-Hale, J., & Saxe, R. (2013). Theory of mind: A neural prediction problem. *Neuron, 79*(5), 836–848.

Kriegstein, K., & Giraud, A. (2006). Implicit multisensory associations influence voice recognition. *PLoS Biology, 4*(10), e326.

Kuo, A. D. (2005). An optimal state estimation model of sensory integration in human postural balance. *J. Neural Eng., 2*, S235–S249.

Kveraga, K., Ghuman, A., & Bar, M. (2007). Top-down predictions in the cognitive brain. *Brain and Cognition, 65*, 145–168.

Kwisthout, J., & van Rooij, I. (2013). Bridging the gap between theory and practice of approximate Bayesian inference. *Cognitive Systems Research, 24*, 2–8.

Laeng, B., & Sulutvedt, U. (2014). The eye pupil adjusts to imaginary light. *Psychol. Sci., 1*, 188–197. doi:10.1177/0956797613503556. Epub 2013 Nov 27.

Land, M. (2001). Does steering a car involve perception of the velocity flow field? In J. M. Zanker & J. Zeil (Eds.), *Motion vision: Computational, neural, and ecological constraints* (pp. 227–235). Berlin: Springer Verlag.

Land, M. F., & McLeod, P. (2000). From eye movements to actions: How batsmen hit the ball. *Nature Neuroscience, 3*, 1340–1345.

Land, M. F., Mennie, N., & Rusted, J. (1999). The roles of vision and eye movements in the control of activities of daily living. *Perception, 28*, 1311–1328.

Land, M. F., & Tatler, B. W. (2009). *Looking and acting: Vision and eye movements in natural behaviour.* Oxford: Oxford University Press.

Landauer, T. K., & Dumais, S. T. (1997). A solution to Plato's problem: The Latent Semantic Analysis theory of the acquisition, induction, and representation of knowledge. *Psychological Review, 104*, 211–240.

Landauer, T. K., Foltz, P. W., & Laham, D. (1998). Introduction to Latent Semantic Analysis. *Discourse Processes, 25*, 259–284.

Landauer, T. K., McNamara, D. S., Dennis, S., & W. Kintsch (Eds.). (2007). *Handbook of latent semantic analysis.* Mahwah, NJ: Lawrence Erlbaum Associates.

Landy, D., & Goldstone, R. L. (2005). How we learn about things we don't already understand. *Journal of Experimental and Theoretical Artificial Intelligence, 17*, 343–369. doi:0.1080/09528130500283832.

Lange, C. G. (1885). *Om sindsbevaegelser: Et psyko-fysiologisk studie.* Copenhagen: Jacob Lunds.

Langner, R., Kellermann, T., Boers, F., Sturm, W., Willmes, K., & Eickhoff, S. B. (2011). Modality-specific perceptual expectations selectively modulate baseline activity in auditory, somatosensory, and visual cortices. *Cerebral Cortex, 21*(12), 2850–2862.

Lauwereyns, J. (2012). *Brain and the gaze: On the active boundaries of vision.* Cambridge, MA: MIT Press.

LeDoux, J. E. (1995). Emotion: Clues from the brain. *Annual Review of Psychology 46*, 209–235.

Lee, D., & Reddish, P. (1981). Plummeting gannets: A paradigm of ecological optics. *Nature, 293*, 293–294.

Lee, M. (2010). Emergent and structured cognition in Bayesian models: Comment on Griffiths et al. and McClelland et al. *Trends in Cognitive Sciences, 14*(8), 345–346.

Lee, R., Walker, R., Meeden, L., & Marshall, J. (2009). Category-based intrinsic motivation. In *Proceedings of the Ninth International Conference on Epigenetic Robotics.* Retrieved from http://www.cs.swarthmore.edu/~meeden/papers/meeden.epirob09.pdf.

Lee, S. H., Blake, R., & Heeger, D. J. (2005). Traveling waves of activity in primary visual cortex during binocular rivalry. *Nature Neuroscience, 8*(1), 22–23.

Lee, T. S., & Mumford, D. (2003). Hierarchical Bayesian inference in the visual cortex. *Journal of Optical Society of America, A, 20*(7), 1434–1448.

Lenggenhager, B., et al. (2007). Video ergo sum: Manipulating bodily self consciousness. *Science, 317*(5841), 1096–1099.

Leopold, D., & Logothetis, N. (1999). Multistable phenomena: Changing views in perception. *Trends in Cognitive Sciences, 3*, 254–264.

Levine, J. (1983). Materialism and qualia: The explanatory gap. *Pacific Philosophical Quarterly, 64,* 354–361.

Levy, D. L., Sereno, A. B., Gooding, D. C., & O'Driscoll, G. A. (2010). Eye tracking dysfunction in schizophrenia: Characterization and pathophysiology. *Current Topics in Behavioral Neuroscience, 4,* 311–347.

Li, Y., & Strausfeld, N. J. (1999). Multimodal efferent and recurrent neurons in the medial lobes of cockroach mushroom bodies. *J. Comp. Neurol., 409,* 603–625.

Limanowski, J., & Blankenburg, F. (2013). Minimal self-models and the free energy principle. *Frontiers in Human Neuroscience, 7,* 547. doi:10.3389/fnhum.2013.00547.

Littman, M.L., Majercik, S.M., and Pitassi, T. (2001). Stochastic boolean satisfiability. *J. Autom. Reason. 27,* 251–296.

Lotze, H. (1852). *Medicinische Psychologie oder Physiologie der Seele.* Leipzig, Germany: Weidmannsche Buchhandlung.

Lovero, K. L., et al. (2009). Anterior insular cortex anticipates impending stimulus significance. *Neuroimage, 45,* 976–983.

Lowe, R., & Ziemke, T. (2011). The feeling of action tendencies: On the emotional regulation of goal-directed behavior. *Frontiers in Psychology, 2,* 346. doi:10.3389/fpsyg.2011.00346.

Lungarella, M., & Sporns, O. (2005). Information self-structuring: Key principles for learning and development. *Proceedings 2005 IEEE Intern. Conf. Development and Learning,* 25–30.

Lupyan, G. (2012a). Linguistically modulated perception and cognition: The label feedback hypothesis. *Frontiers in Cognition, 3,* 54. doi:10.3389/fpsyg.2012.00054.

Lupyan, G. (2012b). What do words do? Towards a theory of language-augmented thought. In B. H. Ross (Ed.), *The psychology of learning and motivation,* 57 (pp. 255–297). New York: Academic Press.

Lupyan, G. (in press). Cognitive penetrability of perception in the age of prediction: Predictive systems are penetrable systems. *Review of Philosophy and Psychology.*

Lupyan, G., & Bergen, B. (in press). How language programs the mind. *Topics in Cognitive Science.*

Lupyan, G., & Clark, A. (in press). Words and the world: Predictive coding and the language-perception-cognition interface. *Current Directions in Psychological Science.*

Lupyan, G., & Thompson-Schill, S. L. (2012). The evocative power of words: Activation of concepts by verbal and nonverbal means. *Journal of Experimental Psychology-General, 141*(1), 170–186. doi:10.1037/a0024904.

Lupyan, G., & Ward, E. J. (2013). Language can boost otherwise unseen objects into visual awareness. *Proceedings of the National Academy of Sciences, 110*(35), 14196–14201. doi:10.1073/pnas.1303312110.

Ma, W. Ji (2012). Organizing probabilistic models of perception. *Trends in Cognitive Sciences, 16*(10), 511–518.

MacKay, D. (1956). The epistemological problem for automata. In C. E. Shannon & J. McCarthy (Eds.), *Automata studies* (pp. 235–251). Princeton, NJ: Princeton University Press.

MacKay, D. J. C. (1995). Free-energy minimization algorithm for decoding and cryptoanalysis. *Electron Lett.*, *31*, 445–447.

Maher, B. (1988). Anomalous experience and delusional thinking: The logic of explanations. In T. F. Oltmanns & B. A. Maher (Eds.), *Delusional beliefs* (pp. 15–33). Chichester: Wiley.

Maslach, C (1979). Negative emotional biasing of unexplained arousal. *Journal of Personality and Social Psychology* 37: 953–969. doi:10.1037/0022-3514.37.6.953.

Maloney, L. T., & Mamassian, P. (2009). Bayesian decision theory as a model of visual perception: Testing Bayesian transfer. *Visual Neuroscience*, *26*, 147–155.

Mamassian, P., Landy, M., & Maloney, L. (2002). Bayesian modeling of visual perception. In R. Rao, B. Olshausen, & M. Lewicki (Eds.), *Probabilistic models of the brain* 13-36 Cambridge, MA: MIT Press.

Mansinghka, V. K., Kemp, C., Tenenbaum, J. B., & Griffiths, T. L. (2006). Structured priors for structure learning. In *Proceedings of the 22nd Conference on Uncertainty in Artificial Intelligence (UAI)* 324–331 Arlington, VA: AUAI Press.

Marcus, G., & Davis, E. (2013). How robust are probabilistic models of higher-level cognition? *Psychol. Sci.*, *24*(12), 2351–2360. doi:10.1177/0956797613495418.

Mareschal, D., Johnson, M., Sirois, S., Spratling, M., Thomas, M., & Westermann, G. (2007). *Neuroconstructivism—I: How the brain constructs cognition*. Oxford, Oxford University Press.

Markov, N. T., Ercsey-Ravasz, M., Van Essen, D. C., Knoblauch, K., Toroczkai, Z., & Kennedy, H. (2013). Cortical high-density counterstream architectures. *Science*, *342*(6158). doi:10.1126/science.1238406.

Markov, N. T., Vezoli, J., Chameau, P., Falchier, A., Quilodran, R., Huissoud, C., Lamy, C., Misery, P., Giroud, P., Ullman, S., Barone, P., Dehay, C., Knoblauch, K., & Kennedy, H. (2014). Anatomy of hierarchy: Feedforward and feedback pathways in macaque visual cortex. *J. Comp. Neurol.*, *522*(1): 225–259.

Marshall, G. D.; Zimbardo, P.G. (1979). Affective consequences of inadequately explained physiological arousal. *Journal of Personality and Social Psychology* 37: 970–988. doi:10.1037/0022-3514.37.6.970.

Marr, D. (1982). *Vision: A computational approach*. San Francisco, CA: Freeman & Co.

Martius, G., Der, R., & Ay, N. (2013). Information driven self-organization of complex robotic behaviors. *PLoS One*, *8*(5), e63400.

Matarić, M. (1990). Navigating with a rat brain: A neurobiologically-inspired model for robot spatial representation. In J.-A. Meyer & S. Wilson (Eds.), *Proceedings, From Animals to Animats: First International Conference on Simulation of Adaptive Behavior (SAB-90)* (pp. 169–175). Cambridge, MA: MIT Press.

Matarić, M. (1992). Integration of representation into goal-driven behavior-based robots. *IEEE Transactions on Robotics and Automation*, *8*(3), 304–312.

Maturana, H. (1980). Biology of cognition. In H. Maturana, R. Humberto, & F. Varela, *Autopoiesis and cognition* (pp. 2–62). Dordrecht: Reidel.

Maturana, H., & Varela, F. (1980). *Autopoiesis and cognition: The realization of the living.* Boston, MA: Reidel.

Maxwell, J. P., Masters, R. S., & Poolton, J. M. (2006). Performance breakdown in sport: The roles of reinvestment and verbal knowledge. *Res. Q. Exerc. Sport, 77*(2), 271–276.

McBeath, M., Shaffer, D., & Kaiser, M. (1995). How baseball outfielders determine where to run to catch fly balls. *Science, 268,* 569–573.

McClelland, J. L. (2013). Integrating probabilistic models of perception and interactive neural networks: A historical and tutorial review. *Frontiers in Psychology, 4,* 503.

McClelland, J. L., Mirman, D., Bolger, D. J., & Khaitan, P. (2014). Interactive activation and mutual constraint satisfaction in perception and cognition. *Cognitive Science, 6,* 1139–1189. doi:10.1111/cogs.

McClelland, J. L., & Rumelhart, D. (1981). An interactive activation model of context effects in letter perception: Part 1. An account of basic findings. *Psychological Review, 88,* 375–407.

McClelland, J. L., Rumelhart, D., & the PDP Research Group (1986). *Parallel distributed processing* (Vol. II). Cambridge, MA: MIT Press.

McGeer, T. (1990). Passive dynamic walking. *International Journal of Robotics Research, 9*(2), 68–82.

Melloni, L., Schwiedrzik, C. M., Muller, N., Rodriguez, E., & Singer, W. (2011). Expectations change the signatures and timing of electrophysiological correlates of perceptual awareness. *Journal of Neuroscience, 31*(4), 1386–1396.

Meltzoff, A. N. (2007a). 'Like me': A foundation for social cognition. *Developmental Science, 10*(1), 126–134.

Meltzoff, A. N. (2007b). The 'like me' framework for recognizing and becoming an intentional agent. *Acta Psychologica, 124*(1), 26–43.

Meltzoff, A. N., & Moore, M. K. (1997). Explaining facial imitation: A theoretical model. *Early Development and Parenting, 6,* 179–192.

Menary, R. (Ed.). (2010). *The extended mind.* Cambridge, MA: MIT Press.

Merckelbach, H., & van de Ven, V. (2001). Another White Christmas: Fantasy proneness and reports of 'hallucinatory experiences' in undergraduate students. *Journal of Behaviour Therapy and Experimental Psychiatry, 32,* 137–144.

Merleau-Ponty, M. (1945/1962). *The phenomenology of perception.* Trans. Colin Smith. London: Routledge and Kegan Paul.

Mesulam, M. (1998). From sensation to cognition, *Brain, 121*(6), 1013–1052.

Metta, G., & Fitzpatrick, P. (2003). Early integration of vision and manipulation. *Adaptive Behavior, 11*(2), 109–128.

Miller, G. A., Galanter, E., & Pribram, K. H. (1960). *Plans and the structure of behavior.* New York: Holt, Rinehart and Winston, Inc.

Miller, L. K. (1999). The savant syndrome: Intellectual impairment and exceptional skill. *Psychol. Bull., 125,* 31–46.

Millikan, R. G. (1996). Pushmi-pullyu representations. In J. Tomberlin (Ed.), *Philosophical perspectives*, 9 (pp. 185–200). Atascadero CA: Ridgeview Publishing.

Milner, D., & Goodale, M. (1995). *The visual brain in action*. Oxford: Oxford University Press.

Milner, D., & Goodale, M. (2006). *The visual brain in action* (2nd ed.). Oxford: Oxford University Press.

Miyawaki, Y., Uchida, H., Yamashita, O., Sato, M. A., Morito, Y., Tanabe, H. C., Sadato, N., & Kamitani, Y. (2008). Visual image reconstruction from human brain activity using a combination of multiscale local image decoders. *Neuron*, 60(5), 915–929. doi:10.1016/j.neuron.2008.11.004.

Mnih, A., & Hinton, G. E. (2007). Three new graphical models for statistical language modelling. *International Conference on Machine Learning*, Corvallis, Oregon. Available at: http://www.cs.toronto.edu/~hinton/papers.html#2007.

Mohan, V., & Morasso, P. (2011). Passive motion paradigm: An alternative to optimal control. *Frontiers in Neurorobotics*, 5, 4. doi:10.3389/fnbot.2011.00004.

Mohan, V., Morasso, P., Sandini, G., & Kasderidis, S. (2013). Inference through embodied simulation in cognitive robots. *Cognitive Computation*, 5(3), 355–382.

Møller, P., & Husby, R. (2000). The initial prodrome in schizophrenia: Searching for naturalistic core dimensions of experience and behavior. *Schizophrenia Bulletin*, 26, 217–232.

Montague, P. R., Dayan, P., & Sejnowski, T. J. (1996). A framework for mesencephalic dopamine systems based on predictive Hebbian learning. *J. Neurosci.*, 16, 1936–1947.

Montague, P. R., Dolan, R. J., Friston, K., & Dayan, P. (2012). Computational psychiatry. *Trends in Cognitive Sciences*, 16(1), 72–80. doi:10.1016/j.tics.2011.11.018.

Moore, G. E. (1903/1922). The refutation of idealism. Reprinted in G. E. Moore, *Philosophical studies*. London: Routledge & Kegan Paul, 1922.

Moore, G. E. (1913/1922). The status of sense-data. *Proceedings of the Aristotelian Society*, 1913. Reprinted in G. E. Moore, *Philosophical studies*. London: Routledge & Kegan Paul, 1922.

Morrot, G., Brochet, F., & Dubourdieu, D. (2001). The color of odors. *Brain and Language*, 79, 309–320.

Mottron, L., et al. (2006). Enhanced perceptual functioning in autism: An update, and eight principles of autistic perception. *J. Autism Dev. Disord.*, 36, 27–43.

Moutoussis, M., Trujillo-Barreto, N., El-Deredy, W., Dolan, R. J., & Friston, K. (2014). A formal model of interpersonal inference. *Frontiers in Human Neuroscience*, 8, 160. doi:10.3389/fnhum.2014.00160.

Mozer, M. C., & Smolensky, P. (1990). Skeletonization: A technique for trimming the fat from a network via relevance assessment. In D. S. Touretzky & M. Kaufmann (Eds.), *Advances in neural information processing*, 1 (pp. 177–185). San Mateo, CA: Morgan Kaufmann.

Muckli, L. (2010). What are we missing here? Brain imaging evidence for higher cognitive functions in primary visual cortex v1. *Int. J. Imaging Syst. Techno. (IJIST)*, 20, 131–139.

Muckli, L., Kohler, A., Kriegeskorte, N., & Singer, W. (2005). Primary visual cortex activity along the apparent-motion trace reflects illusory perception. *PLoSBio, 13*, e265.

Mumford, D. (1992). On the computational architecture of the neocortex. II. The role of cortico-cortical loops. *Biol. Cybern., 66*, 241–251.

Mumford, D. (1994). Neuronal architectures for pattern-theoretic problems. In C. Koch & J. Davis (Eds.), *Large-scale theories of the cortex* (pp. 125–152). Cambridge, MA: MIT Press.

Murray, S. O., Boyaci, H., & Kersten, D. (2006). The representation of perceived angular size in human primary visual cortex. *Nature Reviews: Neuroscience, 9*, 429–434.

Murray, S. O., Kersten, D., Olshausen, B. A., Schrater, P., & Woods, D. L. (2002). Shape perception reduces activity in human primary visual cortex. *Proc. Natl. Acad. Sci. USA, 99*(23), 15164–15169.

Murray, S. O., Schrater, P., & Kersten, D. (2004). Perceptual grouping and the interactions between visual cortical areas. *Neural Networks, 17*(5–6), 695–705.

Musmann, H. (1979). Predictive image coding. In W. K. Pratt (Ed.), *Image transmission techniques* 73-112 New York: Academic Press.

Nagel, T. (1974). What is it like to be a bat? *Philosophical Review, 83*, 435–456.

Nakahara, K., Hayashi, T., Konishi, S., & Miyashita, Y. (2002). Functional MRI of macaque monkeys performing a cognitive set-shifting task. *Science, 295*, 1532–1536.

Namikawa, J., Nishimoto, R., & Tani, J. (2011) A neurodynamic account of spontaneous behaviour. *PLoS Comput. Biol., 7*(10), e1002221.

Namikawa, J., & Tani, J. (2010). Learning to imitate stochastic time series in a compositional way by chaos. *Neural Netw., 23*, 625–638.

Naselaris, T., Prenger, R. J., Kay, K. N., Oliver, M., & Gallant, J. L. (2009). Bayesian reconstruction of natural images from human brain activity. *Neuron, 63*(6), 902–915.

Navalpakkam, V., & Itti, L. (2005). Modeling the influence of task on attention. *Vision Research, 45*, 205–231.

Neal, R. M., & Hinton, G. (1998). A view of the EM algorithm that justifies incremental, sparse, and other variants. In M. I. Jordan (Ed.), *Learning in Graphical Models* (pp. 355–368). Dordrecht: Kluwer.

Neisser, U. (1967). *Cognitive psychology*. New York: Appleton-Century-Crofts.

Newell, A., & Simon, H. A. (1972). *Human problem solving*. Englewood Cliffs, NJ: Prentice-Hall.

Nirenberg, S., Bomash, I., Pillow, J. W., & Victor, J. D. (2010). Heterogeneous Response Dynamics in Retinal Ganglion Cells: The Interplay of Predictive Coding and Adaptation. *Journal of Neurophysiology, 103*(6), 3184–3194. doi:10.1152/jn.00878.2009.

Nkam, I., Bocca, M. L., Denise, P., Paoletti, X., Dollfus, S., Levillain, D., & Thibaut, F. (2010). Impaired smooth pursuit in schizophrenia results from prediction impairment only. *Biological Psychiatry, 67*(10), 992–997.

Noë, A. (2004). *Action in perception*. Cambridge, MA: MIT Press.

Noë, A. (2010). *Out of our heads: Why you are not your brain, and other lessons from the biology of consciousness*. New York: Farrar, Straus & Giroux.

Norman, K. A., Polyn, S. M., Detre, G. J., & Haxby, J. V. (2006). Beyond mind-reading: Multivoxel pattern analysis of fMRI data. *Trends in Cognitive Sciences, 10*, 424–430.

Núñez, R., & Freeman, W. J. (Eds.). (1999). *Reclaiming cognition: The primacy of action, intention and emotion*. Bowling Green, OH: Imprint Academic; NY: Houghton-Mifflin.

O'Connor, D. H., Fukui, M. M., Pinsk, M. A., & Kastner, S. (2002). Attention modulates responses in the human lateral geniculate nucleus. *Nature Neurosci., 5*, 1203–1209.

O'Craven, K. M., Rosen, B. R., Kwong, K. K., Treisman, A., & Savoy, R. L. (1997). Voluntary attention modulates fMRI activity in human MT-MST. *Neuron, 18*, 591–598.

O'Regan, J. K., & Noë, A. (2001). A sensorimotor approach to vision and visual consciousness. *Behavioral and Brain Sciences, 24*(5), 883–975.

O'Reilly, R. C., Wyatte, D., & Rohrlich, J. (ms). Learning through time in the thalamocortical loops. Preprint avail at: http://arxiv.org/abs/1407.3432.

O'Sullivan, I., Burdet, E., & Diedrichsen, J. (2009). Dissociating variability and effort as determinants of coordination. *PLoS Comput Biol., 5*, e1000345. doi:10.1371/journal.pcbi.1000345.

Ogata, T., Yokoya, R., Tani, J., Komatani, K., & Okuno, H. G. (2009). Prediction and imitation of other's motions by reusing own forward-inverse model in robots. *ICRA '09. IEEE International Conference on Robotics and Automation*, 4144–4149.

Okuda, J., et al. (2003). Thinking of the future and past: The roles of the frontal pole and the medial temporal lobes. *Neuroimage, 19*, 1369–1380. doi:10.1016/S1053-8119(03)00179-4.

Olshausen, B. A., & Field, D. J. (1996). Emergence of simple-cell receptive field properties by learning a sparse code for natural images. *Nature, 381*, 607–609.

Orlandi, N. (2013). *The innocent eye: Why vision is not a cognitive process*. New York: Oxford University Press.

Oudeyer, P.-Y., Kaplan, F., & Hafner, V. (2007). Intrinsic motivation systems for autonomous mental development. *IEEE Transactions on Evolutionary Computation, 11*(2), 265–286.

Oyama, S. (1999). *Evolution's eye: Biology, culture and developmental systems*. Durham, NC: Duke University Press.

Oyama, S., Griffiths, P. E., & Gray, R. D. (Eds.). (2001). *Cycles of contingency: Developmental systems and evolution*. Cambridge, MA: MIT Press.

Oztop, E., Kawato, M., & Arbib, M. A. (2013). Mirror neurons: Functions, mechanisms and models. *Neuroscience Letters, 540*, 43–55.

Panichello, M., Cheung, O., & Bar, M. (2012). Predictive feedback and conscious visual experience. *Frontiers in Psychology, 3*, 620. doi:10.3389/fpsyg.2012.00620.

Pariser, E. (2011). *The filter bubble: What the internet is hiding from you.* New York: Penguin Press.

Park, H. J., & Friston, K. (2013). Structural and functional brain networks: From connections to cognition. *Science, 342,* 579–588.

Park, J. C., Lim, J. H., Choi, H., & Kim, D. S. (2012). Predictive coding strategies for developmental neurorobotics. *Front Psychol., 7*(3), 134. doi:10.3389/fpsyg.2012.00134.

Parr, W. V., White, K. G., & Heatherbell, D. (2003). The nose knows: Influence of colour on perception of wine aroma. *Journal of Wine Research, 14,* 79–101.

Pascual-Leone, A., & Hamilton, R. (2001). The metamodal organization of the brain. *Progress in Brain Research, 134,* 427–445.

Paton, B., Skewes, J., Frith, C., & Hohwy, J. (2013). Skull-bound perception and precision optimization through culture. *Behavioral and Brain Sciences, 36*(3), p. 222.

Paulesu, E., McCrory, E., Fazio, F., Menoncello, L., Brunswick, N., Cappa, S. F., et al. (2000). A cultural effect on brain function. *Nat. Neurosci., 3*(1), 91–96.

Pearle, J (1988) *Probabilistic Reasoning in Intelligent Systems,* Morgan-Kaufmann

Peelen, M. V. M., & Kastner, S. S. (2011). A neural basis for real-world visual search in human occipitotemporal cortex. *Proc. Natl. Acad. Sci. USA, 108,* 12125–12130.

Pellicano, E., & Burr, D. (2012). When the world becomes too real: A Bayesian explanation of autistic perception. *Trends in Cognitive Sciences, 16,* 504–510. doi:10.1016/j.tics.2012.08.009.

Penny, W. (2012). Bayesian models of brain and behaviour. *ISRN Biomathematics,* 1–19. doi:10.5402/2012/785791.

Perfors, A., Tenenbaum, J. B., & Regier, T. (2006). Poverty of the stimulus? A rational approach. In *Proceedings of the 28th Annual Conference of the Cognitive Science Society* 663-668 Mahwah, NJ: Lawrence Erlbaum Assoc.

Pezzulo, G. (2007). Anticipation and future-oriented capabilities in natural and artificial cognition. In *50 Years of AI, Festschrift, LNAI,* Berlin: Springer pp. 258–271.

Pezzulo, G. (2008). Coordinating with the future: The anticipatory nature of representation. *Minds and Machines, 18,* 179–225.

Pezzulo, G. (2012). An active inference view of cognitive control. *Frontiers in Theoretical and Philosophical Psychology.* 3: 478–479. doi: 10.3389/fpsyg.2012.00478.

Pezzulo, G. (2013). Why do you fear the Bogeyman? An embodied predictive coding model of perceptual inference. *Cognitive, Affective, and Behavioral Neuroscience, 14*(3), 902–911.

Pezzulo, G., Barsalou, L., Cangelosi, A., Fischer, M., McRae, K., & Spivey, M. (2013). Computational grounded cognition: A new alliance between grounded cognition and computational modeling. *Front. Psychology, 3,* 612. doi:10.3389/fpsyg.2012.00612.

Pezzulo, G., Rigoli, F., & Chersi F. (2013). The mixed instrumental controller: Using value of information to combine habitual choice and mental simulation. *Frontiers in Psychology*, 4, 92. doi:10.3389/fpsyg.2013.00092.

Pfeifer, R., & Bongard, J. (2006). *How the body shapes the way we think: A new view of intelligence.* Cambridge, MA: MIT Press.

Pfeifer, R., Lungarella, M., Sporns, O., & Kuniyoshi, Y. (2007). On the information theoretic implications of embodiment: Principles and methods. In *Lecture Notes in Computer Science (LNCS)*, 4850 (pp. 76–86). Berlin: Heidelberg: Springer.

Pfeifer, R., & Scheier, C. (1999). *Understanding intelligence.* Cambridge, MA: MIT Press.

Philippides, A., Husbands, P., & O'Shea, M. (2000). Four-dimensional neuronal signaling by nitric oxide: A computational analysis. *J. Neurosci., 20,* 1199–1207.

Philippides, A., Husbands, P., Smith, T., & O'Shea, M. (2005). Flexible couplings: Diffusing neuromodulators and adaptive robotics. *Artificial Life, 11,* 139–160.

Phillips, M. L., et al. (2001). Depersonalization disorder: Thinking without feeling. *Psychiatry Res., 108,* 145–160.

Phillips W. A. & Singer W. (1997) In search of common foundations for cortical computation. *Behavioral and Brain Sciences* 20, 657–722.

Phillips, W., Clark, A., & Silverstein, S. M. (2015). On the functions, mechanisms, and malfunctions of intracortical contextual modulation. *Neuroscience and Biobehavioral Reviews* 52, 1–20.

Phillips, W., & Silverstein, S. (2013). The coherent organization of mental life depends on mechanisms for context-sensitive gain-control that are impaired in schizophrenia. *Frontiers in Psychology*, 4, 307. doi:10.3389/fpsyg.2013.00307.

Piaget, J. (1952). *The origins of intelligence in children.* New York: I. U. Press, Ed.

Pickering, M. J., & Clark, A. (2014). Getting ahead: Forward models and their place in cognitive architecture. *Trends in Cognitive Sciences, 18*(9), 451–456.

Pickering, M. J., & Garrod, S. (2007). Do people use language production to make predictions during comprehension? *Trends in Cognitive Sciences, 11*(3), 105–110.

Pickering, M. J., & Garrod, S. (2013). An integrated theory of language production and comprehension. *Behavioral and Brain Sciences, 36*(04), 329–347.

Pinker, S. (1997). *How the mind works.* London: Allen Lane.

Plaisted, K. (2001). Reduced generalization in autism: An alternative to weak central coherence. In J. Burack et al. (Eds.), *The development of autism: Perspectives from theory and research* (pp. 149–169). NJ Erlbaum.

Plaisted, K., et al. (1998a). Enhanced visual search for a conjunctive target in autism: A research note. *J. Child Psychol. Psychiatry, 39,* 777–783.

Plaisted, K., et al. (1998b). Enhanced discrimination of novel, highly similar stimuli by adults with autism during a perceptual learning task. *J. Child Psychol. Psychiatry, 39,* 765–775.

Ploner, M., & Tracey, I. (2011). The effect of treatment expectation on drug efficacy: Imaging the analgesic benefit of the opioid remifentanil. *Sci. Transl. Med.*, *3*, 70ra14.

Poeppel, D., & Monahan, P. J. (2011). Feedforward and feedback in speech perception: Revisiting analysis by synthesis. *Language and Cognitive Processes*, *26*(7), 935–951.

Polich, J. (2003). Overview of P3a and P3b. In J. Polich (Ed.), *Detection of change: Event-related potential and fMRI findings* (pp. 83–98). Boston: Kluwer Academic Press.

Polich, J. (2007). Updating P300: An integrative theory of P3a and P3b. *Clinical Neurophysiology*, *118*(10), 2128–2148.

Popper, K. (1963). *Conjectures and refutations: The growth of scientific knowledge.* London: Routledge.

Posner, M. (1980). Orienting of attention. *Quarterly Journal of Experimental Psychology*, *32*(1), 3–25.

Potter, M. C., Wyble, B., Hagmann, C. E., & Mccourt, E. S. (2013). Detecting meaning in RSVP at 13 ms per picture. *Attention, Perception, & Psychophysics*, 1–10.

Pouget, A., Beck, J., Ma, Wei J., & Latham, P. (2013). Probabilistic brains: Knowns and unknowns. *Nature Neuroscience*, *16*(9), 1170–1178. doi:10.1038/nn.3495.

Pouget, A., Dayan, P., & Zemel, R. (2003). Inference and computation with population codes. *Annual Review of Neuroscience*, *26*, 381–410.

Powell, K. D., & Goldberg, M. E. (2000). Response of neurons in the lateral intraparietal area to a distractor flashed during the delay period of a memory-guided saccade. *J. Neurophysiol.*, *84*(1), 301–310.

Press, C., Richardson, D., & Bird, G. (2010). Intact imitation of emotional facial actions in autism spectrum conditions. *Neuropsychologia*, *48*, 3291–3297.

Press, C. M., Heyes, C. M., & Kilner, J. M (2011). Learning to understand others' actions. *Biology Letters*, *7*(3), 457–460. doi:10.1098/rsbl.2010.0850.

Pribram, K. H. (1980). The orienting reaction: Key to brain representational mechanisms. In H. D. Kimme (Ed.), *The orienting reflex in humans* (pp. 3–20). Hillsdale, NJ: Lawrence Erlbaum Assoc.

Price, C. J., & Devlin, J. T. (2011). The interactive account of ventral occipito-temporal contributions to reading. *Trends in Cognitive Neuroscience*, *15*(6), 246–253.

Price, D. D., Finniss, D. G., & Benedetti, F. (2008). A comprehensive review of the placebo effect: Recent advances and current thought. *Annu. Rev. Psychol.*, *59*, 565–590.

Prinz, J. (2004). *Gut reactions.* New York: Oxford University Press.

Prinz, J. (2005). A neurofunctional theory of consciousness. In A. Brook & K. Akins (Eds.), *Cognition and the brain: Philosophy and neuroscience movement* (pp. 381–396). Cambridge: Cambridge University Press.

Purves, D., Shimpi, A., & Lotto, R. B. (1999). An empirical explanation of the Cornsweet effect. *Journal of Neuroscience*, *19*(19), 8542–8551.

Pylyshyn, Z. (1999). Is vision continuous with cognition? The case for cognitive impenetrability of visual perception. *Behavioral and Brain Sciences*, 22(3), 341–365.

Quine, W. V. O. (1988). On what there is. In *From a Logical Point of View: Nine Logico-Philosophical Essays* (pp. 1–20). Cambridge, MA: Harvard University Press.

Raichle M. E. (2009). A brief history of human brain mapping. *Trends Neurosci.* 32:118–126.

Raichle, M. E. (2010). Two views of brain function. *Trends in Cognitive Sciences*, 14(4), 180–190.

Raichle, M. E., MacLeod, A. M., Snyder, A. Z., Powers, W. J., Gusnard, D. A., & Shulman, G. L. (2001). A default mode of brain function. *Proc. Natl. Acad. Sci. USA*, 98, 676–682.

Raichle, M. E., & Snyder, A. Z. (2007). A default mode of brain function: A brief history of an evolving idea. *Neuroimage*, 37, 1083–1090.

Raij, T., McEvoy, L., Mäkelä, J. P., & Hari, R. (1997). Human auditory cortex is activated by omissions of auditory stimuli. *Brain Res.*, 745, 134–143.

Ramachandran, V. S., & Blakeslee, S. (1998). *Phantoms in the brain: Probing the mysteries of the human mind*. New York: Morrow & Co.

Ramsey, W. M. (2007). *Representation reconsidered*. Cambridge: Cambridge University.

Rao, R., & Ballard, D. (1999). Predictive coding in the visual cortex: A functional interpretation of some extra-classical receptive-field effects. *Nature Neuroscience*, 2(1), 79.

Rao, R., & Sejnowski, T. (2002). Predictive coding, cortical feedback, and spike-timing dependent cortical plasticity. In Rao, R. P. N., Olshausen, B. and Lewicki, M. (Eds.), *Probabilistic Models of the Brain* (pp. 297–316). Cambridge, MA: MIT Press.

Rao, R., Shon, A., & Meltzoff, A. (2007). A Bayesian model of imitation in infants and robots. In C. L. Nehaniv & K. Dautenhahn (Eds.), *Imitation and social learning in robots, humans, and animals: Behavioural, social and communicative dimensions* (pp. 217–247). New York: Cambridge University Press.

Reddy, L., Tsuchiya, N., & Serre, T. (2010). Reading the mind's eye: Decoding category information during mental imagery. *NeuroImage*, 50(2), 818–825.

Reich, L., Szwed, M., Cohen, L., & Amedi, A. (2011). A ventral stream reading center independent of visual experience. *Current Biology*, 21, 363–368.

Remez, R. E., & Rubin, P. E. (1984). On the perception of intonation from sinusoidal sentences. *Perception & Psychophysics*, 35, 429–440.

Remez, R. E., Rubin, P. E., Pisoni, D. B., & Carrell, T. D. (1981). Speech perception without traditional speech cues. *Science*, 212, 947–949.

Rescorla, M. (2013). Bayesian perceptual psychology. In M. Matthen (Ed.), *Oxford Handbook of the Philosophy of Perception*. Oxford University Press, NY.

Rescorla, M. (in press). Bayesian sensorimotor psychology. *Mind and Language*.

Reynolds, J. H., Chelazzi, L., & Desimone, R. (1999). Competitive mechanisms subserve attention in macaque areas V2 and V4. *Journal of Neuroscience, 19*, 1736–1753.

Rieke, F., Warland, D., de Ruyter van Stevenick, R., & Bialek, W. (1997). *Spikes: Exploring the neural code.* Cambridge, MA: MIT Press.

Riesenhuber, M., & Poggio, T. (1999). Hierarchical models of object recognition in cortex. *Nat. Neurosci., 2*, 1019–1025.

Rizzolatti, G., Fadiga, L., Fogassi, L., & Gallese, V. (1996). Premotor cortex and the recognition of motor actions. *Brain Res. Cogn. Brain Res., 3*, 131–141.

Rizzolatti, G., Fogassi, L., & Gallese, V. (2001). Neurophysiological mechanisms underlying the understanding and imitation of action. *Nat. Rev. Neurosci., 2*, 661–670.

Rizzolatti, G., & Sinigaglia, C. (2007). Mirror neurons and motor intentionality. *Functional Neurology, 22*(4), 205–210.

Rizzolatti, G., et al. (1988). Functional organization of inferior area 6 in the macaque monkey: II. Area F5 and the control of distal movements. *Exp. Brain Res., 71*, 491–507.

Robbins, H. (1956). An empirical Bayes approach to statistics. *Proceedings of the Third Berkeley Symposium on Mathematical Statistics and Probability*, Vol. 1: *Contributions to the Theory of Statistics*, 157–163.

Robbins, J. M., & Kirmayer, L. J. (1991). Cognitive and social factors in somatisation. In L. J. Kirmayer & J. M. Robbins (Eds.), *Current concepts of somatisation: Research and clinical perspectives* (pp. 107–141). Washington, DC: American Psychiatric Press.

Roberts, A., Robbins, T., & Weiskrantz, L. (1998). *The prefrontal cortex: Executive and cognitive functions.* New York: Oxford University Press.

Rock, I. (1997). *Indirect perception.* Cambridge, MA: MIT Press.

Roepstorff, A. (2013). Interactively human: Sharing time, constructing materiality. *Behavioral and Brain Sciences, 36*, 224–225. doi:10.1017/S0140525X12002427.

Roepstorff, A., & Frith, C. (2004). What's at the top in the top-down control of action? Script-sharing and 'top-top' control of action in cognitive experiments. *Psychological Research, 68*(2–3), 189–198. doi:10.1007/s00426003-0155-4.

Roepstorff, A, Niewöhner, J, & Beck, S. (2010). Enculturating brains through patterned practices. *Neural Networks, 23*, 1051–1059.

Romo, R., Hernandez, A., & Zainos, A. (2004). Neuronal correlates of a perceptual decision in ventral premotor cortex. *Neuron, 41*(1), 165–173.

Rorty, R. (1979). *Philosophy and the mirror of nature.* Princeton, NJ: Princeton University Press.

Ross, D. (2004). Meta-linguistic signalling for coordination amongst social agents. *Language Sciences, 26*, 621–642.

Roth, M., Synofzik, M., & Lindner, A. (2013). The cerebellum optimizes perceptual predictions about external sensory events. *Current Biology, 23*(10), 930–935. doi:10.1016/j.cub.2013.04.027.

Rothkopf, C. A., Ballard, D. H., & Hayhoe, M. M. (2007). Task and context determine where you look. *Journal of Vision, 7*(14):16, 1–20.

Rumelhart, D., McClelland, J., & the PDP Research Group (1986). *Parallel Distributed Processing* (Vol. 1). Cambridge, MA: MIT Press.

Rumelhart, D. E., Hinton, G. E., & Williams, R. J. (1986a). Learning internal representations by error propagation. In D. E. Rumelhart, J. L. McClelland, & the PDP Research Group (Eds.), *Parallel distributed processing: Explorations in the microstructure of cognition*, Vol. 1: *Foundations* (pp. 318–362). Cambridge, MA: MIT Press.

Rumelhart, D. E., Hinton, G. E., & Williams, R. J. (1986b). Learning representations by back-propagating errors. *Nature, 323,* 533–536.

Rupert, R. (2004). Challenges to the hypothesis of extended cognition. *Journal of Philosophy, 101*(8), 389–428.

Rupert, R. (2009). *Cognitive systems and the extended mind.* New York: Oxford University Press.

Sachs, E. (1967). Dissociation of learning in rats and its similarities to dissociative states in man. In J. Zubin & H. Hunt (Eds.), *Comparative psychopathology: Animal and human* (pp. 249–304). New York: Grune and Stratton.

Sadaghiani, S., Hesselmann, G., Friston, K. J., & Kleinschmidt, A. (2010). The relation of ongoing brain activity, evoked neural responses, and cognition. *Frontiers in Systems Neuroscience, 4,* 20.

Saegusa, R., Sakka, S., Metta, G., & Sandini, G. (2008). Sensory prediction learning: How to model the self and environment. *12th IMEKO TC1-TC7 Joint Symposium on Man Science and Measurement (IMEKO2008)*, Annecy, France, 269–275.

Salakhutdinov, R., & Hinton, G. (2009). Deep Boltzmann machines. *Proceedings of the 12th International Conference on Artificial Intelligence and Statistics (AISTATS), 5,* 448–455.

Salakhutdinov, R. R., Mnih, A., & Hinton, G. E. (2007). Restricted Boltzmann machines for collaborative filtering. *International Conference on Machine Learning*, Corvallis, Oregon. Available at: http://www.cs.toronto.edu/~hinton/papers.html#2007.

Salge, C., Glackin, C., & Polani, D. (2014). Changing the environment based on empowerment as intrinsic motivation. *Entropy, 16*(5), 2789–2819. doi:10.3390/e16052789.

Satz, D., & Ferejohn, J. (1994). Rational choice and social theory source. *Journal of Philosophy, 91*(2), 71–87.

Sawtell, N. B., Williams, A., & Bell, C. C. (2005). From sparks to spikes: Information processing in the electrosensory systems of fish. *Current Opinion in Neurobiology, 15,* 437–443.

Schachter, S., & Singer, J. (1962). Cognitive, social, and physiological determinants of emotional state. *Psychological Review, 69,* 379–399.

Schacter, D. L., & Addis, D. R. (2007a). The ghosts of past and future. *Nature, 445,* 27. doi:10.1038/445027a.

Schacter, D. L., & Addis, D. R. (2007b). The cognitive neuroscience of constructive memory: Remembering the past and imagining the future. *Philosophical Transactions of the Royal Society of London, Series B, 362,* 773–786.

Schacter, D. L., Addis, D. R., & Buckner, R. L. (2007). The prospective brain: Remembering the past to imagine the future. *Nature Reviews Neuroscience, 8*, 657–661.

Schenk, L. A., Sprenger, C., Geuter, S., & Büchel, C. (2014). Expectation requires treatment to boost pain relief: An fMRI study. *Pain, 155*, 150–157.

Schenk, T., & McIntosh, R. D. (2010). Do we have independent visual streams for perception and action? *Cognitive Neuroscience, 1*(1), 52–62. doi:10.1080/17588920903388950. ISSN 1758-8928.

Scholl, B. (2005). Innateness and (Bayesian) visual perception: Reconciling nativism and development. In P. Carruthers, S. Laurence & S. Stich (Eds.), *The innate mind: Structure and contents* (pp. 34–52). New York: Oxford University Press.

Schultz, W. (1999). The reward signal of midbrain dopamine neurons. *Physiology, 14*(6), 249–255.

Schultz, W., Dayan, P., & Montague, P. R. (1997). A neural substrate of prediction and reward. *Science, 275*, 1593–1599.

Schütz, A. C., Braun, D. I., & Gegenfurtner, K. (2011). Eye movements and perception: A selective review. *Journal of Vision, 11*(5), 1–30. doi:10.1167/11.5.9.

Schwartenbeck, P., Fitzgerald, T., Dolan, R. J., & Friston, K. (2013). Exploration, novelty, surprise, and free energy minimization. *Frontiers in Psychology, 4*, 710. doi:10.3389/fpsyg.2013.00710.

Schwartenbeck, P., FitzGerald, T. H. B., Mathys, C., Dolan, R., & Friston, K. (2014). The dopaminergic midbrain encodes the expected certainty about desired outcomes. *Cerebral Cortex*, bhu159. doi: 10.1093/cercor/bhu159

Schwartz, J., Grimault, N., Hupé, J., Moore, B., & Pressnitzer, D. (2012). Introduction: Multistability in perception: Binding sensory modalities, an overview. *Phil. Trans. R. Soc. B., 367*, 896–905. doi:10.1098/rstb.2011.0254.

Seamans, J. K., & Yang, C. R. (2004). The principal features and mechanisms of dopamine modulation in the prefrontal cortex. *Prog. Neurobiol., 74*(1), 1–58.

Sebanz, N., & Knoblich, G. (2009). Prediction in joint action: What, when, and where. *Topics in Cognitive Science, 1*, 353–367.

Sedley, W., & Cunningham, M. (2013). Do cortical gamma oscillations promote or suppress perception? An under-asked question with an over-assumed answer. *Frontiers in Human Neuroscience, 7*, 595.

Selen, L. P. J., Shadlen, M. N., & Wolpert, D. M. (2012). Deliberation in the motor system: Reflex gains track evolving evidence leading to a decision. *Journal of Neuroscience, 32*(7), 2276–2286.

Seligman, M., Railton, P., Baumeister, R., & Sripada, C. (2013). Navigating into the future or driven by the past. *Perspectives on Psychological Science, 8*, 119–141.

Serre, T., Oliva, A., & Poggio, T. (2007). A feedforward architecture accounts for rapid categorization. *Proc. Natl. Acad. Sci. USA, 104*(15), 6424–6429.

Seth, A. K. (2013). Interoceptive inference, emotion, and the embodied self. *Trends in Cognitive Sciences, 17*(11), 565–573. doi:10.1016/j.tics.2013.09.007.

Seth, A. K. (2014). A predictive processing theory of sensorimotor contingencies: Explaining the puzzle of perceptual presence and its absence in synaesthesia. *Cogn. Neurosci., 5*(2), 97–118. doi:10.1080/17588928.2013.877880.

Seth, A. K., Suzuki, K., & Critchley, H. D. (2011). An interoceptive predictive coding model of conscious presence. *Frontiers in Psychology, 2,* 395. doi:10.3389/fpsyg.2011.00395.

Seymour, B., et al. (2004). Temporal difference models describe higher order learning in humans. *Nature, 429,* 664–667.

Sforza, A., et al. (2010). My face in yours: Visuo-tactile facial stimulation influences sense of identity. *Soc. Neurosci., 5,* 148–162.

Shaffer, D. M., Krauchunas, S. M., Eddy, M., & McBeath, M. K. (2004). How dogs navigate to catch Frisbees. *Psychological Science, 15,* 437– 441.

Shafir, E., & Tversky, A. (1995). Decision making. In E. E. Smith & D. N. Osherson (Eds.), *Thinking: An invitation to cognitive science* (pp. 77–100). Cambridge, MA: MIT Press.

Shah, A., & Frith, U. (1983). An islet of ability in autistic children: A research note. *J. Child Psychol. Psychiatry, 24,* 613–620.

Shams, L., Ma, W. J., & Beierholm, U. (2005). Sound-induced flash illusion as an optimal percept. *Neuroreport, 16*(10), 1107–1110.

Shani, I. (2006). Intentional directedness. *Cybernetics & Human Knowing, 13,* 87–110.

Shankar, M. U., Levitan, C., & Spence, C. (2010). Grape expectations: The role of cognitive influences in color–flavor interactions. *Consciousness & Cognition, 19,* 380–390.

Shea, N. (2013). Perception versus action: The computations may be the same but the direction of fit differs. *Behavioral and Brain Sciences, 36*(3), 228–229.

Shergill, S., Bays, P. M., Frith, C. D., & Wolpert, D. M. (2003). Two eyes for an eye: The neuroscience of force escalation. *Science, 301*(5630), 187.

Shergill, S., Samson, G., Bays, P. M., Frith, C. D., & Wolpert, D. M. (2005). Evidence for sensory prediction deficits in schizophrenia. *American Journal of Psychiatry, 162*(12), 2384–2386.

Sherman, S. M., & Guillery, R. W. (1998). On the actions that one nerve cell can have on another: Distinguishing 'drivers' from 'modulators'. *Proc. Natl. Acad. Sci. USA, 95,* 7121–7126.

Shi, Yun Q., & Sun, H. (1999). *Image and video compression for multimedia engineering: Fundamentals, algorithms, and standards.* Boca Raton CRC Press.

Shipp, S. (2005). The importance of being agranular: A comparative account of visual and motor cortex. *Phil. Trans. R. Soc. B, 360,* 797–814. doi:10.1098/rstb.2005.1630.

Shipp, S., Adams, R. A., & Friston, K. J. (2013). Reflections on agranular architecture: Predictive coding in the motor cortex. *Trends Neurosci., 36,* 706–716. doi:10.1016/j.tins.2013.09.004.

Siegel, J. (2003). Why we sleep. *Scientific American,* November, pp. 92–97.

Siegel, S. (2006). Direct realism and perceptual consciousness. *Philosophy and Phenomenological Research, 73*(2), 379–409.

Siegel, S. (2012). Cognitive penetrability and perceptual justification. *Nous,* *46*(2), 201–222.

Sierra, M., & David, A. S. (2011). Depersonalization: A selective impairment of self-awareness. *Conscious. Cogn., 20,* 99–108.

Simon, H. A. (1956). Rational choice and the structure of the environment. *Psychological Review, 63*(2), 129–138.

Skewes, J. C., Jegindø, E.-M., & Gebauer, L. (2014). Perceptual inference and autistic traits. *Autism* [Epub ahead of print]. 10.1177/1362361313519872.

Sloman, A. (2013). What else can brains do? *Behavioral and Brain Sciences, 36,* 230–231. doi:10.1017/S0140525X12002439.

Smith, A. D. (2002). *The problem of perception* Cambridge, MA: Harvard University Press.

Smith, F., & Muckli, L. (2010). Nonstimulated early visual areas carry information about surrounding context. *Proceedings of the National Academy of Science (PNAS), 107*(46), 20099–20103.

Smith, L., & Gasser, M. (2005). The development of embodied cognition: Six lesson from babies. *Artificial Life, 11*(1), 13–30.

Smith, P. L., & Ratcliff, R. (2004). Psychology and neurobiology of simple decisions. *Trends in Neuroscience, 27,* 161–168.

Smith, S.M., Vidaurre, D., Beckmann, C.F, Glasser, M.F., Jenkinson, M., Miller, K.L., Nichols, T., Robinson, E., Salimi-Khorshidi, G., Woolrich M.W., Ugurbil, K. & Van Essen D.C. (2013). Functional connectomics from resting-state fMRI. *Trends in Cognitive Sciences.* 17(12), 666-682.

Smolensky, P. (1988). On the proper treatment of connectionism. *Behavioral and Brain Sciences, 11,* 1–23.

Smolensky, P., & Legendre, G. (2006). *The harmonic mind: From neural computation to optimality-theoretic grammar,* Vol. 1: *Cognitive architecture,* Vol. 2: *Linguistic and philosophical implications.* Cambridge, MA: MIT Press.

Sokolov, E. N. (1960). Neuronal models and the orienting reflex. In M. A. B. Brazier (Ed.), *The central nervous system and behavior* (pp. 187–276). New York: Josiah Macy, Jr. Foundation.

Solway, A., & Botvinick, M. M. (2012). Goal-directed decision making as probabilistic inference: A computational framework and potential neural correlates. *Psychological Review, 119*(1), 120–154. doi: 10.1037/a0026435.

Sommer, M. A., & Wurtz, R. H. (2006). Influence of thalamus on spatial visual processing in frontal cortex. *Nature, 444,* 374–377.

Sommer, M. A., & Wurtz, R. H. (2008). Brain circuits for the internal monitoring of movements. *Annual Review of Neuroscience, 31,* 317–338.

Spelke, E. S. (1990). Principles of object perception. *Cognitive Science, 14,* 29–56.

Spence, C., & Shankar, M. U. (2010). The influence of auditory cues on the perception of, and responses to, food and drink. *Journal of Sensory Studies, 25,* 406–430.

Sperry, R. (1950). Neural basis of the spontaneous optokinetic response produced by visual inversion. *J. Comp. Physiol. Psychol., 43*(6), 482–489.

Spivey, M. J. (2007). *The continuity of mind.* New York: Oxford University Press.

Spivey, M. J., Grosjean, M., & Knoblich, G. (2005). Continuous attraction toward phonological competitors. *Proceedings of the National Academy of Sciences*, *102*, 10393–10398.

Spivey, M. J., Richardson, D., & Dale, R. (2008). Movements of eye and hand in language and cognition. In E. Morsella & J. Bargh (Eds.), *The psychology of action* (pp. 225–249). New York: Oxford University Press.

Spivey, M., Richardson, D., & Fitneva, S. (2005). Thinking outside the brain: Spatial indices to linguistic and visual information. In J. Henderson & F. Ferreira (Eds.), *The interface of vision language and action* (pp.161–190). New York: Psychology Press.

Sporns, O. (2002). Network analysis, complexity and brain function. *Complexity*, *8*, 56–60.

Sporns, O. (2007). What neuro-robotic models can teach us about neural and cognitive development. In D. Mareschal, S. Sirois, G. Westermann, & M. H. Johnson (Eds.), *Neuroconstructivism: Perspectives and prospects*, Vol. 2 (pp. 179–204). Oxford: Oxford University Press.

Sporns, O. (2010). *Networks of the brain*. Cambridge, MA: MIT Press.

Sprague, N., Ballard, D. H., & Robinson, A. (2007). Modeling embodied visual behaviors. *ACM Transactions on Applied Perception*, *4*, 11.

Spratling, M. (2008). Predictive coding as a model of biased competition in visual attention. *Vision Research*, *48*(12), 1391–1408.

Spratling, M. (2010). Predictive coding as a model of response properties in cortical area V1. *Journal of Neuroscience*, *30*(9), 3531–3543.

Spratling, M. (2012). Unsupervised learning of generative and discriminative weights encoding elementary image components in a predictive coding model of cortical function. *Neural Computation*, *24*(1), 60–103.

Spratling, M. (2013). Distinguishing theory from implementation in predictive coding accounts of brain function [commentary on Clark]. *Behavioral and Brain Sciences*, *36*(3), 231–232.

Spratling, M. (2014). A single functional model of drivers and modulators in cortex. *Journal of Computational Neuroscience*, *36*(1), 97–118.

Spratling, M., & Johnson, M. (2006). A feedback model of perceptual learning and categorization. *Visual Cognition*, *13*(2), 129–165.

Sprevak, M. (2010). Computation, individuation, and the received view on representation. *Studies in History and Philosophy of Science*, *41*, 260–270.

Sprevak, M. (2013). Fictionalism about neural representations. *The Monist*, *96*, 539–560.

Stafford, T., & Webb, M. (2005). *Mind hacks*. CA: O'Reilly Media.

Stanovich, K. E. (2011). *Rationality and the reflective mind*. New York: Oxford University Press.

Stanovich, K. E., & West, R. F. (2000). Individual differences in reasoning: Implications for the rationality debate. *Behavioral and Brain Sciences*, *23*, 645–665.

Stein, J. F. (1992). The representation of egocentric space in the posterior parietal cortex. *Behav. Brain Sci.*, *15*, 691–700.

Stephan, K. E., Harrison, L. M., Kiebel, S. J., David, O., Penny, W. D., & Friston, K. J. (2007). Dynamic causal models of neural system dynamics: Current state and future extensions. *J. Biosci., 32,* 129–144.

Stephan, K. E., Kasper, L., Harrison, L. M., Daunizeau, J., den Ouden, H. E., Breakspear, M., & Friston, K. J. (2008). Nonlinear dynamic causal models for fMRI. *Neuroimage, 42,* 649–662.

Stephan, K. E., Penny, W. D., Daunizeau, J., Moran, R. J., and Friston, K. J. (2009). Bayesianmodelselectionforgroupstudies. *Neuroimage 46,* 1004–1017. doi: 10.1016/j.neuroimage.2009.03.025.

Sterelny, K. (2003). *Thought in a hostile world: The evolution of human cognition.* Oxford: Blackwell.

Stewart, J., Gapenne, O., & Di Paolo, E. A. (Eds.). (2010). *Enaction: Towards a new paradigm for cognitive science.* Cambridge, MA: MIT Press.

Stigler, J., Chalip, L., & Miller, F. (1986). Consequences of skill: The case of abacus training in Taiwan. *American Journal of Education,* 94(4), 447–479.

Stokes, M., Thompson, R., Cusack, R., & Duncan, J. (2009). Top–down activation of shape specific population codes in visual cortex during mental imagery. *J. Neurosci., 29,* 1565–1572.

Stone, J., Warlow, C., Carson, A., & Sharpe, M. (2005). Eliot Slater's myth of the non-existence of hysteria. *J. R. Soc. Med., 98,* 547–548.

Stone, J., Warlow, C., & Sharpe, M. (2012a). Functional weakness: Clues to mechanism from the nature of onset. *J. Neurol. Neurosurg. Psychiatry, 83,* 67–69.

Stone, J., Wojcik, W., Durrance, D., Carson, A., Lewis, S., MacKenzie, L., et al. (2002). What should we say to patients with symptoms unexplained by disease? The 'number needed to offend'. *BMJ, 325,* 1449–1450.

Stotz, K. (2010). Human nature and cognitive–developmental niche construction. *Phenomenology and the Cognitive Sciences,* 9(4), 483–501.

Suddendorf, T., & Corballis, M. C. (1997). Mental time travel and the evolution of the human mind. *Genet. Soc. Gen. Psychol. Monogr.* 123, 133–167.

Suddendorf, T., & Corballis, M. C. (2007). The evolution of foresight: What is mental time travel and is it unique to humans? *Behav. Brain Sci., 30,* 299–331.

Summerfield, C., Trittschuh, E. H., Monti, J. M., Mesulam, M. M., & Egner, T. (2008). Neural repetition suppression reflects fulfilled perceptual expectations. *Nature Neuroscience,* 11(9), 1004–1006.

Sutton, S., Braren, M., Zubin, J., & John, E. R. (1965). Evoked-potential correlates of stimulus uncertainty. *Science, 150,* 1187–1188.

Suzuki, K., et al. (2013). Multisensory integration across interoceptive and exteroceptive domains modulates self-experience in the rubber-hand illusion. *Neuropsychologia.* http://dx.doi.org/10.1016/j.neuropsychologia. 2013.08.014 20.

Szpunar, K. K. (2010). Episodic future thought: An emerging concept. *Perspect. Psychol. Sci., 5,* 142–162. doi:10.1177/1745691610362350.

Szpunar, K. K., Watson, J. M., & McDermott, K. B. (2007). Neural substrates of envisioning the future. *Proc. Natl Acad. Sci. USA*, *104*, 642–647. doi:10.1073/pnas. 0610082104.

Tani, J. (2007). On the interactions between top-down anticipation and bottom-up regression. *Frontiers in Neurorobotics*, *1*, 2. doi:10.3389/neuro.12.002.2007.

Tani, J., Ito, M., & Sugita, Y. (2004). Self-organization of distributedly represented multiple behavior schemata in a mirror system: Reviews of robot experiments using RNNPB. *Neural Networks*, *17*(8), 1273–1289.

Tatler, B. W., Hayhoe, M. M., Land, M. F., & Ballard, D. H. (2011). Eye guidance in natural vision: Reinterpreting salience. *Journal of Vision*, *11*(5):5, 1–23.

Tenenbaum, J. B., Kemp, C., Griffiths, T. L., & Goodman, N. D. (2011). How to grow a mind: Statistics, structure, and abstraction. *Science*, *331*(6022), 1279–1285.

Teufel, C, Fletcher, P, & Davis, G (2010). Seeing other minds: Attributed mental states influence perception. *Trends in Cognitive Sciences*, *14*(2010), 376–382.

Thaker, G. K., Avila, M. T., Hong, L. E., Medoff, D. R., Ross, D. E., Adami, H. M. (2003). A model of smooth pursuit eye movement deficit associated with the schizophrenia phenotype. *Psychophysiology*, *40*, 277–284. PubMed: 12820868.

Thaker, G. K., Ross, D. E., Buchanan, R. W., Adami, H. M., & Medoff, D. R. (1999). Smooth pursuit eye movements to extraretinal motion signals: Deficits in patients with schizophrenia. *Psychiatry Res.*, *88*, 209–219. PubMed: 10622341.

Thelen, E., Schöner, G., Scheier, C., & Smith, L. (2001). The dynamics of embodiment: A field theory of infant perseverative reaching. *Behavioral and Brain Sciences*, *24*, 1–33.

Thelen, E., & Smith, L. (1994). *A dynamic systems approach to the development of cognition and action.* Cambridge, MA: MIT Press.

Thevarajah, D., Mikulic, A., & Dorris, M. C. (2009). Role of the superior colliculus in choosing mixed-strategy saccades. *J. Neurosci.*, *29*(7), 1998–2008.

Thompson, E. (2010). *Mind in life: Biology, phenomenology, and the sciences of mind.* Cambridge, MA: Harvard University Press.

Thornton, C. (ms). Experiments in sparse-coded predictive processing.

Todorov, E. (2004). Optimality principles in sensorimotor control. *Nat. Neurosci.*, *7*, 907–915.

Todorov, E. (2008). Parallels between sensory and motor information processing. In M. Gazzaniga (Ed.), *The cognitive neurosciences* (4th ed.) (pp. 613–624). Cambridge, MA: MIT Press.

Todorov, E. (2009). Efficient computation of optimal actions. *Proc. Natl. Acad. Sci. USA*, *106*, 11478–11483.

Todorov, E., & Jordan, M. I. (2002). Optimal feedback control as a theory of motor coordination. *Nature Neuroscience*, *5*, 1226–1235.

Todorovic, A., van Ede, F., Maris, E., & de Lange, F. P. (2011). Prior expectation mediates neural adaptation to repeated sounds in the auditory cortex: An MEG Study. *J. Neurosci., 31*, 9118–9123.

Tomasello, M., Carpenter, M., Call, J., Behne, T., & Moll, H. (2005). Understanding and sharing intentions: The ontogeny and phylogeny of cultural cognition. *Behavioral & Brain Sciences, 28*(5), 675–691.

Tononi, G., & Cirelli, C. (2006). Sleep function and synaptic homeostasis. *Sleep Medicine Reviews, 10*(1), 49–62.

Torralba, A., Oliva, A., Castelhano, M. S., & Henderson, J. M. (2006). Contextual guidance of eye movements and attention in real-world scenes: The role of global features in object search. *Psychological Review, 113*, 766–786.

Toussaint, M. (2009). Probabilistic inference as a model of planned behavior. *Künstliche Intelligenz, 3*(9), 23–29.

Tracey, I. (2010). Getting the pain you expect: Mechanisms of placebo, nocebo and reappraisal effects in humans. *Nat. Med., 16*, 1277–1283.

Treue, S. (2001). Neural correlates of attention in primate visual cortex. *Trends Neurosci., 24*, 295–300. doi:10.1016/ S0166-2236(00)01814-2.

Tribus, M. (1961). *Thermodynamics and thermostatics: An introduction to energy, information and states of matter, with engineering applications.* New York: D. Van Nostrand.

Tsuchiya, N., & Koch, C. (2005). Continuous flash suppression reduces negative afterimages. *Nature Neuroscience, 8*(8), 1096–1101. doi:10.1038/nn1500.

Tsuda, I. (2001). The plausibility of a chaotic brain theory. *Behavioral and Brain Sciences, 24*(5), 829–840.

Tulving, E. (1983). *Elements of episodic memory.* New York: Oxford University Press.

Tulving, E., & Gazzaniga, M. S. (1995). Organization of memory: Quo vadis? In M. Gazzaniga (Ed.), *The cognitive neurosciences* (pp. 839– 847). Cambridge, MA: MIT Press.

Turvey, M., & Carello, C. (1986). The ecological approach to perceiving-acting: A pictorial essay. *Acta Psychologica, 63*, 133–155.

Turvey, M. T., & Shaw, R. E. (1999). Ecological foundations of cognition: I. Symmetry and specificity of animal-environment systems. *Journal of Consciousness Studies, 6*, 85–110.

Tversky, A., & Kahneman, D. (1973). Availability: A heuristic for judging frequency and probability. *Cognitive Psychology, 5*, 207–232.

Ungerleider, L. G., & Mishkin, M. (1982). Two cortical visual systems. In D. J. Ingle, M. A. Goodale, & R. J. W. Mansfield (Eds.), *Analysis of visual behavior* (pp. 549–586). Cambridge, MA: MIT Press.

Uno, Y., Kawato, M., & Suzuki, R. (1989). Formation and control of optimal trajectory in human multijoint arm movement. *Biological Cybernetics, 61*, 89–101.

Van de Cruys, S., de-Wit, L., Evers, K., Boets, B., & Wagemans, J. (2013). Weak priors versus overfitting of predictions in autism: Reply to Pellicano and Burr (TICS, 2012). *I-Perception, 4*(2), 95–97. doi:10.1068/i0580ic.

Van de Cruys, S., & Wagemans, J. (2011). Putting reward in art: A tentative prediction error account of visual art. *i-Perception*, special issue on Art & Perception, *2*(9), 1035–1062.

Van den Berg, R., Keshvari, S., & Ma, W. J. (2012). Probabilistic computation in perception under variability in encoding precision. *PLoS One*, 7(6), e40216.

Van den Heuvel, M. P., & Sporns, O. (2011). Rich-club organization of the human connectome. *J. Neurosci.*, 31, 15775–15786.

Van Essen, D. C., Anderson, C. H., & Olshausen, B. A. (1994). Dynamic routing strategies in sensory, motor, and cognitive processing. In C. Koch & J. Davis (Eds.), *Large scale neuronal theories of the brain* (pp. 271–299). Cambridge, MA: MIT Press.

van Gerven, M. A. J., de Lange, F. P., & Heskes, T. (2010). Neural decoding with hierarchical generative models. *Neural Comput.*, 22(12), 3127–3142.

van Kesteren, M. T., Ruiter, D. J., Fernandez, G., & Henson, R. N. (2012). How schema and novelty augment memory formation. *Trends in Neurosciences*, 35, 211–219. doi:10.1016/j.tins.2012.02.001.

van Leeuwen, C. (2008). Chaos breeds autonomy: Connectionist design between bias and babysitting. *Cognitive Processing*, 9, 83–92.

Varela, F., Thompson, E., & Rosch, E. (1991). *The embodied mind*. Cambridge, MA: MIT Press.

Vilares, I., & Körding, K. (2011). Bayesian models: The structure of the world, uncertainty, behavior, and the brain. *Annals of the New York Acad. Sci.*, 1224, 22–39.

Von Holst, E. (1954). Relations between the central nervous system and the peripheral organs. *British Journal of Animal Behaviour*, 2(3), 89–94.

Voss, M., Ingram, J. N., Wolpert, D. M., & Haggard, P. (2008). Mere expectation to move causes attenuation of sensory signals. *PLoS One*, 3(8), e2866.

Wacongne, C., Changeux, J.-P., & Dehaene, S. (2012). A neuronal model of predictive coding accounting for the mismatch negativity. *Journal of Neuroscience*, 32(11), 3665–3678.

Wacongne, C., Labyt, E., van Wassenhove, V., Bekinschtein, T., Naccache, L., & Dehaene, S. (2011). Evidence for a hierarchy of predictions and prediction errors in human cortex. *Proc. Natl. Acad. Sci. USA*, 108, 20754–20759.

Warren, W. (2006). The dynamics of action and perception. *Psychological Review* 113(2), 358–389.

Webb, B. (2004). Neural mechanisms for prediction: Do insects have forward models? *Trends in Neurosciences*, 27(5), 1–11.

Weber, C., Wermter, S., & Elshaw, M. (2006). A hybrid generative and predictive model of the motor cortex. *Neural Networks*, 19, 339–353.

Weiskrantz, L., Elliot, J., & Darlington, C. (1971). Preliminary observations of tickling oneself. *Nature*, 230(5296), 598–599.

Weiss, Y., Simoncelli, E. P., & Adelson, E. H. (2002). Motion illusions as optimal percepts. *Nature Neuroscience*, 5(6), 598–604.

Wheeler, M. (2005). *Reconstructing the cognitive world*. Cambridge, MA: MIT Press.

Wheeler, M., & Clark, A. (2008). Culture, embodiment and genes: Unravelling the triple helix. *Philosophical Transactions of the Royal Society B*, 363(1509), 3563–3575.

Wheeler, M. E., Petersen, S. E., & Buckner, R. L. (2000). Memory's echo: Vivid remembering reactivates sensory-specific cortex. *Proc. Natl. Acad. Sci. USA*, 97, 11125–11129.

Wiese, W. (2014). Review of Jakob Hohwy: The Predictive Mind. *Minds and Machines, 24*(2), 233–237.

Wilson, R. A. (2004). *Boundaries of the mind: The individual in the fragile sciences—cognition.* Cambridge: Cambridge University Press.

Wolpert, D. M. (1997). Computational approaches to motor control. *Trends in Cognitive Science, 1,* 209–216.

Wolpert, D. M., Doya, K., & Kawato, M. (2003). A unifying computational framework for motor control and social interaction. *Philosophical Transactions of the Royal Society, 358,* 593–602.

Wolpert, D. M., & Flanagan, J. R. (2001). Motor prediction. *Current Biology, 18,* R729–R732.

Wolpert, D. M., Ghahramani, Z., & Jordan, M. I. (1995). An internal model for sensorimotor integration. *Science, 269,* 1880–1882.

Wolpert, D. M., & Kawato, M. (1998). Multiple paired forward and inverse models for motor control. *Neural Networks, 11*(7–8), 1317–1329.

Wolpert, D. M., Miall, C. M., & Kawato, M. (1998). Internal models in the cerebellum. *Trends in Cognitive Sciences, 2*(9), 338–347.

Wurtz, R. H., McAlonan, K., Cavanaugh, J., & Berman, R. A. (2011). Thalamic pathways for active vision. *Trends in Cognitive Sciences, 15,* 177–184.

Yabe, H., Tervaniemi, M., Reinikainen, K., & Naatanen, R. (1997). Temporal window of integration revealed by MMN to sound omission. *Neuroreport, 8,* 1971–1974.

Yamashita, Y., & Tani, J. (2008). Emergence of functional hierarchy in a multiple timescale neural network model: A humanoid robot experiment. *PLoS Computational Biology, 4*(11), e1000220.

Yu, A. J. (2007). Adaptive behavior: Humans act as Bayesian learners. *Current Biology, 17,* R977–R980.

Yu, A. J., & Dayan, P. (2005). Uncertainty, neuromodulation, and attention. *Neuron, 46,* 681–692.

Yuille, A, & Kersten, D (2006). Vision as Bayesian inference: Analysis by synthesis? *Trends in Cognitive Science, 10*(7), 301–308.

Yuval-Greenberg, S., & Heeger, D. J. (2013). Continuous flash suppression modulates cortical activity in early visual cortex. *Journal of Neuroscience, 33*(23), 9635–9643.

Zhu, Q., & Bingham, G. P. (2011). Human readiness to throw: The size-weight illusion is not an illusion when picking the best objects to throw. *Evolution and Human Behavior, 32*(4), 288–293.

Ziv, I., Djaldetti, R., Zoldan, Y., Avraham, M., & Melamed, E. (1998). Diagnosis of 'nonorganic' limb paresis by a novel objective motor assessment: The quantitative Hoover's test. *J. Neurol., 245,* 797–802.

Zorzi, M., Testolin, A., & Stoianov, I. (2013). Modeling language and cognition with deep unsupervised learning: A tutorial overview. *Front. Psychol., 4,* 515. doi:10.3389/fpsyg.2013.00515.

Index